HIDDEN®
Arizona

"Lists out-of-the-way places other guides might skip, but that doesn't mean *Hidden Arizona* forgets the mainstream, tourist-trampled spots."
—*San Diego Union Tribune*

"Have you discovered *Hidden Arizona* yet? If not, you're in for a treat."
—*Travelin' Magazine*

HIDDEN ®

Arizona

Including Phoenix, Tucson, Sedona and the Grand Canyon

Richard Harris

FIFTH EDITION

Ulysses Press ®

BERKELEY, CALIFORNIA

Published by: ULYSSES PRESS
                P.O. Box 3440
                Berkeley, CA 94703
                www.ulyssespress.com

ISSN 1523-5777
ISBN 1-56975-488-8

Printed in Canada by Transcontinental Printing

10 9 8

MANAGING EDITOR: Claire Chun
PROJECT DIRECTOR: Laura Brancella
COPY EDITOR: Steven Zah Schwartz
EDITORIAL ASSOCIATES: Laura Brancella, Leona Benten, Lily Chou,
    Amy Hough, Kate Allen
TYPESETTERS: Lisa Kester, Steven Zah Schwartz, Tamara Kowalski
    Matt Orendorff
CARTOGRAPHY: Pease Press
COVER DESIGN: Sarah Levin, Leslie Henriques
INDEXER: Sayre Van Young
COVER PHOTOGRAPHY: Steve Satushek/Brand X/Gettyimages.com
HIDDEN BOOKS DESIGN: Sarah Levin
ILLUSTRATOR: Glenn Kim

Distributed in the United States by Publishers Group West

HIDDEN is a federally registered trademark
of BookPack, Inc.

Ulysses Press 쯭 is a federally registered trademark
of BookPack, Inc.

The author and publisher have made every effort to ensure the
accuracy of information contained in *Hidden Arizona*, but can
accept no liability for any loss, injury or inconvenience sustained
by any traveler as a result of information or advice contained in
this guide.

Write to us!

If in your travels you discover a spot that captures the spirit of Arizona, or if you live in the region and have a favorite place to share, or if you just feel like expressing your views, write to us and we'll pass your note along to the author.

We can't guarantee that the author will add your personal find to the next edition, but if the writer does use the suggestion, we'll acknowledge you in the credits and send you a free copy of the new edition.

ULYSSES PRESS
3286 Adeline Street, Suite 1
Berkeley, CA 94703
E-mail: readermail@ulyssespress.com

What's Hidden?

At different points throughout this book, you'll find special listings marked with this symbol:

◄ HIDDEN

This means that you have come upon a place off the beaten tourist track, a spot that will carry you a step closer to the local people and natural environment of Arizona.

The goal of this guide is to lead you beyond the realm of everyday tourist facilities. While we include traditional sightseeing listings and popular attractions, we also offer alternative sights and adventure activities. Instead of filling this guide with reviews of standard hotels and chain restaurants, we concentrate on one-of-a-kind places and locally owned establishments.

Our authors seek out locales that are popular with residents but usually overlooked by visitors. Some are more hidden than others (and are marked accordingly), but all the listings in this book are intended to help you discover the true nature of Arizona and put you on the path of adventure.

Contents

Maps

OUTDOOR ADVENTURE SYMBOLS

The following symbols accompany national, state and regional park listings, as well as beach descriptions throughout the text.

▲	Camping		Snorkeling or Scuba Diving
	Hiking		Waterskiing
	Biking		Windsurfing
	Horseback Riding		Canoeing or Kayaking
	Downhill Skiing		Boating
	Cross-country Skiing		Boat Ramps
	Swimming		Fishing

ONE

The Grand Canyon State

If your image of Arizona is all cowboys, ranches and hitching posts, it's time for another look. For while the flavor of the Old West is certainly still in evidence throughout the state, the trappings of the 20th century are everywhere—indeed, flourishing and growing apace. Head to the major cities—including Phoenix, Scottsdale, Tempe and Tucson—and you'll find all the culture and amenities of any cosmopolitan metropolis: vibrant arts communities, professional sports galore, shopping centers and trendy stores as far as the eye can see, fine college campuses and museums, intriguing art galleries and architecture, as well as enough golf, tennis and other activities to satisfy anyone and everyone. But if you're hankering for a taste of the great outdoors or a glimpse of the frontier life, well, they're here, too: miles of open desert, rivers to swim and sail, trails to roam and towns set more in the past than the present. So saddle up, friend, because Arizona has it all. For each cowboy, you'll find a city slicker; for each country music bar, there's a rhythm-and-blues joint; for each thirsty desert view, add a snowcapped mountain; and for each rough 'n' tough dude ranch, imagine a decadently luxurious resort.

Arizona covers a 114,000-square-mile chunk of land on the southwestern corner of the United States and is bordered by Mexico on the south, California and Nevada on the west, Utah to the north and New Mexico to the east. Although it is the sixth largest state in the nation, Arizona has fewer than 5,000,000 residents. Some have called it the most geographically diverse state in the United States, a point that's hard to argue. In the north are high mountains and the Grand Canyon, as well as the Mogollon Rim, a 1500-foot-high wall of land stretching for hundreds of miles. Indian reservations cover the northeast corner, a high plateau dotted with spectacular mesas and buttes and wide open spaces known for their stark beauty. On the western border, the Colorado River is a cool, blue waterway cutting through a hot, semi-barren landscape. The Sonoran Desert, characterized by giant saguaro cacti with their wildly splayed arms and accordion pleats, spreads from Mexico to central Arizona. To the east lie the White Mountains, covered with pine trees and dotted with lakes. From low desert to snowcapped mountains to wide rivers, Arizona is proud to show off its natural jewels.

Plan to spend some time in Arizona; its greatest attractions are not seen in a blur speeding down the highway. Venture off main roads and get to know the people and land. See which of those Western myths you've seen in the movies are true, and which belong only to vivid imaginations.

But most of all, relax. The pace here is slow, the mood casual. Soak up the sun, leave your watch at home and simply enjoy. You're in Arizona.

Where to Go

This book covers everything you need to know about visiting Arizona—where to sleep, shop, dine, dance, be entertained and explore the outdoors. It is divided into ten chapters. This first chapter offers practical details for planning your trip. Chapter Two explores Arizona's natural landscape, while Chapter Three delves into the region's history, including American Indian and Spanish influences. Chapter Four focuses solely on the Grand Canyon, which is worthy of a book in itself. Chapter Five heads to the northeast corner of the state and Indian Country, including the Painted Desert and Petrified Forest. Sedona, Jerome, Flagstaff and Prescott all are covered in Chapter Six, while Chapter Seven travels down the state's western edge from Kingman to Lake Havasu City and the London Bridge. Chapter Eight describes the Phoenix/Scottsdale area, while Chapter Nine ventures east into the mountains and scenic areas from Globe to Pinetop-Lakeside and the Coronado Trail. Chapter Ten moves farther south to Tucson, Tombstone and the Mexican border.

Many visitors begin a visit to Arizona by heading for the **Grand Canyon**, the largest single geological feature in the Southwest, which splits the region between north and south. The "village" on the South Rim of the Grand Canyon, just an hour's drive from interstate Route 40, is developed on a grand scale, complete with an airport. The North Rim, farther by road from major cities and main routes and closed during the winter months, is more relaxed and secluded, though still busy enough to make advance lodging or camping reservations essential. The northern area of Grand Canyon National Park adjoins Glen Canyon National Recreation Area whose focus is manmade Lake Powell. You can rent a houseboat and enjoy a leisurely trip through the region's natural beauty.

Northeastern Arizona, also known as Indian Country, includes the vast, sprawling Navajo Indian Reservation, larger than some East Coast states, as well as the remote, ancient mesa-top pueblos of the Hopi Indian Reservation, a fiercely traditional and independent region although—or perhaps because—it's completely surrounded by Navajo land. The center of the Navajo world according to legend, Canyon de Chelly is still inhabited by people who herd sheep and live without electricity. Visitors can view the hogans (traditional Navajo log homes) and pastures from high up on the canyon rim, but can only enter the labyrinth accompanied by a Navajo guide. Another national park service unit operated by the tribe, Navajo National Monument protects some of the best Anasazi ruins in the Four Corners area—the region where Arizona, Utah, Colorado and New Mexico converge. The monument's biggest Indian ruin is only accessible on horseback. The third major park on the reservation is Monument Valley Navajo Tribal Park, a landscape so familiar from the many films, television shows and advertisements filmed here that visitors may feel like they're driving through a movie as they travel the back-country road around the valley and visit the hogans of the people who live in this, one of the most remote places in the United States. A tour of Hubbell Trading Post National Historic Site and perhaps a stop at a still-operating trading post will round out your Indian Country experience.

Route 40 through **North Central Arizona** will bring you to Flagstaff, a winter ski resort and college town, sitting on the edge of the dramatic San Francisco Peaks at 7000 feet and blanketed with ponderosa pine trees. Drive south through spectacular Oak Creek Canyon to Sedona, an upscale artist community with a New Age bent and an abundance of shopping. This is also the heart of scenic Red Rock Country, where red sandstone has eroded into dramatic formations of incomparable beauty. Jerome, scenically perched in the Mingus Mountains, is a former mining town that's now home to a small community of artists. Just down the road is Prescott, the original territorial capital of Arizona, which draws visitors with its numerous museums and low-key charm.

Never mind that **Western Arizona** is surrounded by parched desert. The 340-mile-long stretch of the Colorado River that establishes the state's "west coast" border has created an aquatic playground spilling over with unparalleled scenic and recreational opportunities. Kingman serves as a northern gateway to a succession of lakes, resorts and riverfront coves, as well as to the historic gold and silver mining ghost towns of Oatman and Chloride. The Lake Mead National Recreational Area extends to include Lake Mohave, where you'll find Bullhead City, the fastest growing city in Arizona. Farther south is Lake Havasu City, home to the authentic London Bridge, which was brought over from England and reassembled here. Continue down State Route 95 and you'll come to Quartzsite, which attracts more than half a million visitors every February for its annual rock and mineral extravaganza.

Phoenix, the state capital and the largest city in the Southwest, is the focus of **South Central Arizona**. It's amazing that a city of over a million people could survive at all in such a sunbaked desert

ANCIENT INDIAN RUINS

Some of the best of the Indian ruins to see in Arizona include the Anasazi ruins of Betatakin and Keet Seel at the Navajo National Monument 18 miles northwest of Kayenta off Route 160; Montezuma Castle National Monument which are cliffside dwellings built by the Sinagua people in Camp Verde; the four-story Hohokam ruins at the Casa Grande Ruins National Monument, 20 miles east of Casa Grande off Route 87; the pueblos of the Hopi ancestors at Homolovi Ruins State Park on Route 87 three miles east of Winslow; the ruins of the apartment-style dwellings of the Salado people at Tonto National Monument on Arizona 88 in Roosevelt; the volcanic rock Mogollon ruins at Casa Malpais Pueblo in Springerville; and the Besh-Ba-Gowah Archaeological Park with the pueblo ruins of the Salado people in Globe.

valley, but a complex system of dams and aqueducts has allowed Phoenix to become the ninth-largest city in the United States. At first, this rectilinear sprawl of suburbs and shopping malls, giant retirement communities, towering office buildings, industrial parks and farmlands full of year-round citrus and cotton crops may seem to offer few charms for the vacationer. But those who take time to explore Phoenix will soon discover that this city, where it is often better to spend daytime hours indoors, has more than its share of fine museums. The winter months are the time for outdoor adventuring in the Phoenix area, and hiking, horseback riding, boating and fishing opportunities abound. Nearby Scottsdale blends the architecture of the Old West with exclusive shops, galleries, restaurants and nightclubs, while other towns within easy day-trip distance of Phoenix, such as Wickenburg, recall grittier and more authentic memories of the rough-and-rowdy mining boomtown era of turn-of-the-20th-century Arizona.

Towering mountain peaks, sparkling streams and lakes, and dense pine forests surprise many travelers to the high country of **Eastern Arizona**. This forest primeval encompasses the mountain hamlets of Show Low, Pinetop and Lakeside, summer resorts famous for their hiking and fishing, and popular with those trying to escape the scorching temperatures on the desert floor. During winter, skiers flock to the downhill runs and cross-country trails at nearby Sunrise ski resort on the White Mountain Apache Indian Reservation. The forests deepen as you travel east to Alpine, a mountain village just a few miles from the New Mexico border. At the heart of the "Arizona Alps," Alpine is a mecca for nature buffs, who love the profusion of outdoor activities—hiking, camping, hunting and fishing. Alpine is also a northern guidepost along the Coronado Trail, which snakes south through some of the most spectacular scenery in the Southwest to the historic mining town of Clifton. Built along the banks of the San Francisco River, Clifton and its historic Chase Creek Street give a glimpse of what Arizona was like at the turn of the century. Traveling south from Clifton, juniper foothills give way to rolling grasslands and the fertile Gila River Valley, where cotton is king and the town of Safford marks Arizona's eastern anchor of the Old West Highway. This strip of Arizona, stretching 203 miles from Apache Junction to the New Mexico state line, is rich in the frontier history of the Old West. Tracing a course first charted by Coronado, Geronimo, the Dutchman, Billy the Kid, Johnny Ringo and pioneers looking for a place to call their own, you'll pass through cactus-studded valleys, pine-topped mountains, rugged and craggy canyons, lost treasure and historic copper mines. Along the way you can sample the area's history in Globe's plantation-style mansions and antique shops and its pre-history at the Besh-Ba-Gowah Archaeological Park.

Text continued on page 8.

Desert
Survival

Car travel can be risky in some desert areas described in this guidebook simply because they are so remote. Once you venture beyond paved, well-used roads, if your vehicle breaks down it may be days before another human being comes along. In such a situation, a little survival know-how can save your life.

• Most important, carry more drinking water in your vehicle than you can imagine needing. In hot desert conditions, a human being may require two gallons of water per day to stay alive. Dehydration is the major threat to survival.

• When stranded in the desert, do not drink beer or other alcoholic beverages. Alcohol actually makes your body dehydrate more quickly. Taking small amounts of salt with your water will help prevent dehydration.

• Water is often more plentiful in the desert than it appears. Birds, especially doves, visit small waterholes frequently, and you can follow them there. Green vegetation indicates that water lies just below the surface, where you can collect it by digging a hole and straining it. Water from natural sources must be distilled or purified by boiling or by water purification tablets. Not all tablets protect against giardia, the most common organic contaminant in desert areas.

If water does not support green plants or algae, it may contain poisonous alkali and can only be made safe by distillation. You can distill water with a simple solar still made from a sheet of plastic such as the rain fly for a backpacking tent. Dig a hole. Place a can, jar or other empty container in the center of it, and lay the plastic over the top. Put rocks on the plastic around the hole to hold it in place, then place a stone in the center of the plastic, over the container. As the sun heats the air beneath the plastic, water will evaporate from the bottom of the hole. It will condense on the underside of the plastic and run down to the lowest point, where it will drip into the container.

• Juice from the red fruit of the prickly pear cactus can provide lifesaving moisture—and it tastes good. (Be careful of the clusters of tiny spines on the outside of the fruit when cutting it open.) Another storehouse of water is the soft flesh inside a barrel cactus. Damaging cacti on federal land is illegal, however, so resort to chopping open a barrel cactus only in desperate circumstances.

• Stay with your vehicle unless someone in your party needs immediate medical attention and you know that help is nearby. If you must walk out in search of help, leave a note on the windshield telling your travel route and direction and the time you left.

• Stay in the shade during midday heat: inside your vehicle with the windows rolled down, under the vehicle or under a lean-to made with a tarp or blanket. If you hide from the hot sun in the shade of a rock formation, bear in mind that rattlesnakes often have the same idea.

• Use any means possible to attract attention. Lay out bright-colored towels, clothing or camping gear in a giant "X"—the international emergency signal for "stranded"—where it can be seen from aircraft. Use oily rags or green leafy brush to build a smokey signal fire. Watch for the dust plumes of distant vehicles and flash sunlight from a mirror in their direction. Keep the hood of your vehicle up at all times so that anyone who sees you can tell immediately that you're in trouble.

• More and more backroad travelers carry cellular phones in case of emergency. Although these phones don't work in the most remote areas or near the huge power lines that run from dams on the Colorado River, they do work more places than not. A CB radio is rarely helpful.

Southern Arizona in the springtime, when the desert flowers bloom, is the closest thing to paradise on earth most of us will find. The secret is well-kept because during the summer tourist season, when most visitors come to the Southwest, Tucson is considerably hotter than paradise—or just about anyplace else. Those who visit at any time other than summer will discover the pleasure of wandering through the stands of giant saguaro cactus that cover the foothills at the edge of town, perhaps learning more about the region by visiting the wonderful Arizona-Sonora Desert Museum and seeing the radiant 18th-century Spanish Mission San Xavier del Bac. For more desert beauty, drive west through the cactus forest of the Tohono O'odham (Papago) Indian Reservation to Organ Pipe Cactus National Monument on the Mexican border. Many people consider the monument to be the most beautiful part of the southwestern desert. Another great side trip from the Tucson area is Cochise County to the east. National monuments in the rugged, empty mountains preserve the strongholds of Apache warlords and the cavalrymen who fought to subdue them. Old Bisbee, until recently the headquarters for one of the nation's largest open-pit copper mining operations, has been reincarnated as a picturesque, far-from-everything tourist town. Tombstone, meanwhile, enjoys its reputation as the site of a famous gunfight that occurred more than a century ago, and remains one of the most authentically preserved historic towns of the Old West.

When to Go

▼ ▼ ▼ ▼ ▼ ▼ ▼ ▼ ▼

SEASONS

Many people imagine Arizona to be a scorching hot place. Part of it—Tucson, Phoenix, southern and western Arizona—lives up to expectations with daytime high temperatures averaging well above the 100° mark through the summer months. Even in January, thermometers in this area generally reach the high 60s in the afternoon and rarely fall to freezing at night. The clement winter weather and practically perpetual sunshine have made the Arizona desert a haven for retired persons and seasonal residents seeking refuge from colder winters.

Yet less than 200 miles away, the North Rim of the Grand Canyon is closed in the winter because heavy snows make the road impassable. Northern Arizona has cold, dry winters with temperatures usually rising above freezing during the day, but often dropping close to zero at night. The high mountains remain snowcapped all winter and boast several popular ski areas. At lower elevations, lighter snowfalls and plenty of sunshine keep roads clear most of the time.

Where rugged mountains collide with the Sonoran Desert, small changes in elevation can mean big variations in climate. As a rule, climbing 1000 feet in elevation alters the temperature as much as going 300 miles north. For instance, the bottom of the Grand Canyon is always about 20° warmer than the top rim. In

Tucson, some people bask by swimming pools during the winter, while others ski on the slopes of nearby Mount Lemmon.

Springtime is a mixed blessing. Flooding rivers, chilly winds and sandstorms sometimes await visitors in March and early April, but those who take a chance are more likely to experience mild weather and spectacular displays of desert wildflowers. Leaves do not appear on the trees until late April at moderate elevations, late May in the higher mountains.

Throughout Arizona, June is the hottest month. In the southern and western parts of the state, the thermometer can, and often does, climb above a sweltering 100°. Lizards are the most active form of life outside air-conditioned houses and buildings. People have even been known to fry eggs on the sidewalks and let popcorn pop inside closed automobiles during the blistering heat. That's when desert dwellers vacation in northern states, or head to higher elevations, where temperatures average in the low 80s in the summer.

Much of the year's rain is dumped in what locals call the monsoon season—July, August and early September. Try to plan outdoor activities in the morning hours because during the afternoons or early evenings, winds gust and dark cumulus clouds roll in, emptying their store of water before moving on. While these thunderstorms usually cool things down on hot afternoons, the storms don't last long and the skies quickly clear. But when the rains do come, be alert to the dangers of flash floods. Water can quickly run off rocky desert surfaces and into canyons and gullies, sweeping away boulders, cars, people—anything in its path.

MONSOON MAYHEM

Although relatively benign from the safety of an indoor shelter, being caught outdoors during an Arizona monsoon should not be taken lightly. Here are a few safety tips to abide by if you find yourself in this precarious situation:

- Take all precautionary road signs seriously. If you are caught in a wash out, make your way to the roof of your vehicle and wait for help. If available, use a cell phone to call 911.
- If you're driving while it's raining, slow down. Oils and auto fluids cause unusually slick conditions, especially at the start of a downpour.
- If heavy rain and dust impedes visibility, pull off as far off to the right of the road as possible. Turn off the car and the headlights, but keep your foot on the brake pedal so that drivers coming up behind you don't assume that you are still in motion.
- Stay away from open fields, high lands, trees and other tall objects, including bodies of water and metal objects to avoid being struck by lightning.

Autumn is the nicest time of year. Locals used to keep this fact to themselves, and until recently tourists in October were about as rare as snowflakes in Phoenix. Nowadays the secret is out, and record numbers of people are visiting during the fall "shoulder season" to experience autumn colors and bright Indian summer days.

CALENDAR OF EVENTS

Besides all-American-style annual community celebrations with parades, arts-and-crafts shows, concerts and rodeos, Arizona has other, less familiar kinds of festivals. Most towns that trace their heritage back to Spanish colonialism observe annual fiestas, normally on the feast day of the town's patron saint. Fiestas tend to mix sacred and secular, with solemn religious processions and dancing in the streets.

JANUARY

Northeastern Arizona   Relive a tradition of the frontier West on the **Hashknife Sheriff Posse's Pony Express Ride** from Holbrook to Scottsdale.

South Central Arizona   Crowds gather in Scottsdale to watch some of the PGA Tour's best golfers at the **Phoenix Open,** one of Arizona's largest spectator events. The **Barrett-Jackson Auction** is a huge classic and collectible car auction in Scottsdale, with over 800 vehicles ranging in price from several thousand to millions of dollars.

Eastern Arizona   Rock hounds and gem collectors will like the **Gila County Gem and Mineral Show** in Globe.

Western Arizona   The **Gemboree,** held the last full two weeks in January, attracts several hundred thousand rock hounds and gem collectors from around the world.

FEBRUARY

North Central Arizona   **Gold Rush Days** in Wickenburg features a parade, rodeo, arts-and-crafts show, melodrama, gold mucking and drilling competitions and a beard-growing contest. More than 400 artists display their wares amidst entertainment, hot-air balloons and sky divers at the **Great Fair** in Fountain Hills. Scottsdale hosts the largest **All-Arabian Horse Show** in the world. Explore turn-of-the-20th-century buildings on Globe's **Historic Home Tour.** At the **Flagstaff Winterfest,** events include star gazing, sled-dog races, snow games, a snow softball tournament, skiing, concerts and winetasting.

Eastern Arizona   The **Arizona Renaissance Festival** in Apache Junction near Phoenix has music, theater, crafts, games and tournaments on weekends February to early April. **Lost Dutchman Days** in Apache Junction is another community celebration full of traditional small-town events—like a Fourth of July in February.

Southern Arizona The Tucson Gem and Mineral Show draws jewelers and collectors from around the world. At Tucson's La Fiesta de los Vaqueros, events include bareback riding, steer wrestling, barrel racing, bull riding and the world's longest nonmotorized parade. One of the oldest arts and crafts shows in Arizona, the Tubac Festival of the Arts features artists from all over the country, as well as entertainment.

South Central Arizona An outstanding selection of Southwest arts and crafts can be found at the Phoenix Heard Museum Guild Indian Fair and Market, which also features American Indian food, music and dance. The Scottsdale Arts Festival, which also takes place in November, features dance and music performances and crafts exhibitions. The unusual Bashas' Chandler Ostrich Festival has ostrich racing for a highlight, in addition to music, a parade, art exhibits, carnival rides and an automobile show. In Tempe the huge Tempe Festival of the Arts features more than 450 national artists, as well as adult and children's entertainment. The festival is held twice each year, in late March or early April and in early December.

MARCH

Southern Arizona The crowning point of Tombstone Territorial Days is a re-enactment of the events leading up to the gunfight at the O.K. Corral.

North Central Arizona The Sedona Art and Sculpture Walk draws artisans from all over the West to participate in one of the region's major arts-and-crafts fairs. An extravaganza of gourmet food and live music fills Scottsdale during its Annual Culinary Festival.

APRIL

Eastern Arizona Superior's Boyce Thompson Arboretum pays homage to the herb with dishes, tours and a Maypole dance at its yearly Herb Festival.

Southern Arizona Tucson is home to the International Mariachi Contest, a week-long celebration of mariachi music with concerts, workshops, an art exhibit and a golf tournament. Search for the elusive wild burro, hunt for bats or learn about dune ecology during Yuma's Birding & Nature Festival.

◆◆

WHAT'S IN A NAME?

Some believe the name "Arizona" comes from the Spanish derivative of the American Indian *al shon* or *aleh zon* meaning "little spring"; others think it's from the Spanish *árida zona* (arid zone). Another possible origin is from the Aztec word *arizuma*, or "silver bearing."

MAY

North Central Arizona Bill Williams Rendezvous Days, held on Memorial Day weekend in Williams, re-creates the days of the mountain men with barn dances, black-powder shoots, a pioneer costume contest and evening "whooplas." The **Prescott Off-Street Festival** transforms the downtown area with over 100 arts and craft displays, live entertainment and food booths. Enjoy music, cuisine, folk dancing and even coffee from the Grecian Isles during Peoria's **Taste of Greece Festival**.

Western Arizona You won't find the Nelson Riddle Orchestra, but you can get your kicks at the Route 66 Classic Car Show n' Shine during the **Route 66 Fun Run Weekend** in Kingman. This fundraiser helps preserve the historic Route 66 between Chicago and Los Angeles. A street dance, car show, pageant and barbecue are all part of the festivities.

Southern Arizona Tombstone's **Wyatt Earp Days** celebration fills the Memorial Day weekend with Old West costumes, staged shootouts in the streets, and arts and crafts.

JUNE

Northeastern Arizona Holbrook's **Old West Celebration** features an arts-and-crafts show, barbecue, American Indian song and dance, a car and truck show and races.

North Central Arizona The **Wool Festival**, which features sheep shearing, weaving and spinning demonstrations as well as textile arts, is in Flagstaff.

Western Arizona You won't need a seatbelt for **Parker's Great Western Tube Float** down a seven-mile stretch of the Colorado River. Townsfolk dress up in frontier clothing to celebrate **Old Miner's Day** in Chloride.

South Central Arizona Phoenix's Heard Museum hosts an **Indigenous Film Festival** complete with movie screenings, workshops and lectures. Payson hosts the **Old-Time Fiddlers Contest and Festival** at the rodeo grounds.

JULY

North Central Arizona Frontier Days and World's Oldest Rodeo in Prescott draws cowboys from all over the country and also has fireworks, a parade and a cowboy golf tournament.

Western Arizona Step off the sidewalk and make room for solar-powered contraptions on July 4th at the **Oatman Sidewalk Egg Frying Challenge**.

AUGUST

North Central Arizona The first weekend of August brings the **Flagstaff Summerfest**, which features more than 250 artisans, live entertainment and children's activities.

South Central Arizona Payson is home to the United States' **Annual Oldest Continuous Rodeo**, which is well into its second century.

Southern Arizona   **Fiesta de San Agustin** honors Tucson's patron saint with a Mexican-style fiesta of live music, food, street dancing and bull fighting.

Grand Canyon   The Shrine of the Ages Auditorium (next to the visitor center) is the setting for world-class music during the **Grand Canyon Chamber Music Festival.**

SEPTEMBER

Western Arizona   Kingman's favorite native son is remembered during **Andy Devine Days and Rodeo.**

Southern Arizona   **Rendezvous of Gunfighters,** one of several practically identical town festivals held in Tombstone throughout the year, features a parade and a costume party on Labor Day weekend.

Western Arizona   In Lake Havasu City, **London Bridge Days** commemorates the relocation of the bridge to this improbable site with a parade, live entertainment, costume contests and lots of Olde English fun.

OCTOBER

South Central Arizona   The **Arizona State Fair,** held in Phoenix, runs until late October or early November.

Southern Arizona   The spicy, flavorful and decorative chile takes center stage during the annual **La Fiesta de los Chiles** at the Tucson Botanical Gardens, where it features tastings of chile-accented foods from around the world, chile cooking and craft demonstrations, chile gift items, Latin jazz and salsa music, and a "Chile Rap" puppet show. **Rex Allen Days** in Willcox honors cowboy movie star Rex Allen the first weekend in October, with country a fair, rodeo, art show and cowboy dances. Tombstone celebrates **Helidorado Days** with music, arts and crafts and gunfight re-enactments.

South Central Arizona   The **Four Corner States Bluegrass Festival** in Wickenburg presents three days of music as bands compete for thousands of dollars in prize money. The **Thunderbird Balloon Classic and Airshow** in Scottsdale has more than 150 balloons, a balloon show and street dance.

NOVEMBER

Southern Arizona   The largest perimeter bicycling event in the U.S., **El Tour de Tucson** is a colorful spectator sport and a charity fundraiser.

Western Arizona   Christmas lights sparkle during Lake Mead Marina's **Harbor Parade of Lights.**

DECEMBER

South Central Arizona   The **Tostitos Fiesta Bowl Parade** in Phoenix has marching bands, equestrian units and floats. Tempe's **New Year's Eve Tostitos Fiesta Bowl Block Party** welcomes the two Fiesta Bowl teams with food, rides, music and fireworks.

CALENDAR OF AMERICAN INDIAN EVENTS

Indian pueblos mark their patron saints' feast days with elaborately costumed ceremonial dances that include a pueblo's entire population, from toddlers to elders. Animal dances are normally held in the winter months and corn dances in the summer. Led by the pueblos' kiva clans, these observances almost certainly evolved from the religious rites of the ancient Anasazi people.

Besides Puebloans, a few other tribes welcome outsiders to ceremonial events. In recent years, however, some Indian groups have opted to minimize the presence of non-Indians. In Arizona, the Hopi people no longer announce the dates or places of their ceremonial dances in advance. To avoid making yourself and future visitors unwelcome, do not carry a camera during any Indian ceremony; videocams and sketch pads are also banned. Do not use alcoholic beverages; possession of alcohol is a crime on Indian lands, and obnoxious drunks are not tolerated. Do accord ancient spiritual traditions the respect they deserve.

In addition to ceremonials, all Indian nations host annual pow-wows—gatherings of people from many tribes around the country who compete for money in colorful contest dances. There are also a growing number of fairs and markets where Indian artisans display and sell their work—often at a fraction of what you'd pay in Santa Fe or Sedona.

FEBRUARY **South Central Arizona** Casa Grande is the site of **O'odham Tash–Casa Grande Indian Days**, including Indian rituals, a rodeo and arts and crafts. Performers from throughout North America converge on Phoenix to compete in the annual **World Championship Hoop Dance Contest.**
Southern Arizona The **Tohono O'odham Nation Fair** at Sells, west of Tucson on the reservation, features outstanding basketry, pottery, rug and jewelry exhibits as well as a rodeo.

MARCH **South Central Arizona** On the first Saturday in March, members of various Arizona tribes gather at the **Phoenix Indian Medical Center Social Pow Wow.** The Heard Museum's **Indian Fair & Market** in Phoenix brings together old and new American Indian traditions with artwork, entertainment and ethnic food.

JULY **North Central Arizona** Traditional arts and crafts can be purchased at the **Annual Hopi Marketplace**, held at Flagstaff's Museum of Northern Arizona. The **Navajo Craftsman Exhibition** at Flagstaff's Museum of Northern Arizona opens later in the month.

SEPTEMBER **Northeastern Arizona** The **Navajo Nation Fair** in Window Rock has carnival rides, a rodeo, horse races, dance competitions, a pretty-baby contest, the Miss Navajo pageant and a wonderful arts-and-crafts pavilion.

South Central Arizona   Mesa is the site of the intertribal **Mesa Pow Wow.**   **OCTOBER**

Eastern Arizona   Traditional dances, folk art and food are featured during **Apache (Jii) Days** in Globe.

South Central Arizona   The annual **Pueblo Grande Indian Market** in Phoenix draws over 700 artisans and also features tribal singers, dancers and Southwestern food booths. The **Tempe Festival of the Arts** brings in hundreds of national artists (see March listing).   **DECEMBER**

Southern Arizona   The Yaqui Indian Reservation on the outskirts of Tucson marks the **Fiesta de Nuestra Señora de Guadalupe** with an 18-hour-long observance that includes masked dancers and processions.

For free visitor information packets including maps and current details on special events, accommodations and camping, contact the **Arizona Office of Tourism.** ~ 1110 West Washington Street, Suite 155, Phoenix, AZ 85007; 602-364-3700, 866-275-5816; www.arizonaguide.com. In addition, most towns have a chamber of commerce or visitor information center. As a general rule, these tourist information centers are not open on weekends.

Before You Go

VISITORS CENTERS

PACKING

Arizonians are casual in their dress and expect the same of visitors. Restaurants with dress codes are few and far between. Even if you attend a fancy $100-a-plate fundraiser or go out for a night at the opera, you'll find that a coat and tie or evening gown and heels instantly brand you as a tourist. Chic apparel in these parts is more likely to mean a Western-cut suit, ostrich-hide boots and a bolo tie with a flashy turquoise-and-silver slide, or, for women, a fiesta dress with a concho belt, long-fringed moccasins and a squash blossom necklace—all fairly expensive items that you may never have occasion to wear back home. Relax. Sporty, comfortable clothing will pass practically anywhere.

> Arizona's official neckwear is the bola tie, invented in 1949 by Wickenburg resident Vic Cedarstaff.

When packing clothes, plan to dress in layers. Temperatures can turn hot or cold in a flash at any time of year. During the course of a single vacation day, you can often expect to start by wearing a heavy jacket, a sweater or flannel shirt and a pair of slacks or jeans, peeling down to a T-shirt and shorts as the day warms up, then putting the extra layers back on soon after the sun goes down.

Other essentials to pack or buy along the way include a good sunscreen and high-quality sunglasses. Bear in mind that in many areas off the beaten path, you'll be unlikely to find a store selling anything more substantial than curios and beef jerky. If you are planning to camp in the mountains during the summer, you'll be glad you brought mosquito repellent. Umbrellas are considered an oddity in these parts. When it rains, the approved means of keeping water from running down the back of your neck is a cowboy hat.

A well-known Southwestern strategy to soothe the palate after spicy eats is the consumption of *sopapillas*, deep-fried dough smothered in honey.

For outdoor activities, tough-soled hiking boots are more comfortable than running shoes on rocky terrain. Even RV travelers and those who prefer to spend most nights in motels may want to take along a backpacking tent and sleeping bag for irresistible urges to stay out under star-spangled skies. A canteen, first-aid kit, flashlight and other routine camping gear are also likely to come in handy. Cycling enthusiasts should bring their own bikes. Especially when it comes to mountain biking, there are a lot more great places to ride than there are towns where you can find bicycles for rent. The same goes for boating, golf and other activities that call for special equipment.

A camera is essential for capturing your travel experience; of equal importance is a good pair of binoculars, which let you explore distant landscapes from scenic overlooks. And don't, for heaven's sake, forget your copy of *Hidden Arizona*.

LODGING   In Arizona, lodgings run the gamut from tiny one-room mountain cabins to luxurious hotels that blend Indian pueblo architecture with contemporary elegance. Bed and breakfasts can be found not only in chic destinations like Sedona but also in such unlikely locales as former ghost towns and the outskirts of Indian reservations. They come in all types, sizes and price ranges. Typical of the genre are lovingly restored old mansions comfortably furnished with period decor, usually with fewer than a dozen rooms. Some bed and breakfasts, however, are guest cottages or rooms in nice suburban homes, while others are larger establishments, approaching hotel size, of the type sometimes referred to as country inns.

Both rims of the Grand Canyon have classic, rustic-elegant lodges built during the early years of the 20th century. Though considerably more expensive than budget motel rooms, the national park lodges are moderate in price and well worth it in terms of ambience and location. Reservations should be made far in advance.

The abundance of motels in towns along all major highway routes presents a range of choices, from name-brand motor inns to traditional mom-and-pop establishments that have endured for the half-century since motels were invented. Older motels along main truck routes, especially interstate Route 40, offer some of the lowest room rates in the United States today.

At the other end of the price spectrum, the height of self-indulgent vacationing is to be found at upscale resorts in destinations such as Tucson and Sedona. These resorts offer riding stables, golf courses, tennis courts, fine dining, live entertainment nightly and exclusive shops right on the premises so that guests can spend their entire holidays without leaving the grounds—a boon for celebrities seeking a few days' rest and relaxation away from the public eye, but a way to miss out on the real Arizona.

Other lodgings throughout the state offer a different kind of personality. Many towns—preserved historic districts like Tombstone, as well as larger communities like Flagstaff—have historic hotels dating back before the turn of the century. Some of them have been lavishly restored to far surpass their original Victorian elegance. Others may lack the polished antique decor and sophisticated ambience, but make up for it in their authentic feel. These places give visitors a chance to spice up their vacation experience by spending the night at a place where they can look out their window onto a Main Street that has changed surprisingly little since the days of the Old West.

Whatever your preference and budget, you can find something in this book to suit your taste. Remember, rooms can be scarce and prices may rise during the peak season, which is summer throughout most of the region and winter in low-lying desert communities such as Phoenix, Scottsdale and Tucson. Travelers planning to visit a place in peak season should either make advance reservations or arrive early in the day, before the "No Vacancy" signs start lighting up. Those who plan to stay in Sedona or Grand Canyon National Park at any time of year are wise to make lodging reservations well ahead of time.

Accommodations in this book are organized by region and classified according to price. Rates referred to are high-season rates, so if you are looking for off-season bargains, it's good to inquire. *Budget* lodgings generally run less than $70 per night for two people and are satisfactory and clean, but modest. *Moderate* hotels range from $70 to $110; what they have to offer in the way of luxury will depend on where they are located, but they generally offer larger rooms and more attractive surroundings. At a *deluxe* hotel or resort you can expect to spend between $110 and $180 for a double; you'll generally find spacious rooms, a fashionable lobby, a restaurant and often a group of shops. *Ultra-deluxe* facilities, priced above $180, are a region's finest, offering all the amenities of a deluxe hotel plus plenty of extras.

Room rates vary as much with locale as with quality. Some of the trendier destinations have no rooms at all in the budget price range. In other communities—especially those along interstate highways where rates are set with truck drivers in mind—every motel falls into the budget category, even though accommodations may range from $19.95 at run-down, spartan places to $45 or so at the classiest motor inn in town. The price categories listed in this book are relative, designed to show you where to get the most out of your travel budget, however large or small it may be.

DINING Within a particular chapter, restaurants are categorized by region, with each restaurant entry describing the establishment according to price. All restaurants listed serve lunch and dinner unless otherwise noted. Dinner entrées at *budget* restaurants usually cost $8 or less. The ambience is informal, service usually speedy and the crowd often a local one. *Moderately* priced restaurants range between $8 and $16 at dinner; surroundings are casual but pleasant, the menu offers more variety and the pace is usually slower. *Deluxe* establishments tab their entrées from $16 to $24; the cuisine may be simple or sophisticated, but the decor is more plush and the service more personalized. *Ultra-deluxe* dining rooms, where entrées begin at $24, are often the gourmet places; here, cooking has become a fine art and the service should be impeccable.

Some restaurants change hands often and are occasionally closed in low seasons. Efforts have been made in this book to include places with established reputations for good eating. Breakfast and lunch menus vary less in price from restaurant to restaurant than do dinner offerings. Many Arizona restaurants offer "New Southwestern" menus featuring offbeat dishes—green chile tempura, snowcrab enchiladas—using local ingredients.

RIDERS OF THE PURPLE SAGE

The allure of Arizona has not gone unnoticed by the publishing and film industries. Zane Grey based many of his Western novels on north central Arizona, including *Riders of the Purple Sage*. Tony Hillerman's contemporary murder mysteries are often set in the Navajo Indian Reservation and Four Corners area and include *The Dark Wind* and *A Thief of Time*. Oliver La-Farge's Pulitzer Prize–winning novel *Laughing Boy* describes Navajo life. Movies filmed at Old Tucson Studios include John Wayne's *El Dorado*; Paul Newman's *The Life and Times of Judge Roy Bean*; and *Gunfight at the O.K. Corral* with Kirk Douglas. Monument Valley was the setting for *How the West Was Won* and *The Legend of the Lone Ranger*. *Oklahoma* and *The Red Badge of Courage* were filmed in Patagonia, while *The Riders of the Purple Sage* was shot in the Sedona/Oak Creek Canyon area.

The canyons, mountains and deserts of Arizona are clearly the area and there are some important things to remember when driving on the side roads throughout the region. First and foremost, believe it if you see a sign indicating four-wheel drive only. These roads can be very dangerous in a car without high ground clearance and the extra traction afforded by a four-wheel drive—and there may be no safe place to turn around if you get stuck. During rainy periods, dirt roads may become impassable muck. And in winter, heavy snows often necessitate the use of snow tires or chains on main roads, while side roads may or may not be maintained at all.

DRIVING NOTES

Some side roads will take you far from civilization, so be sure to have a full radiator and tank of gas. Carry spare fuel, water and food. In winter, it is always wise to travel with a shovel and blankets in your car. Should you become stuck, local people are usually quite helpful about offering assistance to stranded vehicles or in case no one else is around, for extended backcountry driving, a CB radio or a cell phone would not be a bad idea.

Any place that has cowboys and Indians, rocks to climb and limitless room to run is bound to be a hit with youngsters. Plenty of family adventures are available during a stay in Arizona, from man-made attractions to wilderness experiences. A few guidelines will help make travel with children a pleasure.

TRAVELING WITH CHILDREN

Book reservations in advance, making sure that the places you stay accept children. Many bed and breakfasts do not. If you need a crib or extra cot, arrange for it ahead of time. A travel agent can be of help here, as well as with most other travel plans.

If you are traveling by air, try to reserve bulkhead seats where there is plenty of room. Take along extras you may need, such as diapers, changes of clothing, snacks and toys or small games. When traveling by car, be sure to take along the extras, too. Make sure you have plenty of water and juices to drink; dehydration can be a subtle but serious problem. Most towns, as well as some national parks, have stores that carry diapers, baby food, snacks and other essentials, though they usually close early. Larger towns often have all-night grocery or convenience stores.

A first-aid kit is a must for any trip. Along with adhesive bandages, antiseptic cream and something to stop itching, include any medicines your pediatrician might recommend to treat allergies, colds, diarrhea or any chronic problems your child may have.

Arizona sunshine is intense. Take extra care for the first few days. Children's skin is usually more tender than adult skin and severe sunburn can happen before you realize it. A hat is a good idea, along with a reliable sunblock.

Many national parks and monuments offer special activities designed just for children. Visitors-center film presentations and rangers' campfire slide shows can help teach children about the natural history of Arizona and head off some questions. However, kids tend to find a lot more things to wonder about than adults have answers for. To be as prepared as possible, seize every opportunity to learn more.

GAY & LESBIAN TRAVELERS

The unique beauty of the Southwest is appealing to many: the wide open spaces stretching for miles and miles invite people who are looking to get away from it all. It's a region that gives people a lot of space, literally, and encourages you to do your own thing, which allows gay or lesbian travelers to feel comfortable here. Whether you're interested in exploring the area's magnificent scenery, sightseeing in the cosmopolitan cities, or just relaxing by the pool, the Southwest has much to offer.

Arizona boasts the gay and lesbian hot spot of Phoenix, to which this book has dedicated a special "gay-specific" section. Phoenix is home to a large gay and lesbian community and there's a growing number of gay-friendly bars, nightclubs and restaurants.

You'll find news and entertainment listings for Phoenix in *Echo Magazine*, a free biweekly that is distributed in cafés, bookstores and bars. ~ P.O. Box 16630, Phoenix, AZ 85011; 602-266-0550, 888-324-6624; www.echomag.com.

For information on virtually anything from lodging to HIV/AIDS resources in Phoenix, call **1n10**—a gay and lesbian community center—between 10 a.m. and 10 p.m. seven days a week. ~ 602-234-2752, 602-264-5437; www.1n10.org.

WOMEN TRAVELING ALONE

Traveling solo grants an independence and freedom different from that of traveling with a partner, but single travelers are more vulnerable to crime and should take additional precautions.

It's unwise to hitchhike and probably best to avoid inexpensive accommodations on the outskirts of town; the money saved does not outweigh the risk. Bed and breakfasts, youth hostels and YWCAs are generally your safest bet for lodging, and they also foster an environment ideal for bonding with fellow travelers.

Keep all valuables well-hidden and hold onto cameras and purses. Avoid late-night treks or strolls through undesirable parts of town, but if you find yourself in this situation, continue walking with a confident air until you reach a safe haven. A fierce scowl never hurts.

These hints should by no means deter you from seeking out adventure. Wherever you go, stay alert, use your common sense and trust your instincts.

If you are hassled or threatened in some way, never be afraid to yell for assistance. It's a good idea to carry change for a phone call and to know the number to call in case of emergency. Most areas have 24-hour hotlines for victims of rape and violent crime.

In Tucson, call the **Southern Arizona Center Against Sexual Assault** (SACASA). ~ 1632 North Country Club Road, Tucson, AZ 85716; 520-327-1171, 24-hour hotline 520-327-7273, 800-400-1001.

For more helpful hints, get a copy of *Safety and Security for Women Who Travel* (Travelers' Tales).

DISABLED TRAVELERS

Arizona is striving to make public areas fully accessible to disabled persons. Parking spaces and restroom facilities for the handicapped are provided according to both state law and national park regulations. National parks and monuments also post signs that tell which trails are wheelchair accessible.

There are many organizations offering information for travelers with disabilities, including the **Society for Accessible Travel & Hospitality** (SATH). ~ 347 5th Avenue, Suite 610, New York, NY 10016; 212-447-7284; www.sath.org. Also try the **MossRehab ResourceNet**. ~ MossRehab Hospital, 1200 West Tabor Road, Philadelphia, PA 19141; 215-456-9600; www.mossresourcenet. org. For general travel advice, contact **Travelin' Talk**, a networking organization. ~ P.O. Box 1796, Wheat Ridge, CO 80034; 303-232-2979; www.travelintalk.net. Its sister company **Access-Able Travel Source**, provides traveling information on the web: www.access-able.com.

SENIOR TRAVELERS

Arizona is a hospitable place for older vacationers, many of whom turn into part-time or full-time residents thanks to the dry, pleasant climate and the friendly senior-citizen communities that have developed in southern Arizona and, on a smaller scale, in other parts of the state. The large number of national parks and monuments in the region means that persons age 62 and older can save considerable money with a Golden Age Passport, which allows free admission. Apply for one in person at any national park unit that charges an entrance fee. Many private sightseeing attractions also offer significant discounts for seniors.

"Snowbirds" are seasonal residents who come from colder climes to bask in the southern Arizona sun. When summer's 100-plus temperatures arrive, the snowbirds return home and southern Arizonians head for cooler parts of the state.

The **American Association of Retired Persons** (AARP) offers membership to anyone over 50. AARP's benefits include travel discounts with a number of firms. ~ 601 E Street NW, Washington, DC 20049; 800-424-3410; www.aarp.org.

Elderhostel offers educational courses as part of all-inclusive packages at colleges and universities. In Arizona, Elderhostel courses are available in numerous locations including Flagstaff, Nogales, Phoenix, Prescott, Scottsdale and Tucson. ~ 11 Avenue de Lafayette, Boston, MA 02111; 877-426-8056; www.elderhostel.org.

Be extra careful about health matters. In Arizona's change-able climate, seniors are more at risk of suffering hypothermia. High altitudes may present a risk to persons with heart or respiratory conditions; ask your physician for advice when planning your trip. Many tourist destinations in the state are a long way from any hospital or other health care facility.

In addition to the medications you ordinarily use, it's a good idea to bring along written prescriptions from your doctor for obtaining more if needed. Consider carrying a medical record with you, including your history and current medical status, as well as your doctor's name, phone number and address. Make sure that your insurance covers you while you are away from home.

FOREIGN TRAVELERS

Passports and Visas   Most foreign visitors need a passport and tourist visa to enter the United States. Contact your nearest United States Embassy or Consulate well in advance to obtain a visa and to check on any other entry requirements.

Customs Requirements   Foreign travelers are allowed to carry in the following: 200 cigarettes (1 carton), 50 cigars, or 2 kilograms (4.4 pounds) of smoking tobacco; one liter of alcohol for personal use only (you must be 21 years of age to bring in alcohol); and US$100 worth of duty-free gifts that can include an additional quantity of 100 cigars. You may bring in any amount of currency, but must fill out a form if you bring in over US$10,000. Carry any prescription drugs in clearly marked containers. (You may have to produce a written prescription or doctor's statement for the custom's officer.) Meat or meat products, seeds, plants, fruits and narcotics are not allowed to be brought into the United States. Contact the **United States Customs Service** for further information. ~ 1300 Pennsylvania Avenue NW, Washington, DC 20229; 202-927-1700; www.customs.treas.gov.

Driving   If you plan to rent a car, an international driver's license should be obtained before arriving in the United States. Some car rental agencies require both a foreign license and an international driver's license. Many also require a lessee to be at least 25 years of age; all require a major credit card. Seat belts are mandatory for the driver and all passengers. Children under the age of five or under 40 pounds should be in the back seat in approved child-safety restraints.

Currency   United States money is based on the dollar. Bills come in denominations of $1, $2, $5, $10, $20, $50 and $100. Every dollar is divided into 100 cents. Coins are the penny (1 cent), nickel (5 cents), dime (10 cents) and quarter (25 cents). Half-dollar and dollar coins are rarely used. You may not use foreign currency to purchase goods and services in the United States. Consider buying traveler's checks in dollar amounts. You may also use credit

The Cactus League

Each year, 12 major league baseball teams migrate to the sunny Arizona desert during the months of February and March for their Cactus League spring training schedule. And where there's baseball, the fans aren't far behind.

It's become an increasingly popular way to spend a vacation as more and more fans take the opportunity to enjoy a little welcome sunshine, root for their favorite teams, and get a close-up look at some of professional baseball's super stars, all at the same time. If you can't wait for the first ball of the regular season to be thrown out in April, catch the preseason action at Arizona's Cactus League.

National League fans root for the following teams at their practice fields: **San Francisco Giants** (Scottsdale Stadium, 7408 East Osborn Road, Scottsdale; 480-990-7972, 480-312-2586); **Chicago Cubs** (HohoKam Park, 1235 Center Street, Mesa; 480-964-4467); **Colorado Rockies** (Hi Corbett Field, 3400 East Camino Campestre, Tucson; 520-327-9467); and the **San Diego Padres** (Peoria Sports Complex, 16101 North 83rd Avenue, Peoria; 623-878-4337, 800-409-1511).

If the American League teams are your favorites, take a seat in the bleachers to watch the **Oakland A's** (Phoenix Municipal Stadium, 5999 East Van Buren Boulevard, Phoenix; 602-392-0217); **Seattle Mariners** (Peoria Sports Complex, 16101 North 83rd Avenue, Peoria; 623-878-4337, 800-409-1511); and the **Anaheim Angels** (Diablo Stadium, 2200 West Alameda Drive, Tempe).

Adding to the excitement is the intimacy and informality of the small-town ballparks, where stadium bleachers are much closer to the action, and ticket prices are substantially less than regular season prices, although tickets to some games—like the Chicago Cubs'—can be surprisingly hard to come by.

To save on the cost of the tickets, look into package deals offered by many local hotels and tour companies. For general information about all the Cactus League teams, visit www.cactus-league.com. You can also contact the **Mesa Convention and Visitors Bureau**. ~ 120 North Center Street; 480-827-4700, 800-283-6372, fax 480-827-0727; www.mesacvb.com. Contact your local travel agency for information on hotel and ticket prices for other teams.

cards affiliated with an American company such as Interbank, Barclay Card, VISA and American Express.

Electricity and Electronics   Electric outlets use currents of 110 volts, 60 cycles. To operate appliances made for other electrical systems, you need a transformer or other adapter. Travelers who use laptop computers for telecommunication should be aware that modem configurations for U.S. telephone systems may be different from their European counterparts. Similarly, the U.S. format for videotapes is different from that in Europe; National Park Service visitors centers and other stores that sell souvenir videos often have them available in European format.

Weights and Measures   The United States uses the English system of weights and measures. American units and their metric equivalents are: 1 inch = 2.5 centimeters; 1 foot (12 inches) = 0.3 meter; 1 yard (3 feet) = 0.9 meter; 1 mile (5280 feet) = 1.6 kilometers; 1 ounce = 28 grams; 1 pound (16 ounces) = 0.45 kilogram; 1 quart (liquid) = 0.9 liter.

Outdoor Adventures

CAMPING

Tent or RV camping is a great way to tour Arizona. Besides saving money, campers enjoy the freedom of watching sunsets from beautiful places, spending nights under spectacularly starry skies and waking up in lovely surroundings that few hotels can match.

Most towns have commercial RV parks of some sort, and long-term mobile-home parks often rent spaces to RVs by the night. But unless you absolutely need cable television, none of these places can compete with the wide array of public campgrounds available in national and state parks, monuments and forests. Federal campground sites are typically less developed and only the biggest ones have electrical hookups. National forest campgrounds don't have hookups, while state park campgrounds just about always do. The largest public campgrounds offer tent camping loops separate from RV loops, while backcountry camping areas offer the option of spending the night far from the crowds.

With the exception of both rims of the Grand Canyon, where campsite reservations are booked up to 56 days in advance by calling (800-365-2267 credit cards only), you won't find much in the way of sophisticated reservation systems. The general rule in public campgrounds is still first-come, first-served, even though they fill up practically every night in peak season.

For listings of state parks with camping facilities and reservation information, contact the **Arizona State Parks**. ~ 1300 West Washington Street, Phoenix, AZ 85007; 602-542-4174; www.pr.state.az.us. Information on camping in the national forests in Arizona is available from **National Forest Service—Southwestern**

Region. ~ 333 Broadway SE, Albuquerque, NM 87102; 505-842-3292; www.fs.fed.us/r3. Camping and reservation information for national parks and monuments is available from **National Park Service—Intermountain Support**
Office or from the individual parks and monuments listed in this book. ~ 1100 Old Santa Fe Trail, Santa Fe, NM 87504; 505-988-6100; www.nps.gov.

To secure a campsite during peak season, travel in the morning to reach your intended campground by early afternoon. Some may find it more convenient to keep a single location for as much as a week and explore surrounding areas on day trips.

Many Indian lands have public campgrounds, which usually don't appear in campground directories. For information, contact: **Navajo Parks and Recreation.** ~ P.O. Box 2520, Window Rock, AZ 86515; 928-871-6647. **Hopi Tribal Headquarters.** ~ P.O. Box 123, Kykotsmovi, AZ 86039; 928-734-2441. **Havasupai Tourist Enterprise.** ~ P.O. Box 160, Supai, AZ 86435; 928-448-2237. The **White Mountain Apache Game and Fish Department.** ~ P.O. Box 220, Whiteriver, AZ 85941; 928-338-4385. **Zuni Pueblo.** ~ P.O. Box 339, Zuni, NM 87327; 928-782-4481.

Also see the "Parks" sections in each chapter to discover where camping is available.

Tent camping is allowed in the backcountry of all national forests here except in the few areas where signs are posted prohibiting it. You no longer need a permit to hike or camp in national forest wilderness areas, but plan to stop at a ranger station anyway for trail maps and advice on current conditions and fire regulations. In dry seasons, emergency rules may prohibit campfires and sometimes ban cigarette smoking, with stiff enforcement penalties.

PERMITS

For backcountry hiking in national parks and monuments, you must first obtain a permit from the ranger at the visitor center. The permit procedure is simple and free. It helps park administrators measure the impact on sensitive ecosystems and distribute use evenly among major trails to prevent overcrowding.

Most of the large desert lakes along the Colorado and other major rivers are administered as National Recreation Areas and supervised by the U.S. Army Corps of Engineers. Federal boating safety regulations that apply to these lakes may vary slightly from state regulations. Indian reservations have separate rules for boating on tribal lakes. More significant than any differences between federal, state and tribal regulations are the local rules in force for any particular lake.

BOATING & RAFTING

Ask for applicable boating regulations at a local marina or fishing supply store or use the addresses and phone numbers listed in "Parks" or other sections of each chapter in this book to contact the headquarters for lakes you plan to visit.

Boats, from small power boats to houseboats, can be rented for 24 hours or longer at marinas on several of the larger lakes. At most marinas, you can get a boat on short notice if you arrive on a weekday, since much of their business comes from local weekend recreation. The exception is Lake Powell, where houseboats and other craft are booked far in advance. Take a look at Chapter Four for details on how to arrange for a Lake Powell boat trip.

River rafting is a very popular sport and the ultimate whitewater rafting experience, of course, is a trip through the Grand Canyon. Independent rafters are welcome, but because of the bulky equipment and specialized knowledge of river hazards involved, most adventurous souls stick with group trips offered by any of the many rafting companies located in Flagstaff, Page and towns farther upriver. Rafters, as well as people using canoes, kayaks, windsurfers or inner tubes, are required by state and federal regulations to wear life jackets.

FISHING   Many Arizona residents seem to have an irresistible fascination with water. During the warm months, lakeshores and readily accessible portions of streams are often packed with anglers, especially on weekends. Vacationers can beat the crowds to some extent by planning their fishing days during the week.

Fish hatcheries keep busy stocking streams with trout, particularly rainbows, the most popular game fish throughout the region. Catch-and-release fly fishing is the rule in some popular areas, allowing more anglers a chance at bigger fish. Be sure to inquire locally about eating the fish you catch, since some seemingly remote streams and rivers have contamination problems from old mines and mills.

The larger reservoirs offer an assortment of sport fish, including crappie, carp, white bass, smallmouth bass, largemouth bass and walleye pike. Striped bass, an ocean import, can run as large as 40 pounds, while catfish in the depths of dammed desert canyons sometimes attain mammoth proportions.

For copies of state fishing regulations, inquire at a local fishing supply store or marina, or contact the **Arizona Game and Fish Department**. ~ 2222 West Greenway Road, Phoenix, AZ 85023; 602-942-3000; www.gfd.com. State fishing licenses are required for fishing in national parks and national recreation areas, but not on Indian reservations, where daily permits are sold by the tribal governments. For more information about fishing on Indian lands, contact the tribal agencies listed in "Camping" above.

TWO

The Arizona Landscape

GEOLOGY Arizona's geology can be summed up in one word —diverse. Its treasures include everything from spectacular canyons to high mountain peaks, from arid deserts to lush forests, from sparse volcanic fields to abundant alpine meadows.

Arizona's riches lie not only in grand overviews, but also in a myriad of unique details. Dinosaur tracks. Petrified wood. Pure white gypsum sand dunes. Huge underground caverns. Salt domes, arches, natural bridges, hoodoos and goblins fancifully shaped by water and weather.

Some of the state's greatest assets are its mountains, creatively dubbed "sky islands" by biologists. Humphrey's Peak, part of the San Francisco Peaks north of Flagstaff, soars up 12,670 feet to make it the highest point in Arizona. Other high mountain ranges are the White Mountains in the east, and the Santa Catalina and Santa Rita mountains around Tucson.

While the grandeur of Arizona's mountains are hard to miss, its desert beauty is much more subtle. It's a rugged, prickly area that welcomes with wide open vistas, cactus blooms and a profusion of texture and color.

Four deserts sprawl across Arizona. The granddaddy of them all is the Sonoran Desert, which gets more rain than any other desert in North America. Residents of Phoenix and Tucson call it home, as do more than 300 species of birds. The Chihuahuan Desert occupies just a fraction of land in southeastern Arizona, but offers some unusual geological features. One is Texas Canyon, a mountain range made of giant boulders. Another is the Willcox Playa, where what at first appears to be a lake proves instead to be a mirage—an empty, 50-mile-wide basin of glimmering sand. The Mohave Desert in northwestern Arizona is a dry, stark region of sand dunes, but manmade Lake Havasu lends some refreshing contrast. Finally, there's the Great Basin Desert in the Colorado Plateau, a majestic land of mesas, buttes, spires, cliffs and canyons.

Of course, Arizona's most famous geological formation is the Grand Canyon, sculpted by nature over the last five million years. Geological shifting slowly lifted the plateau up to higher elevations as the rushing waters of the Colorado River sliced it in half. The dark rocks at river level, which contain no fossils, are some of the oldest matter on the face of the earth. The different layers of color and texture seen in the cliffs attest to times when the area was sea floor, forest and swamp. Tiny fossilized sea creatures from the Paleozoic era, long before dinosaurs, trace the development of some of the first life on the planet up through strata of shale, limestone and sandstone.

A lesser-known, miniature version of the Grand Canyon also inspires awe— Salt River Canyon in eastern Arizona. Spectacular views await at every corner as you drive down Route 60 between Show Low and Globe. At the Salt Banks, where a series of salt springs deposited travertine formations, visitors find colorful minerals and algae, as well as petroglyphs dating from the 13th century.

You can also trace the past with a visit to the Petrified Forest National Park, which includes the Painted Desert. The barren hills here contain a fossil record of life as far back as 225 million years ago, including fish, reptiles and amphibians. The surrounding hills, mainly devoid of vegetation, have been called the Painted Desert because the sun reflects the iron, manganese and other minerals contained in the rocks, tinting them with shades of red, gray, white and orange.

There are two explanations of how the trees in the Petrified Forest National Park turned to stone—one colorful, one scientific. The more riveting explanation is the Indian legend. They say that a goddess came into the area hungry and tired. She killed a rabbit and tried to make a fire to cook it, but the logs were wet and would not burn. Angrily, she put a curse on the area, turning the logs to stone.

The scientific explanation is that the forest was formed about 170 million years ago while part of a large valley. Over time, the valley filled with sediment, until large trees floated into the lowlands and were buried 3000 feet below the earth's surface. Before the trees could decay, water rich with silica, iron, manganese, copper and other minerals seeped into the trees, eventually turning them into "stone."

South of the Petrified Forest, you'll come eventually to the Mogollon Rim, which slices across east central Arizona like a sheer wall 200 miles long and up to 1500 feet high, dividing eastern Arizona into two halves—the mesalands to the north and the southern deserts.

Yet another unique feature of the Arizona landscape is Sunset Crater, a national monument in the San Francisco Volcanic Fields outside Flagstaff. The highlight here is a 1000-foot-tall volcanic cone that sprayed molten rock and ash when it first erupted in the winter of 1064–65. You can see the cinder and lava fields and climb nearby O'Leary Crater for a closer view. The fields of pumice gravel prevent vegetation from growing, but make hiking easy at the foot of these picture-perfect volcanic cones.

The geological features of Arizona are so spectacular that it is certainly possible to appreciate the various landscapes for their beauty without knowing how they were formed. But travelers who take a little time to learn about the region's geology by visiting the many natural history museums and park visitors centers along the way develop a different perspective. A closer look lets a visitor see how the many different colors and kinds of surface rock connect in a wonderfully complex formation hundreds of miles across. For example, Kaibab limestone

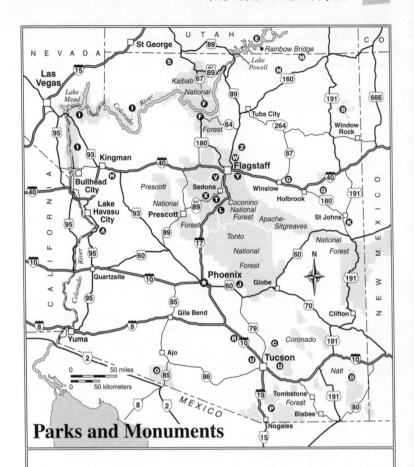

Parks and Monuments

PARKS AND MONUMENTS

- **A** Buckskin Mountain State Park
- **B** Canyon de Chelly National Monument
- **C** Catalina State Park
- **D** Chiricahua National Monument
- **E** Glen Canyon National Recreation Area
- **F** Grand Canyon National Park
- **G** Homolovi Ruins State Park
- **H** Hualapai Mountain Park
- **I** Lake Mead National Recreation Area
- **J** Lost Dutchman State Park
- **K** Lyman Lake State Park
- **L** Montezuma Castle National Monument
- **M** Monument Valley Navajo Tribal Park
- **N** Navajo National Monument
- **O** Organ Pipe Cactus National Monument
- **P** Patagonia Lake State Park
- **Q** Petrified Forest National Park
- **R** Picacho Peak State Park
- **S** Pipe Spring National Monument
- **T** Red Rock State Park
- **U** Saguaro National Park
- **V** Slide Rock State Park
- **W** Sunset Crater Volcano National Monument
- **X** Tuzigoot National Monument
- **Y** Walnut Canyon National Monument
- **Z** Wupatki National Monument

(the 250,000,000-year-old, 300-foot thick, grayish-white layer along the top rim of the Grand Canyon) is also visible at Lee's Ferry, a half-day's drive to the east. By stopping to explore the panorama in three dimensions, not just two, you'll gain a greater appreciation of the geological wonders that form the Arizona landscape.

▼▼▼▼▼▼▼▼▼▼▼
Flora and Fauna

FLORA

Different kinds of plants thrive within Arizona's wide range of altitudes. Arid deserts below 4500 feet stretch over about a third of the state, including Phoenix and Tucson. This is home for saguaro, mesquite and paloverde trees, prickly pear, cholla and barrel cactus and creosote bushes. Climb from 4500 to 6500 feet, and tall grasses, agave plants, evergreen shrubs, oak, piñon and juniper trees will appear. Once every seven years in the fall, piñon trees produce pine nuts, which many consider a delicacy. This zone lies in central Arizona and a few other areas scattered throughout the state. In the fragrant ponderosa pine forests found at the 7000- to 9000-foot-level, mainly in northern Arizona and near Payson, pine trees grow up to 125 feet high.

And from the 7500- to 10,000-foot-level, Douglas and white fir and quaking aspen create thick forests. In some areas, accessible only by hiking trails, fir trees stand that are 100 feet tall and bigger around than a man's reach. This zone includes the Kaibab Plateau of the Grand Canyon North Rim, the San Francisco Peaks, the White Mountains and other high peaks. From desert cacti to mountaintop aspens, studying the flora of Arizona can be endlessly fascinating.

Built in the 1920s as an educational facility, **Boyce Thompson Arboretum** with its large cactus gardens is a good place to study desert plants. A lake showcases plants that need more water, but the arboretum generally features drought-tolerant plants. Don't miss more than 300 species of mammals, birds, reptiles and amphibians that call the arboretum home, and be sure to stop at the visitors center, a building on the National Register of Historic Places. There are also potted plants for sale if you want to take a bit of Arizona with you. Admission. ~

DESERT TREASURE

American Indians have harvested the saguaro cacti's fig-like fruits since prehistoric times. When fermented, the fruit is used in traditional ceremonies during the summer's harvest. Historically, the ribs of the saguaro were useful for building homes, storage containers and animal traps. Saguaro cacti were a precious commodity not to be taken for granted; the saguaro cactus takes between 50 to 100 years to grow an arm. Today, the cactus blossom is Arizona's official state flower.

37615 Route 60 near Superior; 520-689-2811 (event line), 520-689-2723, fax 520-689-5858; www.arboretum.ag.arizona.edu, e-mail btainfo@ag.arizona.edu.

One downright odd-looking plant is the elephant tree. Its massive, contorted papery trunk most closely resembles the roots of a tree turned upside down.

One of the oldest living things on earth makes its home in the Arizona desert—the creosote bush. Some of these humble shrubs have been alive for 11,000 years, which makes the 500-year life span of the Joshua tree look like nothing. And then there's the organ pipe cactus and the saguaro. They may not live as long as the creosote, but they're so rare and interesting that whole monuments have been set up for them—the Organ Pipe Cactus National Monument and Saguaro National Monument.

The senita cactus is found only in Organ Pipe National Monument. Similar to the organ pipe cactus, the senita is called "whisker cactus" because of its long gray hair-like spines. Both it and the organ pipe cactus are night blooming, with flowers closing soon after sunrise. The fruit of the organ pipe cactus was harvested by the Papago Indians.

The most famous of Arizona's plants is the saguaro, the giant, multi-armed cactus that poses for thousands of tourist snapshots and travels through the mail on slick postcards. Arizona's state flower, the saguaro, is found in the Sonoran Desert, the most diverse of Arizona's four deserts. In part, this is because the Sonoran averages seven and a half to ten inches of rain annually, a lot of rain for the desert, and there is rarely a hard freeze. The saguaro reaches a ripe old age of 75 before even sprouting its arms. Most are pockmarked with holes. These are not decay; they're natural houses. The Gila woodpecker drills holes in mature saguaro trunks in order to nest in a cool, humid environment safe from predators. After they leave this "house," other species move in, anything from owls to purple martins. And the saguaro continues to give by providing nectar for bats via its white flowers.

In order to live in the desert, the saguaro cactus has had to be very inventive. The green weight in a mature saguaro is from 75 to 95 percent water. When the weather is so dry that the roots can no longer get water from the soil, there is enough water in the saguaro tissue to stay alive. During dry months, the saguaro's diameters shrink and fold in like an accordion and their ribs become more angled. Even with an 80 percent water loss from their stems, a young saguaro can live. (A human can't live with even a 12 percent water deficit.) The saguaro's roots are shallow—usually not more than three feet below the surface, but extend as much as 100 feet laterally from the plant to eke every bit of moisture from the earth.

There is a fascinating biological association between the yucca plant and the tiny yucca moth. Each is completely dependent on the other to perpetuate its species. The female moths collect pollen from yucca flowers, fly to other yucca blossoms, then lay their eggs and deposit fertilizing pollen. Some of the plant's seeds become food for the moth larvae, while others mature and reproduce. The new larvae fall to the ground, burrow into it and remain there until spring when they become moths and repeat the cycle.

Arizona boasts 60 percent of all types of wildlife species native to North America, including javelina, bear, antelope, elk, bison, mule, white-tailed deer, mountain lion, big horn sheep and turkey.

When spring rains come, which may be only once every few years, the desert bursts forth for a few weeks with a fantastic display of wildflowers. But there can be a downside to desert flora, as well. Many of the desert's plants have a special thorny sting for those who dare to touch them. In addition, it is against the law to destroy or even collect most desert plants and cacti. As one Phoenix man found out, it's not worth the trouble to harass a cactus—after he fired a gun at it, the saguaro cactus toppled and killed him.

Instead, it's better just to enjoy from a distance the beauty of the desert's botanical offerings, especially in spring when they're in bloom. Some of the more colorful you're likely to see are the yellow flowers of the brittlebush, the yellow to orange Mexican poppy, the blue desert lupines that dot roadsides and hills, and the brilliant orange blooms on the whiplike stems of the ocotillo. If you're lucky enough to arrive at the right time, you'll find this wildly colorful mix a truly memorable sight.

FAUNA

Many animals of Western legend still roam free in the forests and canyons of Arizona. Mountain lions, rarely seen because they inhabit remote areas and hunt in the dark, sometimes flash past late-night drivers' headlight beams. Black bears live deep in the mountains—in times of drought, when food is short, they may stray into towns to raid trash cans.

Coyotes, the most commonly seen southwestern predators, have been dubbed "urban coyotes" by wildlife management officials because of their adaptability to the urban landscape. They will eat almost anything, often feasting on rodents, rabbits, garbage can leftovers or, to the owner's dismay, household pets. Intelligence is another of their attributes; they'll look both ways before safely crossing busy highways. Even if you don't see them, it's not uncommon to hear their high-pitched yipping and howling on a desert night or at dawn.

Often found foraging in groups, the javelina is another common Arizona animal. It resembles a pig with its oversized head, short, muscular legs and canine teeth.

Some of the strangest animals are spadefoot toads, who spend most of their life alone in a sealed burrow three feet under the ground. When the ground shakes from thunder during summer storms, they come to the surface to feed and mate.

It's a stunning sight to watch bighorn sheep leaping and climbing on the rocky ranges that jut up from low desert plains. A ram usually weighs in at anywhere from 250 to 300 pounds, with a stocky body and massive, curved horns. They eat thistles, grasses and flowers, and even open barrel cacti with their horns to get to the succulent pulp.

One of the most distinctive regional birds is the magpie, a long-tailed, exotic-looking, iridescent cousin of Asian mynah birds. Another is the roadrunner, with its bristle-tipped topknot and long tail. Named because of their penchant for sprinting along roadways, you'll see them out dodging cars while hunting for lizards.

Large birds often seen by motorists or hikers include turkey vultures, ravens and many different kinds of hawks. Both golden and bald eagles live throughout Arizona and are occasionally spotted soaring in the distance. Eagles and vultures are about the same size, and the easiest way to tell them apart is to remember that eagles glide with their wings horizontal, while vultures' wings sweep upward in a V-shape.

Dozens of hummingbird species fly from Mexico to southwestern Arizona for the summer, while Canadian geese and other northern waterfowl warm up for the winter on rivers and lakes in the desert area.

Many visitors come to Arizona with some trepidation about the area's less attractive species. Sharing the land with humans are 11 species of rattlesnakes, 30 species of scorpions, 30 kinds of tarantulas, as well as Gila monsters with their black and yellow bead-like skin. But these creatures would rather retreat than attack, and even people who live in Arizona rarely see them. Just remember to walk loudly and don't put your hand or foot where you can't see it—like most insects and mammals, these creatures would be just as happy without an introduction.

THREE

History

At one time, nearly 25,000 Indians were the exclusive residents of what is now Arizona. The earliest were the Hohokam, who thrived from A.D. 30 until about A.D. 1450. Signs of their settlements remain intact to this day. Two other major tribal groups followed: the Anasazi (a Navajo word meaning ancient ones) in the state's northern plateau highlands, and the Mogollon People, in the northeastern and eastern mountain belt.

Their hunting/gathering lifestyle changed around 300 B.C., partly because of droughts that drove the antelope and mammoths away. People began cultivating food and shifting their focus to farming. Freed from having to constantly search for food, they developed complex societies and built large pueblos on mesas, in valleys and in the steep cliff walls of canyons.

By A.D. 200, the Anasazi began living in Canyon de Chelly, building spectacular cliff dwellings and living in harmony with nature. Remains of their works can be seen at Keet Seel and Betatakin at Navajo National Monument, and in ruins in Canyon de Chelly. These ruins reveal the dark, tiny, claustrophobic rooms that served as home, but afforded no luxuries. Possibly because of drought, the cliff dwellings were abandoned by 1300.

During this time, the Sinagua culture was developing northeast of what is now Flagstaff and farther south in the Verde River Valley. Settling in arid regions, they were named Sinagua, or "without water" in Spanish. Remnants of the Sinagua stone pueblos remain in Tuzigoot and Wupatki national monuments, and their cliff dwellings are at Walnut Canyon and Montezuma Castle.

By A.D. 450, the Hohokam culture had begun to farm the Gila and Salt River valleys between Phoenix and Casa Grande. Eventually, they spread out across a third of the state and built an impressive 600-mile network of irrigation canals, planting corn, beans and squash. They vanished by 1450. Although few of the Hohokam dwellings remain, one prime example is the four-story-high pueblo at the Casa Grande Ruins National Monument about 20 miles east of Casa Grande.

The Pima, desert farmers who next occupied this region, were the ones who named their predecessors Hohokam, meaning "all used up." No one knows the real reason the Hohokam disappeared, but possible explanations have included a long drought, disease and the arrival of more aggressive tribes.

Some 600 years ago, during the century just before Columbus' ships reached American shores, a new group of people arrived in the region. They were Athabascans, nomads from the far north (from an area that is now Canada) who had gradually wandered down the front range of the Rocky Mountains in small groups. They were to become the Apache and Navajo, warlike hunters who eventually settled down as farmers—but only after another kind of stranger had come to change the character of the Southwest forever.

THE SPANISH

In the mid-1500s, the Spaniards were the first Europeans to explore what is now Arizona. Lured by a Moorish legend about treasures in the Seven Cities of Cibola, the viceroy of New Spain sent explorers from Mexico City to search for the riches. Upon seeing pueblos glittering in the sun, the explorers returned home and reported their finding of a golden city. Francisco Vasquez de Coronado arrived a year later with great hopes, but discovered with disappointment that the "glitter" was only mica embedded in the adobe walls.

The conquistadors were looking not only for gold, but seeking souls to save. They found more souls than gold and in the process introduced the native peoples to cattle, horse raising and new farming methods, augmenting their crops of beans, squash and maize with new grains, fruits and vegetables. The Franciscans made forays into the area in the 1670s, founding missions among the Hopi and converting many of them to Christianity. In 1687, Jesuit priest Eusebio Francisco Kino began establishing missions in Arizona. He taught the American Indians European farming techniques, planted fruit trees and gave them animals to raise. Kino visited the Pima village of Tumacacori in 1691, and in 1700 laid the foundation for the church at Mission of San Xavier del Bac.

The first English-speaking settlers in the region were Mormons, who escaped persecution in the empty desert. From the 1840s on, they settled throughout northern Arizona, often in places that are still remote today.

Although the Spaniards brought some positive improvements, there was also a downside. The Spanish imported European diseases such as measles and smallpox and invaded Indian territory. As a result, the American Indians staged several battles, including the violent revolt of 1680. The Pueblo Revolt created the Navajo nation. To persuade their Athabascan neighbors to help chase away the Spanish, the Pueblo leaders agreed that the Athabascans could keep the livestock driven off from ranches they attacked. In that way, the tribe came to own sheep and horses, which would profoundly change their culture. When the Spanish colonists returned, many Pueblos who had participated in the revolt fled to avoid retaliation and went to live with the nomads, bringing with them such advanced technologies as weaving cloth and growing corn. The Athabascan descendants who herded sheep and farmed became known as the Navajo people, while those who held to the old way of life came to be called Apache. In 1751, the normally peaceful Pima people rebelled, killing more than a hundred Spaniards, while the Apache continued their hit-and-run raids and ambushes on both the Spaniards and the Pima.

In response, the Spanish government built a presidio at Tubac. But after Mexico won its independence from Spain in 1821 and Spanish soldiers were withdrawn, the Indians again attacked. Settlers finally moved to the safety of walled cities such as Tucson.

STATEHOOD In 1848, most of Arizona became part of the United States as a result of the Mexican-American war. The only exceptions were Tucson and part of southern Arizona. This was soon to change. Having this area in Mexican hands became inconvenient during California's Forty-niner Gold Rush—the route to the gold went through what was Mexico. So the U.S. government negotiated the Gadsden Purchase in 1853, acquiring the remainder of southern Arizona and some additional land for a mere ten million dollars.

Still, the American Indians were a problem. Until about the mid-1860s, they accepted the few white miners, traders and farmers who came west, but as the number of settlers grew, friction arose and fighting resulted. The Navajo and Apache especially resented the white settlers. In the minds of many, a final solution had to be found.

The cavalry was called in and one of the most brutal chapters in the history of the Southwest followed. Black troops of the Tenth Cavalry, known as Buffalo Soldiers because of their dark skin and curly black hair, came in large numbers to protect settlers of the Arizona land where Geronimo, Cochise, Mangus, Alchise and other chieftains had dotted the terrain with the graves of thousands of emigrants and prospectors. Numerous sites still exist throughout the state that bring those days of conflict into vivid focus—Cochise Stronghold in the Dragoon Mountains south of Willcox, hideout of the notorious Apache chief; Fort Bowie National Historic Site, an adobe ruin that was a key military outpost during the Indian wars, and nearby Fort Huachuca, an important territorial outpost that's still in operation today as a communications base for the U.S. Army; and Fort Verde State Historic Park, in Camp Verde on Route 17 between Phoenix and Flagstaff, yet another military base that played a key role in subduing the Apache in the 1870s.

In 1864, under the leadership of Colonel Kit Carson, the Navajo were forced to surrender and were shipped to an internment camp in New Mexico. Although they returned to Arizona within five years, the Navajo were required to live on reservations. The longest and most violent army campaign against the American Indians was the Apache Wars. Though never numerous, the Apache were so fierce and elusive that the wars lasted for 19 bloody years. The Apache fell when leader Cochise died in the Chiricahua Mountains and Geronimo was forced to surrender in 1886. Only then could settlers from the United States establish the first towns in Arizona.

During the 1860s and 1870s, the Arizona Territory was symbolic of the Wild West. Saloons did a bang-up business, literally, as shootouts and boisterous behavior were common events. Out-

Reservations

laws who were caught and tried were sent to Yuma, known for its strict Territorial Prison.

Soon the territorial sources of income began to shift toward grazing, farming and mining. Cattlemen established herds in the high desert grasslands of southeastern Arizona and the meadows of north central Arizona. But they created a modern environmental disaster. In 1870, about 5000 cattle grazed in Arizona; by 1891, this number had jumped to 1.5 million. The land simply could not support them. About 50 to 75 percent of the cattle died in the drought of 1892 and 1893. By the time the rains returned, thousands of square miles had been destroyed by hungry cows. The grasslands disappeared forever, replaced by raw desert.

Around this time, Mormons came to colonize farmlands, convert Indians and find refuges isolated enough to discourage the government from harassing the polygamists among them. They settled along the Little Colorado River and in Mesa, leaving behind a legacy of fertile farmland and top public schools.

In 1857, a short-lived gold rush began, followed by silver. The most famous lode was discovered in 1877 by Ed Schieffelin, who found silver ore and named the first stake Tombstone. But in 1886, the mines flooded and Tombstone collapsed. The copper boom followed, transforming the territory from a frontier to a real cash economy. Since large investments were needed, much of the boom was financed by corporations back east. They brought with them their style of architecture; as a result, the boom towns of Jerome, Clifton, Globe and Bisbee still have picturesque Victorian homes perched on their hillsides. But it was the gold prospector who eventually became the very symbol of the Old West—an old man with a white beard, alone with his trusted burro, looking to strike it rich. You only have to head 30 miles east of Phoenix into the Superstition Mountains to find the lore and the legend and the lure of gold still very much alive today.

FLAG FACTS

The red and gold colors on Arizona's state flag represent the colors favored by Spanish conquistadors. The blue on the bottom half is the same hue as that of the national flag, while the 13 red and gold rays depict its 13 stripes. They are also purported to mirror the rays of a scenic Arizona sunset. The copper star represents what was historically the state's most important industry. When the design of the flag was adopted in 1917, there was some protest over its close resemblance to Japan's rising sun flag.

When the Civil War broke out, Arizona sided with the Confederacy. One reason was that citizens were mad at Congress for not making theirs a separate territory. In 1863, the area was declared the Arizona Territory. Over the following years, the capital jumped from the Prescott area to Tucson, and then finally Phoenix. On Valentine's Day in 1912, Arizona became the 48th state.

Arizona didn't boom in the years immediately after statehood and the reason was obvious—a lack of water. Providing water to the desert was quite a task. All that changed in 1911 when the Theodore Roosevelt Dam was completed on the Salt River. Not only did it curb the occasional river flooding, but it also provided irrigation water to Phoenix and the surrounding area. In 1936, the Hoover Dam was completed, forming Lake Mead, the largest artificial lake in North America. Once the water became plentiful, large-scale industry and agriculture followed.

MODERN TIMES

The economy was based on the three C's: cattle, cotton and copper. Copper mining boomed in the 1920s and 1930s and copper was really sought during World War II when it was used for military munitions. Towns that rose with the copper boom and died after the war include Jerome and Bisbee, which have had renaissances as artist communities.

During the postwar years, Arizona moved away from its agricultural economic base; today, electronics, aerospace engineering and other high-tech industries are large employers. In addition, the tourism industry is an important part of the Arizona economy, with people arriving daily to explore the natural and man-made attractions in the state. It has been a winter retreat for the wealthy since the 1920s with its warm climate and healthy, dry air that helped people suffering from allergies. Unfortunately, this is no longer the case. Today, imported plants irritate those with allergies and levels of smog during parts of the year have grown to alarmingly high levels.

As for the American Indians, today there are 20 reservations in Arizona, more than any other state, with an estimated 252,000 Indians from 17 different tribes living in sad testimony to the white settlers' land grabs. The tribes speak 18 languages, and are spread across 31,000 square miles—about a quarter of Arizona. Some 150 miles east of Phoenix in the White Mountain region of eastern Arizona is the Fort Apache Indian Reservation with over a million and a half acres of land. Bordering it, with almost two million acres, is the San Carlos Apache Indian Reservation. The largest reservation in North America, Navajoland, home to over 175,000 Navajos, begins 76 miles north of Flagstaff and extends into northwestern New Mexico and southeastern Utah. Located almost in the center of the Navajo Indian Reservation is the Hopi Indian Reservation, over 11,000 members strong, who have lived on the same site without interruption for more than 1000 years, retaining more of their ancient traditions and cultures than any other indigenous group.

The Spanish-Mexican influence is strongly evident throughout the area. About 25 percent of the state's population is Hispanic, and that number is growing daily. The Hispanic culture permeates much of Arizona. Mexican restaurants are in almost every neighborhood, boasting thick enchiladas and mouth-watering burritos. Some are frequented by strolling mariachi bands, whose music goes back to a ribald Spanish song and dance form of the 18th century. Boisterous celebrations such as Cinco de Mayo liven up the cultural climate, and Hispanic artwork hangs in museums across the state. All this is just part of that unique cultural mix that is Arizona today.

FOUR

The Grand Canyon

Awesome. Magnificent. Breathtaking. It's easy to slip into hyperbole when trying to describe the Grand Canyon, but it's understandable. No matter how many spectacular landscapes you've seen in your lifetime, none can compare with this mighty chasm stretching across the northwest corner of Arizona.

The Grand Canyon comes as a surprise. Whether you approach the South Rim or the North Rim, the landscape gives no hint that the canyon is there until suddenly you find yourself on the rim looking into the chasm ten miles wide from rim to rim and a mile down to the Colorado River, winding silver through the canyon's inner depths. From anywhere along the rim, you can feel the vast, silent emptiness of the canyon and wonder at the sheer mass of the walls, striated into layer upon colorful layer of sandstone, limestone and shale.

More than five million years ago, the Colorado River began carving out this canyon that offers a panoramic look at the geologic history of the Southwest. Sweeping away sandstones and sediments, limestones and fossils, the river cut its way through Paleozoic and Precambrian formations. The layers of rock exposed by erosion on the walls of the Grand Canyon range from 250 million to more than two billion years in age, the oldest exposed rock on Earth. By the time humankind arrived, the canyon extended nearly all the way down to schist, a basement formation.

The Grand Canyon is aptly named—being, perhaps, the grandest geological marvel of them all. It is as long as any mountain range in the Rockies and as deep as the highest of the Rocky Mountains are tall. For centuries, it posed the most formidable of all natural barriers to travel in the West, and to this day no road has ever penetrated the wilderness below the rim. No matter how many photographs you take, paintings you make or postcards you buy, the view from anywhere along the Grand Canyon rim can never be truly captured in two dimensions. Nor can the mind fully comprehend it; no matter how many times you have visited the Grand Canyon before, the view will always inspire the same awe as it did the first time you stood and gazed in wonder at the canyon's immensity and the silent grandeur of its massive cliffs.

The Grand Canyon extends east to west for some 277 miles, from the western boundary of the Navajo Indian Reservation to the vicinity of Lake Mead and the Nevada border. Only the highest section of each rim of the Grand Canyon is accessible by motor vehicle. Most of Grand Canyon National Park, both above and below the rim, is a designated wilderness area that can only be explored on foot or by river raft.

The South Rim and the North Rim are essentially separate destinations, more than 200 miles apart by road. For this reason, we've divided this chapter into five sections covering the developed national park areas on both rims as well as "The Arizona Strip." For the adventuresome, we've also included hiking possibilities in the canyon, as well as two lesser-known areas of the Grand Canyon that are challenging to reach—Toroweap Point in the Arizona Strip on the North Rim and the scenic area below the Indian village of Supai on the South Rim.

With more than five million visitors a year, the Grand Canyon is one of the most popular national parks in the United States. While many come to enjoy the panoramic vistas, others come to tackle the most challenging hiking trails in the country or to explore the narrow canyons and gorges by pack mule. Whatever reason you choose to visit the Grand Canyon, it will be worth it.

▼ ▼ ▼ ▼ ▼ ▼ ▼ ▼ ▼ ▼ ▼
The South Rim

The South Rim is the most accessible area of the Grand Canyon. It's no wonder that you'll find most of the facilities here. The many trailheads leading into the canyon and along the rim make this a good place to start your Grand Canyon tour. Note: Many changes are expected in Grand Canyon National Park in the upcoming years. Road maps may become inaccurate so it is advisable to check with the park for updated information. In addition, fees may change.

SIGHTS   If you enter Grand Canyon National Park via the south entrance from Williams or Flagstaff, as most visitors do, you'll drive through **Tusayan**, about a mile south of the park entrance. The IMAX **Theater** in Tusayan shows films about the Grand Canyon on a seven-story, 82-foot-wide wraparound screen with six-track Dolby sound. These films can add an extra dimension to a Grand Canyon visit because they present river-rafting footage, aerial photography and closeup looks at places in the canyon that are hard to reach on foot. Admission. ~ Route 64; 928-638-2203, fax 928-638-2807; www.grandcanyonimaxtheater.com.

Once inside the park's boundary, the route leads past **Mather Point** lookout and **Yavapai Observation Station**; both offer spectacular views of the canyon. There's a ranger on duty at Yavapai, and from this spot you can see Phantom Ranch, nearly a mile below, the Colorado River and the Suspension Bridge used by hikers of the Kaibab Trail to cross the river.

Text continued on page 46.

Grand Canyon National Park

South Rim
Information

WHEN TO VISIT   The South Rim of Grand Canyon National Park is open all year. Most park visitors go to the South Rim, making it crowded even during the off-season, but the heaviest crowds can be expected during the spring, summer and fall months. Day visitors can expect traffic congestion and even some delays entering the park, especially during the summer. Overnight visitors must plan well in advance. Accommodations within the park are extremely limited and often are booked more than a year in advance. (See "Lodging" listings.)

WEATHER AND ELEVATION   The South Rim of the Grand Canyon is 7000 feet above sea level in a high-desert region. Temperatures during the summer are generally pleasant on the rim, ranging between 50° and 80°. Since the canyon floor lies some 5000 feet below the rim, daytime temperatures there are quite a bit higher, often climbing past 100°. Winter can bring snow, icy roads and clouds that can obscure canyon views. Spring and fall weather can change quickly in the canyon. The park's elevation can affect breathing, and it can take several days to become acclimated.

GETTING TO THE SOUTH RIM   The South Rim of Grand Canyon National Park is about 60 miles north of Williams (via Route 64 from Route 40) and about 80 miles from Flagstaff (via Route 180). Besides the south entrance, through which most visitors enter, the park can be entered from the east near Cameron, off Route 89. **Grand Canyon Railway** operates daily train service from Williams. ~ 928-773-1976, 800-843-8724; www.thetrain.com, e-mail info@thetrain.com. Limited air service is available to Grand Canyon Airport.

ENTRANCE FEES   The tariff for private vehicles is $20; for pedestrians, bicyclists and motorcyclists, it's $10. The fee is nonrefundable, but admission is good for seven consecutive days for both the South and North rims. U.S. seniors over 62 and permanently disabled U.S. citizens may obtain specially priced passes; frequent national-park visitors should inquire about the Golden Eagle Passport. An annual Grand Canyon passport is also available. Camping reservations can be made online at reservations.nps.gov.

GETTING AROUND THE PARK   A free Village shuttle bus system operates nearly year-round and makes stops within Grand Canyon Village and viewpoints along Hermit Road. The eight-mile-long Hermit Road is closed to private vehicles during the same months. The Desert View Drive, however, follows the canyon rim for 25 miles and is open year-round. A hikers shuttle is available to South Kaibab Trail (at Yaki Point). ~ 928-638-3283, fax 928-638-2877. Shuttle transportation between the South and North rims (a four- to five-hour trip) operates seasonally, for a fee. Reservations required. ~ 928-638-2820.

POSTAL, MEDICAL AND OTHER SERVICES   The South Rim has its own post office, located in the shopping center next to Yavapai Lodge. A bank and a general store are also located in the center. Emergency medical service is available 24 hours (dial 911). The South Rim has its own medical clinic (928-638-2551) and dental office (928-638-2395), both operating on limited hours.

SERVICES FOR PERSONS WITH PHYSICAL DISABILITIES   Many buildings in the park are historic and do not meet accessibility standards. However, some structures are accessible with assistance. The *Grand Canyon Accessibility Guide* is available at the visitors center and the Yavapai Observation Station. Free wheelchairs are available at the visitors center, as are special vehicle permits allowing access to Hermit Road during summer months. Wheelchair accessible bus tours are available by prior arrangement (the Village shuttle bus is not wheelchair accessible). ~ 928-638-2631, fax 928-638-6451.

PETS   Pets are permitted in the park but must be leashed, and, with the exception of certified service dogs, they're not allowed in lodgings, on park buses or below the rim. There is a kennel on the South Rim. ~ 928-638-0534.

BIKES   Bikes are not allowed on most park trails. Mountain bikes are allowed on those roads open to automobile traffic and on 11 miles of prototype trails that have been completed and opened as part of the planned Grand Canyon Greenway. This series of paved, wheelchair-accessible pedestrian and cyclist trails will eventually trace both the north and south rims for a total of 73 miles, with rest areas and several bike-rental and dropoff points along the way.

AND DON'T FORGET   Bring moleskin for potential blisters if you plan to go hiking, and a good pair of binoculars.

Grand Canyon Village serves as the commercial hub for the park. It boasts a number of lodges, a bank, a post office, a general store and the Backcountry Information Center. ~ 928-638-7888, 928-638-7644, fax 928-638-6451; www.thecanyon.com.

From the village you can reach **Canyon View Information Plaza**. There's no parking at the plaza, so you'll need to take a shuttle (during slower times of the year it is possible to park at Mather Point and walk to the plaza). Once there, you'll find a comprehensive visitors center where park rangers are on duty to answer questions, and maps and brochures about the park are available. Books about the Grand Canyon, American Indian cultures and related topics are for sale at the nearby Grand Canyon Association Bookstore. You can arrange bike rentals, view an exhibit about the natural and cultural history of the Grand Canyon and find out about ranger programs and audio-visual presentations. If you haven't already received a copy of the park newspaper, *The Grand Canyon Guide*, pick up a copy here. It's full of helpful information, including seasonal events, activities and park services. The plaza is open daily.

The **Rim Trail** is a paved pathway that extends along the edge of the canyon from Yavapai Observation Station, which is three-fourths of a mile east of the visitors center, to Maricopa Point, about three miles west of the center. Beyond Maricopa Point, the Rim Trail continues unpaved to Hermit's Rest. Night and day, the Rim Trail is a busy, at times crowded, walkway leading past all the major historical structures on the South Rim. You can sit on a bench and gaze out over the canyon or, at night, gaze up at a blue-black sky glittering with a zillion stars.

Native stone and Oregon pine were the materials used by architect Charles Whittlesey to build the sprawling **El Tovar Hotel** in 1905. Named for an officer in the expedition led by the Spanish explorer Coronado, the rustic lodge was operated by the Fred Harvey Company. It's still considered to be one of the nation's great historic hotels.

Several of the historic buildings set along the canyon rim were built by Mary Colter, an architect hired by the Fred Harvey Company. **Hopi House**, Colter's first effort for Harvey, was built of stone and adobe to resemble a pueblo building. Inside, ceilings are thatched, and there are niches and corner fireplaces, elements that are typical of Hopi pueblo dwellings. Completed on New Year's Day, 1905, Hopi House was originally used as living quarters for Hopi who danced for guests in the evening.

Bright Angel Lodge is another Colter building, dating to 1935. Built on the site of Bright Angel Camp of tents and cabins, the lodge was intended to provide moderately priced accommodations for tourists. Colter incorporated a stone fireplace that represents the rock layers of the canyon. Colter's **Lookout Studio** was completed in 1914. Perched on the edge of the canyon, the studio was built of native stone profile to make it seem an extension of the canyon wall. It offers exceptional views of the canyon.

Kolb Studio was started in 1904 by photographers Ellsworth L. Kolb and Emery C. Kolb, who took pictures of mule passengers descending Bright Angel Trail. They built their studio at the trailhead. The brothers were the first to film a Grand Canyon river run.

HERMIT ROAD   Hermit Road (formerly West Rim Drive) is open to private vehicles only during the winter months. But a free shuttle bus (white and green) departs from West Rim Interchange, near Bright Angel Lodge. The drive clings to the rim of the canyon as it brings you to a series of overlooks, each more spectacular than the last. **Pima Point** offers one of the best canyon views, and from **Mohave Point** one of longest stretches of river is visible. (Mohave also serves as a good sunset-viewing spot.) The most popular spot to watch the sunset is **Hopi Point.** The road ends at **Hermits Rest.** Shuttle buses run about every 15 minutes from one hour before sunrise to one hour after sunset; it takes about 75 minutes to travel the entire loop if you don't get off the bus.

DESERT VIEW DRIVE   From Grand Canyon Village, Desert View Drive (formerly East Rim Drive) extends 25 miles east along the rim to the park's east entrance at **Desert View.** There are several overlooks along the way—**Grandview, Moran** (named for landscape painter Thomas Moran) and **Lipan** (with views of the river and Unkar Rapids). **Yaki Point** (a favorite for watching the sunrise) is reached by shuttle only, which runs from one hour before sunrise to one hour after sunset.

The turnoff for the **Tusayan Museum and Ruins** comes up between Moran and Lipan points. Hopi ancestors inhabited the

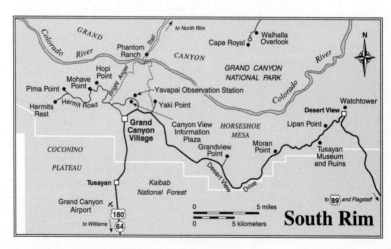

region, and this ruin, believed to be about 800 years old, is what remains of a hamlet of about 30 people who lived at the site for about 20 years. In the Hopi belief system, the canyon is said to contain the *sipapu*, the hole through which the Earth's first people climbed from the mountaintop of their previous world into this one. Visitors can tour the site by themselves or join a ranger-led walk. Signage along the path explains specific features of the construction and uses of the site. The small museum displays artifacts of ancient life along the rim.

From Desert View, the last stop before exiting the park (or the first if you enter at the east entrance), the Painted Desert is visible as is Navajo Mountain, some 90 miles away. Mary Colter built a multilevel observation **Watchtower** here, her interpretation of prehistoric towers scattered over portions of the Four Corners area. Hopi wall decorations depict ceremonial paintings and designs. An observation room on the fourth level provides an incredible panorama of the surrounding landscape. Visitor information, restrooms and a general store are operated at Desert View, as is a service station (open seasonally).

HIDDEN ▶

For the adventuresome, an intriguing Grand Canyon experience that is only accessible by foot is found far downriver near the west end of the canyon. The **Havasu Trail** (10 miles), entirely within the Havasupai Indian Reservation, is reached by leaving the interstate at Seligman (westbound) or Kingman (eastbound) and driving to the Supai turnoff near Peach Springs. From there, the Supai Road (Indian Road 18) goes for 63 miles before it dead-ends and a foot trail descends 2000 feet in eight miles to the Indian village of **Supai,** where about 500 people live. All hikers must check in at tribal headquarters. From there, the main trail continues for about two more miles into Havasu Canyon, a side canyon from the Grand Canyon, which includes a series of three high waterfalls— 75-foot **Navajo Falls,** 100-foot **Havasu Falls** and 200-foot **Mooney Falls**—with large pools that are ideal for swimming. There is a campground near Mooney Falls, and from there the trail continues down to the Colorado River in the bottom of the Grand Canyon. Whether you plan to stay in the campground or the modern lodge at Supai, advance reservations are essential. ~ For camping: Havasupai Tourist Enterprise, P.O. Box 160, Supai, AZ 86435; 928-448-2121, fax 928-448-2237.

LODGING

If you're planning a trip to the Grand Canyon it's important to make reservations for lodging early—at least a year in advance! The first thing to do is to write or call for a free Trip Planner offered by the National Park Service. It has information about accommodations, activities, itineraries, and dos and don'ts. ~ Trip Planner, Grand Canyon National Park, P.O. Box 129, Grand Canyon, AZ 86023; 928-638-7888, fax 928-638-7797; www.nps.gov/grca, e-mail grca_superintendent@nps.gov.

The South Rim offers many lodging choices. For information about South Rim accommodations or same-day reservations, call 928-638-2631. Reservations at any of them can be made up to 23 months in advance by writing to **Xanterra Parks & Resorts, Grand Canyon National Park Lodges**. ~ 14001 East Iliff Avenue, Suite 600, Aurora, CO 80014; 303-338-6000, 888-297-2757, fax 303-338-2045; www.xanterra.com.

Top of the line is the **El Tovar Hotel**. Designed after European hunting lodges, El Tovar was built by the Fred Harvey Company in 1905 and some staff members still wear the traditional black-and-white uniforms of the famous "Harvey Girls" of that era. The lobby retains its original backwoods elegance, with a big fireplace, massive wood ceiling beams and dark-stained pine decor throughout. All have full baths, color televisions and telephones. ~ DELUXE TO ULTRA-DELUXE.

More affordable historic lodging is available nearby at **Bright Angel Lodge**. The main log and stone lodge was built in 1935 on the site of Bright Angel Camp, the first tourist facility in the park. Its lobby features Indian motifs and a huge fireplace. Rooms are clean and modest. Some have shared baths, and none have televisions. Besides the rooms in the main building, the lodge also rents several historic cabins, all with televisions and a few with fireplaces. ~ BUDGET TO MODERATE.

On the rim between El Tovar and Bright Angel Lodge are the modern twin stone lodges, **Thunderbird Lodge** and **Kachina Lodge**. Located on the rim trail, these caravansaries are within easy walking distance of the restaurants at the older lodges. All have televisions and phones. ~ MODERATE TO DELUXE.

The largest lodging facility in the park, **Yavapai Lodge** is situated in a wooded setting about a quarter of a mile from the canyon rim, near the general store and about one mile from Grand Canyon Village. The contemporary guest rooms are equivalent in quality to what you would expect for the same price at a national chain motor inn. ~ MODERATE TO DELUXE.

Maswik Lodge is a half mile from the canyon rim at the southwest end of Grand Canyon Village. It presents a variety of motel-

FRED HARVEY TO THE RESCUE

In 1876, Fred Harvey (with the permission of the railroad) opened a restaurant in the Santa Fe station in Topeka, Kansas, to rescue diners from the rather tasteless food being served on the train. As years went by, a string of Fred "Harvey Houses" (hotels and restaurants) followed the tracks of the Santa Fe line. When the railroad built a spurline to the Grand Canyon in 1901, the Fred Harvey Company was not far behind.

style rooms as well as cabins. All the rooms have TVs and phones. ~ MODERATE TO DELUXE.

HIDDEN ►

No survey of lodgings at the Grand Canyon would be complete without mentioning **Phantom Ranch**. Located at the bottom of the canyon, this 1922 lodge and cabins is at the lower end of the North Kaibab Trail from the North Rim and the Bright Angel and South Kaibab trails from the South Rim. It can only be reached by foot, mule or river raft. In fact, mail sent from Phantom Ranch bears the postmark, "Mailed by Mule from the Bottom of the Canyon." Cabins are normally reserved for guests on overnight mule trips, but hikers with plenty of advance notice can also arrange lodging. Bunk beds are available by reservation only in four ten-person dormitories, separated by gender. There is no television at the ranch, and only one pay phone. Food service is provided in the dining room and must be arranged in advance. Do not arrive at Phantom Ranch without reservations. ~ BUDGET.

HIDDEN ►

Located in a remote red-rock canyon on the Havasupai Indian Reservation, the 24 motel-style units at **Havasupai Lodge** is a truly hidden destination. There's a café next door, swimming in the nearby creek and a convenient barbecue pit. Just two miles away are Navajo, Havasu and Mooney falls. You can also enjoy American Indian–led horseback and hiking tours of this scenic region. ($20 entrance fee for reservation) ~ P.O. Box 1596, Supai, AZ 86435; 928-448-2111, fax 928-448-2551. MODERATE.

Just outside the South Rim entrance gate, the community of Tusayan has several hotels and motor inns that are not affiliated with the national park. If you cannot get reservations at one of the national park lodges, try one of the typical chain motels, such as the **Rodeway Inn Red Feather Lodge**. One and a half miles from the park entrance on Route 64. ~ 928-638-2414, 800-228-2000, fax 928-638-9216; www.redfeatherlodge.com, e-mail rodeway@redfeatherlodge.com. MODERATE TO DELUXE. The **Best Western Grand Canyon Squire Inn** is another such establishment. ~ Two miles from park entrance on Route 64; 928-638-2681, 800-622-6966, fax 928-638-0161; www.grandcanyonsquire.com. DELUXE. Or try the **Grand Canyon Quality Inn & Suites**. ~ One mile from park entrance on Route 64; 928-638-2673, 800-221-2222, fax 928-638-9537; www.grandcanyonqualityinn.com. DELUXE TO ULTRA-DELUXE.

For camping information, see page 52.

DINING

The contact information for all South Rim Grand Canyon restaurants is 928-638-2631, fax 928-638-9247.

The most elegant (in fact, the *only* elegant) South Rim restaurant is **El Tovar Dining Room**. Entrées such as filet mignon with crab legs béarnaise are served on fine china by candlelight. Prices are high and the ambience is classy, but casual dress is perfectly acceptable. Three meals are served daily; dinner reservations required. ~ DELUXE TO ULTRA-DELUXE.

More informal surroundings and lower prices are to be found at the **Bright Angel Restaurant** in the Bright Angel Lodge. Menu selections include chicken piccata, grilled rainbow trout and fajitas. Cocktails and wine are available. ~ BUDGET TO MODERATE.

Adjoining the Bright Angel Lodge, the **Arizona Room** specializes in steaks and seafood. The open kitchen lets you watch the chefs cook while you eat. Dinner only. Closed in January and February. ~ MODERATE TO DELUXE.

In the Yavapai Lodge, the **Canyon Cafe** serves fast food—burgers and fries, pizza and fried chicken—for breakfast, lunch and dinner (open seasonally with varied hours). ~ 928-638-2262, fax 928-638-2593. BUDGET.

There are two other cafeterias in the park. The first is **Maswik Cafeteria** at Maswik Lodge, which serves breakfast, lunch and dinner. ~ Located at the west end of Grand Canyon Village. BUDGET. The **Desert View Trading Post Cafeteria** serves a changing selection of hot meals (seasonal hours). ~ Located 23 miles east of the village along Desert View Drive. BUDGET.

President Theodore Roosevelt once said of the Grand Canyon: "Leave it as it is; you cannot improve on it; not one bit."

Ice cream, sandwiches and soft drinks are available at the **Hermits Rest Snack Bar** at the end of Hermit Road, as well as at the **Bright Angel Fountain**, near the trailhead for the Bright Angel Trail. Open seasonally. ~ BUDGET.

Outside the park entrance, the town of Tusayan has nearly a dozen eating establishments ranging from McDonald's to Taco Bell and Wendy's.

Other options include the **Coronado Room** located at the Best Western Grand Canyon Squire Inn, which serves prime rib, steaks and daily specials in a Southwestern-style dining room. Dinner only. ~ Route 64; 928-638-2681, 800-622-6966, fax 928-638-0162; www.grandcanyonsquire.com. DELUXE.

For standard coffee shop fare check out the **Garden Room**, also located at the Best Western Grand Canyon Squire Inn, which is open for breakfast and lunch. ~ Route 64; 928-638-2681, 800-622-6966, fax 928-638-0162; www.grandcanyonsquire.com. BUDGET.

Of several national park concession tourist stores on the South Rim, the best are **Hopi House**, the large Indian pueblo replica across from El Tovar Hotel, and the adjacent **Verkamp's Curios**. Both have been in continuous operation for almost a century and specialize in authentic American Indian handicrafts, with high standards of quality and some genuinely old pieces.

SHOPPING

Other Grand Canyon shops, at least as interesting for their historic architecture as their wares, include the old **Kolb Studio**, originally a 1904 photographic studio and now a bookstore, and the **Lookout Studio**, which has rock specimens and conventional curios. Both are in Grand Canyon Village. Another souvenir shop is the **Hermits Rest Gift Shop**. ~ End of Hermit Road. The **Desert View Watchtower** has more of the same. ~ Desert View Drive.

NIGHTLIFE   **Bright Angel Lodge** offers live weekly entertainment—usually a folk guitarist. In general, though, Grand Canyon National Park does not have much in the way of hot nightlife. We suggest taking in one of the ranger-produced slideshows presented in the amphitheater or simply sitting in the dark along the canyon rim and listening to the vast, deep silence.

▼▼▼▼▼▼▼▼▼▼▼▼▼▼▼   There are tent/RV sites in Grand Canyon Village

Outdoor Adventures

at **Mather Campground** ($15 per night, no hookups), first-come, first-served. Reservations

CAMPING   may be made up to five months in advance beginning the 5th of each month. ~ 800-365-2267, fax 301-722-1174; reservations.nps. gov. RV sites with full hookups are available at **Grand Canyon Trailer Village** ($25 per night for two people, $2 for each extra person), adjacent to Mather Campground. ~ 303-297-2757. Tent/RV sites are also available on a first-come, first-served basis at **Desert View Campground** ($10 per night, no hookups; closed mid-October to mid-May), 25 miles east of Grand Canyon Village. Outside the park, there's tent and RV camping available on a first-time, first-served basis at the Forest Service's **Ten-X Campground** ($10 per night, no hookups; closed October to mid-April), just south of Tusayan. Closed October to mid-April. ~ 928-638-2443.

Camping at Phantom Ranch or anyplace else below the rim requires a backcountry permit, which costs $10 per permit plus

◆◆◆

DON'T TRAIL OFF

If you're planning a hiking excursion in the Grand Canyon, remember to stick to the designated trails. Trails are in part designed to drain off water with a minimum of soil erosion; forging your own path may cause future problems. If you do need to venture off the beaten track, make sure the members of your group spread out instead of walking single file. Also, try to avoid meadows and wet areas, which are more likely to be affected by footprints and group travel than more forested and rocky land. When in doubt, remember those words of wisdom from camp counselors of yore: "Take only pictures, leave only footprints." Although in this case, try to avoid even that.

$5 per person per night. The number of permits available is limited; to improve your chances of obtaining one, apply four months in advance of your stay. ~ Backcountry Information Center; P.O. Box 129, Grand Canyon, AZ 86023; 928-638-7875, fax 928-638-2125.

At the Grand Canyon, the **Apache Stable** at Moqui Lodge in Tusayan, near the park's south entrance, offers a selection of guided rides to various points along the South Rim, lasting from one to four hours. One- and two-hour rides are available. Horseback rides do not go below the canyon rim. Call for reservations. ~ 928-638-2891, fax 928-638-2783; www.apachestables.com.

RIDING STABLES

For information on mule trips into the canyon, see "Touring the Grand Canyon" in this chapter.

Although trails within the national park are closed to bicycles, Kaibab National Forest surrounding the park on both the North and South Rims offers a wealth of mountain-biking possibilities. The forest areas adjoining Grand Canyon National Park are laced with old logging roads, and the relatively flat terrain makes for low-stress riding.

BIKING

Located at the South Rim of the Grand Canyon, the **Hermit Road** is closed to most private motor vehicles during the summer months but open to bicycles. This fairly level route (eight miles one way) makes for a spectacular cycling tour. Watch out for bus traffic during the summer months. One ride the National Forest Service recommends in the vicinity of the South Rim is the **Coconino Rim Trail** (9.1 miles), a loop trail that starts near Grandview Point and travels southeast through ponderosa forests.

For other suggestions, stop in at the Tusayan Ranger Station just outside the South Rim entrance (928-638-2443) or contact Kaibab National Forest Headquarters. ~ 800 South 6th Street, Williams, AZ 86046; 928-635-8200.

The ultimate hiking experience in Grand Canyon National Park—and perhaps in the entire Southwest—is an expedition from either rim to the bottom of the canyon and back. With an elevation change of 4800 feet from the South Rim to the river, or 5800 feet from the North Rim, the hike is as ambitious as an ascent of a major Rocky Mountain peak, except that the greatest effort is required in the last miles of the climb out, when leg muscles may already be sore from the long downhill trek. Strenuous as it may be, hiking the Grand Canyon is an experience sure to stay vivid for a lifetime.

HIKING

Though some people claim to have done it, hiking roundtrip from the rim to river level and back in a single day is a monumental feat that takes from 16 to 18 hours. Most hikers who plan

Text continued on page 56.

Touring the Grand Canyon

It seems like there are more ways to explore the Grand Canyon than there are routes down its walls. Hikers, mule riders, aviators and even whitewater enthusiasts have all discovered its sporting opportunities.

Of course the most rigorous way to tour the famous chasm is by *hiking*. If you have the time, making your way by foot down to the bottom is an amazing experience. Be forewarned—it is impossible to complete the journey in a day; people are often airlifted out for trying. Rest stops with shade and refreshing cold water are scattered intermittently along the trails. Plan ahead and camp or stay at the Phantom Ranch. (Do not arrive at the Phantom Ranch without reservations!)

For a taste of the Old West, mules are a classic mode of transport. *Mule trips* range from one-day excursions that venture as far as Plateau Point to two- and three-day trips (available November through March) to the bottom of the canyon. The cost is several hundred dollars per person, including meals and accommodations at the Phantom Ranch. Mule trips depart from both the North and South rims. Reservations must be made well ahead of time—as much as a year in advance for weekends, holidays and the summer months. For South Rim departures, contact **Xanterra Parks & Resorts**. ~ 14001 East Iliff Avenue, Suite 600, Aurora, CO 80014; 303-297-2757, fax 303-297-3175; www.grandcanyon lodges.com, e-mail reserve-gcsr@xanterra.com. For North Rim departures, call **Grand Canyon Trail Rides**. Closed mid-October to mid-May. ~ P.O. Box 128, Tropic, UT 84776; 435-679-8665; www.canyonrides.com.

Many *"flightseeing"* tours offer spectacular eagle-eye views of the Grand Canyon. **Grand Canyon Airlines**' fully narrated tour circles the canyon starting at the South Rim and offers views of the Painted Desert and the confluence of the Colorado and Little Colorado rivers. ~ P.O. Box 3038, Grand Canyon, AZ 86023; 928-638-2407, 800-528-2413; www.grandcanyonairlines.com. With **Air Grand Canyon** you can choose from three different trips ranging from a 30- or 50-minute tour of the Eastern Gorge and the confluence of the Colorado and Little Colorado rivers to a 105-minute flight that visits all the major canyon sights. ~ P.O. Box 3399, Grand Canyon, AZ 86023; 928-638-2686, 800-

247-4726, fax 928-776-8099; www.airgrandcanyon.com. Both of these companies operate from Grand Canyon Airport near Tusayan.

Even more thrilling—and more expensive—are *helicopter tours*. Helicopters can fly considerably lower than airplanes, affording an even closer look at the magnificent canyon. Neither helicopters nor planes are allowed to fly beneath the rim, however, keeping the canyon peaceful for hikers and riders. The 45-minute Imperial Flight offered by **Papillon Grand Canyon Helicopters** affords views of the Painted Desert, Marble Canyon and Dragon's Corridor. The shorter North Canyon flight explores the Central Corridor. ~ P.O. Box 455, Grand Canyon, AZ 86023; 928-638-2419, 800-528-2418; www.papillon.com. With **AirStar Helicopters** you can choose the 25- to 30-minute Central Corridor tour, the 40- to 45-minute Eastern Canyon tour or a 50- to 55-minute tour combining the two. ~ P.O. Box 3379, Grand Canyon, AZ 86023; 928-638-2622, 800-962-3869; www.airstar.com.

If simply looking at the bottom of the canyon isn't enough, water adventurers might consider a *rafting trip* down the Colorado River. Raft trips operate from April through September. Most start at Lee's Ferry, northeast of the national park boundary near Page, Arizona, and just below Glen Canyon Dam. The rafts are motorized, with pontoons, and provide seating for about 14 people.

More exciting are the smaller oar-operated dories that ride closer to the water and occasionally tip over in the rough rapids. Rafting the full length of the canyon, 280 miles from Lee's Ferry to Lake Mead, takes a leisurely eight days, providing plenty of time to hike and explore remote parts of the canyon inaccessible by other means. Many rafting companies also offer shorter trips that involve being picked up or dropped off by helicopter part way through the canyon.

One of the leading raft tour companies is **Grand Canyon Expeditions**, offering eight-day motorized expeditions and fourteen-day rowing trips. Transportation, camping gear and all meals are provided. ~ P.O. Box O, Kanab, UT 84741; 435-644-2691, 800-544-2691. Another good organization is **Arizona River Runners** for multiday motorized or oar-powered trips. Meals and equipment are included. ~ P.O. Box 47788, Phoenix, AZ 85068; 602-867-4866, 800-477-7238. A complete list of river trip outfitters is available from **Rivers and Oceans**. ~ 928-526-4575, 800-473-4576. Private parties can take the river route through the Grand Canyon. Contact the South Rim visitors center for additional information.

to go the whole way will want to allow at least two, preferably three, days for the trip. The park service does not recommend attempting to hike from the rim to the canyon bottom during the summer months *unless* starting the trek before 7 a.m. or after 4 p.m. (Though it might be 85° on the rim, it could be 115° at the bottom.) A wilderness permit, required for any overnight trip into the park backcountry, can be obtained free of charge at the backcountry office on either rim. All distances listed for hiking trails are one way unless otherwise noted.

The Grand Canyon's first trail was the Bright Angel Trail, opened in 1891.

The **Bright Angel Trail** (7.8 miles to the river or 9.3 miles to Phantom Ranch), the most popular trail in the canyon, starts at Grand Canyon Village on the South Rim, near the mule corral. It has the most developed facilities, including a resthouse with an emergency phone along the upper part of the trail and a ranger station, water and a campground midway down at Indian Garden, where the Havasupai people used to grow crops. The one-day roundtrip hike will take you along a ridgeline to Plateau Point, overlooking the Colorado River from 1300 feet above, just before the final steep descent. Allow about five hours to hike from the rim down to the river and about ten hours to climb back up. It is therefore advisable to camp and make the return trip the following day. Remember, a permit is required for overnight trips. A lot of hikers use this trail, as do daily mule riders—not the route to take if you seek solitude.

Another major trail from the South Rim is the **South Kaibab Trail** (7.3 miles to Phantom Ranch), which starts from the trailhead on Desert View Drive, near Yaki Point. A free shuttle bus takes hikers to the trailhead. The shortest of the main trails into the canyon, it is also the steepest and, due to lack of water and shade along the route, not recommended during the summer months.

Several less-used trails also descend from the South Rim. All of them intersect the **Tonto Trail** (95 miles), which runs along the edge of the inner gorge about 1300 feet above river level. The **Grandview Trail** (3 miles), an old mine access route that starts at Grandview Point on Desert View Drive, goes down to Horseshoe Mesa, where it joins a loop of the Tonto Trail that circles the mesa, passing ruins of an old copper mine. There is a primitive campground without water on the mesa. All camping in the canyon requires a backcountry permit.

The **Hermit Trail** (8.5 miles) begins at Hermit's Rest at the end of Hermit Road and descends to join the Tonto Trail. Branching off from the Dripping Springs Trail, which also starts at Hermits Rest, the **Boucher Trail** (11 miles) also goes down to join the Tonto Trail and is considered one of the more difficult hiking trails in the park. Ask for details at the Backcountry Information Center.

The paved, handicapped-accessible **Rim Trail** (1.5 miles) goes between the Kolb Studio at the west side of Grand Canyon Village and the Yavapai Observation Station. A one-third-mile spur links the Rim Trail with the visitors center. At each end of the designated Rim Trail, the pavement ends but unofficial trails continue for several more miles, ending at Hopi Point near the Powell Memorial on Hermit Road and at Yaki Point, the trailhead for the South Kaibab Trail, on Desert View Drive.

Williams

This historic mountain town, tucked away in the ponderosa pine forest of northern Arizona, is still somewhat undiscovered. But it's only 60 miles southeast from the Grand Canyon and, working hard to get its name on more visitors maps, has adopted (and legally registered) the moniker "Gateway to the Grand Canyon." Founded in 1882, long before it had a savvy chamber of commerce, Williams was known as a tough, bawdy railroad and logging center. Across the street from the railroad yards, brothels and opium dens sprung up to

Williams

serve the loggers, Chinese laborers, railroad workers and cowboys. At that time, a muddy roadway through town was part of the network of trails known as Old Trails Highway. By the 1920s, the roadway became part of the U.S. highway system and entered cultural lore as Route 66. As the interstate highway system replaced the old Route 66, Williams held out until 1984, when it became the last town along the old route to be bypassed by the interstate.

Today, many of the buildings along Bill Williams and Railroad avenues (the old Route 66 roadways) are listed on the National Register of Historic Places and now house American Indian and Western arts-and-crafts galleries, antique stores and restaurants, as well as a few saloons.

With at least a dozen motels that hark back to the old Route 66 days, this small town (pop. 2900) is something of a quaint, living museum of a bygone era in American culture. Quaint, however, does not mean out of touch: The chamber of commerce in Williams has a website (www.thegrandcanyon.com).

SIGHTS   The first place to stop in Williams is the **Williams Forest Service Visitors Center**, located in the old Santa Fe railroad freight depot, to pick up brochures about attractions or obtain information about lodging, dining or visiting the Grand Canyon. ~ 200 West Railroad Avenue; 928-635-4061, fax 928-635-1417; www.williamschamber.com.

From the visitors center, a walk around downtown Williams is quite manageable. The historical core extends no more than four blocks in either direction along Route 66 and Railroad avenues. Most of the shops and galleries of interest to visitors are on Route 66, which is only a block from the visitors center. Sidewalks have been brick-paved, and most turn-of-the-20th-century buildings have been restored and now house galleries of Western and American Indian art, jewelry and crafts, collectibles, restaurants and a couple of authentic Route 66 saloons.

The **Grand Canyon Railway** is just across the tracks from the visitors center, in the historic 1908 Williams Depot. Using either turn-of-the-20th-century steam engines (summer months) or 1950s diesel engines (winter), the train leaves Williams in the morning for a two-and-a-quarter-hour trip through Kaibab National Forest to the Grand Canyon, tracing the route that brought early tourists to the park. The return trip to Williams departs from the Grand Canyon in midafternoon. Trains run daily year-round. The depot building also houses a small but well-done historical and railroad museum. ~ Williams Depot, Railroad Avenue and Grand Canyon Boulevard, Williams; 928-773-1976, 800-843-8724, fax 928-773-1610; www.thetrain.com, e-mail info@thetrain.com.

The Grand Canyon Railway

More than a century ago, the first tourists to see the Grand Canyon had to endure a long, bumpy, dusty ride on horseback or in a stagecoach. No wonder there wasn't much interest in the the canyon as a tourist attraction. Mining, logging and ranching interests had spurred early partial development of a rail line into the canyon area. But it wasn't until 1901, when the Grand Canyon was made part of a national forest preserve, that the Atchison, Topeka and Santa Fe Railroad completed a spur from Williams to the South Rim. The railroad, along with the Fred Harvey Company, developed the Grand Canyon into a major tourist attraction. Twice a day, steam trains left the Williams Depot for the South Rim. Over the years, until 1968, when the last train pulled out of Williams for the Grand Canyon, millions of visitors, including Theodore Roosevelt, FDR, John Muir and Jimmy Durante, had ridden the Grand Canyon Railway.

In 1989, Arizona businessman Max Biegert and his wife, Thelma, bought the railway. They had steam locomotives and coach cars rebuilt or restored, and on September 17, 1989—88 years after the inauguration of the first passenger service began—they renewed daily steam locomotive passenger service from Williams to the South Rim. More than 200,000 passengers ride the railway each year now, which keeps about 50,000 vehicles a year out of the South Rim part of the Grand Canyon (an important benefit considering the congestion and pollution generated by monumental automobile traffic).

The railway operates year-round, with trains leaving from Williams Depot at 10 a.m. for the two-and-a-quarter-hour, 65-mile journey to the South Rim. Before boarding restored coaches (including the 1923 Harriman coaches), passengers are entertained in the depot plaza by cowboy skits and gunfights. Onboard, musicians perform and move from coach to coach. Snacks and beverages are available. Meanwhile, as the train rounds a bend, the landscape of the Arizona high country changes from ponderosa pine to open plain. Once in the park, there's time for one of two bus tours (with optional lunch) of the South Rim before reboarding at 3:30 p.m. for the return trip to Williams. It's been reported that occasionally on the way back, masked train robbers have held up the train.

Roundtrip fares are $60 for adults, $25 for children (2–10) and $35 for youth (11–16). Four upgrades, from Club Class to Parlor Car, are available, as are one-way options and overnights at the South Rim. ~ 800-843-8724, fax 928-773-1610; www.thetrain.com, e-mail info@thetrain.com.

A drive south about 12 miles on **Perkinsville Road** (referred to locally as the South Road) will bring you to open meadows, where, at dusk, it's not uncommon to spot deer and elk emerging from the forest to graze. Early October, when the aspen trees have turned golden and flame, is an especially lovely time to make the drive during the day to see the fall colors.

The summer months, June through August, are a good time to visit **Grand Canyon Deer Farm Petting Zoo**. That's when the fawns are born at the small, walk-through park. Although most of the animals, including pronghorn antelope, buffalo, turkeys, wallabies and reindeer, are enclosed, several types of deer and some of the goats have free reign and will demand to eat right out of your hand. If you buy some feed before entering the park grounds, you'll be guaranteed an upclose visit. Open year-round, weather permitting in winter. Admission. ~ 6752 East Deer Farm Road on Route 40, Exit 171, eight miles east of Williams; 928-635-4073, 800-926-3337, fax 928-635-2357; www.deerfarm. com, e-mail deerfrmr@aol.com.

Aviation history buffs might want to stop at **Planes of Fame Air Museum** on Route 64 in Valle, about halfway between Williams and the Grand Canyon. The historic aircraft on display, many of them restored to flying condition, represent a spectrum of aviation history from World War I through the supersonic jet age. Besides a 1930s Travel Air (one of the first aircraft to tour the Grand Canyon) there are several fighter craft, as well as General Douglas MacArthur's Lockheed Constellation transport called "Bataan." (There's an extra charge to tour this craft.) Admission. ~ 755 Mustang Way, Valle; 928-635-1000; www. planesoffame.org.

Just down the road from the Planes of Fame Air Museum is an odd sight: **Bedrock City**, a cartoon-colored, life-size theme park of sorts where you can walk into the Flintstones' and Rubbles' homes, as well as the jail and the schoolhouse. But there's not much of the fun and wild antics of the Hanna-Barbera cartoons: no costumed Fred and Barney wandering around, no animated Dino or Pebbles. You can, however, catch a ride on the train that lurches through a volcano and around town. The cinder pathways are hard to walk on. A campground, coffee shop and souvenir store are on the premises. Admission. ~ Routes 64 and 180, Valle; 928-635-2600.

LODGING   Williams has several choices for motel accommodations located along historic Route 66, many offering low prices as well as nostalgia. The chamber of commerce can provide a list. ~ 200 West Railroad Avenue; 928-635-4061, fax 928-635-1417; www.williamschamber.com, e-mail info@williamschamber.com.

Visitors looking for a historical connection to Williams' rowdy railroad and mining past might consider booking a room at the **Red Garter Bed and Bakery**. Innkeeper John Holst has completely restored and renovated an 1897 Victorian Romanesque building that was used as a saloon and a bordello. The original eight cribs on the second floor have been remodeled into four guest rooms and furnished with antiques. Each room has a private three-quarter bath. Of course, the rooms tend be smaller than standard hotel or motel rooms, and two of the rooms don't have windows, but 12-foot ceilings, over-the-door transoms, skylights and ceiling fans keep things cheerful, bright and airy. The "best" girl's room is a small bedroom–sitting room suite in the front of the building. An extended continental breakfast is served each morning in the bakery downstairs. Innkeeper Holst has lived in Arizona for many years and is extremely knowledgeable about Williams and the region. He's glad to help out with suggestions for itineraries, day trips and activities in the area. Closed December and January. ~ 137 West Railroad Avenue; 928-635-1484, 800-328-1484; www.redgarter.com, e-mail john@redgarter.com. DELUXE.

◄ *HIDDEN*

Metate-shaped stone bowls, once used by American Indians to grind corn, are commonly found throughout Southwest ruins.

Adjacent to the Grand Canyon Railway depot is the **Fray Marcos Hotel**, built in the same architectural style as the Williams Depot. The large, comfortable rooms have two queen-size beds; smoking and nonsmoking rooms are available. The hotel has a restaurant, a spa, a fitness room and an indoor pool. ~ Williams Depot, 235 Grand Canyon Boulevard; 928-635-4010, 800-843-8724, fax 928-635-2180; www.thetrain.com, e-mail info@the train.com. DELUXE.

The **Best Western Inn of Williams**, perched on a hillside just off Route 40, is a AAA three-diamond-rated motel. The inn features an outdoor pool and spa and provides hairdryers and laundry facilities. ~ 2600 West Route 66, Route 40 Business Loop, Exit 161; 928-635-4400, 800-635-4445, fax 928-635-4488; www.bestwestern.com. MODERATE TO DELUXE.

The only hostel located on the highway to the Grand Canyon, **Grand Canyon Red Lake Hostel** has a total of 32 beds; private rooms are available. Facilities include a common room (equipped with TV and VCR) and a kitchen area (with microwave, toaster and mini-refrigerators); showers are coin-operated. ~ 8850 North Route 64, ten miles north of Williams; 928-635-4753, 800-581-4753, fax 928-635-4753. BUDGET.

This is still cowboy country when it comes to food, and steak and ribs are popular on local menus. You can't miss the big neon cow in front of **Rod's Steak House**, a Route 66 landmark that's been

DINING

around since 1946. A casual, no-frills place, Rod's keeps the menu straightforward: steak (prepared eight different ways), prime rib (four cuts), fish and chicken. There's a children's menu available. Closed Sunday. ~ 301 East Route 66; 928-635-2671, fax 928-635-9557; www.rods-steakhouse.com, e-mail rods@rods-steakhouse.com. MODERATE TO DELUXE.

Besides platters of steak, barbecued ribs or prime rib, **Miss Kitty's Steakhouse and Saloon** offers up live country music each evening during tourist season. It's a big place, with lots of wood and brick and high beamed ceilings. A balcony rings two sides of the room and a stage and dancefloor occupy one end of the room. It's fast, efficient and fun. Dinner only; closed Monday through Wednesday during the off-season. ~ In the Ramada Inn Canyon Gateway, 642 East Route 66; 520-635-9161. MODERATE TO DELUXE.

Pancho McGillicuddy's Mexican Cantina is located in the downtown Williams historic district, next to the Red Garter Bed and Bakery. The atmosphere is cheerful and friendly, and the food is fresh tasting and generously portioned. They serve a limited Mexican breakfast. Call ahead for winter schedule. ~ 141 West Railroad Avenue; 928-635-4150, fax 928-832-9687. BUDGET TO MODERATE.

Set in a renovated gas station, **Cruiser's Café 66** generates the spirit of Route 66 with antiques and memorabilia galore. Sidle up to gas pumps, neon signs, old photographs and road signs for a closer look at those magical motoring days. Grab a drink at the horseshoe bar before ordering burgers, chicken, steaks or ribs. ~ 233 West Route 66; 928-635-2445, fax 928-635-9800. BUDGET TO MODERATE.

SHOPPING   Get your kicks—or at least handmade American Indian jewelry, arts, crafts and Route 66 souvenirs—at **Native American Williams**. ~ 117 East Route 66; 928-635-4600.

AUTHOR FAVORITE

Old Smoky's Restaurant looks like a typical small-town roadside greasy spoon from the outside, but that doesn't deter the breakfast crowds of both locals and Grand Canyon visitors fueling up for a day of sightseeing. Crossing the threshold of this neighborhood pancake house is like stepping back in time. The decor features cowboy and Western memorabilia, and hard-to-find collectibles. Expect huge portions of homestyle cooking that include biscuits and gravy, fluffy omelets, thick chunks of homemade bread and bottomless cups of Joe. No dinner. ~ 624 West Route 66, Williams; 520-635-2091, fax 520-635-9276; e-mail oldsmoky@aol.com. BUDGET.

If hanging out in a Route 66 saloon or motel lounge isn't your **NIGHTLIFE**
idea of a fun evening, there isn't too much to do in Williams after
dark. But on most Saturday evenings you can head over to the
Red Garter Bed and Bakery and peek into the bakery, where ◄ *HIDDEN*
you'll probably find a group of local musicians playing and
singing. Come in, have a cup of coffee and observe the proceedings or, perhaps, join in them. The friendly, informal gathering is
a great way to meet local people. Closed December and January.
~ 137 West Railroad Avenue; 928-635-1484; e-mail john@red
garter.com.

The 18-hole **Elephant Rocks at Williams**, sur-   ▼▼▼▼▼▼▼▼▼▼▼▼▼▼
rounded by ponderosa forest, is fairly difficult.   **Outdoor Adventures**
The 18th hole, for instance, starts at an eleva-
tion of 7000 feet and drops some 80 feet to the cup. Besides that,   **GOLF**
it has a distractingly enjoyable view of the surrounding countryside and Bill Williams Mountain a few miles away. Open March   ◄ *HIDDEN*
through November, weather permitting. You'll find a putting
green, a driving range and club and cart rentals. ~ Country Club
Road, Williams; 928-635-4935.

The family-oriented **Williams Ski Area**, atop 9256-foot Bill Wil-   **SKIING**
liams Mountain, offers beginners and intermediate skiers a variety
of groomed slopes and trails on which to practice. Snowboarding
and tubing are allowed here. Downhill and snowboard rentals,
as well as lessons, are available. Open depending on conditions.
~ 928-635-9330, fax 928-635-9339; or the chamber of commerce
at 928-635-4061; www.williamsskiarea.com, e-mail wmskia@
infomagic.net.

Stable in the Pines offers easy guided trail rides through the coun-   **RIDING**
try just outside Williams. The emphasis is on enjoying the outdoors,   **STABLES**
with trail guides pointing out flora and fauna. Children must be
six and older; there are hay rides on the weekend for the younger
kids. Closed October through April. ~ Circle Pines KOA Campground, Route 40, Exit 167, Williams; 928-635-1930, 800-562-
9379, fax 928-635-2627; e-mail najudymo@grm.net.

All distances listed are one way unless otherwise noted.   **HIKING**
    Bill Williams Mountain offers two especially pleasant day
hikes lasting no more than six hours roundtrip. The trailhead for
Benham Trail (4.5 miles) is about a 15-minute trek from Williams, on Forest Road 140 off Perkinsville Road. The trail starts
at the 7200-foot level, in ponderosa pine and oak thickets, and
climbs up moderately difficult slopes to about 9200 feet into
mixed conifer forest. At several places along the trail, hikers have
good views of the valley below and distant peaks.

Bill Williams Mountain Trail #2 (4 miles) also starts out in ponderosa pine and oak thickets, near the Williams Ranger Station at Clover Hill. The trail then leads hikers through stands of aspen and fir. The ancestors of the Hopi inhabited the land here at one time, and the area is still considered sacred. Trail guides are available at the Williams Visitors Center and at the ranger station.

The North Rim

The North Rim of the Grand Canyon receives only about one-tenth of the number of visitors the South Rim gets. Snowbound during the winter because it is 1200 feet higher in elevation, the North Rim is only open from mid-May through October, while the South Rim is open year-round. The South Rim is more convenient for more travelers since it is much closer to a major interstate highway route and to the large population centers of southern Arizona and California. But if your tour of the Southwest includes destinations such as the Navajo Indian Reservation, Lake Powell, Page, Bryce Canyon and Zion national parks, or even Las Vegas, then your route will take you closer to the North Rim, giving you an opportunity to explore the cooler, quieter side of the canyon.

SIGHTS

Before starting the drive into the park from Jacob Lake, stop at the **Kaibab Plateau Visitors Center**. A small exhibit details information on human habitation and wildlife on the plateau, and a ranger is on duty to answer questions. Closed late October through April. ~ Routes 89 and 67, Jacob Lake; 928-643-7298 except on the weekends, fax 928-635-8208; www.fs.fed.us/r3/kai.

The drive across the **Kaibab Plateau** into the park on Route 67 (also called the Kaibab Plateau North Rim Parkway) winds through a forest of ponderosa pine, quaking aspen, blue spruce and Douglas fir, and large open mountain meadows. Mule deer and other wildlife can be seen occasionally in the meadows (early morning and early evening are the best times to spot them grazing). In the fall, stands of aspen trees set the landscape ashimmer in a trembling glow of yellow and flame orange.

Several miles into the park, a turnoff at Fuller Canyon Road leads to the scenic drives on **Point Imperial Road** and **Cape Royal Road**. At 8803 feet, **Point Imperial** is the highest point on either rim and commands a stunning view of Mt. Hayden, a huge carved sandstone spire, and the sprawling vistas of the eastern canyon. Cape Royal Road leads to **Vista Encantadora, Painted Desert Overlook** and **Walhalla Overlook**. There's an ancient Anasazi ruin across the road from Walhalla. The drive ends at **Cape Royal**, where you can take a self-guided nature walk and get a look at the Colorado River and the large natural arch called **Angels Window**. Cape Royal is also a popular spot to watch the sun rise or set. (Narrated tours to both Cape Royal and Point Imperial are available. Check at the information desk in the lobby of Grand Canyon Lodge.)

Route 67 dead-ends at the **Grand Canyon Lodge**, built of native stone and timber and perched right on the edge of the rim. Verandas on either side of the lodge offer sunny, open spots to view the canyon. At night, the lights of Grand Canyon Village, 11 miles away on the South Rim, are visible.

From the lodge, to the east, a path leads out to **Bright Angel Point**. Though paved, the quarter-mile path clings precipitously to the canyon rim, and rises and falls in some spots. A pamphlet to a self-guided walking tour to Bright Angel Point is available for a quarter. It points out places to look for fossils and where to see **Roaring Springs**, some 3800 feet below and the North Rim's source of water. From Bright Angel Point, which is at an elevation of 8200 feet, there are good views of the South Rim and the San Francisco Peaks near Flagstaff, some 50 miles away. The high elevation, however, can make breathing difficult for some people. Other viewpoints on the North Rim are reached by foot trails. (See "Hiking" under "Outdoor Adventures.")

On Route 389, nine miles from the Fredonia turnoff and six miles before you reach Pipe Springs, an unpaved road known as the Mount Trumbull Loop turns off to the south. (The other end of the

North Rim

HIDDEN ►

200-mile "loop" is near St. George, Utah.) This road provides the main access to **Grand Canyon–Parashant National Monument**. Don't forget to fill up the gas tank in Fredonia because you won't find a single gas station or telephone along this route. In fact, you may not even see another vehicle—just wide-open countryside as empty as all of Arizona used to be long ago. The newly created national monument has no visitor facilities, though future plans call for an interpretive center and camping areas. It spans a vast plateau of sagebrush flats and piñon-juniper forests teeming with mule deer, bighorn sheep and mountain lions. The monument includes **Parashant Canyon**, the largest side canyon of the Grand Canyon, reached via primitive roads in a four-wheel-drive vehicle. It also includes the westernmost part of the Grand Canyon north rim.

HIDDEN ►

The most striking feature of Grand Canyon–Parashant National Monument is **Toroweap Point,** a dramatic vista on the edge of the Grand Canyon. The well-maintained unpaved road to Toroweap Point turns off the Mount Trumbull Loop about 50 miles from the highway; several other dirt roads branch off along the way but if you keep to the road that goes south and looks well used, following the "Toroweap" and "Grand Canyon National Monument" signs wherever you see them, it's hard to get lost. The elevation is 2000 feet lower than at the main North Rim visitor area, so instead of pine forest the vegetation is desert scrub, its roots clinging tenuously to slickrock. Being closer to the river, still nearly 3000 feet below, you can watch the parade of river rafts drifting past and even eavesdrop on passengers' conversations. There is a small, primitive **campground** at Toroweap Point, but no water, restrooms or other facilities. As likely as not, you may find that you have the place all to yourself.

LODGING

On the North Rim, the only lodging within the park is the **Grand Canyon Lodge**, which consists of a beautiful 1930s-vintage main lodge building overlooking the canyon and a number of cabins—some rustic, others modern, a few with canyon views. Clean and homelike, both rooms and cabins have an old-fashioned feel, though when I visited they seemed a little noisy. North Rim accommodations are in very high demand, so reservations should be made far ahead. They are accepted up to 23 months in advance. Reservations for the lodge are booked through Xanterra, which also handles reservations for the lodges at Bryce Canyon and Zion national parks. The lodge is closed from mid-October to mid-May. ~ Lodge: 928-638-2611, fax 928-638-2554. Reservations: 14001 East Iliff Avenue, Suite 600, Aurora, CO 80014; 303-297-2757, fax 303-297-3175; www.xanterra.com. MODERATE.

Just five miles from the entrance to the park, the **Kaibab Lodge** offers basic sleeping accommodations—29 small rooms with private bathroom in cabin-style buildings set around the main lodge

North Rim
Information

WHEN TO VISIT Although the park remains open for day use until December (or until heavy snow closes the road), visitor facilities on the North Rim of the Grand Canyon are open only from mid-May to mid-October.

WEATHER AND ELEVATION The North Rim's elevation is 8200 feet. Summers are temperate, with warm days and mild evenings. Winter snow can accumulate to over 12 feet.

GETTING TO THE NORTH RIM The distance across the canyon from the South Rim to the North Rim is only about ten miles as the crow flies. But the distance in road miles is about 200. Access is on Route 67, from Routes 89 and 89A. From Jacob Lake to the Grand Canyon Lodge, the distance is 45 miles. Page and Lake Powell are about 120 miles to the east. Shuttle transportation between the rims is available daily from mid-May to mid-October for a fee. ~ 928-638-2820.

ENTRANCE FEES The tariff for private vehicles is $20; for pedestrians, bicyclists and motorcyclists, it's $10. The fee is nonrefundable, but admission is good for seven consecutive days for both the North and South rims. U.S. seniors over 62 and physically disabled U.S. citizens may obtain specially priced passes; frequent national park visitors should inquire about the Golden Eagle Passport. An annual Grand Canyon passport is also available.

GETTING AROUND THE PARK The main road into the park dead-ends at the Grand Canyon Lodge. From there you can walk along a paved but precipitous path to one of the park's most popular overlooks, Bright Angel Point. Before reaching the lodge, a turnoff leads to Cape Royal Scenic Drive, a 20-mile drive to several other lookouts. Van tours are also available; a schedule is posted in the lobby of the lodge.

POSTAL, MEDICAL AND OTHER SERVICES A general store and a service station are located near the campground. The post office is located in the lodge complex. Dial 911 for emergency medical service. Water is not available along scenic drives or at viewpoints.

SERVICES FOR PERSONS WITH PHYSICAL DISABILITIES The *Accessibility Guide* is available at the information desk in the lodge lobby. Many of the viewpoints and other facilities are wheelchair-accessible or accessible with assistance.

building. There are no televisions or phones in the rooms (you'll find them in the lobby of the main lodge). There are three more developed and larger cabins available, two with microwaves and refrigerators. Reserve rooms well in advance. ~ Grand Canyon North Rim Parkway (Route 67); 928-638-2389 (May to mid-October only), 928-526-0924, 800-525-0924, fax 928-527-9398; www.canyoneers.com. MODERATE.

Forty-four miles from the North Rim is the **Jacob Lake Inn**. This small, rustic resort complex surrounded by national forest offers motel rooms and cabins, both smoking and nonsmoking, including some two-bedroom units. All cabins have decks and forest views (cabins 28 and 29 front the edge of the forest). Reservations should be made well in advance. ~ Junction of Routes 89 and 67, Jacob Lake; 928-643-7232, fax 928-643-7235; www.jacoblake.com, e-mail jacob@jacoblake.com. MODERATE.

For camping information, see page 69.

DINING

The **Grand Canyon Lodge Dining Room** offers breakfast, lunch and dinner at affordable prices. The food is good, conventional meat-and-potatoes fare and the atmosphere—a spacious, rustic log-beamed dining room with huge picture windows overlooking the canyon—is simply incomparable. Reservations are required for dinner. The lodge also operates a budget-priced snack shop serving breakfast, lunch and dinner in plain, simple surroundings, as well as a saloon offering pizza and sandwiches. Nearby, the camper store sells pizza sandwiches. Closed mid-October to mid-May. ~ 928-638-2611. MODERATE TO DELUXE.

PARKS

KAIBAB NATIONAL FOREST 🚶 🚴 🐎 ⚓ This 1,500,000-acre expanse of pine, fir, spruce and aspen forest includes both sides of the Grand Canyon outside the park boundaries. Most recreational facilities are located near the North Rim, where they supplement the park's limited camping facilities. Wildlife in the forest includes mule deer, wild turkeys, several other bird species and even a few bison. There are picnic areas, restrooms and a visitors center. The facilities in the forest close from about October to April. ~ The national forest visitors center is at Jacob Lake, the intersection of Routes 89A and 67; 928-643-7298 (North Rim visitors center), 928-635-4061, fax 928-635-1417 (South Rim); www.fs.fed.us/r3/kai. Jacob Lake Campground is at the same location, while Demotte Campground is 23 miles south on Route 67, about five miles from the national park entrance.

▲ Demotte Campground has 23 sites, $12 per night, and Jacob Lake Campground has 52 sites, $12 per night. ~ 928-643-7770. RV hookups are available at the privately owned Kaibab Camper Village, $12 for tent sites (two people, $2 each additional person), $22 for motor homes (two people, $2 each additional person). ~ 928-643-7804, 928-526-0924 (mid-October to mid-April).

North Rim Campground ($15 to $20 per night, no hookups) is open from mid-May to mid-October. Reservations may be made at 800-365-2267 or online at reservations.nps.gov up to five months in advance beginning the 5th of each month. Rangers at a booth just south of Jacob Lake can advise motorists whether campsites are available within the park and, if not, will direct them to alternate camping in Kaibab National Forest, where there are developed campgrounds at **Demotte Park** ($12 per night, no hookups), seven miles north of the canyon rim, and **Jacob Lake** ($12 per night, no hookups). In addition, dispersed primitive camping is allowed beside forest roads within Kaibab National Forest, though not within a quarter mile of the highway.

Outdoor Adventures

CAMPING

Although trails within the national park are closed to bicycles, Kaibab National Forest surrounding the park on the North Rim offers a wealth of mountain-biking possibilities. The forest areas adjoining Grand Canyon National Park are laced with old logging roads and the relatively flat terrain makes for low-stress riding.

Toward the west end of the Grand Canyon on its North Rim, visitors to **Toroweap Point** will find endless mountain biking opportunities along the hundreds of miles of remote, unpaved roads in the Arizona Strip.

BIKING

All distances listed for hiking trails are one way unless otherwise noted.

The main trail into the canyon from the North Rim is the **North Kaibab Trail** (14.2 miles). The trail starts from the trailhead two miles north of Grand Canyon Lodge and descends abruptly down Roaring Springs Canyon for almost five miles to Bright Angel Creek. This is the steepest part of the trip. Where the trail reaches the

HIKING

AUTHOR FAVORITE

Of more than 250 miles of hiking trails in Grand Canyon National Park, my personal favorite is the North Rim's **Widforss Trail** (5 miles), named after artist Gunnar Widforss, who painted landscapes in the national parks during the 1920s. The trail winds along the lip of the plateau through scrubby oak, piñon pines, ponderosa pines and juniper to a remote canyon viewpoint. The viewpoint overlooks a side canyon known as Haunted Canyon.

creek, there are several swimming holes, a good destination for a one-day roundtrip. The trail then follows the creek all the way to Phantom Ranch at the bottom of the canyon. Park rangers recommend that hikers allow a full day to hike from the rim to the ranch and two days to climb back to the rim, stopping overnight at Cottonwood Camp, the midway point. Because of heavy snows on the rim, this trail is not recommended during the winter months.

Without descending below the canyon rim, hikers can choose from a variety of trails ranging from short scenic walks to all-day hikes. The easy, paved, handicapped-accessible **Transept Trail** (2 miles) runs between the campground and the lodge, then continues gradually downward to Bright Angel Point, which affords the best view of the Bright Angel Trail down into the canyon.

The **Uncle Jim Trail** (2.5 miles) starts at the same trailhead as the Roaring Springs Canyon fork of the Bright Angel Trail, two miles north of the lodge. It circles through the ponderosa woods to an overlook, Uncle Jim Point.

The **Ken Patrick Trail** (10 miles) runs from Point Imperial to the Kaibab Trail parking lot.

HIDDEN ▶   Visitors to remote Toroweap Point may wish to try the **Lava Falls Route** (1.5 miles), which begins as a jeep road midway between the old ranger station and the point. Although this trail is not long, it is recommended for experienced hikers only, as it is rocky, edgy, very steep, and marked only by cairns, descending 3000 feet to the Colorado River and the "falls"—actually a furious stretch of white water formed when lava spilled into the river. Allow all day for the roundtrip hike and do not attempt it during the hot months.

▼▼▼▼▼▼▼▼▼▼
Arizona Strip   The rectangular-shaped stretch of Arizona sandwiched between the Colorado River and the borders of Utah and Nevada is referred to as the Arizona Strip. Most of the area is remote, with few paved roads and, aside from Colorado City, Fredonia and Jacob Lake, few towns or settlements for visitors. In January 2000, President Clinton signed an executive order creating Grand Canyon–Parashant National Monument to protect more than a million acres of the Arizona Strip from mining, hunting, off-roading and other environmental abuses.

Along the eastern edge of the Arizona Strip, on the Colorado River, however, the manmade Lake Powell is an increasingly popular resort, especially well-known for houseboat vacations. The nearby town of Page offers ample accommodations and dining options. Page is about 120 miles from the North Rim of the Grand Canyon. Glen Canyon Dam, Lee's Ferry (a prized spot for trophy trout), Marble Canyon and Vermillion Cliffs are along the route to the North Rim from Page.

Once a remote fortresslike Mormon ranching outpost, **Pipe Spring** **SIGHTS**
National Monument had the only telegraph station in the Arizona Territory north of the Grand Canyon, and was home to the
Winsor family and their employees, thus its historical nickname,
Winsor Castle. The ranch buildings and equipment are well preserved, and the duck pond provides a cool oasis. Park rangers
costumed in period dress re-create the pioneer lifestyle during the
summer months. Admission. ~ Route 389, 13 miles west of Fredonia; 928-643-7105, fax 928-643-7583; www.nps.gov/pisp.

Like life, **Lake Powell** is grand, awesome and filled with con-
tradictions. Conservationists considered it a disaster when Glen
Canyon Dam was built in Page, flooding beautiful Glen Canyon
and creating a 186-mile-long reservoir that extended deep into the
heart of Utah. Today, the lake is part of the Glen Canyon National
Recreation Area and covers one and a quarter *million* acres in two
states. It is an enormously popular recreation area, and the desert
canyon landscape of multihued sandstone mesas, buttes and spires

Arizona Strip

to Escalante

0 |————| 20 miles
0 |————| 20 kilometers

Grand Staircase-
Escalante National
Monument

Glen Canyon
National
Recreation
Area   Ferry

276
276

Mt Carmel   **Old Paria**

Warm   Creek   River

Paria   **Lake Powell**   *San   Juan*

Kanab   89   89

U T A H
Fredonia   A R I Z O N A

389   ALT
89   *River*   **Rainbow Bridge**
National Monument

▲ Tower Butte   ▲ *Navajo Mountain*
Marble Canyon   **Page**
Navajo   Creek

VERMILLION CLIFFS   ALT
89   98

Jacob
Lake   **Bitter Springs**   **Navajo National**
Monument

Kaibab National
Forest   67

Kaibab
Lodge   *River*   Navajo   98   160

Grand Canyon   N   Indian
National Park   89   Reservation

NORTH   RIM   *Colorado*

Havasupai
Indian
Reservation   **Tuba City**

Grand   **Little**   **Moenkopi**
Canyon   *Colorado*
Village   SOUTH   RIM   64   Little Colorado
River Gorge   264
Kaibab National
180   Forest   **Cameron**

POINTS OF INTEREST	
Ⓐ	Bullfrog Marina
Ⓑ	Dangling Rope Marina
Ⓒ	Glen Canyon Dam
Ⓓ	Hall's Crossing Marina
Ⓔ	Lee's Ferry
Ⓕ	Navajo Bridge
Ⓖ	Wahweap Marina

is spectacular. The shoreline of Lake Powell exceeds 1900 miles, more than the length of the west coast of the U.S.

The depth of Lake Powell's turquoise waters varies from year to year depending on mountain runoff and releases from Glen Canyon Dam. An interesting cave discovered on one trip may well be under water the next season. The same holds true for favorite sandy beaches, coves and waterfalls. But part of the fun of exploring this multi-armed body of water is finding new hidden treasures and hideaways around the next curve. Sunset is a favorite time of day to be on Lake Powell because natural-rock amphitheaters appear to change colors before your very eyes as the late afternoon sun makes its curtain call.

Page started out as a construction camp for the workers building the Glen Canyon Dam in 1956. The U.S. government had to trade land with the Navajo tribe to acquire the 17-square-mile site, and a road was cut into the remote region from Route 89. The town incorporated in 1975, and today, Page has a population of 8200 residents and an annual visitor count of over three million.

The Page–Lake Powell Chamber of Commerce Visitor Bureau can provide you with information. Closed Sunday. ~ 644 North Navajo Drive, Page; 928-645-2741, 888-261-7243, fax 928-645-3181; www.pagelakepowellchamber.org.

Wedged into a sandstone gorge, **Glen Canyon Dam** took ten years to construct, starting in 1956. Over 400,000 buckets of concrete (a "bucket" holds 24 tons) were poured to build the dam. The dam, which holds back the Colorado River, flooded Glen Canyon and created Lake Powell, the nation's second-largest man-made lake. The powerplant at the toe of the dam produces nearly 1.3 million kilowatts of power, which is sold to municipalities, government agencies and public utilities in seven Western states.

Each year, about a million visitors begin their visit to the dam at the **Carl Hayden Visitor Center**. Exhibits explain the dam's con-

TREAT WITH RESPECT

Rainbow Bridge is considered sacred by many American Indians, and the site has religious significance. To the Navajo, Rainbow represents guardians of the Universe. Boat tour passengers approach the bridge on a quarter-mile walkway that's part pontoon. The bridge may be photographed from a viewing area, but visitors are not permitted to walk under the bridge. Although signs that advise of the site's sacred status are clearly posted, many visitors tend to ignore the request to remain in the viewing area and must be called back by tour guides or boat crew members.

struction and benefits. If you join a free guided tour you'll find yourself descending in a large elevator to a depth of more than 500 feet below the crest of the dam. At one point on the tour, over 100 feet of concrete separates you from the waters of Lake Powell. ~ Route 89, Page; 928-608-6404, fax 928-608-6283; www.nps. gov/glca, e-mail glca_chvc@nps.gov.

You can become acquainted with Powell from atop its sky-high buttes and adjacent byways, but those truly interested in getting to know the complex personality, curves and quirks must travel by vessel to the quiet box canyons and deep, gleaming pools for an experience akin to spiritual cleansing. Aficionados claim the best season to visit is early fall when rates and temperatures drop to a comfortable level.

By mid-May, Lake Powell's waters are usually warm enough to engage in a variety of water sports. All the marinas except for Dangling Rope rent boats and houseboats in which to explore the area. Contact **Lake Powell Resorts & Marinas** for rentals at Wahweap, Bullfrog and Hite marinas (though Hite may be closed due to low water levels). ~ Lakeshore Drive off Route 89, near Glen Canyon Dam; 928-645-6000, 602-331-5200, 800-528-6154, fax 602-331-5258; www.lakepowell.com.

Another way to explore Lake Powell is to take a **boat tour**— a float trip down the Colorado River, a half-day tour to Rainbow Bridge, a full-day tour that enters many of the lake's high-walled canyons and includes a box lunch, or a sunset or dinner cruise aboard a paddle wheeler. The boat tours, paddle-wheel cruises and float trips depart Wahweap Lodge & Marina. ~ 100 Lakeshore Drive; 928-645-2433, 800-528-6154, fax 602-331-5258; www.lakepowell.com.

The highlight of the Lake Powell boat tours is **Rainbow Bridge National Monument**, the world's largest natural bridge located about 50 miles from Wahweap. "Nonnezoshi"—or rainbow turned to stone, as it's called by the Navajos—spans 275 feet and rises 290 feet above the canyon floor. Declared a national monument in 1910, it wasn't until Glen Canyon Dam was completed 53 years later, and the lake started to fill, that the site became a favorite destination. Well touristed and commercialized on countless posters and cards, the stone arch with its awesome girth and prisms of color never ceases to amaze. Rainbow Bridge is reached only by boat, foot or horseback.

South of the awesome bridge, between Warm Creek and Wahweap bays, is **Antelope Island**, site of the first known expedition of whites to the area. Franciscan priests Francisco Dominguez and Silvestre Vélez de Escalante trekked across a low point in the river (before it became a lake) and established camp on the island.

Nearby **Padre Bay** was also named for the priests. Within these waters is the rock fortress called **Cookie Jar Butte**.

A landmark visible from the Wahweap section of the lake is the hump-backed, 10,388-foot **Navajo Mountain** and the striking **Tower Butte**, both located on the Navajo Indian Reservation. They are good landmarks to keep in mind when your directional sense gets churned in the water.

A primitive Indian "art gallery" is located approximately ten miles east of the Rainbow Bridge Canyon up the San Juan River arm in **Cha Canyon**. You must motor past what are termed the Bob Hope Rock (check out the profile) and Music Temple Canyon to reach Cha.

The concentration of peregrine falcon nesting aeries around Lake Powell is one of the highest in the U.S.; chalk this up to an abundance of food sources near the lake.

For more extensive history and sightseeing tips on Lake Powell, Stan Jones' *Boating and Exploring Map* is essential to your enjoyment and is available at any Lake Powell shop.

The name John Wesley Powell pops up everywhere in this area. Major Powell, a Civil War veteran, led two expeditions down the Colorado River through the Grand Canyon, in 1869 and 1871. Powell mapped and kept journals of the 1000-mile journey through the largest uncharted section of the United States. A small museum in Page, the **John Wesley Powell Museum**, chronicles his expeditions and presents a small exhibition of American Indian basketry. Call for schedule. Admission. ~ Lake Powell Boulevard and North Navajo Drive, Page; 928-645-9496, fax 928-645-3412; www.powellmuseum.org.

One of the most extraordinary sights of this high-desert region around Page is a **slot canyon**, a narrow passage cut by flash-flood water and wind into the sandstone. The erosion cuts striated patterns into the rock walls, like ripples of water, and as sunlight drifts down from the opening 120 feet above, rock shapes and forms seem to undulate in the light and shadow. Quartz crystals in the rock reflect the light, while magnesium and iron create the dark, reddish colors and calcium and lime give the lighter tones. Photographers love slot canyons. **Carolene Ekis** conducts **photographic and sightseeing tours** to the most impressive and accessible slot canyon in the area. It's located on a Navajo land, so it's not otherwise accessible to the public. ~ 928-660-0739 (mobile), 928-645-9102, fax 928-645-2564; www.antelopecanyon.com.

LODGING   If you've never slept under the stars, being on a **houseboat** on Lake Powell is a great introduction. These floating homes are fully equipped with bunk beds, kitchens, showers and toilets. To make reservations more than a week in advance, contact **Lake Powell Resorts & Marinas**. If preparing less than a week ahead, call Wahweap Marina (928-645-2433) or the marina you're interested in directly. ~ Lakeshore Drive off Route 89, near Glen Canyon Dam; 800-528-6154, fax 602-331-5258; www.lake powell.com. ULTRA-DELUXE.

Accommodations on the Arizona side of Lake Powell are limited to **Wahweap Lodge,** which is set on the lake's westernmost bay. Guest rooms are bright and airy; those facing the lake have especially lovely views of the marina, blue waters and rugged lakeshore. Wahweap gets bonus points for its two swimming pools, spa and manicured grounds. ~ 100 Lakeshore Drive; 928-645-2433, 800-528-6154, fax 928-645-1031; www.lakepowell.com. DELUXE.

Courtyard by Marriott occupies a prime spot where the local business loop of Route 89 starts to swing up the mesa into Page. The property has fine views of Glen Canyon and is surrounded by a golf course. The Southwest adobe-style design fits into the sandstone butte landscape. Each of the 153 rooms are comfortably furnished with two double beds and have a balcony. There is room service, an exercise room, a pool and a spa. ~ 600 Clubhouse Drive, Page; 928-645-5000, 800-321-2211, fax 928-645-5004; www.marriott.com. MODERATE TO DELUXE.

Several motels are located along Lake Powell Boulevard, the main drag in Page, including three Best Westerns. The 102-room **Best Western Arizona Inn** has a pool and spa. ~ 716 Rimview Drive; 928-645-2466, 800-826-2718, fax 928-645-2053; www.bestwesternarizonainn.com. MODERATE. Somewhat bigger, the **Best Western Lake Powell,** with 132 rooms offers similar amenities (pool and spa). ~ 208 North Lake Powell Boulevard; 928-645-5988, 800-528-1234, fax 928-645-2578; www.best western.com. MODERATE. The smaller, 99-room **Page Travelodge** also has a pool. ~ 207 North Lake Powell Boulevard; 928-645-2451, 800-637-9183, fax 928-645-9552. MODERATE.

The city of Page has licensed and approved several **bed and breakfast** accommodations; the chamber of commerce will provide a list. ~ 928-645-2741, 888-261-7243, fax 928-645-3181; www.pagelakepowellchamber.org. BUDGET TO MODERATE.

Aside from having dinner on your rented houseboat or at a campsite along the shore, dining on Lake Powell is limited to the **Rainbow Room** at Wahweap Lodge. Considering the volume of traffic handled in the round, large, two-tiered dining room, the food—prime rib, seafood, chicken, salads and a few American Indian dishes—isn't bad, and it's served in generous proportions. Service is friendly and efficient. Three meals are served. There's also a budget-priced pizza café on the Wahweap launch dock, open May through September. ~ Wahweap Lodge, 100 Lakeshore Drive, Lake Powell; 928-645-2433, fax 928-645-1031; www.lakepow ell.com. MODERATE TO DELUXE.

DINING

HIDDEN ▶   In Page, the **Dam Bar & Grill** is an unexpected upscale and kind of hip restaurant and bar. The dam theme may be a bit overdone—a "transformer" at the entrance shoots off neon bolts of electricity, one wall of concrete is sculpted like the dam, and heavy wire mesh used to hold back sandstone walls of the gorge becomes decorative partitions between booths. But other touches—a huge etched glass panel separating the bar and the dining room, generous use of wood, linen napkins—and the surprisingly good food show that someone is paying attention. Steak and prime rib are the main events here, but fish also receives excellent attention in the kitchen. Pasta, chicken, sandwiches, burgers and salads round out the menu. No lunch in Winter. Closed Sunday and Monday from mid-November through April. ~ 644 North Navajo Drive, Page; 928-645-2161; www.damplaza.com, e-mail dambar@damplaza.com. MODERATE TO ULTRA-DELUXE.

Even just a slice of pizza (it's huge) at **Strombolli's Restaurant and Pizzeria** is enough to fill you up if you're not too hungry. Otherwise you can order from a menu of traditional Italian dishes, calzones and salads. There's an outdoor covered patio, if the weather's nice, but the view of the commercial strip doesn't offer much to look at. Closed November through February. ~ 711 North Navajo Drive, Page; 928-645-2605. BUDGET TO MODERATE.

For a quick sandwich to eat on the run or for a picnic, try the **Sandwich Place**, where you can also get hot subs and burgers. ~ 662 Elm Street, next to Safeway, Page; 928-645-5267; e-mail dtt@aztrail.com. BUDGET.

NIGHTLIFE   Celebrate the night with a sunset dinner cruise aboard the **Canyon King Paddlewheeler**, which departs (June to August) from the Wahweap Marina. ~ 928-645-2433, 800-528-6154, fax 602-331-5258; www.lakepowell.com.

AUTHOR FAVORITE

I was thrilled to discover that Lake Powell's waters usually warm to a comfortable temperature for swimming by May or early June. During the summer months, when the majority of the three million-plus annual visitors come, the surrounding temperatures can exceed a sizzling 100°. That's my cue to seek cool relief and a relaxing getaway in this stark desert ocean. Even at peak periods like July 4th and Labor Day weekends, when all the rental boats are checked out and hotel rooms booked, Lake Powell still manages to provide ample shoreline for docking and camping and, as always, clear, blue-green water for aquatic pursuits.

GLEN CANYON NATIONAL RECREATION AREA 🏃 ⛵ 🚣 🛶   **PARKS**

🛶 🚤 ⛴ ↙ The Colorado River–fed Lake Powell, formed by the Glen Canyon Dam, is the world's second-largest manmade reservoir. Although all sorts of water sports can be enjoyed at all of its five marinas, the biggest and busiest is the Wahweap Marina, located on the Arizona side. Facilities here include hotels, restaurants, two boat ramps, boat rentals, visitors centers, picnic areas and restrooms. Day-use fee, $10 for a seven-day pass. ~ Both Routes 98 and 89 lead to Lake Powell. Reach Wahweap Marina via Route 89, six miles north of Page; 928-608-6404, fax 928-608-6283; www.nps.gov/glca, e-mail glca_chvc@nps.gov.

▲ There are campsites at Wahweap Marina (928-645-1059), $15 to $27 per night; RV hookups are available through a private concessionaire, Wahweap RV Park (928-645-1009, 800-528-6154), $15 to $27 per night. Free backcountry camping is allowed with a permit. Camping is not allowed within one mile of any developed area.

RAINBOW BRIDGE NATIONAL MONUMENT 🏃 🚤 Greatest of the world's known natural bridges, this symmetrical salmon-pink sandstone span rises 290 feet above the floor of Bridge Canyon. Rainbow Bridge sits on one square mile within the Navajo Indian Reservation in Glen Canyon. Tours of the monument leave regularly from Wahweap Marina. Facilities are limited to restrooms. Permit fee. ~ Accessible by boat or on foot. To go the land route means traversing 13 miles of mostly unmarked trails through Navajo Indian Reservation land and requires a permit (928-871-6647); the number for the monument is 928-608-6404, fax 928-608-6204; www.nps.gov/rabr, e-mail glcachvc@nps.gov.

▼▼▼▼▼▼▼▼▼▼▼▼
Lee's Ferry

When Europeans began exploring this part of the country in the late 18th century, there were very few places that the Colorado River could be crossed from both sides. Lee's Ferry was one of them. But not since the Anasazi had inhabited the area centuries before had there been any permanent residents. John Wesley Powell and nine companions charted the Colorado River in 1869 and 1871—by rowboat. Around 1872, John Doyle Lee and one of his 17 wives, Emma, arrived to set up a ferry across the river. Lee, a Mormon, had been sent by church leaders to establish the ferry as a way to help the Mormons settle in Northern Arizona. Some years before, Lee had been involved in an incident known as Mountain Meadow Massacre, an attack on a wagon train involving Paiute Indians, Lee and other Mormons. Lee was eventually apprehended by authorities and executed. Today, Lee's Ferry is part of the Glen Canyon National Recreation Area.

SIGHTS There are only seven land crossings of the Colorado River within 750 miles. **Navajo Bridge**, which spans Marble Canyon Gorge, is one of them. There are actually two bridges: a newer structure for vehicles traveling on Route 89A and the older bridge, which pedestrians may walk across to get a look at the 470-foot gorge. Pick up area maps and general books at the visitors center, which also has a permanent exhibit covering geological and historical facts about Lee's Ferry. Closed November to May. ~ Route 89A at the western side of the new bridge; 928-355-2319, fax 928-645-5409.

Just to the west of Navajo Bridge, a turnoff to **Lee's Ferry** winds back to the spot where the Colorado and Paria rivers join. At the **ranger station** you can pick up maps and limited information about hiking and fishing in the area. ~ Located five miles north of Marble Canyon, at the top of the hill below the water tower; 928-355-2234, fax 928-645-5409.

A few historical structures still stand at the **old ferry crossing** and at the settlement site known as **Lonely Dell** so called because Emma Lee is reported to have said, "Oh, what a lonely dell" when she first saw the site of her new home. Parking is available at the launch ramp, and from there you can set off on one of several hikes along the river or into the cliffs above. A self-guided walking tour booklet and a hiking map are available at the ranger station.

In 1928, Navajo Bridge replaced Lee's Ferry Bridge as the only place to cross the Colorado River for 600 miles.

Back on Route 89A, heading toward Jacob Lake, **Vermillion Cliffs** dominate the landscape to the north. The Navajo sandstone cliffs are clearly reddish even during the bright light of the day but at sunset they take on a more brilliant color. A pullout on the flatlands (about 20 miles east of Jacob Lake) as well as in the foothills (about 11 miles east of Jacob Lake) as the road climbs up the plateau toward Jacob Lake both provide good viewing.

LODGING **Marble Canyon Lodge** is at the turnoff to Lee's Ferry on Route 89A, just west of Navajo Bridge. Motel accommodations are basic but clean. No in-room phones. The lodge also has a restaurant serving breakfast, lunch and dinner, a general store, a gas station and a fly-and-tackle shop. ~ Route 89A at Lee's Ferry turnoff, Marble Canyon; 928-355-2225, 800-726-1789, fax 928-355-2227. BUDGET.

About three miles west of Marble Canyon, **Lee's Ferry Lodge** offers quainter (read knotty pine) motel accommodations at the base of the Vermillion Cliffs. The lodge is popular with anglers and has an angler's shop (928-355-2352) offering complete guide services. Reserve ahead of time. ~ Route 89A at Vermillion Cliffs; 928-355-2231, fax 928-355-2371; www.leesferrylodge.com, e-mail info@leesferrylodge.com. BUDGET TO MODERATE.

DINING

In these parts, there's not much to choose from in the way of restaurants. The restaurant at **Marble Canyon Lodge** serves an American-style menu for breakfast, lunch and dinner. ~ Marble Canyon Lodge, Route 89A at Lee's Ferry turnoff, Marble Canyon; 928-355-2225, 800-726-1789, fax 928-355-2227. MODERATE TO DELUXE.

About the only other choice is **Vermillion Cliffs Bar & Grill** at Lee's Ferry Lodge, which, happily, serves good food—steaks, chops, sandwiches and baby back ribs—in a pleasantly rustic and friendly atmosphere. Besides that, it stocks 150 different kinds of beer. Three meals are served. ~ Route 89A at Vermillion Cliffs; 928-355-2231, fax 928-355-2371; www.leesferrylodge.com. DELUXE.

LEE'S FERRY, GLEN CANYON NATIONAL RECREATION AREA Halfway along the most direct route between the North Rim and South Rim of the Grand Canyon, this beach area on the river below Glen Canyon Dam makes a good picnic or camping spot. It is situated at the confluence of the Colorado and Paria rivers, which often have distinctly different colors, giving the water a strange two-toned appearance. Today, Lee's Ferry is the departure point for raft trips into the Grand Canyon. Lunch at one of the shaded picnic tables; restrooms are available. Groceries are 55 miles away in Page. Day-use fee, $5 for a seven-day pass. ~ Located in Marble Canyon about five miles off Route 89A, 85 miles from the North Rim entrance to Grand Canyon National Park and 104 miles from the east entrance to the South Rim; 928-355-2234. To reach Lee's Ferry Campground, take Lee's Ferry Road north about three miles from Marble Canyon. Wahweap Campground and Wahweap RV Park are off Route 89, one mile north of Page. Page Lake Powell Campground is half a mile outside of Page on Route 98.

▲ Within Glen Canyon National Recreation Area, **Lee's Ferry Campground** (928-355-2234) has 49 tent/RV sites (no hookups); $10 per night. **Wahweap Campground** (928-645-1059) has over 200 tent/RV sites; $15 to $27 per night for tents, $28 per night for RVs. The **Wahweap RV Park** (520-645-1009, 800-528-6154) has 87 sites; $15 to $27 per night. The privately owned **Page Lake Powell Campground** (928-645-3374) has 16 tent sites, $17 per night; and 120 RV sites, $24 to $28 per night.

PARKS

The Grand Canyon's North Rim is at the end of **Route 67**, which forks off of **Route 89A** at the resort village of Jacob Lake. It is more than 150 miles from the nearest interstate highway—**Route 15**, taking Exit 15 north of St. George, Utah—but is within an easy morning's drive of either Zion National Park or Bryce Canyon National Park or Lake Powell.

Transportation

CAR

Although only 12 miles of straight-line distance separate them, the shortest driving distance between the North Rim and South Rim visitors areas of the Grand Canyon is 216 miles around the eastern end of the canyon via Route 67, Route 89A, **Route 89** and **Route 64**, crossing the Colorado River at Navajo Bridge. The only other alternative for driving from rim to rim is to go by way of Las Vegas, Nevada—a trip of more than 500 miles.

From Route 40, eastbound motorists can reach Grand Canyon Village on the South Rim by exiting at Williams and driving 60 miles north on Route 64. Westbound travelers, leaving the interstate at Flagstaff, have a choice between the more direct way to Grand Canyon Village, 80 miles via Route 180, or the longer way, 105 miles via Route 89 and Route 64, which parallels the canyon rim for 25 miles. These routes combine perfectly into a spectacular loop trip from Flagstaff.

AIR

Flights can be booked from most major cities to **Grand Canyon Airport**, which is located near Tusayan just outside the south entrance to the national park. Airlines that fly there include Air Vegas, Eagle Canyon, Scenic Airlines, Sunshine Airlines and Vision Airlines. A shuttle service runs hourly between the airport and Grand Canyon Village. ~ 928-638-2446.

BUS

Trans Canyon Shuttle operates a daily shuttle bus service between the two rims of Grand Canyon National Park (reservations are required). ~ Tusayan; 928-638-2820.

CAR RENTALS

A car-rental agency at the Grand Canyon Airport is **Casa Grande**. ~ 520-836-9050, 800-736-8222.

FIVE

Northeastern Arizona

East of the Grand Canyon stretches a land of sandstone monuments and steep-walled canyons that turns vermilion by dawn or dusk, a land of foreign languages and ancient traditions, of sculptured mesas and broad rocky plateaus, of pine forests and high deserts. This is the heart of the Southwest's Indian Country.

It is home to the Navajos, the biggest American Indian tribe, and the Hopis, one of the most traditional. To them belongs the top northeastern third of Arizona, 150 miles in length and 200 miles across the state. In addition to this impressive expanse, Navajoland spills into New Mexico, Utah and Colorado.

Here, by horseback or jeep, on foot or in cars, visitors can explore the stark beauty of the land, delve into its uninterrupted centuries of history, then dine on mutton stew and crispy blue-corn piki bread. You can watch dances little changed in centuries or shop for a stunning array of crafts in American Indian homes, galleries and trading posts dating back to the end of the Civil War. And here, in the pit houses, pueblos and cliff dwellings of people who have occupied this land for 12,000 years, are more remnants of prehistoric American Indian life than anywhere else in the United States.

Five generations of archaeologists have sifted through ruins left by the region's dominant prehistoric culture, the Anasazi—Navajo for "ancient enemy." None are more beautiful or haunting than Betatakin and Keet Seel at Navajo National Monument, 45 miles due north of today's Hopi mesas.

Archaeologist have found evidence of human habitation on the Hopi Indian Reservation dating back 8000 years, and Hopi traditions today offer insights about life in those older cities. Traditional and independent, most villages are run by their religious chiefs. Each maintains an ancient, complex, year-long dance cycle tied to the renewal and fertility of the land they regard with reverence. As one Hopi leader put it, the land is "the Hopi's social security." Their multistoried architecture, built on mesa tops, has influenced many 20th-century architects.

Surrounding the Hopis is Navajoland, the largest Indian reservation in the United States. At 26,000 square miles, it is twice the size of Israel. Unlike the village-dwelling Hopis, most of the more than 200,000 Navajos still live in far-flung family compounds—a house, a hogan, a trailer or two, near their corrals and fields. (Some clans still follow their livestock to suitable grazing lands as seasons change.)

This is both an arid, sun-baked desert and verdant forested land, all of it situated on the southeastern quarter of the Colorado Plateau. At elevations of 4500 to 8000 feet above sea level, summer temperatures average in the 80s. July through September is monsoon season, when clear skies suddenly fill with clouds that turn a thunderous lightning-streaked black. These localized, brief, intense summer rains bearing wondrous smells have been courted by Hopi rituals for centuries and are crucial to the survival of their farms.

For the modern adventurer, September and October can be the most alluring months to visit—uncrowded, less expensive, sunny, crisp, with splashes of fall color.

The Colorado Plateau is famous for its rainbow-colored canyons and monuments that have been cut by rivers and eroded by weather. Erosion's jewels here are Monument Valley on the Arizona–Utah border, a stunning pocket of towering red spires, bluffs and sand dunes, and Canyon de Chelly, a trio of red-rock canyons that form the heart of Navajo country.

At Navajoland's southernmost boundary, the world's densest, most colorful petrified logs dot Petrified Forest National Park. They're located amid bare hills that look like they were spray painted by a giant artist and aptly named the Painted Desert.

This mesmerizing geography serves as a backdrop to the region's riveting history. Navajos probably began arriving from the north a century or two before the Spaniards rode in from the south in the 1540s. The conquistadors brought horses, sheep, peaches, melons, guns and silversmithing—all of which would dramatically change the lives of the indigenous Indians. The Navajos had arrived in small groups, nomadic hunters, primitive compared to their Pueblo neighbors.

Cultural anthropologists now believe the turning point in Navajo history followed the Pueblo Indian Revolt of 1680 when all the village-dwelling Indians of the Southwest united to push the hated Spanish out of what is now New Mexico. When the Spaniards returned a dozen years later, heavily armed and promising slavery for unyielding villagers, many Pueblo people from the Rio Grande fled west to the canyons of Navajo country, intermarrying and living as neighbors for three-quarters of a century.

During that time the Navajos grew in wealth due to their legendary raiding parties—helping themselves to Indian- or Anglo-owned sheep, horses and slaves. By the late 1700s, a much-changed race of part Athabascan and part Pueblo blood—the Dineh, Navajo for "the people"—had emerged. Powerful horsemen, wealthy sheepherders and farmers, they had developed a complex mythology and had surpassed their Pueblo teachers at the craft of weaving.

Navajo "shopping spree" raids continued along the Spanish, Mexican and Anglo frontiers. The United States army built Fort Defiance, near present-day Window Rock, and dispatched Colonel Kit Carson to end the incursions. Carson's tactic was to starve the Navajos out of Canyon de Chelly and neighboring areas by killing their livestock and burning their fields. On March 14, 1864, the first of some 8000 Navajos began what is known as their "long walk"—300 miles at 15 miles a day—to Fort Sumner, New Mexico. Here a 40-square-mile government compound became home to the Navajo for four of their bitterest years. They were plagued by crop failures, hunger, sickness, death and gross government mismanagement. Finally, on June 1, 1868, a treaty was signed, and some 7000 survivors moved back home.

Trading posts became the Indians' new supply source and conduit to the white man's world. While modern shopping centers, crafts galleries and convenience stores have replaced most of them, a few originals remain. The most famous is the rural, creek-side Hubbell Trading Post, a National Historic Site at Ganado. Others worth seeking out include Oljato near Monument Valley and posts at Cameron, Tuba City and Keams Canyon.

During the 20th century the Navajos and the Hopis have moved from a subsistence to a cash economy. The Indian Reorganization Act of 1934 ended overt

Northeastern Arizona

Text continued on page 86.

Exploring the Navajo and Hopi Nations

This detour from Route 40 offers memorable glimpses of traditional Navajo and Hopi ways of life and a dramatic cross-section of the vast reservations' terrain in just eight hours. It bypasses 124 miles of interstate, including Petrified Forest National Park. All highways on this route are two-lane blacktop unless otherwise indicated.

- Driving eastbound on Route 40, exit on Route 87 just east of Winslow and turn left (north).

- Don't miss **Homolovi Ruins State Park** (page 87), three miles north of the interstate. Abandoned for eight centuries, this archae-ological site is striking in its resemblance to the Hopi Mesa villages, which are still inhabited today. Allow a half hour to one hour.

- Continue north on Route 87 for 60 miles across dry, struggling grasslands to the junction with Route 264. Allow one hour.

- Turn left (west) to the **Hopi Cultural Center** (page 100) and visit the museum, where the most traditional tribe in the U.S. tells its own story. Allow a half hour, or more if you plan to shop at the nearby **Hopi Arts & Crafts–Silvercraft Cooperative Guild Shop** (page 103).

- Head east on Route 264 for eight miles to the turnoff for the First Mesa Villages. While ancient villages thrive on top of all three Hopi mesas, those of First Mesa are most accessible for a quick visit. Drive up to the mesa top and the villages of **Hano** and **Sichomovi** (page 101); if time permits, hire a guide to take you on foot to **Walpi** (page 101), where there are no cars, electricity or running water. Allow a half hour to two hours.

- Continue east on Route 264 for 49 miles through an arid basin of marginal grazing land to Ganado. Allow one hour.

- Visit **Hubbell Trading Post** (page 106), more than a century old and still doing business (thanks to the National Park Service), for a fascinating look at the way many Navajos first encountered the outside world's cash economy. Allow one hour.

- Continue east on Route 264 for 30 miles through the junipers and pines of Defiance Mesa in Navajo Nation Forest to Window Rock. Allow 45 minutes.

- Visit the **Navajo Nation Museum Library and Visitors Center** (page 108) for a look at the history, art and culture of the Navajo people. Allow a half hour to one hour—or more if you also take in the neighboring **Navajo Nation Zoological and Botanical Park** (page 108).

- Take Route 264 west back to Ganado. Turn south (left) on Route 191 until it joins Route 40, and head back to Flagstaff through Holbrook and Winslow.

IF YOU HAVE MORE TIME

From Ganado, follow Route 191 north for 30 miles across Ganado Mesa and up Beautiful Valley to **Canyon de Chelly National Monument** (page 111). You can catch glimpses of Canyon de Chelly and Canyon del Muerto in a few hours from two scenic rim drives; for a more memorable experience, stay an extra day and take a horse or jeep trip into Canyon de Chelly with a Navajo guide.

repressive government policies toward American Indians and launched an era of increased self-government. Since 1961, when oil and coal reserves were found on reservation lands, both tribes have parlayed millions of resulting dollars into paved roads, schools, hospitals, civic centers, low-cost housing, expanded electrical services and running water for more homes. Three mines, three power plants, a 60,000-acre farming project, forest industries and scattered electronic assembly plants are gradually providing jobs for Navajos. But the most widespread employment is the cottage industry—creation of their own arts and crafts.

Today in every village and town you will find the rich and wonderfully evolving legacy of American Indian arts and crafts. From the Navajo—weavings respected worldwide, sand paintings and silver and turquoise jewelry. From the Hopis—some of the finest pottery in the Southwest, superb carvings of wooden kachinas, woven basketry and plaques and masterful incised silver jewelry. You will hear Indian languages and see rich spiritual traditions carried on by new generations. You will experience the history of this Western region, the blend of Indian, Spanish and Anglo cultures. All this in a setting of striking geography.

Southern Navajo Country

▼ ▼ ▼ ▼ ▼ ▼ ▼ ▼ ▼ ▼ ▼ ▼ ▼ ▼ ▼ ▼ ▼ ▼

Indian Country is a concept that barely does justice to the astonishing diversity of the southern Navajo realm. There is so much to see and do in this region, which also embraces the pastel realm of the Painted Desert, that you may be tempted to extend your stay. Ancient Anasazi ruins and colorful badlands are just a few of the highlights. (Note that Prohibition is still observed throughout the Hopi and Navajo country. It is illegal to bring or drink alcoholic beverages here.)

SIGHTS

On the southwest corner of the Navajo Indian Reservation, during spring runoff—usually March and April—a detour off Route 40 brings you to the thundering, muddy **Grand Falls** of the Little Colorado River—plummeting 185 feet into the canyon of the Little Colorado River. A lava flow from Merriam Crater ten miles to the southwest created the falls about 100,000 years ago. Some years the falls are only a trickle, and even during the best years they dry up by May, resuming again briefly during abundant summer monsoons. It is wise to inquire in Winslow or Flagstaff about the level of the Little Colorado River before making the trip. To get there, turn off Route 40 either at Winona, 17 miles northeast of Flagstaff to Route 15, or at the Leupp Junction (Route 99), ten miles west of Winslow to Route 15. Either way, ask at the turnoff for exact directions. The Winona route is the shortest from the highway— about twenty miles, the last eight unpaved. *Note:* Do not try to drive on this road after local rainfall.

HIDDEN ►

Many locals contend the most colorful and dramatic concentration of Painted Desert hills in central Arizona is at **Little Painted Desert County Park**, 15 miles northeast of Winslow. A one-mile hiking trail and picnic tables overlook this vast basin where clay and silt deposited by ancient rivers have eroded into gray, red, purple, ochre and white striped badlands—300 feet to 400 feet tall. Colors are most vivid at dawn and dusk. ~ Route 87, 15 miles north of Winslow; 928-524-6407, fax 928-524-4252.

The scattered broken pottery, rock drawings and crumbling walls speak with quiet eloquence of an ancient past at **Homolovi Ruins State Park** five miles northeast of Winslow. The park contains four major 14th-century pueblos of 40 to 2000 rooms, with over 300 identified archaeological sites, a visitors center and museum where interpretive programs are presented. Nine miles of paved roads and a mile of hiking trails lead to the two largest village ruins, inhabited between A.D. 1150 and A.D. 1450. The park also includes petroglyphs and a pithouse village dating from A.D. 600 to A.D. 900. Hopis believe this was home to their ancestors just before they migrated north to today's mesas. They still consider the ruins—located on both sides of the Little Colorado River—sacred and leave *pahos* (prayer feathers) for the spirits. Admission. ~ Route 87; 928-289-4106, fax 928-289-2021; e-mail homolovi@ pr.state.az.us.

Winslow, the hub of Northeastern Arizona, is a railroad town and was an early trade center. Its current history goes back to Mormon pioneers who arrived in 1876 and built a small rock fort known as Brigham City, as well as a few other small settlements. The town grew, and soon a water system, stores and an opera house appeared, along with a school, saloons and, that harbinger of all frontier civilizations, sidewalks. The Aztec Land and Cattle Company purchased a million acres of land from the railroad in the late 1800s and thousands of head of cattle were brought in to be handled by local cowboys. The town was incorporated in 1900. For information contact **Winslow Chamber of Commerce**. Closed

Southern Navajo Country

on weekends. ~ 300 West North Road; 928-289-2434, fax 928-289-5660; www.winslowarizona.org, e-mail winslowchamber@cybertrails.com.

The **Old Trails Museum** houses changing exhibits related to Winslow's history, including American Indian and pioneering artifacts, and a collection of railroad and Route 66 memorabilia. Closed Sunday and Monday. ~ 212 Kinsley Avenue, Winslow; 928-289-5861; e-mail oldtrails@cybertrails.com.

HIDDEN ►

The **Brigham City Restoration** on the northeastern outskirts of Winslow re-creates one of the earliest settlements in northern Arizona. In 1876, 20 Mormon families and 15 bachelors from Salt Lake City built homes inside the sandstone walls of this fortress, where they manufactured crockery and sponsored meetings of the region's ranchers. Brigham City lasted only five years before crop failures from both flash floods and drought forced its abandonment. The original walls of the fort were later moved to the grounds of the La Posada Hotel, where they can still be seen today. Reconstruction on the original site began in 1998. ~ North Road, just past the municipal golf course, Winslow.

To the east of Winslow on Route 40 you'll come to **Holbrook**. Headquarters for the Apache Sitgreaves National Forest, Holbrook was named for H. R. Holbrook, first engineer of the Atlantic and Pacific Railroad, forerunner of the Santa Fe Line. It was once a tough cowboy town—the Aztec Land and Cattle Company drove cattle here, a rough-and-tough bunch that shot up everything and earned the name the Hashknife Posse. Each January, members of the present-day Hashknife Posse carry the mail Pony Express–style from Holbrook to Scottsdale—the only mail run on horseback authorized by the U.S. Postal Service. There are probably more people still wearing ten-gallon hats and cowboy boots here than in any other small town in the West.

The **Historic Navajo Courthouse Museum** is located in the County Courthouse, which flourished from 1898 until 1976. It's now a museum focusing on Holbrook's past, including the town's original one-piece iron jail. The museum is like a musty attic, stuffed with old photos, pioneer utensils and tortoise-shell

ROCKIN' WINSLOW

Mention the name "Winslow, Arizona" and the response you're likely to get is a humming of the Eagles' classic "Take it Easy." The well-known rock tune put Winslow on the map with its famous lyric, "Well I'm a-standin' on the corner in Winslow, Arizona." You too can stand on the corner in historic downtown Winslow at **Standin' on the Corner Park**, the site of special events, festivals or folks just plain standin' around.

combs, and even features an old parlor. There's a turn-of-the-20th-century apothecary complete with snake oil and other wonder tonics. It also houses the Holbrook Tourism Information Center, where you can pick up maps and brochures, as well as a historic downtown tour map. ~ 100 East Arizona Street, Holbrook; 928-524-6558, fax 928-524-1719; e-mail holbrookcham@cyber trails.com.

PETRIFIED FOREST NATIONAL PARK   The signs advertising sale of "gems" and "petrified wood" on every other block in Holbrook offer a good clue that **Petrified Forest National Park** can't be far away. Entrances at the northern and southern gateways to this park are located 22 miles east of Holbrook—the northern entrance on Route 40, the southern one on Route 180. Visitors centers located at the north and south entrances provide maps, brochures, books and posters, as well as exhibits of the park's geology and history. Either entrance launches you on the 28-mile scenic drive, the best way to see the park. Admission. ~ 928-524-6228, fax 928-524-3567; www.nps.gov/pefo.

Eons ago, trees fell into an ancient swamp and were converted over time to rainbow-colored rock—much of it still in massive logs. These colorful rare stone trees lie scattered throughout the 100,000-acre park, which may be the largest forest of petrified wood in the world. There are also many other types of fossils, both plant and animal, as well as evidence of the American Indians who once lived here.

The national monument was established in 1906, in response to the large number of logs and fossils that were being poached. It became a national park in 1962. Despite the barren desert environment, the park is dotted with prickly pear, cholla cacti and other natural vegetation. Look closely and you may find evening primrose, Indian paintbrush, mariposa lily and other plants.

The most frequently visited area of the park is the southern section, which holds the greatest concentration of petrified wood. Here, you'll find a wide variety of specimens—from giant logs, to small agatized chunks. Farther north are ancestral Pueblo sites and petroglyphs. The northern end of the park penetrates the Painted Desert, an eerie landscape of colorful, heavily eroded mudstone and siltstone that resembles the moon's surface, except for the brightly hued formations.

The scenic drive begins off Route 40 (north) at the **Painted Desert Visitors Center.** Here you'll see a 20-minute film on the mysteries of the making of the forest—silica crystals replacing wood cells—as well as archaeology and problems with petrified wood theft. Adjacent to the visitors center are a cafeteria and gift-shop amenities. ~ 928-524-6228, fax 928-524-3567; www.nps.gov/pefo.

The **Painted Desert Inn National Historic Landmark** is a 1930s pueblo-style building, originally a trading post, restaurant and inn. Detailed hand-carved wood and tin furnishings were made by the Civilian Conservation Corps (CCC). Murals painted by the late Hopi artist Fred Kabotie depict scenes of Hopi life: a winter buffalo dance to ensure return of buffalo each spring, the journey of two Hopis to Zuni lands to gather salt. The inn closed for a year-long restoration project in summer 2004, call for details. ~ Two miles north of the visitors center, at Kachina Point on the scenic drive; 928-524-6228, fax 928-524-3567; www.nps. gov/pefo.

The overlooks at the north end of the park provide good views of the Painted Desert. If you're ready for a rest stop, there are sheltered tables, seasonal water and restrooms (closed in winter) at the **Chinde Point Picnic Area**. At the **Nizhoni Point Overlook**, the hills below appear to sparkle with crystals. The minerals are actually selenite gypsum. From the **Whipple Point Overlook** and the **Lacey Point Overlook** you'll see bands of red, white and pink—the effect of the sun reflecting on mudstone and siltstone stained by iron, manganese and other minerals. Colors are the most intense at sunrise and sunset or on cloudy days.

South of Route 40 on the scenic drive, the park's midsection contains ancestral sites of ancient American Indian cultures dating from A.D. 300 to A.D. 1400. Scientists have discovered petroglyphs here used as solar calendars. A trail at the **Puerco Pueblo**, the first pullout south of Route 40, leads through the pueblo. Built of stone and masonry walls, the pueblo was home to about 75 people from A.D. 1100 to 1300. The ruin has been partially excavated and restored.

Although named **The Tepees**, these giant cone-shaped mounds look more like ant hills, wrinkled through erosion and colored blue and gray by iron, manganese and other mineral deposits. Nearby, **Newspaper Rock**, a huge sandstone block, is covered with a fine collection of petroglyphs. You'll need binoculars to get a good look, or you can use the coin-operated telescopes.

The petrified wood at **Blue Mesa**, where a trail leads through dramatic towering hills, is a favorite of photographers because of its blue, gray and white cone-shaped hills with chunks of agatized wood scattered about. The eroded sandstone formations suggest a mini Grand Canyon. This is also one of the best overlooks of the Painted Desert, whose strange multicolored buttes seem to glow in the distance.

The southern third of the park holds the greatest concentration of petrified logs. **Jasper Forest Overlook** provides a panorama of the area and includes barren hills sprinkled with petrified logs. Notice how the softer claylike soil has eroded from around the heavier petrified wood, creating a mosaic on the desert floor. Some logs are complete with root systems indicating they had grown nearby.

A trail at **Crystal Forest** leads you close to dense pockets of logs, many over 100 feet long and a foot or two in diameter. The large concentration of petrified wood here is mostly chunks scattered about like the remains of an ancient woodpile. Look closely at the logs and you'll see hollows and cracks where early souvenir hunters and gem collectors chipped away clear quartz and amethyst crystals. In fact, fossil destruction and poaching in this area prompted the Arizona Territory to petition Congress to preserve the petrified wood sites.

At the **Rainbow Forest Museum**, photographs, drawings, dioramas and samples tell the story of the area's paleontological history. Outside, the half-mile-long Giant Logs trail leads past enormous rainbow-hued trees. Many of the longest petrified logs (up to 170 feet) are found across the road at the **Long Logs** spur. A side trail leads to **Agate House**, a small eight-room pueblo-style structure built nearly 900 years ago entirely from chunks of petrified wood. Two of the rooms have been partially restored. The scenic drive ends two miles farther south at Route 180. ~ Two miles in from Route 180, near the park's southern entrance; 928-524-6822, fax 928-524-3567; www.nps.gov/pefo.

Inspired by 18th-century Mexican haciendas, the grand **La Posada** was constructed by Henry Harvey and the Santa Fe Railway with beautiful painted ceilings, stone floors and adobe walls as well as eight acres of gardens. Its 35 large, lavish rooms and suites are individually decorated with antiques and historic photos; furniture is made by hand on the premises. Some have courtyard views and full baths with oversized tubs. The hotel is basically a museum open to the public. ~ 303 East 2nd Street, Winslow; 928-289-4366, fax 928-289-3873; www.laposada.org, e-mail info@la posada.org. MODERATE TO DELUXE.

LODGING

◄ *HIDDEN*

The two-story **Adobe Inn** has 72 rooms, each decorated in typical motel fashion. You'll find a restaurant and an indoor pool

AUTHOR FAVORITE

The last and most elegant of the Southwestern resort hotels built by Fred Harvey's son Henry and the Santa Fe Railway, **La Posada** soon became a favorite haunt of celebrities, tycoons and presidents. The decline of rail travel forced the hotel to close in 1959, and it remained an abandoned shell for nearly 40 years. Reopened in 1998, it is undergoing a room-by-room restoration. See above for more details.

on the premises. A buffet breakfast is included. ~ 1701 North Park Drive, Winslow; 928-289-4638, 800-937-8376, fax 928-289-5514; www.bestwestern.com. moderate.

On the western edge of town, the **Town House Travelodge** has 68 rooms with modern furnishings all on the first floor. Amenities here include a laundry and an outdoor pool. ~ 1914 West 3rd Street, Winslow; 928-289-4611, 800-578-7878, fax 928-289-4428. BUDGET.

Fifteen dazzling white stucco wigwams, the sort of kitsch old Route 66 was famous for, are found in Holbrook. They make up one of the world's most novel motels, and affordable yet! Built in 1950 by Chester Lewis (six other cities had wigwam motels of similar design; only one other survives), **Wigwam Motel's** wigwams were restored by his children and grandchildren who still operate them. Inside each, matching red-plaid curtains and bedspreads adorn original handmade hickory furniture. Scenes from the film version of Tony Hillerman's *The Dark Wind* were filmed here in 1990. There's no extra charge for lulling vibrations as trains rumble by in the night. ~ 811 West Hopi Drive, Holbrook; 928-524-3048; www.nephi.com, e-mail clewis97@cybertrails.com. BUDGET.

For a more conventional resting spot there's the **Adobe Inn**, a two-story, 54-room Best Western that has typical motel furnishings and a pool. ~ 615 West Hopi Drive, Holbrook; 928-524-3948, fax 928-524-3612; www.bestwestern.com. BUDGET.

Another Best Western motel is the **Arizonian Inn,** with 70 guest rooms, contemporary furnishings, a restaurant and a pool. Continental breakfast is included. ~ 2508 East Navajo Boulevard, Holbrook; 928-524-2611, 877-280-7300, fax 928-524-2253; www.bestwestern.com/arizonianinn. MODERATE.

With 40 rooms, the **Best Inn** falls into the small, no-frills category. But all of the modern, well-maintained rooms have refrigerators, microwaves and Southwest paintings on the walls. ~ 2211 East Navajo Boulevard, Holbrook; 928-524-2654, 800-551-1923, fax 928-524-1496. BUDGET.

DINING

HIDDEN ►

Celebrated by locals and in newspapers from New York to San Francisco, the **Casa Blanca Cafe** is known for its tacos, chimichangas, cheese crisps and burgers. Choose between booth and table seating at this ceramic-tiled establishment where cactus baskets grace the walls. The dining room is cooled by Casablanca fans but, alas, there's no trace of Bogie. ~ 1201 East 2nd Street, Winslow; 928-289-4191. BUDGET.

In Holbrook, the best spot for Mexican cuisine is **Romo's Cafe,** which has been serving tasty south-of-the-border dishes since the 1960s. The decor isn't fancy in this storefront café, but the rear dining room, with its used-brick walls and hanging plants, is a more private setting than the bustling area out front for enjoying green-chile chimichangas or traditional enchilada dinners, as well as American food. In your world travels, don't be surprised to see a Romo sweatshirt—they've turned up as far away as Munich, Germany. Closed Sunday. ~ 121 West Hopi Drive, Holbrook; 928-524-2153. BUDGET.

For a taste of the Old West, saddle up and head for the **Butterfield Stage Company Restaurant**. The specialty here is sizzling porterhouse steak served with all the fixin's, as well as barbecue beef and prime rib. In addition to the cowboy tack and memorabilia on the walls, outside there's a stagecoach on display. Dinner only. ~ 609 West Hopi Drive, Holbrook; 928-524-3447, fax 928-524-3380. MODERATE TO DELUXE.

> With the exception of the Navajo Indian Reservation, Arizona does not observe daylight-saving time and operates year-round on mountain standard time.

Rock walls add an earthy note to **The Plainsman**. For casual dining try the coffee shop, where there's booth seating. Enjoy meals such as liver and onions, veal cutlet and turkey sandwiches. The dining room is a favorite of the local chamber of commerce, which meets here monthly. Popular items include châteaubriand, prime rib, frogs' legs and grilled halibut. No dinner on Sunday. Closed Monday. ~ 1001 West Hopi Drive, Holbrook; 928-524-3345. BUDGET TO DELUXE.

SHOPPING

Most of the souvenir and gift shops in Holbrook contain a blend of American Indian handiwork and Old Route 66 memorabilia. One of the best is **Julien's Roadrunner** on Old Route 66. The well-stocked shop sells everything from railroad and Route 66 memorabilia to nostalgic signs. The proprietor, Ted Julien, is a long-time resident of Holbrook and a veritable expert on the area's history and attractions. Feel free to ask him anything (even about his competition), but be prepared for thorough and unabbreviated answers. Closed Sunday. ~ 109 West Hopi Drive, Holbrook; 928-524-2388; e-mail julienaz66@cybertrails.com.

Linda's Indian Arts and Crafts is a small shop, but it offers a good selection of American Indian jewelry and Navajo skirts, as well as porcelain dolls and Route 66 memorabilia. Closed weekends. ~ 405 Navajo Boulevard, Holbrook; 928-524-2500.

For the biggest selection of top-of-the-line American Indian arts and crafts, visit **McGee's Beyond Native Tradition**, which sells everything from Hopi jewelry and kachinas to Navajo blankets. ~ 2114 North Navajo Boulevard, Holbrook; 928-524-1977.

Nakai Indian Cultural Trade Center, in business for about three decades, also features top-quality American Indian products as well as jewelry made on the premises. Closed Sunday. ~ 357 Navajo Boulevard, Holbrook; 928-524-2329.

Outside of Petrified Forest National Park, check in at the **Petrified Forest Gift Shop** to pick up sample minerals and geo-

◀ HIDDEN

des (cut on the premises). A variety of natural and polished petrified wood is for sale, from tiny $2 chunks to massive coffeetable slabs costing thousands of dollars. ~ Route 180, 19 miles southeast of Holbrook; 928-524-3470, fax 928-524-6924.

Painted Desert Visitors Center Gift Shop sells books, postcards and music. ~ Route 40 entrance to the Petrified Forest National Park, exit 311; 928-524-6228 ext. 236.

Fred Harvey Painted Desert Gift Shop sells polished and natural petrified wood, from tiny stones to great slabs, plus other gems as well as Southwestern Indian crafts and curios, books, postcards and music. You will also find silver-and-turquoise Navajo jewelry, which originated as "wearable wealth" that could be pawned when necessary. ~ Route 40 entrance to the Petrified Forest National Park; 928-524-3756.

> The largest Indian reservation in the United States, the Navajo Nation's territory claims nearly 24,000 square miles.

At **R. B. Burnham & Co. Trading Post** is a room lined with naturally dyed yarns. Behind that room is a shrine to Hopi and Navajo crafts. Assembled with much care, and for sale, are gallery-quality Navajo rugs, carved furniture upholstered in Navajo weavings, plus the whole array of American Indian arts and crafts. It's worth a stop even just to look. ~ Route 191 at Exit 339 in Sanders; 928-688-2777, fax 928-688-3777.

NIGHTLIFE   It's pretty quiet out this way. For nightlife activities, the choices are limited.

PT's boasts live entertainment on some Friday and Saturday nights. Otherwise, there's a nice outdoor patio (with a full bar!) and karaoke machine inside. ~ 1500 East 3rd Street, Winslow; 928-289-0787.

All the action in Holbrook happens at **Young's Corral Bar** where some weekends are filled with the sounds of deejay-spun dance tunes. ~ 865 East Navajo Boulevard, Holbrook; 928-524-1875.

PARKS   **LITTLE PAINTED DESERT COUNTY PARK** 🏃 One of the nicest, most colorful chunks of the 40-mile-long Painted Desert is concentrated in this 900-acre park, at 5500-foot elevation near the southern boundary of the Navajo Indian Reservation north of Winslow. In fact, many locals contend that the most colorful and dramatic concentration of Painted Desert hills is located right here. Large 300- to 400-foot-tall fragile mounds of mud slate in grays, reds, purples and yellows tend to change in color intensity throughout the day. Colors are most vivid at dawn and dusk. There's an overlook, two picnic ramadas and restrooms. ~ Route 87, 15 miles north of Winslow; 928-524-6407, fax 928-524-6824.

MCHOOD PARK/CLEAR CREEK RESERVOIR
Once an important water source for Winslow, the deep canyon five miles from town is now a favorite boating, swimming and picnic area. Fishing is good for trout, bass and catfish. Facilities include a picnic area and restrooms. ~ Take Route 87 south to Route 99, then turn left; 928-289-5714, fax 928-289-3742.

▲ The park's 24 campsites are free; primitive only and park gates remain open at night.

CHOLLA LAKE COUNTY PARK   One of the larger bodies of water in northeastern Arizona, the park is adjacent to a power station. This manmade lake offers swimming, boating, fishing (for bass, catfish, bluegill and carp) and picnicking. You'll find a playground, picnic tables, restrooms and showers. The park closes for maintenance from October through March. Day-use fee, $2 to $3. ~ Take Route 40 east from Winslow for about 20 miles to Exit 277, then follow the power plant road to the park; 928-524-6407, fax 928-524-6824; e-mail parks rec@co.navajo.az.us.

▲ There are 25 sites (14 with RV hookups); $10 per night for standard sites, $14 for hookups.

PETRIFIED FOREST NATIONAL PARK   Straddling Route 40 and abutting the southern boundary of the Navajo Indian Reservation, this 28-mile-long (north to south) park features rolling badlands of the Painted Desert—mainly red-hued hills—north of Route 40. South of Route 40 lies one of the densest concentration of petrified wood in the world. Each section has a wilderness area. At each entrance is a visitors center with a restaurant, restrooms and a museum. A 28-mile road leads visitors past nine Painted Desert vistas and 13 Petrified Forest stops. Day-use fee, $10. ~ Both park entrances are 18 miles east of Holbrook: the northernmost on Route 40, the southern one on Route 180; 928-524-6228, fax 928-524-3567; www.nps.gov/pefo.

▲ Backcountry only; a wilderness permit (free at the visitors center) is required.

Western Navajo Country

The Western Navajo Indian Reservation, bordering such wonders as the Grand Canyon National Park and Lake Powell National Recreation Area, is a land of great beauty and ancient sights. President William McKinley signed an order January 8, 1900, deeding these one and a half million acres of land to the Navajos who had migrated westward 32 years earlier after outgrowing their original reserve.

SIGHTS

Where Routes 89 and 64 meet, the Navajos operate **Cameron Visitors Center**, offering advice and brochures on tribal attractions. ~ 928-679-2303, fax 928-679-2330.

Follow Route 64 west ten miles to an unpaved spur road and walk a few hundred feet to a dramatic **overlook**. At the bottom of hundreds of feet of sheer canyon walls is a muddy ribbon of the Little Colorado River. Upper limestone cliffs, layered like flap-jack stacks, contrast with massive sandstone slabs below, evidence of a shallow sea 250 million years ago. This **Grand Canyon of the Little Colorado Gorge Tribal Park** is owned by the Navajos. A festive air reigns year-round as Indians set up their flag- and banner-bedecked crafts booths in the parking area.

A mile north of the visitors center is **Cameron Trading Post, Motel and Restaurant**, a stone pueblo-style complex established in 1916 by Hopis and Navajos. Long known as an oasis of hos-pitality, it's located by Tanner's Crossing, the last place wagons could cross the Little Colorado before the river enters gorges too deep to navigate. Quicksand pockets made this crossing espe-cially treacherous. ~ Route 89, Cameron; 928-679-2231, 800-338-7385, fax 928-679-2350; www.camerontradingpost.com, e-mail info@camerontradingpost.com.

Today this mini-city is a great place to people watch: old Na-vajo women in traditional velvet blouses, men in tall, black reser-vation hats and turquoise jewelry accompanied by youngsters in mod T-shirts and tennies. Inside the post, packed with curios and quality crafts, you'll often see a weaver at work.

HIDDEN ►

Next door, don't miss **Cameron Collector's Gallery**, offering antique Indian crafts and outstanding works of contemporary American Indian art—rare chief's blankets, pottery, dolls, weap-onry and ceremonial garb. Behind the gallery, **Mrs. Richardson's Terraced Garden** is an oasis of vegetables and flowers.

North of Cameron, continuing on Route 89 to The Gap, lies the northernmost extension of the **Painted Desert**, an ancient land of silt and volcanic ash hills barren of vegetation. The Painted Desert draws its name from the undulating mounds of multihued sediments that grace the strange landscape. Red sphinx shapes astride crumbling pyramids of eroded solidified sand, these bad-lands are red and white along some miles; gray and white along others. They're part of the Chinle Formation beloved by geologists for its dinosaur-era fossils.

HIDDEN ►

At **Dinosaur Tracks**, jewelry shacks mark the spot where scien-tists believe a 20-foot-long carnivorous Dilophosaurus left tracks. For a small fee locals escort you to the several impressions—three-toed footprints twice as big as adult hands. (Look for the recon-structed skeleton of this dinosaur in Window Rock at the Navajo Tribal Museum.) ~ The turnoff is seven miles west of Tuba City on Route 160, then north one-eighth mile along a dirt road.

Worth a stop in Tuba City, named for a 19th-century Hopi leader, is the hogan-shaped, native stone **Tuba Trading Post**. Built in 1905 during a tourism boom, its door faces east to the rising sun; crafts, groceries and sundries are for sale. Next door, you can enter a built-for-tourists hogan replica. Now administrative and trade center for western Navajos, Tuba City was founded by Mormons in 1877. ~ Main Street and Moenave Avenue, Tuba City; 928-283-5441, fax 928-283-4144.

LODGING

Lodging in Navajo and Hopi country can be summed up in one word: scarce. In an area about the size of Massachusetts, only about 700 guest rooms are available, so it's no wonder reservation motels claim 100 percent occupancy most nights from Memorial Day through Labor Day. If you get stuck, reservation border towns (Holbrook, Winslow and Flagstaff) usually have vacancies, though they too can sell out, especially on weekends of special events.

Padded headboards and brown Santa Fe–style bedspreads and drapes cozy up 112 simple, cement-block rooms in the **Anasazi Inn**, located 42 miles north of Flagstaff. It boasts the Western Navajo Indian Reservation's only swimming pool. ~ Route 89, Gray Mountain; 928-679-2214, 800-678-2214, fax 928-679-2334. MODERATE.

Cameron Trading Post and Motel, 40 miles east of the Grand Canyon's east entrance, and 54 miles north of Flagstaff, is a favorite overnight stop in Indian Country. This tiny, self-contained, 112-acre, employee-owned outpost sits on a bluff overlooking the eastern prelude to the Grand Canyon of the Colorado. From 6 a.m. until 10 p.m. or later, the trading post is a beehive of tourists and Navajos mingling to shop, dine or pick up everything from mail and tack to baled hay. It's mainly the tourists who stay overnight in 62 rooms and 4 suites. Established in 1916, the motel

AUTHOR FAVORITE

Ambiance is everything at the **Cameron Trading Post Restaurant** on the western Navajo reservation. The food is fine—and you're lucky to find any restaurant at all out here—but for me the hand-carved furniture and view of the Little Colorado make this place very special. After walking through the typically low, open-beam ceiling trading post, you enter a lofty room lined with windows looking out onto the Little Colorado River. Tables and chairs are of carved oak and the ceiling glimmers silver from its patterned pressed tin squares. Forty-one breakfast choices include Navajo taco with egg, *huevos rancheros* and hot cakes; for dinner, try the deep-fried fish and chicken or steak entrées. ~ Route 89, Cameron; 928-679-2231, 800-338-7385, fax 928-679-2350; www.camerontradingpost.com/restaurant.html, e-mail info@camerontradingpost.com. BUDGET TO DELUXE.

rooms are of native stone and wood architecture (variously called Pueblo style or Victorian territorial), as is the rest of the compound. The rooms tend to be a little funkier here than elsewhere on the reservation. ~ Route 89, Cameron; 928-679-2231, 800-338-7385, fax 928-679-2350; www.camerontradingpost.com, e-mail info@camerontradingpost.com. MODERATE TO DELUXE.

Off Tuba City's main thoroughfare sits **Dine Inn Motel**, a modern one-story affair with 20 guest rooms. Four of these are furnished with a refrigerator, microwave and couch. ~ Route 160 at Peshlakai Avenue, Tuba City; 928-283-6107. MODERATE.

Students at Tuba City's Greyhills High School are learning the hotel management business by operating the 32-room **Greyhills Inn**. Open year-round to all ages, rooms are comfy and carpeted, with modern interiors. Guests share bathrooms and, for a modest fee, can share meals with Navajo students in their cafeteria during the school year. Closed during school holidays. ~ 160 Warrior Drive, northeast of Bashas off Route 160, near Tuba City; 520-283-6271, fax 520-283-4432. BUDGET TO MODERATE.

DINING
If you're not on a cholesterol-free diet, you'll find Indian Country food, as with everything else here, an adventure. Fry bread appears at lunch and dinner with taco trimmings as a Navajo taco, or as bread for a sandwich, or as dessert dripping with honey. Other favorites include mutton stew (usually served with parched corn), chili, Mexican food, burgers and steaks, and for breakfast, biscuits with gravy.

Anasazi Gray Mountain Restaurant fills its walls with Southwestern kitsch. Entrées (hamburgers, chicken-fried steak, halibut, pepper steak) come with soup or salad, hot rolls, baked potato, cowboy beans or french fries and salsa. ~ Route 89, Gray Mountain; 928-679-2203, fax 928-679-2334; www.anasaziinn.com, e-mail info@anasaziinn.com. BUDGET TO DELUXE.

Hogan Restaurant, amid open-beam and wood decor, offers dinners of steak, shrimp and chicken-fried steak, plus the inevitable Navajo taco and a variety of Mexican entrées. Look for the large historic photos of Charles H. Algert, pioneer Indian trader and founder of Tuba Trading Post, shown on horseback in 1898, and an 1872 photo of the Hopi leader Tuba, standing with arms folded. ~ Main Street, Tuba City; 928-283-5260, fax 928-283-5078. BUDGET TO MODERATE.

SHOPPING
The 1916 stone **Cameron Trading Post** is like a department store of Indian crafts, crammed with a good selection of nearly everything—lots of Navajo rugs, cases of jewelry from all Southwestern tribes, kachinas, sand paintings, baskets and pottery. Navajo ceramics are simple, unadorned brown pieces glazed with hot pitch. The adjoining Cameron Gallery offers the most

expensive crafts including antique Indian weavings, Apache baskets, Plains beadwork, weaponry and ceremonial garb. ~ Route 89, Cameron; 928-679-2231; www.camerontradingpost.com, e-mail info@camerontradingpost.com.

Tuba Trading Post emphasizes Navajo rugs, sometimes including small pictorials. Also for sale are kachinas, jewelry and the Pendleton blankets Indians like to give one another for births, graduations and other celebrations. ~ Main Street and Moenave Avenue, Tuba City; 928-283-5441, fax 928-283-5078.

Hopi Indian Country

Three sand-colored mesas stacked and surrounded by a dozen ancient villages form the core of the Hopi Indian Reservation. Completely surrounded by the Navajo Indian Reservation, the villages are strung along 90 miles of Route 264. Home for several centuries to the Hopi, some structures standing today have been used by the same families for 900 years. This fascinating high-desert place (about 4000-foot elevation) is a study in contrasts: it looks stark and poor one minute, then ancient and noble the next.

SIGHTS

Looking for crafts to buy at the homes of Hopi craftsmakers or attending dances are good reasons to visit the villages. Hopi Indian Dances, nearly all of them involving prayers for rain for their dry farm plots, occur year-round. Dates are rarely announced more than two weeks in advance. Whether or not you can attend will vary with the dance and the village. Don't miss a chance to attend one. Instructions for visitors will be posted outside most villages. In all cases, leave cameras, tape recorders and sketching pads in the car. Photography is not permitted in the villages or along Hopi

AUTHOR FAVORITE

sights

I felt a sense of privilege when I witnessed the beauty of a Hopi ceremonial dance, as though I were being let in on a secret ritual. Although some Hopi dances are held in plazas and are open to the public, others are held privately in underground kivas. Many of their dances are appeals for rain or to improve harmony with nature. Starting times are determined by Hopi elders according to the position of the moon, sun and vibrations. The **Powamu Ceremony** or **Bean Dance** in late February is a fertility ritual to help enhance the summer harvest, while the **Snake Dance** is done near the end of August. Live rattlesnakes are used during the ceremony as a form of communication with the Underworld. If you attend a ceremony, remember to respect the proceedings and not take pictures or use tape recorders.

roads. To ask for permission to attend, contact the **Hopi Office of Public Relations**. ~ 928-734-3283, fax 928-734-3289; www.hopi. nsn.us, e-mail vcharles@hopi.nsn.us.

Two miles southeast of Tuba City at **Moenkopi** ("the place of running water"), a village founded in the 1870s by a Hopi chief from Oraibi, note the rich assortment of farm plots. This is the only Hopi village that irrigates its farmland—water comes from a nearby spring. Elsewhere farmers tend small plots in several locations, enhancing their chance of catching random summer thundershowers. The villages of upper and lower Moenkopi are the only Hopi villages not situated on or just below one of the three mesas.

It's some 40 miles to the next two villages. **Bacavi**, consisting mostly of prefab homes, was built in 1909 following a political upheaval at Old Oraibi. **Hotevilla**, also a relatively new (built in 1906) village, with its mix of adobe and cinderblock homes at the edge of a mesa, is nonetheless a traditional village known for its dances and crafts. A few miles down the road, on the edge of Third Mesa, **Old Oraibi** is one of the oldest continuously inhabited villages in North America. Hopis lived here as early as 1150. Try the ten-minute walk from the south edge of the village to ruins of a church built in 1901 by H. R. Voth, a Mennonite minister. It was destroyed by lightning. At **Kykotsmovi**, "mound of ruined houses," two miles east, then south one mile on Route 2, the Hopi Office of Public Relations provides visitor information. ~ Route 2; 928-734-3283, fax 928-734-3289; www.hopi.nsn.us, e-mail vcharles@hopi.nsn.us.

Continue east on Route 264 a half dozen miles to **Shungopavi**, Second Mesa's largest village, built at a cliff's edge. It's two more miles to the **Hopi Cultural Center**, the biggest social center for Indians and visitors. Hopi staffers of this pueblo-style museum-restaurant-motel-gift shop complex are also pretty knowledgeable about events on the reservation. ~ At Second Mesa on Route 264; 928-734-2401, fax 928-734-6651; www.hopi.nsn.us.

Just 100 feet west of the complex at the **Hopi Arts & Crafts–Silvercraft Cooperative Guild**, silversmiths work amid the biggest assortment of Hopi-made crafts on the reservation. Closed weekends. ~ 928-734-2463, fax 928-734-6647.

East of the Cultural Center, the two weathered villages of **Sipaulovi** and **Mishongnovi** are strikingly placed above the desert floor on Second Mesa, many of their dwellings carved from stone. It's a steep climb north to both up an unnamed road from Route 264. Founded in the 1680s, both are known for their dances and are worth a visit for the views. Mishongnovi is currently closed, but you can still wander around. Photographs are not allowed. ~ Information: 928-737-2570, fax 928-737-9444.

FIRST MESA   If you have time to make only one stop, visit the trio of villages on First Mesa—**Hano**, **Sichomovi** and **Walpi**. Perched atop the flat oblong mesa, its sides dropping precipitously 300 feet to the desert below, the village locations help you understand why the Hopis believe they live at the center of the universe. Accessible only by a thrilling curvy drive up a narrow road with no guardrails (signs off Route 264 point the way), all three villages seem to grow out of the mesa's beige-colored stone. Vistas are uninterrupted for miles amid an eerie stillness. A guided walking tour (fee) is offered daily. Call ahead, especially February to July during the ceremonial season. ~ Eight miles east of the Secakuku Trading Post; 928-737-2262, fax 928-737-2347.

Most awesome is Walpi. Built some 300 years ago on a promontory with panoramas in all directions, Walpi's houses stack atop one another like children's blocks, connected with wooden ladders. From the parking lot (no cars are permitted in Walpi) the vil-

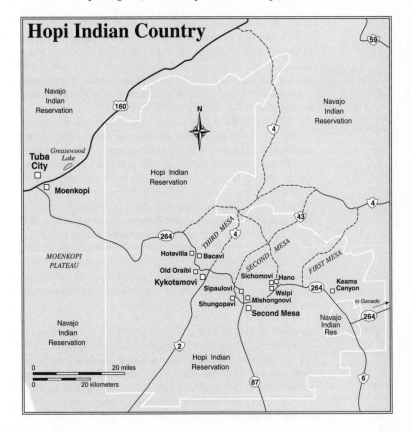

Hopi Indian Country

lage resembles a great stone ship suspended on a sea of blue sky. Leaders keep the village traditional so that neither electricity nor running water is permitted. Year-round guided **walking tours of Walpi** are offered daily. Sign up at Ponsi Hall. ~ 928-737-2262, fax 928-737-2347.

Here, as in the other villages, kivas or ceremonial chambers dug into the earth serve as they have since Hisatsinom days, a refuge where clan dancers fast and observe rituals for days prior to dances. Then on dance days, no longer farmers in denims, the Hopis slowly emerge through ladders on kiva roofs to the hypnotic rhythm of drums and rattles. Transformed in feathers, bells and pine boughs, they appear as sacred beings.

Everyday activities include women baking bread out of doors in beehive ovens or tending clay firings. These are excellent pottery villages. Crude signs in windows invite you into homes of kachina and pottery makers, a wonderful chance to get acquainted with these hospitable people.

Know your American Indian lingo: a tepee is a conical dwelling, made from buffalo hides and supported by poles; a wigwam is more rounded, made from woven mats or birch bark.

Like Walpi, Sichomovi is a medieval-looking little stone town around an ancient ceremonial plaza. Unlike Walpi, you can reach Sichomovi by car (though probably not in a motor home) and wander the narrow, dusty streets without a guide's supervision. There is parking at the Ponsi Hall administrative offices and near the gate that closes off the road to Walpi.

Hano resembles its neighboring Hopi villages, but in language and custom it remains a Tewa settlement of Pueblo Indians who fled Spanish oppression in the Rio Grande region in the late 1690s.

Continuing east on Route 264, Hopi Indian Country ends at Keams Canyon, the federal government administrative center, with tourist facilities (restaurant, Indian art gallery, grocery) clustered around **Keams Canyon Shopping Center**. Well-chosen Hopi and Navajo crafts are for sale. Closed Sunday. ~ Route 264; 928-738-2294, fax 928-738-5250; www.ancientnations.com.

Follow the canyon northeast into the woods. About two miles in, on the left, near a ramada and a small dam, you'll find **Inscription Rock** where Kit Carson signed his name on the tall sandstone wall about the time he was trying to end Navajo raiding parties.

LODGING   Designed by Arizona's award-winning architect Benny Gonzales, Second Mesa offers the only tribal-owned tourist complex. Here are 33 rooms of the **Hopi Cultural Center Inn** with their white walls, rosewood furniture, television, desk and vanity. This is a nonsmoking establishment. ~ Route 264 at Second Mesa; 928-734-2401, fax 928-734-6651; www.hopiculturalcenter.com, e-mail info@hopiculturalcenter.com. MODERATE.

Hopi's primary meeting place, the **Hopi Cultural Center Restaurant,** with open-beam ceiling and sturdy, wood-carved furniture, offers Hopi options at all meals. Breakfasts include blue-corn pancakes, blue-corn cornflakes with milk and fry bread. For lunch or dinner, *nok qui vi*—traditional stew with corn and lamb, served with fresh-baked green chiles and fry bread—as well as steak, chicken and shrimp entrées round out the menu. For dessert there is strawberry shortcake. ~ Route 264 at Second Mesa; 928-734-2401 ext. 306, fax 928-734-6651. BUDGET TO MODERATE.

Murals depicting Hopi mesa life decorate the exterior at **Keams Canyon Cafe.** This simple eatery has such entrées as T-bone steak, roast beef, barbecued ribs and enchiladas, all served on formica tables. Closed Sunday. ~ Route 264 in Keams Canyon; 928-738-2296. BUDGET TO MODERATE.

Roadside Hopi galleries and shops are abundant. Owned by individual families, by groups of artists or by craftsmakers with national reputations, many of these Hopi crafts enterprises are located on or near Route 264. A growing number are in private homes in the mesatop villages, where artisans put out makeshift hand-lettered signs—often propped up by rocks—when they have wares for sale.

Third Mesa's **Monongya Gallery** has large rooms filled with Indian jewelry, some pottery and kachina doll sculptures. ~ Third Mesa; 928-734-2344.

Driving east a half-mile, follow the Old Oraibi signs south to **Old Oraibi Crafts,** specializing in Hopi *dawas*—wall plaques made of yarn. This tiny shop with a beam ceiling also sells stuffed Hopi clown dolls.

In Second Mesa, west of the Hopi Cultural Center, the pueblo-style **Hopi Arts & Crafts–Silvercraft Cooperative Guild Shop** sells work by more than 350 Hopi craftsmakers, often introducing new artists. You'll see fine, reasonably priced samples of all Hopi crafts —coil baskets, wicker plaques, kachina dolls—from traditional to the contemporary baroque and even the older-style flat dolls, plus silver jewelry, woven sashes and gourd rattles. Prices are good. Staff members are knowledgeable about who the best craftsmakers are in any specialty and where to find them. In the shop you'll occasionally see Hopi silversmiths at work. ~ Second Mesa; 928-734-2463, fax 928-734-6647; www.hopiguild.com.

East of the Hopi Cultural Center one and a half miles, on the left, stop at an unassuming-looking **Tsakurshovi** to find the funkiest shop en route, the only place you can buy sweetgrass, bundled sage, cottonwood root, fox skins, elk toes, warrior paint, dance fans, the oldest-style kachina dolls and the largest selection of Hopi baskets on the reservation, amid a delightful hodgepodge of crafts

Text continued on page 106.

The Fine Craft
of Shopping

While shopping for arts and crafts in Indian Country we've been invited into Hopi homes to eat corn fresh from the field, have discussed tribal politics with college-educated shopkeepers and met traditional basketmakers who spoke no English. At the same time we've longingly admired contemporary Indian-crafted jewelry that would dazzle New York's Fifth Avenue crowd.

Shopping can occur anywhere in Indian Country. Once we bought sand-paintings from the trunk of an Indian artist's car while camping in the Chuskas. But Indian Country's main shopping avenue is Route 264, from Tuba City to Window Rock where you'll find two fine old trading posts. **Tuba Trading Post** offers an assortment of Indian-crafted merchandise. ~ Main Street and Moenave Avenue, Tuba City; 928-283-5441. Expect more of the same at **Hubbell Trading Post**, including the best selection of Navajo rugs along this route. ~ Route 264, Ganado; 928-755-3254. Throughout Hopi country, shopping is the best way to get to know the locals. Shops line entrances to all three mesas and most villages have at least a few signs in home windows inviting visitors in to look at family-made crafts. (*Note:* Tribal officials caution against making a deposit on any craft you can't take with you unless you know the craftsmaker or have a reliable personal reference.) What should you be you looking for when shopping? Both Hopi and Navajo offer crafts unique to their tribes.

HOPI CRAFTS

Baskets   Hopi wedding and other ceremonial baskets are still woven by Hopi women. Third Mesa villages are also known for their wicker plaques of colorfully dyed sumac and rabbit brush. Coiled yucca plaques are preferred at Second Mesa. Trays of plaited yucca over a willow ring serve as sifters and are made at First and Second Mesa villages.

Jewelry   The favorite Hopi jewelry form is overlay—designs cut from silver sheets, then soldered onto a second silver piece. Cut-out areas are oxidized black.

Kachinas   The Hopi believe that kachinas are ancestral spirits who periodically visit the pueblo. Elaborately costumed dancers dressed up as kachinas during important ceremonies. Kachinas are often carved in dancers' poses, then painted or dressed in cloth, feathers and bright acrylics. The newer trends feature stylized, intricately detailed figures carved from one piece of cottonwood root, then stained. (Navajos now make imitation kachinas too, to the irritation of Hopi carvers.)

Pottery   Nampeyo, a First Mesa woman inspired by ancient pottery shards, started the revival of yellow-to-orange Sikyatki pottery a century ago. First Mesa remains a major producer of pottery decorated with black thin-curved-line motifs.

Weaving   Traditionally, Hopi men do the weaving in this tribe—mostly ceremonial belts, wedding clothes and some rugs.

NAVAJO CRAFTS

Baskets   The most popular basketry of the Navajos is the coiled wedding basket, with its bold-red, zigzag pattern. Other baskets found in Navajo trading posts are likely to be made by Paiutes who also live in the area. During the 1980s, a renaissance resulted in some large, intricately designed coil baskets—both plate and jug-shaped.

Jewelry   Since the 1860s, Navajos have engaged in the art of silver-smithing, shaping silver to fit turquoise stones. Other popular items are stoneless silver rings, bolos, earrings, necklaces—especially the squash blossom—made by handwrought or sand-cast methods.

Pottery   Navajo ceramics are simple, unadorned brown pieces glazed with hot pitch. The pieces look wonderful when made by a master; clunky and amateurish otherwise.

Sandpaintings   Medicine men sing curing ceremonies while assistants create elaborate pictures on the ground with sands and crushed minerals in an astonishing assortment of colors. Each is destroyed at the ceremony's end. Similar designs glued onto wood are sold as sandpaintings. Widely available, these are made mainly in the Shiprock, New Mexico area.

Weaving   According to the Navajo creation story, Spider Woman wove the world then taught the Navajo to weave. Thousands of Navajo women and a few dozen Navajo men weave rugs today on the reservation, but only a small percentage are considered masterweavers, commanding the highest prices. Still, even a saddle blanket can be a treasured memento. It takes up to two years to weave a single Navajo blanket on a traditional loom.

and trade items adored by Hopi dancers. (Owners invented the "Don't Worry, Be Hopi" T-shirts.) ~ Second Mesa; 928-734-2478.

Honani Crafts Gallery, with its stained-glass windows of Hopi dancer designs, sells jewelry made by 16 silversmiths from all three mesas plus kachinas, pottery, books and concho belts. ~ Five and a half miles east of the Hopi Cultural Center, Route 264; 928-737-2238.

It's seven more miles to First Mesa, where Walpi residents welcome you to see pottery and kachinas they've made in Hopi's most picturesque village.

Thirteen miles east, visit **McGee's Indian Art Gallery** at Keams Canyon Shopping Center, distinctive for its Hopi village murals. For sale are a tasteful variety of Hopi and Navajo crafts—concho belts, silver jewelry, wicker plaques, kachinas, sand paintings, moccasins and rugs. Closed Sunday. ~ Route 264, Keams Canyon; 928-738-2295; www.hopiart.com, e-mail rmcgee@hopiart.com.

Central Navajo Country

This is the heart, soul and capital of Navajoland—a strikingly beautiful expanse of canyons, red rocks, forests and mountains where the Navajos have recorded their proudest victories and most bitter defeats. The longer you stay and explore, the more you'll appreciate the ever-evolving culture that is the Navajo Way.

The ruins of ancient cities you'll see also remind us that long before the Navajo arrived this too was homeland to ancestors of the Hopis—the Anasazi.

SIGHTS   Forty-five miles east of Keams Canyon, near the small village of Ganado, follow a shaded road a half mile west along a creek to **Hubbell Trading Post National Historic Site**, which still operates as it did when Lorenzo Hubbell, dean of Navajo traders, set up shop here in the 19th century. Now owned by the National Park Service and operated by Western National Parks, Hubbell's remains one of only a few trading posts with the traditional "bullpen" design—shoppers stand outside a wooden arena asking for canned goods, yards of velvet and other household goods. Built in the 1870s, this adobe building looks and smells its age. The floors are uneven from years of wear. Walls are jammed to their open-beam ceilings with baskets, pottery, books, rugs, historical photos, jewelry, postcards, dry goods and grocery items. Tack and tools still dangle from the rafters. ~ Route 264, Ganado; 928-755-3254, 928-755-3475 (visitor center), fax 928-755-3405; www.nps.gov/hutr.

Self-guiding tours of the 160-acre complex and exhibits in the **Visitors Center** explain how trading posts once linked the Navajo with the outside world, and how Hubbell was not just a trader but a valued friend of the Indian community until his death in 1930. The Hubbell family continued to operate the post until it was given to the National Park Service in 1967. Also in the Visitors Center is a good selection of Indian-related books. And for a tip, Navajo weavers demonstrating their crafts will pose for photos—but be sure to ask first. (Please obtain consent before snapping pictures on Navajo land.) ~ Ganado; 928-755-3475, fax 928-755-3405; www.nps.gov/hutr.

Half-hour-long tours of the **Hubbell House**, with its excellent collection of crafts, give further insights into frontier life and the remarkable trader who lies buried on a knoll nearby.

Navajo-owned ponderosa pine forest lands comprise part of the 30-mile drive to Window Rock, eastward along Route 264. Picnickers may wish to stop a while at **Summit Campground**, where the elevation reaches 7750 feet. ~ Located 20 miles east of Ganado.

Nine miles east of Summit Campground in Window Rock, on your left, before the stateline, stop at the office of **Navajo Nation Tourism**. Here you'll be able to obtain Central Navajo Country maps and tourism information. Closed Saturday and Sunday. ~ 928-871-6436, fax 928-871-7381; www.discovernavajo.com, e-mail info@discovernavajo.com.

Nearby is **St. Michaels Mission Museum** in the white, hand-hewn native stone building that in the late 1890s was the chapel

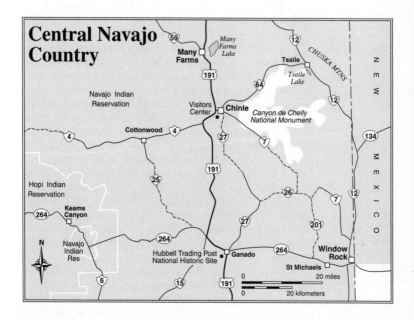

and four-bedroom living quarters for Franciscan friars from Cincinnati. (Sleeping must have been tough on such thin mattresses atop box crates!) Other displays—everything from uncomfortable-looking wooden saddles to vintage typewriters—include old photographs that depict their work and life. You'll see pages of the first phonetic systems they made to help create the written Navajo language. Outside, towering cottonwoods and a friar's three-quarter-acre flower garden create a parklike oasis. Open only from Memorial Day to Labor Day. ~ Three miles west of Window Rock off Route 264, St. Michaels; 928-871-4171, fax 928-871-4186.

Next door, the **St. Michaels Prayer Chapel** houses a 16-foot wood carving entitled "The Redemption of Humankind," created by German artist Ludwig Schumacher as a gift to American Indians.

East on Route 264 three miles, a rare Indian Country traffic light (at Route 12) marks "downtown" **Window Rock**, a growing, modern Navajo Nation capital. East of the Navajo Nation Inn, the **Navajo Nation Museum Library and Visitors Center** leads visitors through an overview of historic and contemporary Navajo life and traditions with rotating exhibits. **Navajo Arts & Crafts Enterprise**, located west of the inn, encourages innovation among its members and guarantees the quality of everything it sells. The museum is closed on Sunday. Admission. ~ At the intersection of Route 264 and Loop Road, Window Rock; Navajo Nation Museum: 928-871-7941, fax 928-871-4924; Navajo Arts & Crafts Enterprise: at the intersection of Routes 12 and 264, 928-871-4095, fax 928-871-3340.

The natural setting of **Navajo Nation Zoological and Botanical Park** serves as the stomping ground for domestic and wild animals that figure in Navajo culture and folklore—everything from coyote, wolves, cougars, bears, deer, elk, bobcats, rattlesnakes and prairie dogs to goats. In all, 58 species live here. Look for the Navajo-churro sheep, brought here by the Spanish. Herds are being increased because of their proven resistance to disease and the excellent weaving quality of their wool. Displays here include fork-stick and crib-log examples of hogan architecture. A modest botanical garden labels typical high-desert plants: Indian rice grass, Navajo tea, lupine, asters and junipers. ~ North of Route 264, Window Rock; 928-871-6573, fax 928-871-6637; www.navajonationparks.org.

A row of towering red-sandstone pinnacles that resemble the **Haystacks**, for which they are named, forms the zoo's western boundary.

When you arrive at the street light at the town of Window Rock, follow Route 12 north past Window Rock's shopping center, then drive right a mile to **Tseghahodzani**—"the rock with the hole in it." Here you'll find a sweeping wall, several stories tall,

Kit Carson and the Long Walk

The memory of famed frontiersman Kit Carson was tarnished by a military action against the Navajo in 1863, when he was instructed to remove the Indians from their homeland. Carson began his campaign by encouraging the neighboring Ute tribe to raid Navajo bands, destroying their hogans. The army paid the Utes money for stolen livestock and allowed them to keep Navajo slaves captured in the raids.

As Carson's troops advanced, most of the Navajo took refuge in Canyon de Chelly, where the army surrounded them, burned their cornfields, and laid seige until the Navajo surrendered. The seige lasted nearly six months, during which time the Indians staved off starvation by butchering and eating stolen army mules.

The people, numbering about 8000, along with 2000 horses and 10,000 sheep and goats, were driven on a forced march to Fort Sumner in eastern New Mexico, more than 300 miles across arid desert. Many Navajos grew ill from exposure to snowstorms and freezing temperatures as they crossed the windswept high desert. The soldiers gave them white flour and coffee beans, but being unfamiliar with these foods, the Indians mixed the flour with water and drank it, and tried to boil the coffee beans in stew. The combination gave them severe stomach cramps. People who fell by the wayside were shot or left behind to freeze to death. In all, an estimated 3000 people died. The march east is remembered in Navajo lore as the "Long Walk"; along with the subsequent incarceration, it was the biggest factor in galvanizing the Navajo from scattered nomads to a unified tribe.

Moving the Navajo at Fort Sumner proved to be a colossal blunder. Between fuel shortages and crop failures, it cost the U.S. government $1.1 million dollars to intern them for 18 months. Reviewing the situation, General William Sherman reported that it would have cost less to provide them with room and board in a New York hotel. A survey of the Navajo lands revealed nothing of value, and they were eventually marched back to their homeland.

Kit Carson's ruthless campaign against the Navajo was praised by his commanding officer, General James Carleton, as "the crowning act of his long career fighting the savages of the Rocky Mountains." Looking back at the conflict, however, we might draw a different conclusion as to who the real savages were.

of vermilion-colored sandstone. Almost dead center is an almost perfectly circular "window" 130 feet in diameter eroded in it, offering views to the mountains beyond. John Collier, Commissioner of Indian Affairs in the 1930s, was so stirred by it, he declared it the site for the Navajo administrative center. Visitors can picnic and walk here.

Nearby, stop by the octagonal stone **Council Chambers**, designed as a great ceremonial hogan. Murals painted by the late Gerald Nailor depict tribal history. It is here the 88-member Tribal Council meets four times a year to set policy. You'll hear Navajo and English spoken at all proceedings. Visitors are free to tour the building and watch the meetings. ~ Window Rock; 928-871-6417.

The prettiest route in Indian Country is **Route 12** from Route 40 through Window Rock and on north another 65 miles. The road hugs red-rock bluffs while skirting pine forests, lakes, Navajo homes and hogans surrounded by pasture, orchards and cornfields.

HIDDEN ▶

Follow signs to the pine-clad Dine College's (formerly the Navajo Community College) **Tsaile Campus** and its tall glass hogan-shaped Ned Hatathli Cultural Center with two floors devoted to the **Hatathli Museum**. From prehistoric times to the present—dioramas, murals, photographs, pottery, weaponry and other artifacts interpret Indian cultures including the Navajo. Wonderfully detailed murals tell the Navajo story of Creation, but you'll need to find someone to interpret it for you as there's little text. Visitors are also welcome in the college's library and dining hall. Closed Saturday and Sunday. ~ Route 12, about 60 miles north of Window Rock; college: 928-724-3311, museum: 928-724-6654, fax 928-724-3327; www.dinecollege.edu.

JOHN LORENZO HUBBELL—HERO

To American Indians at the turn of the 20th century, John Lorenzo Hubbell was a local hero. He operated a trading post at Ganado, giving the Indians important contact with the outside world. They traded silver work, wool, sheep and rugs for essentials such as flour, coffee, sugar, tobacco and clothing. To smooth the trading process, Hubbell spoke English, Spanish, Navajo and Hopi. He was also a sheriff and a member of the territorial legislature. Hubbell tried improving the lot of American Indians by bringing in a silversmith from Mexico to teach them silver working. But he really gained their respect during a smallpox epidemic. Having had smallpox, he had developed an immunity to it. So he was able to treat the Navajo without getting the disease himself.

CANYON DE CHELLY NATIONAL MONUMENT Route 64, to the left off of Route 12, leads to a favorite spot of tourists from around the world, **Canyon de Chelly National Monument** (access is also available three miles east off Route 191 on Route 7, although it's hazardous in winter). By the time the Spanish arrived in the 1540s the Navajos already occupied this trio of slick, towering red-walled canyons that converge in a Y. The canyons and rims are still home to Navajo families, their sheep and horses grazing. Water near the surface moistens corn, squash and melon crops, apple and peach orchards.

It's hard to decide if Canyon de Chelly is most impressive from the rim drives, with their bird's-eye views of the hogan-dotted rural scenes, or astride a horse or an open-air jeep, sloshing (during spring runoff) through Chinle Wash. The best introduction for any adventure is the **Visitors Center**. Chinle, the shopping and administrative center for this part of the reservation, is as plain as its famed canyons are spectacular. ~ Along the main road through Chinle; 928-674-5500, 928-674-5507; www.nps.gov/cach.

Be sure to stop at the visitors center **museum**, where exhibits on 2000 years of canyon history plus cultural demonstrations, local artists' exhibits and a ranger-staffed information desk will enlighten you about the area. Next door is a typical Navajo hogan. The center is also the place to hire **Navajo guides**—required if you hike, camp or drive your own four-wheel-drive vehicle into the canyons.

Proud tales of the Navajos' most daring victories are retold daily by guides who also point out bullet holes in the walls from brutal massacres. Thousands of much older ruins leave haunting clues to a people who lived and died here from about A.D. 200 until the late 1300s, when prolonged drought throughout the Four Corners region probably caused them to move to the Rio Grande and other regions of Arizona and New Mexico. Each bend in the canyon reveals ever-taller canyon walls, more pictographs and petroglyphs (historic and prehistoric art drawn on rock walls). Each turn showcases vivid red walls and the yellow-green of leafy cottonwoods thriving along the canyon floor.

North and South Rim drives, each approximately 16 miles one way, take about two hours each to complete. (It's a good idea to bring along brochures that point out geological, botanical and historical sites at each overlook.) **South Rim Drive** follows the Canyon de Chelly, which gives the monument its name. Highlights include **White House Overlook** (located at 5.7 miles; the only nonguided hike into the canyon begins here), to view remains of a multistory masonry village where about 100 persons lived about 800 years ago. On a narrow ledge across the canyon,

Text continued on page 114.

In the Land of Kachinas

Buying a kachina "doll" is spiritually different from shopping for, say, turquoise jewelry or a Navajo rug, crafts that were developed specifically for sale to non-Indians. Each kachina effigy represents part of a religious tradition that dates back more than a thousand years to the time of the Anasazi and is still vital today among several Pueblo groups, especially the Hopi.

Kachinas are the spirit essence of natural phenomena. Godlike, they live within sacred mountains—particularly the San Francisco Peaks (page 142), also known as the Kachina Peaks. All things in the Hopi world—rain clouds, corn, wild animals, insects, smoke, even death—are represented by their own individual kachinas. Since it is not easy to interact with the kachinas in their spirit form, every Hopi man inherits the duty to represent a single kachina within his village and kiva clan. He does this by dressing in a prescribed costume and participating in day-long dances held frequently between the winter solstice and mid-July. Most important to this impersonation is the kachina mask, believed to give a man the ability to see the world through his kachina's eyes and embody its spirit. Such masks are passed on from one generation to the next and never sold.

At birth, each male Hopi child is given a *tihu* (as kachina "dolls" are called in Hopi), as a reminder of the kachina whose spirit he will adopt upon kiva initiation at age ten. Women are also given *tihu* as a way to bring them the benefits of supernatural allies, since they cannot participate in kiva ceremonies. Once accepted, the kachina effigies are not used as toys but rather displayed in the home, usually hung from a roof beam or wall.

The Hopi have been selling kachina "dolls" to non-Indians since 1857. Most Hopi craftsmen have ethical standards about which *tihu* they will and will not carve for sale. Modern Hopi kachinas are carved in dancers' poses, then painted or dressed in cloth, feathers and bright acrylics. The newer trends feature stylized, intricately detailed figures carved from a single piece of cottonwood root, then stained. In recent years, Navajo craftsmen have begun making commercial "counterfeit" kachinas, against strong objections from Hopi carvers. Some of the most popular dolls made for sale to tourists do not represent authentic kachinas at all. Among these are snake dancers, hoop dancers, Hopi maidens and butterfly girls.

There are sound economic and spiritual reasons to buy your *tihu* directly from a Hopi craftsman. When you visit a village atop one of the three Hopi mesas, watch for handmade signs outside homes announcing kachinas for sale. But first take every opportunity to educate yourself about them. Visit Indian arts museums such as the Hopi Cultural Center (page 100) and the Museum of Northern Arizona (page 136) to see what constitutes a "museum-quality" kachina. Stop at fine-quality Indian arts and crafts galleries and ask plenty of kachina questions.

Keep in mind that when you buy a *tihu*, that kachina's spirit will become a presence in your home. Hopi mythology contains myriad kachinas, not all of them pleasant company. It may be better to share your home with Aholi, who sprouts seed corn and brings the flowers of summer, or Tsil, the running kachina who wears chile peppers on his head, than with someone like Wiharu, the child-eating ogre, or Mastop, the death fly kachina, who sneaks up on women and copulates with them from behind.

Animal kachinas are the friends, advisors, doctors and helpers of the Hopi people. Among the many kachinas whose likenesses you may encounter while traveling in Indian country, the most sacred is Ichivota, the White Buffalo, who symbolizes the unity of all humanity in a oneness of heart, mind and spirit. Other buffalo kachinas serve as advisors in healing rituals. Honan, the badger kachina, another powerful healer, shows people how to find where curative herbs and roots grow. Kweo, the wolf kachina, embodies the hunting spirit, and offerings of cornmeal and prayer feathers are made to him before group hunts.

Other common categories of kachinas include clown kachinas, who act rudely and provide comic relief during ceremonial dances, and bird kachinas, who reprimand the clowns during dances and also carry messages to the supernatural world. The spirits of cloud and thunder kachinas are invoked to bring rain.

ancients built retaining walls to try to keep their homes from sliding off the sloping floor into the canyon.

Spider Rock Overlook (at 16 miles) is a vista of the steepest canyon walls, about a 1000-foot vertical drop. Look right to see Monument Canyon; left to see Canyon de Chelly. The 800-foot-tall spire at their junction is **Spider Rock**, where Spider Woman is said to carry naughty Navajo boys and girls. Those white specks at the top of her rock, Navajo parents say, are the bleached bones of boys and girls who did not listen to mother and father.

North Rim Drive explores the **Canyon del Muerto** ("Canyon of the Dead"), named in 1882 by Smithsonian Institution expedition leader James Stevenson after finding remains of prehistoric Indian burials below Mummy Cave. Highlights include:

Antelope House Overlook (at 8.5 miles), which is named for paintings of antelope, probably made in the 1830s, on the canyon wall left of this four-story, 91-room ruin. Prehistoric residents contributed hand outlines and figures in white paint. Viewers from the overlook will see circular structures (kivas, or ceremonial chambers) and rectangular ones (storage or living quarters). Across the wash in an alcove 50 feet above the canyon floor is where 1920s archaeologists found the well-preserved body of an old man wrapped in a blanket of golden eagle feathers; under it was a white cotton blanket in such good shape it appeared brand new. It is believed he was a neighborhood weaver. Also here, at Navajo Fortress Viewpoint, the isolated high redstone butte across the canyon was once an important Navajo hideout from Spanish, American and perhaps other Indian raiders.

Mummy Cave Overlook (at 15.2 miles) is site of the largest, most beautiful ruins in Canyon del Muerto. The 1880s discovery of two mummies in cists found in the talus slope below the caves inspired this canyon's name.

Massacre Cave Overlook (at 16 miles) is site of the first documented Spanish contact with Canyon de Chelly Navajos. In the

STAFF OF LIFE

Made of flour tortilla dough, deep-fried and sometimes served with honey butter, fry bread is a staple of Navajo cuisine and pow wows. Considered a food of inter-tribal unity, fry bread didn't evolve until 1863, when thousands of Navajo were driven from their homes and imprisoned in Fort Sumner, New Mexico, by American scout Kit Carson. Given little to eat except wheat flour and lard, Navajo women (used to cooking native game) made the best of what they considered to be low-quality rations in the reservation camp, including learning how to fry with the iron pot, new to the Navajo culture.

winter of 1805 a bloody battle is believed to have occurred at the rock-strewn ledge to your left, under a canyon rim overhang. Hoping to end persistent Navajo raiding on Spanish and Pueblo Indian villages, Antonio de Narbona led an expedition here and claimed his forces killed up to 115 Navajos, another 33 taken captive.

The Navajo Nation's only tribally owned motel, **Navajo Nation Inn** bustles with a mix of Navajo politicians and business people in suits and cowboys in black "reservation hats." The 56 rooms are pleasantly decorated with turquoise carpet, Southwest-style wood furniture and matching bedspreads. ~ 48 West Route 264, Window Rock; 928-871-4108, 800-662-6189, fax 928-871-5466; www.navajonationinn.com. BUDGET.

LODGING

A parklike scene is the setting for the historic stone and pueblo-style **Thunderbird Lodge**. All 73 adobe-style rooms handsomely blend Navajo and Southwestern architectural traditions. Each features American Indian prints and is an easy walk to the canyon entrance. There's a gift shop and cafeteria. ~ A quarter-mile southeast of Canyon de Chelly National Monument Visitors Center, Chinle; 928-674-5841, 800-679-2473, fax 928-674-5844; www.tbirdlodge.com, e-mail tbirdlodge@cybertrails.com. BUDGET TO MODERATE.

Best Western Canyon de Chelly Motel makes up for its sterile architecture by providing Chinle's only indoor swimming pool (guests only); it has 100 rooms, some for nonsmokers. Pets are welcome. ~ A block east of Route 191 on Navajo Route 7, Chinle; 928-674-5875, 800-327-0354, fax 928-674-3715; www.canyondechelly.com, e-mail bwcdc@cybertrails.com. MODERATE.

In a modern, spacious room, **Navajo Nation Inn Dining Room** is the Navajo capital's biggest restaurant, seating 250 and decorated with Navajo art. The menu includes chicken, steak, Navajo sandwiches, Navajo burgers, beef stew, vegetable stew and mutton buffet on the first Thursday of the month. Lunch is always busy, the restaurant filled with politicians from nearby tribal headquarters offices. No dinner on weekends. ~ 48 West Route 264, Window Rock; 928-871-4108, fax 928-871-5466. BUDGET TO MODERATE.

DINING

If traditional American Indian food isn't your desire, Window Rock has a few fast-food restaurants (McDonald's, KFC) to tide you over.

Junction Restaurant is one of only two sit-down (nonbuffet) restaurants in Chinle. A mix of peach and blue booths and blonde-wood tables and chairs seat patrons dining on everything from *huevos rancheros* or biscuits and gravy for breakfast to a crab Louis or hot sandwiches for lunch to American and Navajo specialties for dinner. ~ Adjacent to Canyon de Chelly Motel, a block east of Route 191 on Navajo Route 7, Chinle; 928-674-8443, fax 928-674-3715. MODERATE.

Located in the original 1896 trading post built by Samuel Day, **Thunderbird Restaurant** serves up half a dozen entrées cafeteria-style for each meal. The menu offers a good variety, and changes some each day. You sit in a choice of booths or tables surrounded by walls with top-quality, for-sale Navajo crafts. ~ Thunderbird Lodge, a quarter-mile southeast of Canyon de Chelly National Monument Visitors Center, Chinle; 928-674-5841; www.tbirdlodge.com/dining.htm, e-mail info@tbirdlodge.com. BUDGET TO MODERATE.

SHOPPING   Be sure to stop at the **Hubbell Trading Post**, whose low stone walls, little changed in 90 years, contain the best Navajo rug selection en route, plus several rooms crammed with jewelry, dolls, books, baskets and historic postcards. ~ Route 264, Ganado; 928-755-3254.

Navajo Arts & Crafts Enterprise sells the work of some 500 Navajo craftsmakers. Selection is excellent and quantity is large—rugs of all styles, Navajo jewelry of all kinds, stuffed Navajo-style dolls. Closed Sunday. ~ At the intersection of Routes 12 and 264, Window Rock; 928-871-4095.

The **Thunderbird Lodge Gift Shop** provides a good selection of rugs, many of them made in the Chinle area, as well as kachinas, jewelry, baskets and souvenirs. Some of the fine-quality arts and crafts decorating the neighboring cafeteria walls are also for sale. ~ Thunderbird Lodge, a quarter-mile southeast of Canyon de Chelly National Monument Visitors Center, Chinle; 928-674-5841; www.tbirdlodge.com.

PARKS   **LAKE ASAAYI BOWL CANYON RECREATION AREA** 🏃 ↳ One of the prettiest of the Navajo fishing lakes, located in the Chuska Mountains known as the "Navajo Alps," Asaayi Lake (elevation

NATIVE ARCHITECTURE

The first talented architects of Arizona were the local tribes, with their handiwork ranging from cliff dwellings to pit houses. The Anasazi specialized in pueblos on cliff walls in northern Arizona. They mortared together cut stones for walls, while using logs and earth for the ceiling. Considering that rooms were small and without windows, they spent much time on their flat roofs, a perfect surface for chores. The Anasazi also built pit houses, flat-roofed stone houses partially dug into the ground. The Sinagua built pueblos similar to the Anasazi, but they preferred hills rather than canyons. And the Navajo people favored six-sided hogans made of logs and earth.

7600 feet) is popular for fishing (rainbow trout), picnicking and primitive camping. The 36-acre lake and creek are fishable year-round (ice fishing in winter); fishing permits are available from the Navajo Fish and Wildlife Department (928-871-6451) in Window Rock. You'll find picnic areas, barbecue grills and pit toilets. ~ From Window Rock, take Route 12 to Route 134. Drive northeast four miles then south seven miles on a graded dirt road to the lake; 928-871-6647, fax 928-871-6637; www.navajonationparks.org.

▲ Camping is allowed; $15 to $25 depending on the number of campers. Permits are available at the recreation area or at the Navajo Parks and Recreation (928-871-6647, fax 928-871-6637), both in Window Rock.

CANYON DE CHELLY NATIONAL MONUMENT 🏃🏇 The most famous and popular Navajo Indian Reservation attraction is this 84,000-acre land of piñon and juniper forests cut by a trio of red-walled sandstone canyons. Extending eastward from Chinle to Tsaile, the canyon's rim elevations range from 5500 to 7000 feet while the canyon bottoms drop from 30 feet nearest Chinle to 1000 feet farther east. Cottonwood trees and other vegetation shade farms connected by miles of sandy wash along the canyon bottom. Two major gorges, 27 and 34 miles long, dramatically unveil walls of 250-million-year-old solidified sand dunes in a strata geologists call the Defiance Plateau. Facilities include a motel, restaurant, bookstore, visitors center, museum, crib-log hogan, restrooms, jeep and horse tours, and guided hikes. ~ Located in Chinle, via Route 191; 928-674-5500, fax 928-674-5507; www.nps.gov/cach. Spider Rock Campground is east of the visitors center on South Rim Canyon Drive.

▲ There are two campgrounds available. Cottonwood Campground has 96 sites (no hookups); no fee. Spider Rock Campground, run by a private concessionaire, offers 47 sites (no hookups); $10 to $15 per night. ~ 928-674-8261; e-mail spiderrock@cybertrails.com.

Nature's handiwork in this part of the state exemplifies her unabashed use of warm tones to paint her landscapes, **Northern Navajo Country**
from flame-colored sandstone buttes to red-rock pillars. Traveling here also allows you an experience unachievable in any other part of the United States: being in four states at once, all at the Four Corners Monument. The inevitable Navajo crafts booths offer up necklaces, bracelets, earrings, T-shirts, paintings, sandpaintings, fry bread and lemonade—a splendid way to make something festive out of two intersecting lines on a map.

To get to Northern Navajo Country from the south, you'll have to pass by **Teec Nos Pos Arts and Crafts Center**, the usual road-

SIGHTS

side gallery of Southwest Indian crafts, with an emphasis on area sand paintings and Navajo rugs. Closed Sunday. ~ Routes 160 and 64; 928-656-3228.

Heading westbound on Route 160, even before travelers reach Kayenta, amazing eroded shapes emerge on the horizon—like the cathedral-sized and -shaped **Church Rock**. Kayenta, originally a small town that grew up around John Wetherill's trading post at 5564-feet elevation, today is both Arizona's gateway to Monument Valley and a coal-mining center.

The 24 miles north to Monument Valley on Route 163 is a prelude to the main event, huge red-rock pillars. **Half Dome** and **Owl Rock** on your left form the eastern edge of the broad Tyende Mesa. On your right rise **Burnt Foot Butte** and **El Capitan**, also called Agathla Peak—roots of ancient volcanoes whose dark rock contrasts with pale-yellow sandstone formations.

MONUMENT VALLEY   A half-mile north of the Utah state line on Route 163 is a crossroads; go left two miles to Gouldings Trading Post and Lodge, or right two miles to **Monument Valley Navajo Tribal Park Headquarters** and Monument Valley Visitors Center. Inside you can see excellent views from a glass-walled observatory. This was the first Navajo Tribal Park, set aside in 1958. Within you'll see more than 40 named and dozens more unnamed red and orange monolithic sandstone buttes and rock skyscrapers jutting hundreds of feet. It is here that you can arrange Navajo-owned jeep tours into the Valley Drive. Admission. ~ P.O. Box 360289, Monument Valley, UT 84536; 435-727-5874.

For a small fee, you can explore the **17-mile Loop Drive** over a dirt road, badly rutted in places, to view a number of famous landmarks with names that describe their shapes, such as **Rain God Mesa, Three Sisters** and **Totem Pole**. At **John Ford's Point**, an Indian on horseback often poses for photographs, then rides out to chat and collect a tip. A 15-minute roundtrip walk from **North Window** rewards you with panoramic views.

The Navajos and this land seem to belong together. A dozen Navajo families still live in the park, and several open their hogans to guided tours. For a small fee, they'll pose for your pictures. A number of today's residents are descendants of Navajos who arrived here in the mid-1860s with Headman Hoskinini, fleeing Kit Carson and his round-up of Navajos in the Canyon de Chelly area. Hoskinini lived here until his death in 1909.

The ultimate cowboy-Indian Western landscape, Monument Valley has been the setting for many movies. Seven John Ford Westerns, including *Stagecoach* and *She Wore a Yellow Ribbon*, were filmed in Monument Valley between 1938 and 1963. Other films shot here include *How the West Was Won*, *Billy the Kid* and *The Trial of Billy Jack*.

Gouldings Trading Post, Lodge and Museum, a sleek, water-melon-colored complex on a hillside, blends in with enormous sandstone boulders stacked above it. The original Goulding two-story stone home and trading post, now a museum, includes a room devoted to movies made here. Daily showings can be seen in a small adjacent theater. ~ Two miles west of Route 163, Monument Valley; 435-727-3231, fax 435-727-3344; www.gouldings.com, e-mail gouldings@gouldings.com.

From Gouldings it's nearly 11 miles northwest on paved Oljato Road to the single-story stone **Oljato Trading Post,** its Depression-era gas pumps and scabby turquoise door visible reminders of its age. Inside ask to see a dusty museum room filled with Navajo crafts hidden behind the turquoise bullpen-style mercantile. Often you can buy a fine Navajo wedding basket for a good price. ~ Oljato; 435-727-3210; www.a-aa.com/trailride.   ◄ HIDDEN

Back to Kayenta and Route 160, it's a scenic 18-mile drive southwest to the turnoff for the **Navajo National Monument,** which encompasses some of the finest Anasazi ruins (open only from Memorial Day to Labor Day). This stunning region show-cases the architectural genius of the area's early inhabitants.

To gain an overview of the monument, stop by the **Visitors Center and Museum,** featuring films and exhibits of the treasures

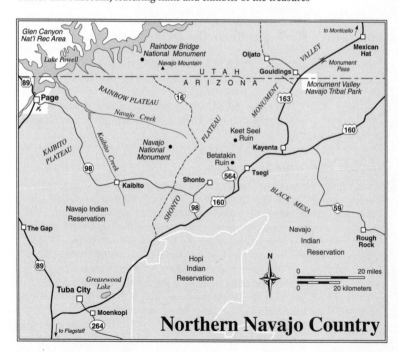

Northern Navajo Country

tucked away beneath the sandstone cliffs, including a replica of an Anasazi ruin. You'll be impressed by pottery, jewelry, textiles and tools created by the Kayenta Anasazi who lived in these exquisite canyons. There's also a craft gallery selling Zuni, Navajo and Hopi artwork. ~ Route 564, nine and a half miles north of Route 160, or 27 miles west of Kayenta; 928-672-2366, fax 928-672-2703; www.nps.gov/nava.

From the visitors center you can hike an undemanding forest trail to **Betatakin Point Overlook**. Here you'll get an overview of Betatakin Ruin and Tsegi Canyon. One of the ruins here, **Inscription House,** is closed to protect it for posterity. However, it is possible to make the strenuous but rewarding hike to **Betatakin Ruin**, located in a dramatic alcove 700 feet below the canyon's rim. On this trip back in time, you'll see a 135-room ledge house that rivals the best of Mesa Verde. Also well worth a visit is remote **Keet Seel.** Even some of the roofs remain intact at this 160-room, five-kiva ruin. You can only reach this gem with a permit obtained at the visitors center. For more information on the ranger-led walks to these two well-preserved ruins, see "Hiking" at the end of the chapter.

Back on Route 160, it's about 28 miles southwest to **Elephant Feet**, roadside geologic formations that resemble legs and feet of a gigantic sandstone elephant.

LODGING   **Best Western Wetherill Inn** has 54 spacious rooms sporting dark-brown furniture, upholstered chairs, multicolored spreads and matching curtains in Southwest style. ~ Route 163, a mile north of Route 160, Kayenta; 928-697-3231, fax 928-697-3233; e-mail wetherill@gouldings.com. DELUXE.

Tour buses full of French, German, Italian and Japanese guests frequent the 162-room **Holiday Inn Monument Valley.** All rooms

---

NAVAJO CEREMONIAL DANCES

Three popular Navajo dances, which you may be lucky enough to see, are the Corral Dance, the Night-Way Dance and the Enemy-Way Dance. The Corral Dance seeks divine help to avoid dangerous lightning and snake bites; it's so named because part of the ceremony takes place within a corral of branches around a bonfire. The nine-day-long Night-Way Dance supposedly helps people suffering from nervousness or insanity. And the Enemy-Way Dance performed during the summer is a purifying ceremony to help people suffering from nightmares and other "enemies of the mind." Activities are held in a different place for each of the three nights of the ceremony and, at the conclusion, a sheep is slaughtered for breakfast.

in the two-story adobe brick buildings offer floral carpets in hall-ways, whitewashed furniture, upholstered chairs and spacious bathrooms. There's also an outdoor pool. ~ At the junction of Routes 160 and 163, Kayenta; 928-697-3221, 800-465-4329, fax 928-697-3349; www.ichotels.com. MODERATE TO DELUXE.

The only lodging right at Monument Valley, **Gouldings Lodge** is nestled at the base of a towering sandstone cliff that provides afternoon shade. The long, low two-story lodge has sliding glass doors leading to balconies for each of the 62 rooms, taking brilliant advantage of the monoliths that dot the landscape. The air-conditioned rooms are decorated in colorful Navajo motifs. The indoor pool is for guests only. ~ Two miles west of Route 163, Monument Valley; 435-727-3231, 800-874-0902, fax 435-727-3344; www.gouldings.com, e-mail gouldings@gouldings.com. BUDGET TO DELUXE.

Anasazi Inn at Tsegi Canyon, with 57 rooms and a view of the canyon, is the closest lodging to Navajo National Monument. ~ Route 160, ten miles west of Kayenta; 928-697-3793, fax 928-697-8249; www.anasaziinn.com, e-mail info@anasaziinn.com. BUDGET TO MODERATE.

DINING

An American Indian theme prevails at the Holiday Inn's **Wagon Wheel Restaurant**, complete with Anasazi-style walls and sand-painting room dividers. Tables for four and matching chairs are decorated in Southwest style. There's a continental breakfast buffet for diners in a hurry; a salad bar and burgers, sandwiches, Navajo tacos for lunch or dinner; meat and fish entrées for dinner. ~ At the junction of Routes 160 and 163, Kayenta; 928-697-3221, fax 928-697-3349. MODERATE TO DELUXE.

Old West saloon architecture signals Kayenta's **Golden Sands Cafe**. Inside, the walls are lined with photographs of old movies and commercials shot in Monument Valley. Breakfast specials include omelettes or blueberry pancakes; dinner entrées include rib steak, chicken-fried steak and Navajo tacos. ~ Adjacent to the Wetherill Inn on Route 163, a mile north of Route 160, Kayenta; 928-697-3684, fax 928-697-3734. BUDGET TO MODERATE.

Chances are you already know what's on the menu at **Burger King**. This one, however, is special because of its "museum"—actually a display case between two seating sections—dedicated to the Navajo Code Talkers. Memorabilia recall the unique way 5000 Navajo men served in World War II, transmitting military radio messages in their native language throughout the Pacific theater of operations. It was the only code the Japanese never succeeded in breaking. The Code Talkers' historical role continues to be a source of great pride among the Navajo people—including the Burger King's owner, whose father was one of them. ~ Route 160, Kayenta; phone/fax 928-697-3534. BUDGET.

HIDDEN ►   Lively, crowded and cheery, **Amigo Cafe** serves fresh (nothing served here comes out of a can) Mexican, American and Navajo entrées. Popular with locals. Closed Sunday. ~ On the east side of Route 163, a mile north of Route 160, Kayenta; 928-697-8448. BUDGET TO MODERATE.

Three levels of dining stairstep a bluff so that the **Stage Coach Dining Room** patrons can enjoy the panoramas of Monument Valley. The peach and burnt umber booths and tables of this former cafeteria complement the stunning sandstone bluffs and views outside. The restaurant is known for its Navajo tacos, beef stew and fry bread. There's a salad bar, and nonalcoholic wine and beer are offered. ~ Gouldings Lodge, Monument Valley; 435-727-3231 ext. 404; www.gouldings.com, e-mail gouldings@gouldings.com. MODERATE TO DELUXE.

The term "Indian power" is a tongue-in-cheek reference to eating four or five Indian tacos, a favorite food at pow wows, fairs, festivals and outdoor summer shows, a night.

An all-American menu at **Anasazi Inn Café** offers burgers, steak, chicken and a few Navajo dishes. Open 24 hours during the summer. ~ Route 160, ten miles west of Kayenta; 928-697-3793, fax 928-697-8249; www.anasaziinn.com, e-mail info@anasaziinn.com. BUDGET TO MODERATE.

SHOPPING   Ask to see the crafts room at the 1921 **Oljato Trading Post**, 11 miles northwest of Gouldings near Monument Valley, and you'll be led into a dusty museum-like space. The room is crammed with crafts—some for sale, some for admiring. Best buys here are Navajo wedding baskets popular with today's local brides and grooms. Simple, brown-pitch Navajo pottery made in this area is also sold here as well as cedar cradleboards, used on the "res" as a baby's safety seat. ~ Oljato; 435-727-3210.

Yellow Ribbon Gift Shop provides Southwestern tribal crafts and souvenirs for all budgets. ~ Part of Gouldings Trading Post complex, Monument Valley; 435-727-3231.

PARKS   **MONUMENT VALLEY NAVAJO TRIBAL PARK** 🚶 🚵 🐎 Straddling the Arizona–Utah border is the jewel of tribally run Navajo Nation parks. With its 92,000 acres of monoliths, spires, buttes, mesas, canyons and sand dunes—all masterpieces of red-rock erosion—it is a stunning destination. With dozens of families still living here, it is also a sort of Williamsburg of Navajoland. There's a visitors center with shops, showers, restrooms and picnic tables. You must arrange for a guide if you want to explore the park. Admission. ~ Route 163, 24 miles northeast of Kayenta. The visitors center is east another four miles. The Gouldings complex is west three miles; 435-727-5874; www.navajonationparks.org.

▲ Mitten View has 99 sites; $10 per night up to six people in summer; in winter, the restrooms are closed and the fee is $5.

NAVAJO NATIONAL MONUMENT 🏃 Three of the Southwest's most beautiful Anasazi pueblo ruins are protected in the canyons of this 360-acre park, swathed in piñon and juniper forests at a 7300-foot elevation. Inscription House Ruin is so fragile it is closed. Betatakin Ruin, handsomely set in a cave high up a canyon wall, is visible from an overlook. But close looks at Betatakin and the largest site, Keet Seel, require fairly strenuous hikes permitted between Memorial Day and Labor Day. Facilities include a visitors center, a museum, a gift shop, restrooms and picnic areas. ~ Take Route 160 west of Kayenta, turn right at Route 564 and continue nine miles; 928-672-2700.

▲ There are 31 sites in the campground, plus a handful of primitive overflow sites; no hookups, no fee.

Outdoor Adventures

CAMPING

The largest campgrounds on the Navajo reservation are at **Canyon de Chelly** (96 sites, no hookups, free; 47 sites at Spider Rock, no hookups, $10 to $15; Navajo hogans, $25) and **Monument Valley** (99 sites, full hookups, $10). There are also campgrounds at **Lake Asaayi** (open camping, no hookups, $15 to $25) and **Navajo National Monument** (31 sites, no hookups or water, free). Camping is not permitted on the Hopi Reservation.

FISHING

There's fishing year-round in Indian Country with a one-day to one-year Navajo tribal license required at all lakes, streams and rivers in the Navajo Nation. No fishing tackle or boats are for rent on the reservation. Boats are permitted on many of the lakes; most require electric motors only.

WESTERN NAVAJO COUNTRY There's trout fishing in the small **Pasture Canyon Lake** just east of Tuba City. Anglers can reach the **Little Colorado River** at Cameron and the Colorado River at Lee's Ferry (see Chapter Two). Although these rivers define most of the reservation's western boundary, sheer rock gorges put them beyond reach in most other places. Get fishing licenses and boating permits from CSWTA **Inc. Environmental Consultant**. Closed Sunday and Monday. ~ Tuba City; 928-283-4323, fax 928-283-4804.

CENTRAL NAVAJO COUNTRY **Whiskey Lake** and **Long Lake** are known for their trophy-size trout, located in the Chuska Mountains, a dozen miles south of Route 134 via logging routes 8000 and 8090. Their season is May 1 through November 30.

All-year lakes stocked with rainbow trout each spring include **Wheatfields Lake** (44 miles north of Window Rock on Route 12) and **Tsaile Lake** (half-mile south of Navajo Community College in Tsaile). Tsaile Lake is also popular for catfish.

Good for largemouth bass and channel catfishing is **Many Farms Lake** (three miles via dirt road east of Route 191 in Many Farms). You can get licenses and permits from **Navajo Fish & Wildlife**.

~ Window Rock; 928-871-6451. **Wilkinson's Tsaile Trading Post** also has a few supplies. ~ Tsaile; 928-724-3484.

NORTHERN NAVAJO COUNTRY There are no tribal lakes in northern Navajo country, but the reservation boundary follows **Lake Powell** and its tributary, the **San Juan River**. Trout, catfish and bass from Lake Powell take refuge in side-canyon creeks, a few of which can be reached in a four-wheel-drive vehicle. Small boats can put in at **Piute Farms Wash**, north of Oljato and Monument Valley, at one of the most remote parts of Lake Powell. The **Kayenta Trading Post** has fishing licenses and boating permits. ~ 1000 Main Street, Kayenta; 928-697-3541.

JOGGING

Navajos and Hopis, who pride themselves on their long distance–running traditions that date back to first contact with whites in the 1540s, host races at every tribal fair. Races are open to non-Indians as well. Since it is common to see American Indian joggers daily along virtually any route, bring your togs and run, too.

CENTRAL NAVAJO COUNTRY At Canyon de Chelly, try the **White House Ruins trail** or either of the **rim trails**.

NORTHERN NAVAJO COUNTRY The four-mile road leading into Monument Valley or roads to Oljato and around Gouldings Lodge are good places for a jog.

GOLF

The nine-hole **Hidden Cove Golf Course** is carved out of the high desert grasslands and surrounded by scenic mountains and hillsides. Club and cart rentals are available. ~ Exit 283, two miles west of Route 40, Holbrook; 928-524-3097; www.hidden cove.com.

RIDING STABLES

Horses have been an important icon of Navajo culture since the Spanish introduced them in the mid-16th century. They're a grand way to connect with a Navajo guide while seeing awesome country through his eyes. Most offer one-hour to overnight or longer options, and there's flexibility on where you go and how long you stay.

NORTHERN NAVAJO COUNTRY In Monument Valley, **Sacred Monument Tours** can be an hour around The Mittens, or all day or longer into the valley. ~ Located via a dirt road west of the visitors center two miles. Call for specific directions and reservations; 435-727-3218.

Statisticians claim Navajos host more rodeos per year than all other United States tribes combined. Rarely does a summer weekend pass without Navajo cowboys and cowgirls of all ages gathering somewhere on the reservation. To find one when you visit, call *The Navajo Times*, a weekly, in Window Rock (928-871-6641), the Navajo Nation Visitors Center (928-871-6436) or Navajo Radio Station KTNN 660 AM (928-871-2582).

BIKING

Biking is permitted on any paved roads in Navajo Country but only on the main paved highways on the Hopi Indian Reservation.

SOUTHERN NAVAJO COUNTRY Petrified Forest National Park routes will often be too hot for daytime summer riding but offer a splendid way to sightsee in cooler spring and fall seasons.

CENTRAL NAVAJO COUNTRY While you'll find no designated bike paths or trails within the reservation, bicycles are well suited to both rim roads at Canyon de Chelly. Cyclists from around the world are attracted to the uphill challenges of the Chuska Mountain Routes 134 (paved), 68 and 13 (partially paved).

NORTHERN NAVAJO COUNTRY Bicycling is popular along the paved, pine-clad nine miles of Route 564 into Navajo National Monument. Mountain bikes are particularly suited to the 17-mile rutted dirt loop open to visitors in Monument Valley.

HIKING

Because most of the land covered in this chapter is tribally owned or in national parks and monuments, hiking trail options are limited. Hopi backcountry is not open to visitors; it is, however, on the Navajo Indian Reservation. For the mountains, ask for suggestions from area trading posts, or hire an Indian guide by the hour or overnight or longer. Guides know the way and can share stories about the area.

A hat, sunglasses and drinking water are recommended for all hikes; add a raincoat during the July and August monsoon season. All distances listed for hiking trails are one way unless otherwise noted.

SOUTHERN NAVAJO COUNTRY Little Painted Desert County Park has a strenuous one-mile hiking trail descending 500 feet into some of the most colorful hills in all the Painted Desert. Colors are most intense early and late in the day.

Petrified Forest National Park's summertime temperatures often soar into the 90s and 100s. Hiking is best early or late in the day. Water is available only at the visitors center at the north and south end of the park, so you're wise to carry extra with you.

AUTHOR FAVORITE

Other outdoor experiences in Navajo country pale in comparison to a day-long horseback ride into **Canyon de Chelly** with a native guide. **Justin Stables**, located right at the entrance of the reservation, offers two-hour, half-day, all-day and overnight guided tours to White House Ruins and elsewhere in and beyond the canyon. Groups range from 1 to 25 people. ~ 928-674-5678.

A loop that begins and ends at the Crystal Forest stop on the park's 28-mile scenic loop, **Crystal Forest Interpretive Trail** (.5 mile) leads past the park's most concentrated petrified wood stands. You can see how tall these ancient trees were (up to 170 feet), and the variety of colors that formed after crystal replaced wood cells.

An introduction to the Chinle Formation, **Blue Mesa Hike** (1 mile) is a loop interpretive trail that leads past a wonderland of blue, gray and white layered hills. Signs en route explain how the hills formed and are now eroding.

The Flattops (unlimited miles) trailhead descends off sandstone-relic mesas several hundred feet into Puerco Ridge and other areas of the 10,000-acre Rainbow Forest Wilderness at the park's south-eastern end. A quarter-mile trail leads into the area, and then you are on your own, exploring a vast gray-and-brown mudstone and siltstone badlands with wide vistas around every hill. The back-country permits required to visit this remote portion of the park are free from any of the three visitors centers; you can stay up to 14 days.

Painted Desert Wilderness Area trailhead begins at Kachina Point at the park's north end. A brief trail descends some 400 feet, then leaves you on your own to explore cross-country some 35,000 acres of red-and-white-banded badlands of mudstone and siltstone, bald of vegetation. The going is sticky when wet. Get free backcountry permits at either visitors center.

CENTRAL NAVAJO COUNTRY Canyon de Chelly's only hike open to visitors without a guide is **White House Ruin Trail** (2.5 miles roundtrip), beginning at the 6.4-mile marker on the South Rim Drive. The trail switchback winds down red sandstone swirls, and crosses a sandy wash (in rainy seasons you will do some wading in Chinle Creek; bring extra socks) to a cottonwood-shaded masonry village with 60 rooms surviving at ground level and an additional ten rooms perched in a cliff's alcove above.

Four-hour, four-and-a-half-mile Navajo-led hikes up the canyon to White House Ruin start at the visitors center at 9 a.m. Navajo guides can be hired at the **Canyon de Chelly National Monument Visitors Center** to take you on short or overnight hikes into the canyon. The maximum group size for private guided hikes is 15 people. ~ 928-674-5500, fax 928-674-5507.

NORTHERN NAVAJO COUNTRY Hiking is not permitted in **Monument Valley** without a Navajo guide. Hire one at the visitors center (435-727-5874) for an hour, overnight or longer. Fred Cly (505-860-6799, or ask at the visitors center) is a knowledgeable guide especially good for photo angles and best times of day. Reservations cannot be made in advance of arrival; as soon as you pull into Monument Valley, go to the visitors center parking lot and make tour arrangements for the following day.

Navajo National Monument trails include **Sandal Trail** (.5 mile), a fairly level self-guided trail to Betatakin Ruin overlook; bring binoculars. The ranger-led hike (2.5 miles) to **Betatakin Ruin**, or "ledge house" in Navajo, is strenuous, requiring a return climb up 700 steps. But it's worth the effort for the walk through the floor of Tsegi Canyon. National Park Service guides lead one tour of no more than 25 hikers each day, May through September. Tokens are awarded on a first-come, first-served basis at the visitors center. The hike to **Keet Seel** (8.5 miles), the biggest Anasazi ruin in Arizona (160 rooms dating from A.D. 950 to 1300) is open to hikers May through September. Much of the trail is sandy, making the trek fairly tiresome, and hikers must wade through cold, shallow water along the way. You can stay only one night; 20 people a day may hike in. A free backcountry permit is required. To get a permit, you must first make a reservation five months in advance. Call 928-672-2700, fax 928-672-2703. Or take your chances and ask about cancellations when you get there.

Transportation

CAR

This is a land of wide-open spaces, but don't despair. Roads have vastly improved in the last decade, easing the way for travelers. Bounded on the south by **Route 40**, two parallel routes farther north lead east and west through Indian Country: the southern **Route 264** travels alongside the three Hopi mesas and Window Rock; the northern **Route 160**, en route to Colorado, is gateway to all the northern reservation attractions. **Route 89**, the main north-to-south artery, connects Flagstaff with Lake Powell, traversing the Western Indian Reservation. Five other good, paved north–south routes connect Route 40 travelers with Indian Country. **Route 99/2** and **Route 87** connect the Winslow area with Hopi villages. **Route 191** leads to Ganado, Canyon de Chelly and Utah. **Route 12**, arguably the prettiest of all, connects Route 264 with Window Rock and the back side of Canyon de Chelly. This is desert driving; be sure to buy gas when it is available.

BACKBONE OF THE NAVAJO NATION

Many Navajos still favor traditional cradleboards (fashioned out of pine, cottonwood or cedar, and laced together with leather strips) to keep babies protected. Navajos believe that the flat boards will give the baby a strong back, and that the supporting pad will help form a rounded head.

AIR   There is no regularly scheduled commuter air service to Hopi or Navajo lands. The nearest airports are Gallup, New Mexico; Flagstaff, Arizona; and Cortez, Colorado.

BUS   **Navajo Transit System** offers weekday bus service between Fort Defiance and Window Rock in the east and Tuba City in the west. The system also heads north from Window Rock to Kayenta on weekdays with stops including Navajo Community College at Tsaile. ~ Based in Fort Defiance; 928-729-4002, fax 928-729-4116; www.navajotransitsystem.com.

TRAIN   **Amtrak**'s daily "Southwest Chief" connects Los Angeles with Chicago and stops at three Indianland gateway cities: Flagstaff, Winslow and Gallup. ~ 800-872-7245; www.amtrak.com.

JEEP TOURS   Jeeps, either with tops down or with air conditioning on (not all jeeps have air conditioning, so ask operators before you pay money), are a popular way to see Navajo Indian Reservation attractions noted for occasional sand bogs and even quicksand pockets. Navajo guides often live in the region and can share area lore and American Indian humor.

At Canyon de Chelly, **Thunderbird Lodge Canyon Tours** takes visitors on outings in large, noisy, converted all-terrain army vehicles. There are eight-hour trips that cover both Canyon de Chelly and Canyon del Muerto, as well as three-and-a-half-hour trips to either canyon. (Full-day tours are not available year-round.) ~ Thunderbird Lodge, Chinle; 928-674-5841; www.tbirdlodge. com, e-mail tbirdlodge@frontiernet.net.

Monument Valley tour operators all offer half-day and all-day tours of Monument and adjoining Mystery Valley. It's the only way visitors can see the stunning backcountry. Most tours include visits to an inhabited hogan. Some offer lunch or dinner.

Gouldings Monument Valley Tours takes visitors on morning and all-day tours in 20-passenger open-air vehicles. ~ At Gouldings Lodge near Monument Valley; 435-727-3231; www. gouldings.com/tours. Depending on the group's size, **Bill Crawley Monument Valley Tours** uses vehicles ranging from a seven-passenger Suburban to a 30-person bus. ~ Kayenta; 928-697-3463; www.crawleytours.com. **Unimog Tours** does three-hour treks covering 24 miles on the canyon floor. ~ 928-674-5433; www.canyondechellytours.com.

SIX

North Central Arizona

When it comes to north central Arizona, visitors soon discover that it's a region of vivid contrasts. The many unusual places to be found in this area vary dramatically in everything from altitude to attitude, from climate to culture. Here, you'll find communities that range from Old West to New Age, from college town to artist colony, along with lava cones and red-rock spires, American Indian ruins and vast pine forests, even a meteor crater, all just waiting to be explored.

Set at the edge of a huge volcano field, Flagstaff grew up as a railroad town in the midst of the world's largest ponderosa pine forest. The town was founded in 1882, less than a year before the first steam train clattered through, and thrived first on timber and later on tourism. Today, both freight and passenger trains still pass through Flagstaff (population 53,000). The largest community between Albuquerque and the greater Los Angeles area on Route 40, one of the nation's busiest truck routes, Flagstaff's huge restaurant and lodging industry prospers year-round. In fact, casual visitors detouring from the interstate to fill up the gas tank and buy burgers and fries along the commercial strip that is Flagstaff's Route 40 business loop can easily form the misimpression that the town is one long row of motels and fast-food joints. A closer look will reveal it as a lively college town with considerable historic charm. A short drive outside of town takes you to fascinating ancient Indian ruins as well as Arizona's highest mountains and strange volcanic landscapes.

Less than an hour's drive south of Flagstaff via magnificent Oak Creek Canyon, Sedona is a strange blend of spectacular scenery, chic resorts, Western art in abundance and New Age notions. You can go jeeping or hiking in the incomparable Red Rock Country, play some of the country's most beautiful golf courses, shop for paintings until you run out of wall space or just sit by Oak Creek and feel the vibes. People either love Sedona or hate it. Often both. You'll also have the chance to visit one of the state's best-preserved ghost towns. Jerome, a booming copper town a century ago, was abandoned in the 1950s and then repopulated in the 1960s by artists and hippies to become a tourist favorite today. Prescott is a quiet

129

little town with a healthy regard for its own history. Long before Phoenix, Flag-staff or Sedona came into existence, Prescott was the capital of the Arizona Territory. Today, it is a city of museums, stately 19th-century architecture and century-old saloons. Change seems to happen slowly and cautiously here. As you stroll the streets of town, you may feel that you've slipped back through time into the 1950s, into the sort of all-American community you don't often find any more.

▼▼▼▼▼▼▼▼▼▼
Flagstaff Area

Flagstaff has been called "The City of Seven Wonders" because of its proximity to the Grand Canyon, Oak Creek Canyon, Walnut Canyon, Wupatki National Monument, Sunset Crater, Meteor Crater and the San Francisco Peaks. Visitors who view Flagstaff from the heights of the San Francisco Peaks to the north will see this community's most striking characteristic: It is an island in an ocean of ponderosa pine forest stretching as far as the eye can see. At an elevation of 7000 feet, Flagstaff has the coolest climate of any city in Arizona. Because of its proximity to slopes on 12,000-foot Agassiz Peak, Flagstaff is the state's leading winter ski resort town. It is also a lively college town, with students accounting for 10 percent of the population.

SIGHTS   A good place to start exploring the area is downtown, toward the west end of Route 66 (the business loop of Route 40). The downtown commercial zone retains its early-20th-century frontier architecture. Neither run-down nor yuppified, this historic district specializes in shops that cater to students from Northern Arizona University, on the other side of the interstate and railroad tracks.

Take time to stroll through the old residential area just north of the downtown business district. Attractive Victorian houses, many of them handmade from volcanic lava rock, give the neighborhood its unique character.

The **Flagstaff Visitors Center** provides ample information on the Flagstaff area. ~ 1 East Route 66, Flagstaff; 928-774-9541, fax 928-556-1308; www.flagstaffarizona.org, e-mail cvb@flagstaff arizona.org.

San Francisco Street is the main thoroughfare through the historic downtown district. Neither rundown nor yuppified, the district retains much of its turn-of-the-20th-century frontier architecture. The **Weatherford Hotel** was built partially of locally quarried sandstone and opened in 1899. It was the first structure in Flagstaff to be listed on the National Register of Historic Places, and is still operated as a hotel. The present owners restored the structure by uncovering original fireplaces and rebuilding balconies that overlook downtown. ~ 23 North Leroux Street, Flagstaff; 928-774-2731.

The 1888 **McMillan Building** now houses an art gallery. ~ 2 West Route 66 at Leroux Street, Flagstaff. The **Hotel Monte Vista**, also listed on the register, dates from the 1920s and was popular with movie stars in the 1930s and 1940s. ~ 100 North San Francisco Street, Flagstaff.

Take time to stroll through the old residential area just north of the downtown business district. Attractive Victorian houses, many of them handmade from volcanic lava rock, give the neighborhood its unique character.

South of downtown, on the other side of the interstate and across the railroad tracks, is **Northern Arizona University**. The original structure, Old Main, was built in 1894 and now houses the Northern Arizona University Art Museum & Galleries. Campus tours are available. ~ Butler Avenue and South Beaver Street, Flagstaff; 928-523-5511.

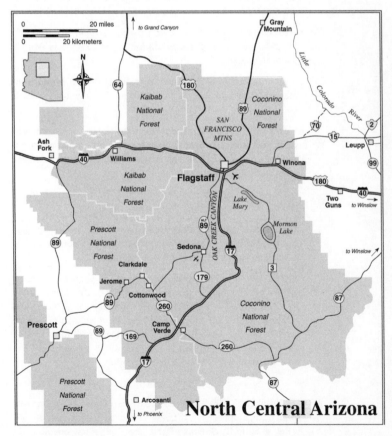

Text continued on page 134.

Two-day Getaway

Exploring North Central Arizona

It's easy to fill a day exploring the unique places that surround Flagstaff. Then take a second day for Route 89A, a two-lane blacktop route 122 miles long that returns you to Route 40 just 47 miles from where you turned off. It's one of Arizona's best scenic drives.

Day 1
- From Flagstaff, take Route 40 a short distance east to Exit 204.

- Visit **Walnut Canyon National Monument** (page 138) and discover the world of the ancient Sinagua cliff dwellers on a short but strenuous hike. Allow one hour.

- Returning to Route 40, head west to Exit 201 and take Route 89 north for ten miles to the turnoff for Sunset Crater and Wupatki national monuments.

- Stop in at the **Sunset Crater Volcano National Monument** (page 137) and take in the beauty of the 1000-foot-tall volcanic cone.

- Follow the 36-mile loop road through the fantastic and varied volcanic landscape of **Sunset Crater** and **Wupatki national monuments** (page 137), stopping at the Wupatki visitors center and ruins. Allow two hours.

- From where the loop road rejoins Route 89, return south to the marked turnoff for Schultz Pass Road.

- Take unpaved **Schultz Pass Road** (page 136) through the pine woods on the slopes of the San Francisco Peaks. Before you know it, you'll be back in Flagstaff. Allow a half hour.

- After a late lunch, take your pick among the various sightseeing possibilities Flagstaff has to offer. You might ride the chairlift at the **Arizona Snowbowl** (page 136), visit the **Museum of Northern Arizona** (page 136) with its excellent Indian and natural history exhibits, or tour **Lowell Observatory** (page 134) for a look at the antique telescope used in the early 1900s to "discover" the nonexistent canals of the Martian civilization.

Day 2
- Leaving Flagstaff, take a leisurely drive down **Oak Creek Canyon** (page 150), stopping for a splash in the chilly mountain stream water at **Slide Rock State Park** (page 150). Allow one hour.

- Arriving in Sedona, take time out to explore a little of Red Rock Country. There are as many possibilities as you have time; for a quick introduction to this unique area, visit **Red Rock State Park** (page 163) and hike the trail along Oak Creek. Allow one hour or more.

- Follow Route 89A west through West Sedona to Clarksdale, a 26-mile drive through pretty Verde Valley.

- Visit the white stone Indian ruins at **Tuzigoot National Monument** (page 164). Allow one hour.

- Continue west on Route 89A for another four miles to Jerome, on a hillside above the Verde Valley. It's a good place to stretch your legs and find lunch. Then drive over the forested hills to the Prescott Valley.

- In Prescott, visit the **Sharlot Hall Museum** (page 167) for a look at 19th-century Arizona. Allow one and a half hours.

- If time permits, also check out the **Phippen Museum of Western Art** (page 168), one of the best Western art museums anywhere. Allow one hour.

- Drive north on Route 89 for 51 miles to rejoin Route 40 at the little crossroads town of Ash Fork.

IF YOU HAVE MORE TIME

If you have extra time in central Arizona, ride the **Verde Canyon Railroad** (page 164), one of the most spectacular scenic train trips anywhere.

A sightseeing highlight in the university area is **Riordan Mansion State Historic Park**, a block off Milton Road north of the intersection of Route 40 and Route 17. The biggest Territorial-day mansion in Flagstaff, it was built in 1904 by two brothers who were the region's leading timber barons. Constructed duplex-style with over 40 rooms and 13,000 square feet of living space, the mansion blends rustic log-slab and volcanic rock construction with early-20th-century opulence and plenty of creative imagination. Tour guides escort visitors through the home to see its original furnishings and family mementos. Most of the house is fully accessible. Reservations are required. Admission. ~ 409 Riordan Road, Flagstaff; 928-779-4395, fax 928-556-0253; www.pr.state.az.us, e-mail mdavis@pr.state.az.us.

On a hilltop just a mile west of downtown is **Lowell Observatory**. The observatory was built by wealthy astronomer Percival Lowell in 1894 to take advantage of the exceptional visibility created by Flagstaff's clean air and high altitude. His most famous achievement during the 22 years he spent here was the "discovery" of canals on the planet Mars, which he submitted to the scientific community as "proof" of extraterrestrial life. Building the observatory proved to be a great accomplishment in itself, though. The planet Pluto was discovered by astronomers at Lowell Observatory 14 years after Dr. Lowell's death, and the facility continues to be one of the most important centers for studying the solar system. Take a guided tour of the observatory and see Dr. Lowell's original Victorian-era telescope. The Steel Visitors Center presents interactive, hands-on exhibits about astronomers' tools. On most summer evenings, staff holds star talks and help visitors stargaze through one of the center's smaller telescopes. Call for hours. Admission. ~ 1400 West Mars Hill Road, Flagstaff; 928-774-3358, fax 928-774-6296; recorded schedule information, 928-774-2096; www.lowell.edu.

HIDDEN ▶   Overshadowed by Lowell Observatory, the **Northern Arizona University Campus Observatory** actually offers visitors a better chance to look through a larger telescope. Public viewing sessions are held on Friday evenings from 7:30 to 10 p.m. when the sky is clear. (Cardio alert: there's quite a steep climb required to reach this heavenly view.) The observatory is open to the public on Friday night or by special arrangement. ~ Northeast corner of San Francisco Street and University Drive on campus, Flagstaff; 928-523-7170, fax 928-523-1371; www.physics.nau.edu/~naaa.

HIDDEN ▶   The **Arboretum at Flagstaff** occupies 200 acres of meadows and ponderosa forest west of town. There's a passive solar greenhouse; outdoors you'll find constructed wetlands, a 1.2-mile nature trail, shade gardens, butterfly gardens, rare and endangered plant species of the Colorado Plateau, and 250 kinds of herbs.

Flagstaff Area

Meteor Crater

Two Guns

to Winslow

Navajo Indian Reservation

Sunrise

PAINTED DESERT

Navajo Indian Reservation

N

Grand Falls

Little Colorado River

Wupatki National Monument

Winona

Sunset Crater Volcano National Monument

Mormon Lake

Walnut Canyon National Monument

Lake Mary

to Tuba City

Antelope Hills

Coconino National Forest

Schultz Pass Rd

Arizona Snowbowl

Snowbowl Rd

Flagstaff

to Williams

Oak Creek Canyon Natural Area

to Slide Rock State Park

OAK CREEK CANYON

Kaibab National Forest

10 miles

10 kilometers

Downtown Flagstaff

Betrand St

to 89

Old US 66

Butler Ave

Elden St

San Francisco St

Phoenix Ave

Leroux St

Beaver St

Cottage Ave

Benton Ave

Clay Ave

Verde St

Ave

Humphreys St

Sitgreaves St

Mikes Pike

Dupont

Franklin

Humphreys St

Runke Dr

University Dr

Cherry St

Aspen Ave

Santa Fe Ave

Milton Rd

Old US 66

1 mile

1 kilometer

POINTS OF INTEREST

Ⓐ Arizona Historical Society— Pioneer Museum
Ⓑ Flagstaff Visitors Center
Ⓒ Hotel Monte Vista
Ⓓ Lowell Observatory
Ⓔ McMillan Building (Bank Hotel)
Ⓕ Museum of Northern Arizona
Ⓖ Northern Arizona University
Ⓗ Northern Arizona University Campus Observatory
Ⓘ Riordan Mansion State Historic Park
Ⓙ Weatherford Hotel

The abundance of native wildflowers (one of the nation's largest collections) during the summer months includes brilliant penstemon, Indian paintbrush, wild rose and scarlet gilia. There's also a tranquil picnic area. Closed mid-December through March. Admission. ~ 4001 Woody Mountain Road, Flagstaff; 928-774-1442, fax 928-774-1441; www.thearb.org, e-mail leslie.fauset@nau.edu.

The **Arizona Historical Society–Pioneer Museum** presents a program of changing exhibits. Themes are drawn from the history of northern Arizona, including logging, livestock-raising and social life. Highlights include early-day photos of the Grand Canyon. The museum is housed in the historic Coconino County Hospital, also known as the "poor farm." Three annual "living history" festivals are held here: the **Flagstaff Wool Festival**; the **Independence Day Festival**, featuring mountain men, crafts and skills and a Civil War artillery unit; and **Playthings of the Past**, featuring toys, dolls and games. Closed Sunday. Admission. ~ 2340 North Fort Valley Road, Flagstaff; 928-774-6272, fax 928-774-1596; www.arizonahistoricalsociety.org.

The **Museum of Northern Arizona** is known worldwide for its changing exhibits of American Indian artifacts, geology, biology and the fine arts of the Grand Canyon region, as well as a few permanent fixtures like the life-size replica skeleton of a dilophosaurus, a giant carnivorous dinosaur that once roamed the Colorado Plateau. This exhibit in the archaeology gallery charts the history and characteristics (such as foodstuffs) of the plateau's human inhabitants since prehistoric times. In the Branigar/Chase Discovery Center, an exhibit of fine arts, part of the museum's collection of five-million-plus objects, now has a regular home. A reception room in this wing has been furnished with Mission-style furniture and a fireplace and is a cozy, comfortable spot to relax. Outside the museum is a half-mile nature trail, which follows along a canyon rim and creek. The gift shop has an excellent collection of American Indian artworks. Admission. ~ 3101 North Fort Valley Road, Flagstaff; 928-774-5213, fax 928-779-1527; www.musnaz.org, e-mail info@musnaz.org.

HIDDEN ►

Not far beyond the Museum of Arizona on Route 180 is the turnoff for **Schultz Pass Road**. The unpaved road is rough and dusty, but as a drive it offers glimpses of the spectacular San Francisco Peaks, which tower above Flagstaff. About 14 miles long, the road comes out on Route 89 a short distance south of the turnoff to Sunset Crater National Monument.

The **Arizona Snowbowl**, one of the state's largest ski areas, runs its chairlift as a scenic skyride during the summer months, carrying visitors to timberline at 11,500 feet elevation on the side of Agassis Peak. From there, spectacular panoramic views stretch out 70 miles and take in the Grand Canyon. Open daily mid-June through Labor Day, open Friday through Sunday to mid-October. Admission. ~ Snowbowl Road, seven miles off Route 180; 928-779-1951, fax 928-779-3019; www.arizonasnowbowl.com, e-mail marketing@arizonasnowbowl.com.

North of Flagstaff, off Route 89, are Wupatki National Monument and Sunset Crater Volcano National Monument. A paved 36-mile loop road connects both monuments and links up with Route 89 at both ends.

Sunset Crater Volcano National Monument, a bright-colored 1000-foot-tall volcanic cone in the San Francisco Volcano Field, is of recent origin. It first erupted in the winter of 1064–65 and covered the surrounding area in a blanket of black cinder. Admission. ~ Forest Service Road 545; 928-526-0502, fax 928-714-0565; www.nps.gov/sucr.

North of Sunset Crater, **Wupatki National Monument** preserves several pueblo ruins on the fringes of the San Francisco Volcano Field. They were inhabited in the 12th and 13th centuries, at the same time the volcanic activity was at its peak. Repeatedly, fiery (albeit slow-moving) eruptions would drive the American Indians out of the area and volcanic ash would fertilize the land and lure them back. The result was a mixture of many Southwestern cultures including the Anasazi, Cohonina and Sinagua people. A ball court at Wupatki Pueblo suggests that they were also influenced by the more advanced Toltec civilization of central Mexico. Most archaeologists now believe that violence between the tribes was rare and that cultural exchange brought about a renaissance that radiated to other parts of the region. Some Hopi villages today trace their origins to pueblos at Wupatki. Park at the visitors center, where pottery, tools and other artifacts from the various sites are displayed, and take the self-guided walking tour around the Wupatki Pueblo, a remarkably intact 700-year-old stone structure that was the largest community in the area. North of the visitors center, side roads go to three other ruins—Wukoki, Citadel and Lomaki—that are typical of the 2000-plus sites contained within the monument boundaries. To protect such sites, the backcountry is off-limits to visitors. However, rangers guide 16-mile overnight hikes to Crack-in-Rock Ruin in the spring and fall; make reservations at least six months ahead. Admission. ~ Forest Road 545; 928-679-2365, fax 928-679-2349; www.nps.gov/wupa.

A mere 900 years old, Sunset Crater is the youngest volcano on the Colorado Plateau.

Sinagua Indians (the name is Spanish for "without water," referring to a nearby mountain) lived from the Grand Canyon southward throughout central Arizona and are thought to be ancestors of the Hopi people. Small Sinagua cliff dwellings can be found in many canyons near Flagstaff, Sedona and the Verde

WALKING TOUR
Historic Flagstaff

Long before motels and restaurants started springing up along old Route 66 in Flagstaff, the town was already a major stopover for travelers seeing the Southwest by train. Not surprisingly, many of the century-old buildings that still stand in Flagstaff were originally built as hotels or saloons. You can glimpse into the town's past on a 20-minute stroll around the compact historic district.

FLAGSTAFF VISITORS CENTER   Start, as old-time visitors did, at the train station near the west end of Historic Route 66, which Amtrak now shares with the Flagstaff Visitors Center (page 130); there's free public parking nearby. Looking directly across the street, you'll see the ornate Italianate facade of the oldest building in town, the Bank Hotel (see below). You can't cross the street here, though.

THE VAIL BUILDING   Walk one block east to the stop light at San Francisco Street and cross Historic Route 66. The Vail Building on the northwest corner is Flagstaff's second-oldest building. After two previous saloons had burned to the ground on this site in two years, the owner rebuilt his saloon of brick in 1888. Today, extensively renovated to give the exterior a pink-and-blue art deco look that seems strangely out of place in Flagstaff, it houses a metaphysical shop. ~ 1 San Francisco Street.

K. J. NACKARD BUILDING   Continuing a half block north on the same side of San Francisco Street will bring you to the K. J. Nackard Building, built by a recent immigrant in 1912. He started Nackard's New York Store here, selling hard-to-get goods that his relatives shipped to him from New York. The building later became Flagstaff's post office and now houses Wolf and Swan Music and Fine Arts. ~ 13 San Francisco Street.

BABBIT BROTHERS BUILDING   Across Aspen Street is the graceful red sandstone Babbit Brothers Building. It was built in 1888 as a mercantile store by the forefathers of Bruce Babbitt, former Arizona governor and

Valley. One of the most interesting Sinagua sites is at **Walnut Canyon National Monument.** Here, the Indians built more than 80 cliff dwellings containing about 300 rooms in the walls of a 400-foot-deep gorge. The overhanging stone ledges above and sheer cliffs below protected them from invaders and animal predators. A paved one-mile trail takes visitors around an "island in the sky" for a close-up look at the largest concentration of cliff dwellings—about 25 of them—and views of many others. A second trail follows the rim of this beautiful canyon for about half

Secretary of the Interior during the Clinton administration. The store is still in operation, though its inventory now leans heavily toward outdoor gear. ~ 101 San Francisco Street.

KINLANI BUILDING   Turn west down Aspen Street for one block to the Kinlani Building on the northwest corner of Aspen and Leroux. It was built in 1925 to house the town's new JC Penney store, but the store vacated the building after less than a year. After decades as an apartment hotel, the Kinlani Building became Flagstaff's first supermarket. It now houses Maloney's Tavern. ~ 31 North Leroux Street.

WEATHERFORD HOTEL   Across Aspen Street, the old Weatherford Hotel ranked among Flagstaff's finest hotels during the railroad era. Western author Zane Grey wrote his classic novel *Riders of the Purple Sage* while staying here. The hotel deteriorated to become a youth hostel and pool hall before being closed down for renovation. The ground floor has been restored to period elegance and houses Charly's Pub and Grill (page 134); the upper floors contain the hotel. ~ 23 North Leroux Street.

RAYMOND BUILDING   Continuing back toward the train station on Leroux Street, you'll pass the Raymond Building, a well-preserved stone building that has massive sandstone block cornices and a decoratively carved archway. R. O. Raymond came to Flagstaff as the doctor for the local logging company but became a rancher and real estate speculator, building this one-story structure in 1911 to serve as his business office. It now houses a gift shop. ~ 13 North Leroux Street.

BANK HOTEL   Leroux Street brings you back to Historic Route 66 at the old Bank Hotel across from the train station. Formally known as the McMillan Building, the oldest building in town was built in 1886 by Flagstaff's first settler, sheep rancher Thomas F. McMillan, and simultaneously housed the town's first hotel and first bank. It later became Flagstaff's opera house. Today it is an arts-and-crafts gallery and offices. ~ 3 North Leroux Street.

a mile. Visitors are not permitted in the national monument backcountry, including the canyon floor. Admission. ~ Take Exit 204 from Route 40 just east of Flagstaff; 928-526-3367; www.nps.gov/waca.

Another fascinating bit of north central Arizona's flamboyant geology is **Meteor Crater**. A shooting star 150 feet in diameter and traveling 30,000 to 40,000 miles per hour struck the earth here 50,000 years ago. The impact blasted a crater 550 feet deep and a mile across. All life within a 100-mile radius was destroyed. Geologist Daniel Barringer theorized a century ago that this was a meteor impact crater. Experts scoffed at the idea, especially since volcanic craters, so common east of Flagstaff, suggested a rational explanation for the phenomenon. He staked a mining claim to search for the huge, valuable mass of iron and nickel that, he was convinced, lay buried beneath the crater. An ambitious drilling operation did not strike a mother lode from outer space but did come up with fragments proving the theory and the geologist's family has been operating the claim as a tourist attraction ever since. The Apollo astronauts trained at Meteor Crater before their moon landings in the late 1960s. The visit is worth the fairly steep admission fee if you take time to go on a guided tour along the main trail. Admission. ~ About 30 miles east of Flagstaff, five miles off Route 40 at Exit 233; 928-289-2362, fax 928-289-2598; www.meteorcrater.com, e-mail info@meteorcrater.com.

LODGING For a directory of bed and breakfasts throughout Arizona, call or write to the **Arizona Association of Bed & Breakfast Inns**. ~ P.O. Box 36656, Tucson, AZ 85740; 800-284-2589; www.arizona-bed-breakfast.com, e-mail info@arizona-bed-breakfast.com.

The large, elegant **Radisson Woodlands Hotel** has spacious and modern guest rooms, with pastel color schemes and king-size beds. Facilities for guests include indoor and outdoor whirlpool spas, a steam room, sauna, fitness center and heated swimming pool. Room service and complimentary shuttle service are also among the hotel's amenities. ~ 1175 West Route 66, Flagstaff; 928-773-8888, 800-333-3333, fax 928-773-0597; www.radisson.com. DELUXE.

Flagstaff's **Hotel Monte Vista** is the only remaining hotel in the heart of the town's historic district. A 1927 hotel now listed on the National Register of Historic Places, the Monte Vista has spacious

AUTHOR FAVORITE

A soothing retreat at the foot of Mount Elden, the **Starlight Pines Bed and Breakfast** offers all the comforts of home. The four accommodations feature clawfoot tubs, polished hardwood floors, colorful Tiffany lamps, and pastel-colored walls. Some rooms have a private balcony, while others overlook the inn's vast wraparound porch. Snuggle up with a book by the front room's crackling fireplace, or visit with the two resident dogs. A full gourmet breakfast is served. ~ 3380 East Lockett Road, Flagstaff; 928-527-1912, 800-752-1912; www.starlight pinesbb.com, e-mail romance@starlightpinesbb.com. DELUXE.

rooms that feature oak furniture, brass beds, velvet wall coverings and gold-tone bathroom fittings—a touch of old-time elegance. During the hotel's glory days, movie stars used to stay here, and some rooms bear plaques naming the most famous person who ever slept in them: Humphrey Bogart, Jayne Russell, Gary Cooper and John Wayne, to name a few. ~ 100 North San Francisco Street, Flagstaff; 928-779-6971, 800-545-3068, fax 928-779-2904; www.hotelmontevista.com. BUDGET TO MODERATE.

Flagstaff offers a good selection of bed-and-breakfast accommodations. Among the antique-furnished vintage lodgings available in the downtown area is **The Inn at 410 Bed and Breakfast**, a 1907 home. The nine guest suites are individually decorated in various themes including Victorian, Santa Fe and cowboy. All have fireplaces. Gourmet breakfast is served on the patio during the summer. ~ 410 North Leroux Street, Flagstaff; 928-774-0088, 800-774-2008, fax 928-774-6354; www.inn410.com, e-mail info@inn410.com. DELUXE TO ULTRA-DELUXE.

Another bed and breakfast located in the historic district is the homelike **Birch Tree Inn**. Built in 1917, the two-story inn was once a Northern Arizona University fraternity house. You'd never know it today, though, looking at the five guest rooms, each featuring its own unique decor—Southwest, Dutch, Shaker pine, heirloom antique, white wicker. The game room has a billiard table, and there's a garden gazebo to laze about in. It has five rooms (three with private baths), and air conditioning. ~ 824 West Birch Avenue, Flagstaff; 928-774-1042, 888-774-1042, fax 928-774-8462; www.birchtreeinn.com, e-mail info@birchtreeinn.com. MODERATE TO DELUXE.

There is also the **Dierker House**, where two of the three guest rooms have king-size beds (the other has a queen). All have down comforters and share a common sitting room and bath. Two-night minimum on weekends. ~ 423 West Cherry Street, Flagstaff; 928-774-3249. BUDGET.

Theodore Roosevelt and William Randolph Hearst once slept at the **Weatherford Hotel**, now refurbished to show off original fireplaces, balconies and early-20th-century style. See if the door Wyatt Earp shot through still stands in the ballroom, which features an antique bar and stained-glass windows. ~ 23 North Leroux Street, Flagstaff; 928-774-2731, fax 928-773-8951; www.weatherfordhotel.com, e-mail weathtel@infomagic.com. BUDGET.

Flagstaff has two hostels. Especially in the summer months, both of these affordable accommodations host backpack travelers of all ages from all parts of the world, and solitary travelers are sure to make instant friends. Try the **Grand Canyon International Hostel**, which has private and dormitory accommodations. It is just one block from the Amtrak station and offers free pick-up service from the Greyhound station. Rates include breakfast. ~ 19 South San Francisco Street, Flagstaff; 928-779-9421, 888-442-2696, fax 928-774-6047; www.grandcanyonhostel.com, e-mail info@grandcanyonhostel.com. BUDGET.

Also with private and four- to eight-person dormitory rooms is **Du Beau International Hostel**. Tours of the Grand Canyon are offered daily in the summer and less frequently during the rest of the year. Rates include a continental breakfast. They close sometimes when business is slow, so call ahead. ~ 19 West Phoenix Avenue, Flagstaff; 928-774-6731, 800-398-7112; www.dubeau hostel.com. BUDGET.

For lodging convenient to the great outdoors, try **Fall Inn to Nature,** a modern four-room bed and breakfast in a quiet country setting at the north edge of town. Guests can hike or ride horses on trails near the inn or fish at Upper Lake Mary a few short miles away. ~ 4555 South Lake Mary Road, Flagstaff; 928-714-0237, 888-920-0237; e-mail fallin@infomagic.com. MODER-ATE TO DELUXE.

If you get your kicks on Route 66, there are still wigwam motels to pull into for a night's stay. There are no wigwams or other relics of kitsch at **Flagstaff Travelodge**, a rather large motel that's horseshoed around a wide lawn where there's a small playground for the kids. Most of the rooms, which are large, clean and cheerful, face the lawn and are far enough off the highway to afford a peaceful night's sleep (rooms 149, 150 and 230 are the ones to avoid). Besides that, many of the bathrooms have windows. ~ 2610 East Route 66, Flagstaff; 928-526-1399, 800-578-7878, fax 928-527-8626; www.travelodgeflagstaff.com. MODERATE.

The **Marriott Residence Inn** offers beautifully maintained apartment-like accommodations near the Flagstaff Mall. Granted, there's a generic "this could be anywhere" feel to the setup, but

AUTHOR FAVORITE

A bustling eatery that's packed on the weekends, **Beaver Street Brewery & Whistle Stop Cafe** is one of a handful of brewpubs in Flagstaff. Its limited menu offers a winning combination of seasonal ales, friendly service, and inventive wood-fired pizzas. Of particular note is the Enchanted Forest pizza, topped with portobello mushrooms, brie, artichoke pesto and walnuts. Beaver Street also serves up sandwiches, salads and pub-style platters of bratwurst and catfish that complement any of its regular half-dozen microbrews on tap. ~ 11 South Beaver Street, Flagstaff; 928-779-0079; www.beaverstreetbrewery.com, e-mail info@beaverstreetbrewery.com. BUDGET TO MODERATE.

the privacy, fireplaces, fully equipped kitchens and pool make up for any lack of local character. "Extras," like grocery-shopping service, complimentary newspapers and complimentary continental breakfast, also make life a bit easier. If you've been traveling for several days, you'll appreciate the laundry facilities. ~ 3440 North Country Club Road, off Route 40, Flagstaff; 928-526-5555, 800-331-3131, fax 928-527-0328; www.marriott.com. DELUXE TO ULTRA-DELUXE.

In the pines just five minutes out of town, the **Arizona Mountain Inn** offers B&B rooms in the main inn (rates include a continental breakfast), and one- to five-bedroom cottages with fireplaces and cooking facilities. Amenities include volleyball, horseshoe and basketball areas as well as hiking trails. ~ 4200 Lake Mary Road, Flagstaff; 928-774-8959, 800-239-5236, fax 928-774-8837; www.arizonamountaininn.com, e-mail arizonamountaininn@msn.com. MODERATE.

DINING

For fine dining, one good bet is the small, homey-feeling **Cottage Place Restaurant**. Specialties include châteaubriand and duet of duckling with cherry demiglaze, as well as seafood fettuccini. Reservations are recommended. Dinner only. Closed Monday. ~ 126 West Cottage Avenue, Flagstaff; 928-774-8431, fax 928-774-4071; www.cottageplace.com. DELUXE TO ULTRA-DELUXE.

In the mood for a romantic dinner? Try the **Woodlands Café** at the Radisson Woodlands Hotel. There's booth and table seating at this spacious yet intimate dining room that features atrium windows and forest views. White walls are decorated with photographs of local scenery; the chandelier is crafted from deer racks. You can select from such entrées as sunflower seed–crusted trout, roasted chicken *molé* and salmon Florentine. You can also order a plain old hamburger. Reservations are recommended. **Sakura,** a popular Japanese restaurant, shares the premises and has the same address and phone number. ~ 1175 West Route 66, Flagstaff; 928-773-9118, fax 928-773-1827. MODERATE TO DELUXE.

A standout among Flagstaff's numerous Chinese restaurants, the **China Star** offers an all-you-can-eat buffet with more than 40 dishes such as Mongolian beef, jalapeño chicken, Szechuan shrimp and five-flavored broccoli. The brightly lit interior is spic-and-span, with hardly a hint of Asian decor. ~ 1802 East Route 66, Flagstaff; 928-774-8880, fax 928-774-1862. BUDGET.

One contemporary restaurant in Flagstaff's downtown area emphasizes creative Southwestern dining. Stop in for lunch or dinner at **Charly's Pub and Grill**, on the ground floor of the Weatherford Hotel. ~ 23 North Leroux Street, Flagstaff; 928-779-1919, fax 928-773-8951; www.weatherfordhotel.com, e-mail weathotel@infomagic.com. MODERATE TO DELUXE.

Text continued on page 146.

In the Land
of Volcanos

The raw power of geology presents itself in the Southwest as dramatically as any place on earth. Consider, for instance, Arizona's Grand Canyon, Utah's Bryce Canyon and Colorado's Great Sand Dunes. Yet visitors often drive right past one of the most awe-inspiring of these earth phenomena—the 2000-square-mile San Francisco Volcano Field northeast of Flagstaff.

The **San Francisco Peaks**, Arizona's tallest mountains, were once part of a huge volcano that, according to some geologists, may have approached the elevation of Mt. Everest. But that was back when dinosaurs roamed the earth and the red rocks of Sedona and Canyon de Chelly were mere sand on the sea floor.

Imagine how surprised the Anasazi people who lived at the base of these ancient mountains must have been when, around A.D. 1065, new volcanos began erupting out of their cornfields. They scattered to other areas as their pueblos were buried in red-hot cinders. Volcanic activity continued for 200 years, then died down as quickly as it had started, leaving prime agricultural land fertilized by the deep layer of ash. Rival Indian groups moved in to compete for the rich farmland, which accounts for the variety of architectural styles and fortresslike defenses at the numerous 13th-century pueblo sites of **Wupatki National Monument** (page 137). ~ Forest Service Road 545; 928-679-2365, fax 928-679-2349; www.nps.gov/wupa.

South of Wupatki, **Sunset Crater Volcano National Monument** (page 137) protects a colorful red-and-black cinder cone 1000 feet tall. A one-mile, self-guided nature trail, which starts one and a half miles away from the visitors center, leads through cinder and lava fields. Hiking is no longer permitted on the slopes of Sunset Crater, since footprints erode and mar the beauty of the perfect cone.

Admission. ~ Forest Service Road 545; 928-526-0502, fax 928-714-0565; www.nps.gov/sucr.

Several volcanos in Coconino National Forest, however, can be climbed, including **O'Leary Peak**. One of the most unusual trails in the Flagstaff area is the **Red Mountain Trail**, 33 miles north of Flagstaff off Route 180. A gap in the base of this 1000-foot-high volcanic cone lets you hike from the end of the national forest access road straight into the crater without climbing. Not often visited by tourists, this is a great place to explore with older children.

For a more ambitious adventure, trek the **Strawberry Crater Wilderness**, a roadless area surrounding the volcano cone for which it is named. Among jet-black lava flows that look fresh, bubbly and almost liquid lie the ruins of ancient pueblos and cornfields. There's a hiking trail up the northwest side of the crater to the summit. Of several unofficial paths through the wilderness, the shortest route to the crater starts at Painted Desert Vista, located midway between the Sunset Crater and Wupatki visitors centers.

You can also explore the chilly interior of the mile-long **Lava River Cave**, a subterranean tube of rippled rock dripping with stone icicles. To get there, take Route 180 for nine miles north of Flagstaff, turn west (left) onto Forest Road 245, go three more miles, turn south (left) on Forest Road 171, and go one more mile to the short, marked road to the cave entrance. Bring your own light (and warm clothes).

The San Francisco Volcano Field is close to Flagstaff, which has a wide choice of lodging and restaurants. To maximize the experience, though, why not spend the night at Coconino National Forest's **Bonito Campground** near Sunset Crater Volcano National Monument, where a two-mile hiking trail leads across a lava flow so recent that it almost looks like it's still moving.

Or you can try **Café Espress**, which specializes in vegetarian, poultry and fish selections. Changing exhibits by local artists adorn the walls. No dinner Sunday through Tuesday. ~ 16 North San Francisco Street, Flagstaff; 928-774-0541. MODERATE.

Dara Thai Restaurant offers a wide assortment of both traditional and innovative Thai entrées are served in an ambience of subdued lighting and rich adornments. Try the house specialty, "evil jungle princess"—strips of chicken stir-fried in coconut milk with lemongrass, straw mushrooms and secret spices. There's also an abundance of vegetarian options including vegetable curries and spicy tofu creations. ~ 14 South San Francisco Street, Flagstaff; 928-774-0047. MODERATE.

HIDDEN ►   **Main Street Catering**, located in the Gateway Plaza, is a favorite among locals. Dishes include Philly cheesesteaks, fresh soups, stuffed sandwiches on homemade bread, barbecued ribs and daily specials. Closed Sunday. ~ 16 East Route 66, Suite 103, Flagstaff; 928-774-1519. MODERATE.

Across from Heritage Square, **Pasto** features atmosphere and food that are pure Old Italy, but service that is the studied elegant graciousness found in higher-end restaurants. The extensive menu has some chef-conceived specialties. Try the lamb osso buco served with parmesan polenta. And whatever else you sample, make sure to save room for *tiramisu*, a dessert favorite. Reservations are recommended. Dinner only. ~ 19 East Aspen Avenue, Flagstaff; 928-779-1937, fax 928-779-5951; www.pastorestaurant.com. MODERATE TO DELUXE.

A bit of Old West burlesque lives on at **Black Bart's Steak House, Saloon, and Musical Revue**, just east of downtown off Interstate 40, where local college students not only serve your steak, prime rib or chicken but also entertain you with show songs and a bit of choreography. Children (and the young at heart) should enjoy the lively proceedings as well as the Old West decor. Dinner only. ~ 2760 East Butler Avenue, Flagstaff; 928-779-3142, fax 928-774-1113; www.blackbartssteakhouse.com, e-mail blackbarts@safeaccess.com. MODERATE TO DELUXE.

HIDDEN ►   For an unusual dining environment, head out of town to the **Mormon Lake Lodge Steak House & Saloon**, which has been in operation since 1924 and is reputed to be one of the West's finest steak houses. The restaurant also features ribs, chicken and trout, all cooked over a bed of mountain mesquite embers. The authentic brands from ranches all across Arizona that have been seared into the wood paneling of the restaurant's walls are said to be the result of one of the wildest branding parties ever. Closed Monday through Thursday from Labor Day to Memorial Day. ~ Located 28 miles southeast of Flagstaff on Mormon Lake Road, Mormon Lake Village; 928-354-2227; www.foreverresorts.com/mormon

lakelodge, e-mail scottgoldmll@cybertrails.com. MODERATE TO ULTRA-DELUXE.

SHOPPING

Wander around Flagstaff's downtown area and you will find a number of "trading posts." East of downtown is **Jay's Indian Arts**. The store sells rugs, jewelry, pottery, kachinas and the like direct from artists on the Navajo, Hopi, Tohono O'odham, Apache and Pueblo reservations. Closed Sunday. ~ 2227 East 7th Avenue, Flagstaff; 928-526-2439; www.jaysindianarts.net, e-mail jayslflag @aol.com.

The **Museum of Northern Arizona**'s gift shop is the best place in town to buy authentic native works. You'll find an excellent collection of American Indian kachina dolls, rugs, sand paintings, as well as other arts and crafts. ~ 3101 North Fort Valley Road, Flagstaff; 928-779-1703, fax 520-774-1229.

The **Art Barn**, in Fort Valley Historical Park, offers works of local and reservation artists for sale, emphasizing Navajo and Hopi art. A nonprofit, member-supported organization, the Art Barn provides artist facilities including exhibition space. Call for hours. ~ 2330 North Fort Valley Road, Flagstaff; 928-774-0822.

Several of Flagstaff's downtown arts-and-crafts galleries host an **Art Walk** with artist receptions on the first Friday of each month from 6 to 8 p.m. This includes **The Artists Gallery**, which features the works of three different local crafters each month. ~ 17 North San Francisco Street; 928-773-0958. **Father Wolf Designs and Gallery** carries quality art, handcrafts and jewelry from American Indian tribes throughout the country. ~ 8620 Marys Drive; 928-527-1139; www.fatherwolf.com.

NIGHTLIFE

Because of the university, Flagstaff boasts both a busy cultural events calendar and a lively nightclub scene. On the cultural side, the performing arts roster includes the **Flagstaff Symphony Orchestra**. The main season runs September through March. ~ 928-774-5107; www.flagstaffsymphony.org. Classical fans may also want to attend a performance of the **Master Chorale of Flagstaff**. ~ 928-714-0300. Also in town is the **NAU Choral Studies Office**; www.nau.edu. ~ 928-523-2642. Most performances are held at the **Northern Arizona College of Fine Arts**. ~ Corner of Riordan Road and Knoles Drive; 928-523-3731; www.nau.edu/spa.

A bustling college town, Flagstaff has an array of nightspots to suit a wide range of crowds and tastes.

The **Theatrikos Theatre Group** performs at the Flagstaff Playhouse. ~ 11 West Cherry Avenue, Flagstaff; 928-774-1662; www.theatrikos.com. For current performance information, inquire at the Flagstaff Visitors Center or tune in to the university's National Public Radio station, KNAU, at 88.7 on your FM dial. ~ Visitors center: 1 East Route 66; 928-774-9541; www.flagstaffarizona.org.

The Blues Project has been packing 'em in at Monday Blues Night at **Charly's Pub and Grill** in the Weatherford Hotel for years. This band performs between 9 and closing time. It occasionally appears other nights as well, and doesn't always play Monday, so check the schedule. Tuesday is open-mic night; other musical genres fill out the week's schedule. Cover. ~ 23 North Leroux Street, Flagstaff; 928-774-2731, fax 928-773-8951; www.weather fordhotel.com, e-mail weathotel@infomagic.com.

A mixed crowd likes the happy hour at **Granny's Closet**. Friday and Saturday are karaoke nights. ~ 218 South Milton Road, Flagstaff; 928-774-8331; www.grannyscloset-az.com.

A microbrewery located in a landmark building with exposed brick walls and Old West antiques, the **Flagstaff Brewing Company** serves a changing selection of house-brewed beers, ranging from pale ales to stout, on tap every night. Budget-priced burgers, salads and soups are available for those with the munchies. Live acoustic, blues and bluegrass music is featured weekend nights on the patio. ~ 16 East Route 66, Flagstaff; 928-773-1442.

Another favorite is the **Mad Italian Public House**, known as the "Mad I." Diversions such as pool and TV should keep you entertained; if not, there's usually a local band pumping out tunes. Occasional cover. ~ 101 South San Francisco Street, Flagstaff; 928-779-1820.

"Take me to the Zoo." That's what locals say when they want to go to **The Museum Club**, one of the West's best examples of a cowboy roadhouse. Oftentimes rowdy, but always fun, the Zoo began as a trading post and taxidermy shop in 1931. It has operated as a nightclub since 1936, and is now listed on the National Register of Historic Places. The huge log cabin–style building is decorated with an ornate 1880 mahogany bar and an astonishing number of big-game trophies mounted on the walls. The dancefloor was built around five ponderosa pine tree trunks. A forked trunk forms the entryway into the club. Legendary country artists who have performed here include Willie Nelson, Bob Wills and the Texas Playboys, and Commander Cody and the Lost Planet Airmen. The owners have arranged with a local cab company to provide free taxi service from the club. Cover on weekends. ~ 3404 East Route 66, Flagstaff; 928-526-9434, fax 928-526-5244; www.museumclub.com.

PARKS   **LAKE MARY** 🚶 🚴 ⚓ 🏊 🛶 🚤 ⛵ 🎣 Actually two long reservoirs, Upper and Lower Lake Mary provide the primary water supply for Flagstaff. They were created by damming Walnut Creek, which explains why there is no longer any water flowing through Walnut Canyon National Monument. The National

Forest Service operates picnic areas on the wooded lakeshore and the small Lakeview Campground overlooks the upper lake. Both lakes are popular places to fish for northern pike, walleye pike and catfish. The upper lake is also used for powerboating and water-skiing. ~ Located eight miles south of Flagstaff on Lake Mary Road. From Route 40, take Exit 195-B and follow the signs; 928-774-1182, fax 928-214-2460.

▲ Lakeview Campground has 30 sites; $12 per night. Pine-grove Campground has 46 sites; $15 per night. Campgrounds are closed mid-October to mid-April, depending on the weather.

MORMON LAKE 🚶 🚲 🐎 ⛺ The largest natural lake in Arizona, covering over 2000 acres when full, is very shallow, averaging only ten feet in depth and can shrink to practically nothing during spells of dry weather. As a matter of fact, more often than not, the lake is dry. Several hiking trails run along the lakeshore and into the surrounding forest. You'll find a nature trail, lodge, restaurant and groceries. ~ Lake Mary Road, 26 miles southeast of Flagstaff; 928-774-1182, fax 928-214-2460.

▲ There are 30 sites at Dairy Springs and 15 sites at Double Springs; $10 per night. Campgrounds are closed October to May, depending on the weather.

Sedona. The creative and the mystical have always been intrigued by the place. Indians once came here to worship, New Agers to feel the "vibrations," artists to capture the beauty. But no matter the number of its devotees, no one knows exactly why this place has such appeal. Its essence remains elusive. Perhaps part of the seduction is the colors—red-rock mountains that rise from the earth to nestle in brilliant blue sky. The landscape is a dreamy mix of fancifully shaped hoodoos, buttes and spires rising above green piñon and juniper trees, low shrubs and stark patches of reddish rock. Adjacent to Sedona is the spectacular Oak Creek Canyon, named after the creek that formed it by carving into the southern edge of the Colorado Plateau. All of these natural elements are highlighted by an intense sunlight that brings out contrast and color.

Sedona Area

Considered sacred by early American Indians, Red Rocks was believed to be a home of the gods, and was the site of many spiritual ceremonies.

The first to discover this special spot were the Indians. About 800 years ago, the Southern Sinagua Indians settled here, leaving behind a 600-room cliff dwelling ruin called Honaki, which is now on the National Register of Historic Places. If you're out hiking, it's worth a side trip to discover these ruins. However, don't be surprised if you are turned away. The ruins are very fragile and are almost disappearing due to impact. They're located on an alcove on the west side of Loy Butte next to Lincoln Canyon.

More settlers came at the turn of the 20th century. At the time, the economic base of the economy was ranching and farming, and apple orchards dotted the area. Writer Zane Grey was also charmed by the area, drawing attention to it in the book *Call of the Canyon* in the 1920s. The film version was also shot here.

With all this attention, it was only a matter of time before tourism became the main attraction. Today about four million people visit the town annually to shop at the numerous art galleries, to nurture their spirits, and to relax amidst a red-rock fantasy.

SIGHTS   **Oak Creek Canyon** is the most accessible of several magnificent canyons that plunge from the high forests of northern Arizona down toward the low deserts of southern Arizona. A major highway—Route 89A from Flagstaff—runs the length of Oak Creek Canyon, making for a wonderful, though often crowded, scenic drive. After a long, thrilling descent from Flagstaff to the bottom of the canyon, where the creek banks are lined with lush riparian vegetation, the highway passes a number of picnicking, camping and fishing areas sandwiched between clusters of rental cabins and private vacation homes. Unfortunately, these areas are almost always packed to capacity during the summer months, and even finding a place to park so you can dabble your toes in the creek is a problem. Though a hiking trail leads up the less-visited west fork of Oak Creek, no side roads branch off the main highway through the canyon. Adventurous travelers can try Forest Road 535, a good unpaved road that turns off to the west above the beginning of the

HIDDEN ►   descent into the canyon. It leads to lush, little-known **Fry Canyon**; another road branches off to a rarely seen vista on the rim of Oak Creek Canyon.

Midway down the canyon is one of Arizona's most popular state parks, **Slide Rock State Park** (see "Parks" below). At the lower end of the canyon, travelers emerge into the spectacular Red Rock Country, the labyrinth of sandstone buttes and mesas and verdant side canyons surrounding Sedona.

Sedona is a town for shopping, for sports, for luxuriating in spectacular surroundings. It is not the kind of place where you will find tourist attractions in the usual sense. Sedonans refer to the junction of Routes 179 and 89A as "the Y." The commercial district at the Y is known as "uptown Sedona," while the fast-growing, seemingly endless strip of shopping-center development along Route 89A is called "West Sedona."

If you stay on the main roads during your visit, you may wonder what attracts people to Sedona, which at first glance seems to lack the unique personality of other Southwestern towns. To find out what's special about this place, talk to some locals—you'll find them behind the counters of New Age stores and in real es-

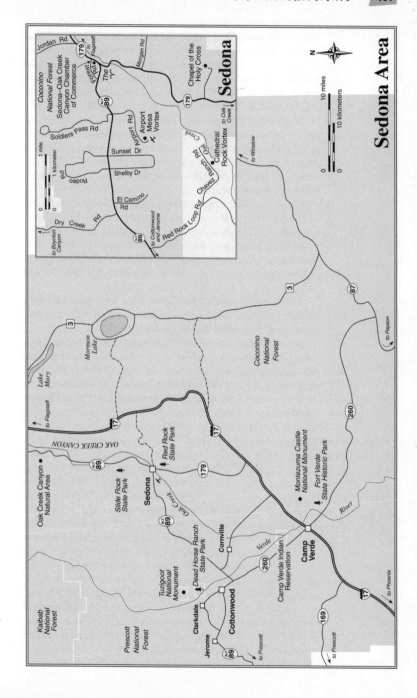

Sedona Area

tate offices—and follow side roads into the wild red-rock country that surrounds the town. A close-up look at the monumental rock formations and canyons will reveal the amazing complexity of nature in this colorful area balanced midway between cool high-altitude forest and blistering low-altitude desert. The elevation drop from Flagstaff to Sedona is 2500 feet, and the temperature is often 20° higher in Sedona than in Flagstaff.

A good place to get your bearings, pick up brochures and have your questions answered is the visitors center at the **Sedona–Oak Creek Canyon Chamber of Commerce**. ~ Corner of Forest Road at Route 89A, just above the Y; 928-282-7722, 800-288-7336, fax 928-204-1064; www.sedonachamber.com, e-mail info@sedonachamber.com.

Other than Oak Creek Canyon, Sedona's most popular tourist spots are spiritual in nature. The **Chapel of the Holy Cross**, south of town, is a Catholic "sculpture church" built between two towering red sandstone rock formations. It is open to visitors daily from 9 a.m. to 5 p.m. (Sunday from 10 a.m.). Parking is very limited. ~ Chapel Road off Route 179, Sedona; 928-282-4069, fax 928-282-3701.

The **Shrine of the Red Rocks**, on Table Top Mesa two miles off Route 89A on Airport Road, features a large wooden cross and a great view of the Red Rock Country.

And then there are Sedona's "vortexes." The vortex idea was "channeled" through members of the town's highly visible New Age community several years ago and keeps evolving. For more information, see "In the Land of Vortexes" in this chapter.

A 45-minute drive south of Sedona via Route 179 and Route 17, **Montezuma Castle National Monument** protects 900-year-old cliff dwellings built by the Sinagua people, ancestors of the Hopi. The ruins got their name from early explorers' mistaken belief that Aztecs fled here and built the structures after the Spanish conquest of Mexico. Though there is no truth to the old theory, archaeologists now know that several centuries before the Spanish arrived, traders used to visit the Southwest, bringing with them architectural methods from central Mexico. The main "castle" is a five-story, 20-room residential structure set high on the cliff. Although visitors cannot climb up to the ruin, the view from the nature trail below will tingle the imagination. The visitors center displays artifacts of the Sinagua and Hohokam cultures. Admission. ~ 2800 Montezuma Castle Highway, Camp Verde; 928-567-3322, fax 928-567-3597; www.nps.gov/moca, e-mail moca_administration@nps.gov.

The cliffside location of the Montezuma Castle made it a natural fortress. Its inhabitants were somewhat protected by the fact that their "highrise" was accessible only by ladder from above and below.

South of Montezuma's Castle via Route 17, in the small town of Camp Verde, portions of an old cavalry fort from the Apache Wars in the 1870s and early 1880s are preserved as **Fort Verde State Historic Park**. Visitors can walk through the former quarters and officer buildings, and there is also a museum of Arizona military history. The fort formed the start of the **General Crook Trail**, the major patrol and supply route during the Apache Wars, which followed the Mogollon Rim west for more than 100 miles to Fort Apache. Today, the trail is used for hiking and horseback riding. Admission. ~ 125 Hollamon Street, Camp Verde; 928-567-3275, fax 928-567-4036; www.pr.state.az.us.

For Sedona visitors who wish to explore the surrounding Red Rock Country, there are numerous companies offering jeep tours. They'll usually pick you up at any Sedona lodging. For more information see "Jeep Tours" later in "Outdoor Adventures."

LODGING

As you drive down Oak Creek Canyon from Flagstaff to Sedona, you will notice several privately owned lodges and cabin complexes in the midst of this spectacular national forest area. You can reserve accommodations at these places and enjoy the canyon in the cool of the evening and early morning, avoiding the midday throngs and traffic of peak season and weekends. Several places are located near Slide Rock State Park.

Top of the line **Junipine Resort** offers modern suites and one- and two-bedroom "creekhouses." These individually decorated one- and two-story units are all crafted from wood and stone. Offering mountain, forest or creek views, each 1300- to 1500-square-foot unit comes with a kitchen and redwood deck overlooking the canyon. ~ 8351 North Route 89A, Sedona; 928-282-3375, 800-742-7463, fax 928-282-7402; www.junipine.com, e-mail creekside@junipine.com. DELUXE TO ULTRA-DELUXE.

Canyon Wren Cabins consists of one old-fashioned log cabin and three chalets with loft bedrooms, kitchens, fireplaces, whirlpool tubs and patios, all within walking distance of swimming holes, fishing spots and hiking trails. Rates include continental breakfast. No telephones or televisions; no smoking indoors or out. ~ 6425 North Route 89A, Sedona; 928-282-6900, 800-437-9736, fax 928-282-6978; www.canyonwrencabins.com, e-mail cnynwren@sedona.net. DELUXE.

In the same part of the canyon, there are more simple accommodations at **Don Hoel's Cabins**. Cabins are being remodeled one at a time, so call ahead for availability. Continental breakfast is included. Closed the weekend after New Year's to the first week of February. ~ 9440 North Route 89A, Sedona; 928-282-3560, 800-292-4635, fax 928-282-3654; www.hoels.com, e-mail cabins@hoels.com. MODERATE TO DELUXE.

Text continued on page 156.

In the Land of Vortexes

Just about every Sedona resident professes to believe in vortexes—power places where energies enter and leave the earth—and can tell you exactly where to find them. The absence of any scientific basis for the notion doesn't seem to bother them. Sedonans share similar experiences at these sites, and this is sufficient confirmation that they are real. They claim that visiting a vortex enhances your psychic powers, emotions and talents, and forces you to face yourself—for better or worse.

Although local visionaries now claim the vortexes were known to ancient Indians, the notion apparently originated in 1987, when more than 10,000 New Agers descended on Sedona to celebrate the Harmonic Convergence, a worldwide weekend of meditation "to awaken and balance the energies of Earth," held simultaneously at sacred sites from Chaco Canyon to Stonehenge. In Sedona, the gathering took place around and on top of Bell Rock. Afterwards, believers coined the term "vortex" to describe the energy they had unleashed, and Sedona has been a metaphysical mecca ever since. Reporting on the Harmonic Convergence, a *Detroit News* reporter quoted Sedona's mayor, Ivan Finley: "As far as I could tell, the earth didn't move—but it was good for the economy."

Before either accepting the vortexes as real or dismissing them, why not go there yourself and see whether you can feel the power that draws many thousands of people to Sedona every year? While some locals identify as many as 13 vortexes in the area, only four are generally recognized:

- The **Airport Mesa Vortex** is a little more than a mile south of Route 89A on Airport Road.

- The **Cathedral Rock Vortex** is near a lovely picnic area alongside Oak Creek, reached from Route 89A in West Sedona via Red Rock Loop Road and Chavez Ranch Road; the rock itself is one of the most photographed places in the area.

- The **Bell Rock Vortex**, a popular spot for UFO watchers, is just off Route 179 south of Sedona near the village of Oak Creek.

- The **Boynton Canyon Vortex**, said to be the most powerful of Sedona's vortexes, is several miles north of West Sedona via Dry Creek Road and Boynton Pass Road. From the well-marked trailhead, a nearly level two-and-a-half-mile hiking trail goes up the canyon through woods and among red-rock formations, passing several small, ancient Sinagua Indian cliff dwellings along the way.

Each vortex reportedly has a radius of ten miles, so you don't need to be standing in one particular spot to feel the force. Many people say they can even sense the power of the vortexes right in the town center of Sedona.

To research the subject of vortexes for yourself, visit one of Sedona's metaphysical book and gift stores such as **Crystal Castle**. ~ 313 Route 179; 928-282-5910. Another good source is **Crystal Magic**. ~ 2978 West Route 89A; 928-282-1622. Both stores have "networking" bulletin boards that let you scan the array of alternative professional services in town—channels, clairvoyants, geomancers and many more. The **Center for the New Age** has vortex information, networking for New Age activities, daily psychic readings and a psychic fair every Saturday. ~ 341 Route 179; 928-282-1949. *Four Corners Magazine* and other free periodicals providing information for and about the local New Age community are widely distributed around town.

Tour companies offering guided trips to the vortexes include **Sedona Red Rock Jeep Tours** (270 North Route 89A; 928-282-6826, 800-848-7728), and **Earth Wisdom Jeep Tours** (293 North Route 89A; 928-282-4714, 800-482-4714).

To get your mind, body and spirit tuned up for your personal vortex experience, consider staying at the **Healing Center of Arizona**. Rates are mid-range, and inexpensive gourmet vegetarian meals are available to groups. Reasonably priced amenities include a sauna and a spa. Guests at the center can receive acupressure treatments, herbology, rebirthing, crystal healing, psychic channeling and other holistic therapies. ~ 25 Wilson Canyon Road; 928-282-7710, 877-723-2811; www.sedonahealing center.com, e-mail johnpaul@sedonahealingcenter.com. MODERATE.

Houses, all with fireplaces and fully equipped kitchens, are available at **Forest Houses Resort**. A four-night minimum stay is required from Memorial Day through Labor Day and on major holidays; a two-night minimum applies at all other times. Children and pets are welcome. Closed January to early March. ~ 9275 North Route 89A, Oak Creek Canyon; 928-282-2999, fax 928-282-0663; www.foresthousesresort.com. MODERATE TO DELUXE.

Farther down the canyon, **Oak Creek Terrace** has resort accommodations ranging from motel-style rooms with queen-size beds and jacuzzis to one- and two-bedroom suites. ~ Route 89A, Oak Creek Canyon; 928-282-3562, 800-224-2229, fax 928-282-6061; www.oakcreekterrace.com, e-mail octresor@sedona.net. MODERATE TO ULTRA-DELUXE.

Rising from Sedona's red rock, the stunning **Casa Sedona Bed and Breakfast** echoes its dramatic surroundings. Each of the 16 beautifully decorated units, from the Safari Room to the Cowboy Room, has a fireplace, a private bath and a private deck or balcony complete with postcard-perfect views. A sumptuous breakfast is usually served outside in the courtyard. If you can move after that, you can wander the grounds or make the short trip into town. A two-night minimum stay on weekends may be required. ~ 55 Hozoni Drive, Sedona; 928-282-2938, 800-525-3756, fax 928-282-2259; www.casasedona.com, e-mail casa@sedona.net. DELUXE TO ULTRA-DELUXE.

Renowned for its superior lighting, Sedona is a mecca for photographers and moviemakers. In fact, it was the backdrop for such films as John Wayne's *The Angel and the Badman* and Robert Mitchum's *Blood on the Moon*.

Charming, affordable lodging in Sedona can be found at the **Rose Tree Inn**, which strives for an "English garden environment" and has patios and a jacuzzi. Some rooms have kitchens and fireplaces. This small inn is close to uptown. ~ 376 Cedar Street, Sedona; 928-282-2065, 888-282-2065; www.rosetreeinn.com, e-mail info@rosetreeinn.com. MODERATE TO DELUXE.

Near Uptown Sedona, the **Star Motel** offers standard rooms with telephones, cable TV and refrigerators, plus one deluxe-priced apartment with a fireplace. ~ 295 Jordan Road, Sedona; 928-282-3641. BUDGET.

A Touch of Sedona Bed and Breakfast, in the uptown area, offers panoramic views from five cozy rooms with corresponding motifs—the "Eagle," "Hummingbird," "Kachina," "Roadrunner" and "Wolf's Den." Rooms boast fireplaces and enclosed outdoor hot tubs. The B&B is close to hiking, shopping and restaurants. A full breakfast comes with the room. ~ 595 Jordan Road, Sedona; 928-282-6462, 800-600-6462, fax 928-282-1534; www.atouchofsedona.com, e-mail info@atouchofsedona.com. DELUXE.

Another top-of-the-line Sedona lodging is **L'Auberge de Sedona**. Individually designed guest rooms and cottages are decorated with furnishings imported from Provence, France, to recreate the atmosphere of a French country inn on 11 acres of creekside grounds within walking distance of uptown Sedona. ~ 301 L'Auberge Lane, Sedona; 928-282-1661, 800-272-6777, fax 928-282-1064; www.lauberge.com, e-mail info@lauberge.com. ULTRA-DELUXE.

Among the poshest accommodations in town is **Los Abrigados Resort & Spa**. Situated next to the atmospheric Tlaquepaque shopping area, Los Abrigados features fanciful Mexican-inspired modern architecture throughout and elegantly stylish suites with kitchenettes, fireplaces and patios or balconies. Guest facilities include tennis courts, swimming pool, weight room and spa. ~ 160 Portal Lane, Sedona; 928-282-1777, 800-521-3131, fax 928-282-2614; www.ilxresorts.com. ULTRA-DELUXE.

Enchantment Resort, secluded five miles west of town in Boynton Canyon, sits in the shadow of magnificent red rocks. Over 60 adobe-style casitas, which convert from studio to two-bedroom accommodations, are well appointed with Southwest-style furnishing, fireplaces, kitchenettes, skylights and private patios. Resort facilities include pools, spas and tennis courts, as well as massages, aromatherapy and other spa treatments. Provençal and regional Southwest dishes with an Asian accent are served in the restaurant. More casual fare is available in the café. ~ 525 Boynton Canyon Road, Sedona; 928-282-2900, 800-826-4180, fax 928-282-9249; www.enchantmentresort.com, e-mail info@enchantmentresort.com. ULTRA-DELUXE.

South of the Y, on Route 179, **Radisson Poco Diablo Resort** is built around a private nine-hole golf course. Their 28 deluxe rooms, called *poco casitas*, are quite large (480 square feet) and luxurious with fireplaces, wet bar and refrigerators, whirlpool bathtubs and private patios that look out over the golf course to the red rocks beyond. ~ 1752 South Route 179, Sedona; 928-282-7333, 800-333-3333, fax 928-282-2090; www.radisson.com/sedonaaz, e-mail info@radissonsedona.com. ULTRA-DELUXE.

A comfortable ranch-style home bordering a national forest, the **Cozy Cactus** is a bed-and-breakfast inn that has single rooms as well as one- and two-bedroom suites, decorated with personal touches from the owners' collections of theatrical memorabilia. All rooms have private entrances and baths, TVs, refrigerators, microwave ovens, and coffeemakers. The terrace has great views of Sedona's stunning red-rock formations. Gay-friendly. ~ 80 Canyon Circle Drive, Sedona; 928-284-0082, 800-788-2082, fax 928-284-4210; www.cozycactus.com, e-mail info@cozycactus.com. DELUXE TO ULTRA-DELUXE.

The award-winning **Canyon Villa Inn** has 11 guest rooms, each with French doors leading to balconies. There's a beautiful heated pool, gourmet cuisine and, of course, views of the red rocks. ~ 125 Canyon Circle Drive, Sedona; 928-284-1226, 800-453-1166, fax 928-284-2114; www.canyonvilla.com, e-mail can villa@sedona.net. ULTRA-DELUXE.

Another inn is **The Adobe Village Graham Inn**, where each individually decorated room has views of Sedona's famous red rocks. The inn features seven guest rooms with king-sized beds, marble showers, private balconies, fireplaces and jacuzzis. Its four villas include waterfall showers and private decks. Additional amenities are the outdoor pool, hot tub and bicycles available for guest use. Breakfast is included. ~ 150 Canyon Circle Drive, Sedona; 928-284-1425, 800-228-1425, fax 928-284-0767; www.sedonasfinest.com. ULTRA-DELUXE.

Surrounded by spruce, piñon and juniper trees is the aptly named **Apple Orchard Inn**, built on the site of the old Jordan Apple Farm. Despite its wooded location, this bed and breakfast is just a hop, skip and a jump away from uptown. Luxuriate in seven plush, unique rooms, many sporting whirlpool tubs, fireplaces and patios. There's a "cooling pool" with a waterfall on a deck overlooking the mountains. For added pampering, summon the on-call massage therapist for a session. In the morning, drink in majestic mountain views while enjoying breakfast in the cozy dining room. Reservations suggested. ~ 656 Jordan Road, Sedona; 928-282-5328, 800-663-6968, fax 928-204-0044; www.appleorchardbb.com, e-mail appleorc@sedona.net. DELUXE TO ULTRA-DELUXE.

For basic motel rooms in Sedona, the **White House Inn** in West Sedona, located just before the Dry Creek Road turnoff, provides lodging with phone and cable television. ~ 2986 West Route 89A, Sedona; 928-282-6680, fax 928-203-0467; www.whitehouseinn.netfirms.com. BUDGET.

HIDDEN ▶   Visitors seeking to change their lives in Sedona might want to consider staying at the **Healing Center of Arizona**. Rates for accommodations in this dome complex are mid-range, and inexpensive gourmet vegetarian meals are served to groups only. There is a large holistic healing and metaphysical library as well as a meditation dome with pyramid. Amenities, offered for reasonable fees, include a sauna and steam bath, flotation tank and outdoor spa. Holistic therapies available to guests at the center include massage, acupressure treatments, herbology, rebirthing, crystal healing, psychic channeling and more. ~ 25 Wilson Canyon Road, Sedona; 928-282-7710, 877-723-2811; www.sedonahealingcenter.com, e-mail johnpaul@sedonahealingcenter.com. MODERATE.

DINING   **L'Auberge de Sedona** has an outstanding French restaurant with a view of Oak Creek and memorable prix-fixe dinners. The six-course menu, which changes nightly, typically features pâté, soup, a small baby green salad and entrées such as poached salmon, grilled lamb, venison, quail or chicken. ~ 301 L'Auberge Lane, Sedona; 928-282-1667; www.lauberge.com, e-mail info@lauberge. com. ULTRA-DELUXE.

An exceptional Continental restaurant in Sedona is **Rene at Tlaquepaque**, which specializes in rack of lamb carved tableside and tableside flambé. The most elaborate French Provincial decor in the Southwest makes this restaurant extra special. Open-air patio dining is available. ~ Route 179 at Tlaquepaque, Sedona; 928-282-9225, fax 928-282-5629. DELUXE TO ULTRA-DELUXE.

El Rincón Restaurante Mexicano is one of those not-too-spicy Mexican restaurants operated with the gringo palate in mind, but whatever it may lack in piquance it makes up for in presentation. A centerpiece of the Tlaquepaque shopping complex's overstated Old Mexico ambience, the restaurant specializes in chimichangas and creative entrées such as shrimp and green chile enchiladas. The menu also features a wide choice of combination plates. ~ Route 179 at The Bridge, Sedona; 928-282-4648; www.elrincon restaurant.com, e-mail information@rinconrestaurants.com. MODERATE.

Italian cuisine is featured at the **Hideaway Restaurant**, with tables on balconies over the creek, surrounded by a stand of sycamore trees. ~ Route 179 near Route 89A, Sedona; 928-282-4204; www.sedona.net/hideaway, e-mail hideaway@sedona.net. BUDGET TO MODERATE.

For health-conscious Thai food, made with all natural, organic ingredients, try **Thai Spices Natural Cuisine of Thailand**, a restau-

AUTHOR FAVORITE

Back in the 1940s, Oak Creek Cabin was a gathering spot for Hollywood stars who were in town filming, and local cowboys and ranchers who cozied up to them. Today, it's the **Cowboy Club Grille**, complete with wooden walls, plush earth-red and turquoise-colored booths, and Western memorabilia, including the second-largest set of longhorns in the U.S. mounted on the wall. A Western flair is also reflected in its "High Desert Cuisine," which highlights buffalo and rattlesnake brochettes and cactus fries. Those of us not feeling experimental can choose from chicken, seafood and angus beef dishes. For a quieter evening, the on-site **Silver Saddle Room** offers dining in a more formal setting. ~ 241 North Route 89A, Sedona; 928-282-4200; www.cowboyclub.com, e-mail info@cowboyclub.com. MODERATE TO ULTRA-DELUXE.

rant located in the White House Inn motel in West Sedona. Closed Sunday. ~ 2986 West Route 89A, Sedona; 928-282-0599, fax 928-282-0533; www.thaispices.com, e-mail info@thaispices.com. BUDGET TO MODERATE.

Amidst Aegean blue walls and artistic tablecloths topped with fresh flowers, diners enjoy Greek and Continental food at **Fournos Restaurant**. Watch the chef cook in the open kitchen, whipping up such specialties as flaming shrimp Santorini flambéed in *ouzo* and baked with feta cheese and Santorini sauce, fish baked in a sauce of yogurt, steamed onions and olive oil, or any one of their many roasted lamb specialties. Closed Sunday through Wednesday. Dinner only. ~ 3000 West Route 89A, Sedona; 928-282-3331. MODERATE TO DELUXE.

HIDDEN ▶

A choice of 101 omelettes is the main attraction at the **Coffee Pot Restaurant**, a local dining spot since the 1950s. Although the brass rails and sautillo tile floors add charm, the brown booths give away the casual atmosphere. On the wall hangs artwork by White Bear, a former Hopi Indian chief. A nice touch is the outdoor patio. Breakfast and lunch only. ~ 2050 West Route 89A, Sedona; 928-282-6626, fax 928-282-1118. BUDGET.

When a sushi craving strikes in the middle of the desert, feast on authentic tempura and sashimi at **Sasaki**. Owned and operated by a seasoned Japanese chef, this sleek, minimalistically decorated restaurant has a sushi bar and a tatami room. The patio offers outdoor dining with an impressive view of Sedona's most familiar red-rock landmark. Dinner only. ~ 65 Bell Rock Boulevard, Sedona; 928-284-1757; www.sedona-sasaki.com. MODERATE TO ULTRA-DELUXE.

To experience an eclectic synthesis of cuisines from all over the world, head for the **Heartline Cafe**, where you can enjoy dishes such as *cioppino* and pecan-crusted local trout with dijon cream sauce. ~ 1610 West Route 89A, Sedona; 928-282-0785, fax 928-204-9206; www.heartlinecafe.com. MODERATE TO ULTRA-DELUXE.

Another good spot is the **Red Planet Diner**, offering everything from Cajun and Italian food to seafood and steaks in an entertaining "intergalactic" environment. Check out the spaceship fountain and sci-fi scenes. ~ 1655 West Route 89A, Sedona; 928-282-6070, fax 928-282-1840; www.redplanetdiner.com. BUDGET TO MODERATE.

More views and an elegant setting await diners at the **Yavapai Dining Room** at Enchantment Resort. Typical of the Southwest cuisine served here is the rack of olive-crusted Colorado lamb with grilled vegetables, goat cheese, and potato tart. And don't miss the Sunday jazz champagne brunch. ~ 525 Boynton Canyon Road, Sedona; 928-282-2900. DELUXE TO ULTRA-DELUXE.

Contemporary furnishings adorn the long, narrow patio where diners can enjoy seafood and steak at the **T. Carl's Res-**

taurant at the Radisson Poco Diablo Resort. The well-prepared cuisine has a Continental flair. ~ 1752 South Route 179, Sedona; 928-282-7333. MODERATE TO DELUXE.

Sedona's shopping district is one of the three or four best in Arizona. Many of the galleries, boutiques and specialty shops are labors of love, the personal creations of people who spent years past daydreaming about opening a cute little store in Sedona. The town has more than 60 art galleries, most of them specializing in traditional and contemporary American Indian art, "cowboy" art and landscape paintings. Quality is relatively high in this very competitive art market. You can easily spend a whole day shopping your way up and down the main streets of town, leaving your feet sore and your credit cards limp.

SHOPPING

Located about halfway between Phoenix and the Grand Canyon, Sedona is named after Sedona Schnebly, the wife of the town's first postmaster.

Uptown Sedona has an abundance of fine little galleries. One that's easily overlooked but worth checking out is the gallery at the **Sedona Arts Center**. The paintings, ceramics, art glass and jewelry of local artists are featured; quality is high and prices are reasonable. ~ Located at the north end of the uptown commercial core on Route 89A at Art Barn Road, Sedona; 928-282-3809, 888-954-4442, fax 928-282-1516; www.sedonaartscenter.com.

The most relaxing and enjoyable place in Sedona to browse is **Tlaquepaque**, a picturesque complex of two-story Mexican-style buildings that houses specialty shops and restaurants below the "Y" on Route 179. Built with old-looking stone walls, courtyards, tile roofs and flowers in profusion, the Spanish Colonial–style Tlaquepaque looks more like Old Mexico than the real thing. **Environmental Realists** features metal jewelry and handcrafted knives and wood accessories. ~ 928-282-4945. **The Storyteller** carries all sorts of books about Sedona and the Southwest, from cookbooks to history. ~ 928-282-2144.

There are numerous other stores in the same vein in Sedona, such as **Heartsong**. ~ 3150 West Route 89 A; 928-282-7089.

Sedona has numerous stores for "enlightened" shoppers. The **Golden Word Book Centre** offers New Age literature. ~ 3150 West Route 89A; 928-282-2688. Get your chakras aligned at **Crystal Magic**. ~ 2978 West Route 89A; 928-282-1622. Can't get enough? The **Center for the New Age** has vortex information, networking for in-store New Age activities, daily psychic readings and a "Psychic Faire" every Saturday. ~ 341 Route 179; 928-282-1949; www.sedonanewagecenter.com.

Garland's Navajo Rugs has one of the largest collections of Navajo rugs in the world, with a selection of more than 5000. They hang on rafters, grouped according to subjects ranging from people to storm patterns. There are also kachina dolls in stock. ~ 411 Route 179, Sedona; 928-282-4070; www.garlands rugs.com.

There are a variety of specialty shops and galleries at **Hozho** shopping center, including the **Lanning Gallery** with contemporary artwork made by people from the Southwest. ~ 431 Route 179, Sedona; 928-282-6865; www.lanninggallery.com.

For the largest art gallery in Arizona, visit **Exposures International—Gallery of Fine Art**. Housed in its own building, Exposures offers life-size and monumental bronze sculptures, as well as works in other mediums. ~ 561 Route 179, Sedona; 928-282-1125, 800-526-7668; www.exposuresfineart.com, e-mail clientsupport@exposuresfineart.com.

The **Hillside Courtyard** is a two-level center with about 25 shops, galleries and restaurants set amidst waterfalls and sculptures. The **Compass Rose Gallery** (928-282-7904) offers a fascinating collection of antique maps, hand-colored prints and historic photographs, many pertaining to the region. **The Clay Pigeon** (928-282-2845) specializes in hand-crafted Southwestern crafts such as the whimsical rabbit sculptures of Jeanne Stevens-Sollman and handmade musical instruments. ~ 671 Route 179, Sedona.

Shopping enthusiasts will also want to visit **Oak Creek Factory Outlet**, a mall located south of town. This is factory-direct outlet shopping with a difference. The factories represented include Nine West (928-284-1910), Jones of New York (928-284-1919), Izod/Gant (928-284-9844) and Anne Klein (928-284-0407) —designer goods at discount prices. ~ Route 179, Oak Creek.

NIGHTLIFE Sedona has surprisingly little nightlife. One exception is the **Dahl and DiLuca**, where you can enjoy piano music nightly. Weekends offer a jazz band. This is a favorite gathering spot for locals who come here to relax, socialize and enjoy the tasty Italian special-

AUTHOR FAVORITE

The best way to discover what's unique about Sedona's culture, as far as I'm concerned, is to browse the bulletin boards at one of the town's largest metaphysical shops, **Crystal Castle**. According to many, the Castle is the New Age capital of the known cosmos. It carries unusual books, incense, jewelry, runes, visionary art and, of course, crystals. In front of the store, a "networking" bulletin board lets you scan the array of alternative professional services in town—channelers, psychic surgeons, clairvoyants, kinesiologists, numerologists and many more. ~ 313 Route 179, Sedona; 928-282-5910; www.crystalcastle.com, e-mail ccastle@sedona.net.

ties. ~ 2321 West Route 89A, Sedona; 928-282-5219; e-mail dah landdiluca@sedona.net.

Other than that, try the lounges in the major resort hotels, or call the **Sedona Arts Center** for its current schedule of theatrical and concert performances. ~ Route 89A at Art Barn Road, Sedona; 928-282-3809; www.sedonaartscenter.com.

SLIDE ROCK STATE PARK 🚶 🏊 Very popular with students from Northern Arizona University, this swimming area midway between Flagstaff and Sedona in the heart of Oak Creek Canyon is almost always packed during warm-weather months. It is a natural water park, with placid pools, fast-moving chutes and a wide, flat shoreline of red sandstone for sunbathing. The state park also includes the Pendley homestead, which is listed on the National Register of Historic Places, and acres of apple orchards. Visitors are not allowed to pick the apples but, during fall, cider made from them is sold at a stand on the trail to the swim area. When rangers are available they lead nature/historical walks on Saturdays. You'll find a picnic area, restrooms, a volleyball court, a nature trail and a snack bar. Day-use fee, $8 per vehicle. ~ Located seven miles north of Sedona via Route 89A in Oak Creek Canyon; 928-282-3034, fax 928-282-0245.

PARKS

RED ROCK STATE PARK 🚶 🚴 🛶 Beautiful Oak Creek runs through this 286-acre park situated in the heart of Red Rock Country. Naturalists offer guided walks daily along the six-mile trail system dotted with sycamore and cottonwood trees. One route leads to a 1948 house that resembles an Indian pueblo and, sitting atop a hill, affords great views of the area. The visitors center has natural history exhibits and videos. Fishing is allowed on Oak Creek, with catches including warm-water catfish and sunfish. There are picnic areas, restrooms and a visitors center. Day-use fee, $6 per vehicle. ~ Drive four miles southwest of Sedona on Route 89A, then turn south on Lower Red Rock Loop Road; the park appears in three miles; 928-282-6907, fax 928-282-5972; e-mail garbeiter@pr.state.az.us.

DEAD HORSE RANCH STATE PARK 🚶 🛶 This 325-acre park, located along the Verde River, has both desert and lush areas that can be enjoyed by walking the extensive hiking trails. Fishing is allowed in the Verde River and the four-acre lagoon, which is stocked with catfish and trout. There are picnic tables, restrooms and showers. Day-use fee, $5 per vehicle. ~ From Cottonwood, take Main Street to 10th Street, then go north for about a mile; 928-634-5283, fax 928-639-0417; e-mail lbovee@pr.state.az.us.

▲ There are over 100 sites (some with water and electricity,) $12 per night for no hookups, $19 per night with hookups.

▼▼▼▼▼▼▼▼▼▼
**Verde Valley &
Jerome Area**

Jerome, located southwest of Sedona on Route 89A, is one of Arizona's most intriguing ghost towns. In the first decades of the 20th century it was a rich silver mining district and, with a population of 15,000, was the fifth-largest city in Arizona. After having been completely abandoned in the 1950s, it was resettled by hippies in the late 1960s and now is a thriving artist's colony with a population of about 500 people.

The century-old wooden buildings of Jerome line only the uphill side of the main street, which winds up the steep slope of Cleopatra Hill in a series of switchbacks. The downhill side looks over the roofs of houses and stores on a lower level, offering a spectacular vista of the entire Verde Valley, where the small towns of Cottonwood and Clarkdale, two miles apart, are undergoing a gradual transition from agriculture to a tourism-based economy.

SIGHTS

Near the little town of Cottonwood, en route from Sedona to Jerome, is **Tuzigoot National Monument**, an uncharacteristically large Sinagua Indian pueblo ruin. Once home to about 225 people, the fieldstone pueblo stood two stories high and had 110 rooms. Today its white walls still stand on the hilltop and command an expansive view of the valley. Although the vista is marred by tailings fields from a refinery that used to process Jerome's copper ore, the museum at the national monument offers a good look at the prehistoric culture of the Sinagua people. Admission. ~ Off Route 89A between Cottonwood and Clarkdale; 928-634-5564, fax 928-639-0552; www.nps.gov/tuzi.

One of the most beautiful canyons in the area is remote and rugged **Sycamore Canyon**, which parallels Oak Creek Canyon. Designated wilderness area, this means that no wheeled or motorized vehicles are allowed. The Parsons Trail takes you up the lushly wooded canyon bottom, along Sycamore Creek, for most of its four-mile length, passing several small cliff dwellings resting high above. Camping is not permitted in the lower part of the canyon. For additional information, call the Sedona Rangers Station. ~ Turn off at Tuzigoot National Monument and follow the rough and ready maintained dirt road for about 12 miles to the trailhead at the end of the road; 928-282-4119.

A historic railroad that carries sightseers through some of Arizona's most spectacular country is the **Verde Canyon Railroad**. Revived in November 1990, this train achieved instant popularity as a major tourist attraction. It takes passengers on a 40-mile roundtrip from Clarkdale, just below Jerome. The diesel-powered train winds along sheer cliffs of red rock in curve after curve high above the Verde River, through a long, dark tunnel, over bridges, past gold mines and Sinagua Indian ruins, to the ghost town of Perkinsville and back. Closed Tuesday; check website for train schedule. Admission. ~ 300 North Broadway Street, Clarkdale; 928-639-0010, 800-293-7245, fax 928-639-1653; www.verdecanyonrr.com, e-mail info@verdecanyonrr.com.

The hillside town of Jerome is six miles past Clarkdale on Route 89A. The pleasure of Jerome lies in strolling (or climbing) the main street, browsing in the shops along the way and admiring the carefully preserved early-20th-century architecture.

The history of Jerome's mining era is brought to life in three museums. The old Douglas Mansion in **Jerome State Historic Park** at the lower end of town offers an informative 25-minute video called "Ghost Town of Jerome," a three-dimensional model of Jerome showing the underground shafts and tunnels, and a mineral exhibit. Admission. ~ Douglas Road, Jerome; 928-634-5381, fax 928-639-3132.

> The Douglas Mansion, built out of adobe bricks, served as a hotel for mining officials and investors. It came complete with a billiard room, wine cellar, steam heat, marble shower and central vacuum system.

For a look at mining tools, old photos, and other exhibits about old-time copper mining enter the **Jerome Historical Society Mine Museum**. Admission. ~ Main Street, Jerome; 928-634-5477; www.jeromehistoricalsociety.org.

The **Gold King Mine Museum** has a re-created assay office, a replica mine shaft and a petting zoo. Admission. ~ Perkinsville Road, Jerome; 928-634-0053; www.goldkingmine.net.

LODGING

One of the chief delights of visiting Jerome is the chance to stay in a historic landmark, a growing number of which are being converted to bed-and-breakfast inns. Some even claim to be haunted by their colorful past residents.

Built for the mining company's chief surgeon in 1916, the **Surgeon's House** is a stately blonde stucco, tile-roofed home with colorful terraced gardens facing the Verde Valley. Along with three spacious rooms and suites in the main house, there is a guest cottage decorated with vibrant Guatemalan textiles, stained-glass window hangings, terra-cotta tiles, an old-fashioned upright bathtub painted Chinese red and a secluded patio. Guests have access to the gardens. Complimentary beverages, snacks and a hearty breakfast are included. ~ P.O. Box 998, Jerome, AZ 86331; 928-639-1452, 800-639-1452; www.surgeonshouse.com, e-mail surgehouse1@wildapache.net. MODERATE TO DELUXE.

Hillside House is a charming and historic old home nestled on the slopes of Cleopatra Hill and surrounded by fruit orchards. The inn is a private home with just one accommodation: a two-room suite located downstairs with its own private entrance and access to a garden patio. In addition to the bedroom, the suite has a sitting area with a bunk bed, refrigerator and microwave. ~ P.O. Box 305, Jerome, AZ 86331; 928-634-5667. MODERATE.

An 1898 Victorian bed and breakfast, the **Ghost City Inn** features six rooms with private baths. Visit the Old West in "The Western Room" or soak up the stunning vistas from the "Verde View Room." There's also a jacuzzi to relax in. ~ 541 Main Street, Jerome; phone/fax 928-634-4678, 888-634-4678; www.ghostcity inn.com. MODERATE TO DELUXE.

DINING

For a bit of Arizona history with your meal, visit the **English Kitchen**, the state's oldest continually operating restaurant. Founded by a Chinese immigrant in 1899, the eatery serves standard American comfort food: charbroiled burgers, hot dogs, soups, salads and homemade pies for dessert. Breakfast and lunch only. Closed January and Monday. ~ 119 North Jerome Avenue, Jerome; 928-634-2132. BUDGET.

Many of Jerome's buildings were constructed of massive blocks of quarried stone to withstand the blasts that frequently shook the ground from the nearby mine. The entire town has been declared a National Historic Landmark.

Jerome Palace Haunted Hamburger is a meateater's delight, specializing in grilled steaks, chicken and ribs served in a cozy dining room with a fireplace and 90-mile views of the Verde Valley. Both indoor and outdoor seating are available. ~ 410 Clark Street, Jerome; 928-634-0554. MODERATE.

The walls at the **Jerome Grill** are decorated with picks, axes and scores of photographs outlining the town's mining heyday. Breakfast goodies include omelets, french toast and *huevos rancheros*. For lunch, fill up on burgers, sandwiches, meatloaf, chicken-fried steak, or any of their delicious Mexican dishes. Try a locally brewed beer or margarita from the bar. No dinner. ~ 309 Main Street, Jerome; 928-634-5094; e-mail inn@jerome.com. BUDGET.

For breakfast or lunch, try the **Flatiron Café**, serving pastries, vegetarian dishes and panini sandwiches along with gourmet coffees and teas in historic surroundings. Call ahead for hours. ~ 416 Main Street, Jerome; 928-634-2733. BUDGET TO MODERATE.

SHOPPING

Many of Jerome's residents are arts-and-crafts people, and a stroll up and down the town's switchback Main Street will take you past quite a few intriguing shops that offer pottery, jewelry, handmade clothing, stained glass and other such wares.

Designs on You is a two-story shop that sells women's casual and natural-fiber clothing and lingerie. ~ 233 Main Street, Jerome; 928-634-7879.

You can watch jewelers create contemporary designs at **Aurum Jewelry**. About 40 local artists show their work here, which ranges from a sculptured iron spoon and fork to belt buckles, bolo ties, custom knives and jewelry. ~ 369 Main Street, Jerome; 928-634-3330; www.aurumjewelry.com.

In the last few years, the heart of the working art movement in town has been centered at the **Old Mingus Art Center**, which is now filled with studios and galleries carrying everything from paintings to sculpture. The biggest is the **Anderson/Mandette Art Studios**. One of the largest private art studios in the country, it feels more like a museum as you walk through it. Paintings by Robin Anderson and Margo Mandette hang upstairs. ~ Route 89A, Jerome; 928-634-3438; www.robinjohnanderson.com, e-mail mandette@sedona.net.

The Old West saloon tradition lives on in Jerome, where the town's **NIGHTLIFE** most popular club is the **Spirit Room** in the old Connor Hotel. There is live music on weekend afternoons and evenings and the atmosphere is as authentic as can be. Occasional cover (evenings only). ~ 166 Main Street at Jerome Avenue, Jerome; 928-634-8809, fax 928-649-0981; www.spiritroom.com.

Continuing southwest on Route 89A, in the next valley, ▼▼▼▼▼▼▼▼▼
sits the city of Prescott, the original territorial capital of **Prescott**
Arizona from 1864 to 1867. President Abraham Lincoln decided to declare it the capital because the only other community of any size in the Arizona Territory, Tucson, was full of Confederate sympathizers. Until recently, Prescott was a low-key, all-American town that seemed stuck in a 1950s time warp. Within the past few years, however, relatively low real estate prices have spurred explosive suburban development, making Prescott the fastest-growing community in Arizona. Yet its downtown historic district retains a certain quiet charm with few concessions to tourism. Incidentally, Prescott is located at the exact geographic center of the state of Arizona.

Built in 1916, the **Yavapai County Courthouse** sits at the heart **SIGHTS** of Prescott, surrounded by a green plaza where locals pass the time playing cards and chatting, and tourists rest awhile on park benches. Surrounding the plaza are many of the town's shops, in addition to historic Whiskey Row, where at one time some 20 saloons were open day and night.

The major sightseeing highlight in Prescott is the **Sharlot Hall Museum**, which contains a large collection of antiques from Arizona's territorial period, including several fully furnished houses and an excellent collection of stagecoaches and carriages, as well as a history of the Prescott area in photographs. Sharlot Mabridth Hall was a well-known essayist, poet and traveler who explored the wild areas of the Arizona Territory around the turn of the

20th century. Seeing that Arizona's historic and prehistoric artifacts were rapidly being taken from the state, Ms. Hall began a personal collection that grew quite large over the next three decades and became the nucleus of this large historical museum. The museum's collections are housed in several Territorial-era buildings brought from around the county, including a home that was built of ponderosa pine logs in 1864 and used as a governor's mansion until 1867. The complex occupies a large park in downtown Prescott. ~ 415 West Gurley Street; 928-445-3122, fax 928-776-9053; www.sharlothall.org.

The **Smoki Museum** houses a large collection of American Indian artifacts from throughout the Southwest. The museum also houses a library and the largest collection of works by Kate Cory, a painter and photographer of Hopi life during the early 20th century. Closed Tuesday through Thursday from January through March. Admission. ~ 147 North Arizona Street; 928-445-1230, fax 928-777-0573; www.smokimuseum.org, e-mail info@smoki museum.org.

Prescott also has some other noteworthy museums. The **Phippen Museum of Western Art**, six miles north of town, honors cowboy artist George Phippen and presents changing exhibits of art of the American West. It is generally considered one of the best Western art museums in the country. Closed Monday from January to Memorial Day. Admission. ~ 4701 Route 89 North; 928-778-1385; www.phippenmuseum.org, e-mail phippen@phippen museum.org.

Thirty-four miles east of Prescott you'll find **Arcosanti**, a planned city that will eventually be home to 6000 people. Arcosanti was designed by famed Italian designer Paulo Soleiri, who came to Arizona to study with Frank Lloyd Wright and never left, as a synthesis of architecture and ecology. The complex, which presently houses a gallery, a bakery and café, a foundry, residences and visitor accommodations, a concert stage and more, is pedestrian-oriented. From a distance, its strange skyline looks like some kind of psychedelic theme park, but on closer examination it is a busy construction site where unusual buildings with domes, arches, portholes and protruding cubes expand constantly like living organisms, making maximum use of passive solar heat. Although construction has been continuous since 1970, plans for future development extend decades into the future. Tours are offered daily. Continuing construction is financed in part by the sale of handmade souvenir items, particularly bronze-and-ceramic Soleiri wind bells. Other funding comes from the many seminars, conferences, workshops and music events presented each year. ~ Route 17, Exit 262 at Cordes Junction; 928-632-7135; www.arcosanti.org, e-mail arcoinfo@arcosanti.org.

LODGING

Prescott has several historic downtown hotels. The most elegant of them is the **Hassayampa Inn**, a 1927 hotel listed on the National Register. The lobby and other common areas have been restored to their earlier glory and furnished with antiques. The rooms have been beautifully renovated and all have private baths. Room rates include a complimentary breakfast in the Peacock Dining Room. ~ 122 East Gurley Street; 928-778-9434, 800-322-1927, fax 928-445-8590; www.hassayampainn.com, e-mail inn1@mindspring.com. DELUXE.

With 160 rooms and suites, **Prescott Resort and Conference Center** is the largest lodging facility in the area. It sits on a hill just outside town with a commanding view of the surrounding countryside. Although rooms are large and come with cable TV, refrigerators and coffeemakers, the resort's biggest draw is probably the adjacent 24-hour casino, Bucky's, which has slots, poker machines and keno machines. ~ 1500 Route 69; 928-776-1666, 800-967-4637, fax 928-776-8544; www.prescottresort.com. ULTRA-DELUXE.

A smaller hotel on a quiet side street is the **Hotel Vendome**. Rooms in this historic 21-unit 1917 hotel have been nicely restored and decorated in the style of the era. There are four two-room suites. Some have modern bathrooms, while others feature restored clawfoot tub/showers. ~ 230 South Cortez Street; 928-776-0900, 888-468-3583, fax 928-771-0395; www.vendomehotel.com, e-mail vendomehotel@aol.com. MODERATE TO DELUXE.

For added privacy, try **The Cottages at Prescott Country Inn**. With twelve two-, three- and four-room abodes, this hideaway offers all the comforts of home. Each cottage has its own complete kitchen (with the exception of one) and all are tastefully decorated. Most have a fireplace and patio. The pricing is wonderfully reasonable, too. Continental breakfast served in bed or at your cottage table. ~ 503 South Montezuma Street; 928-445-7991, 888-757-0015, fax 928-717-1215; www.guestinnusa.com/prescott countryinn. MODERATE TO DELUXE.

A cozy bed and breakfast in a 1934 main house with three guesthouses is the **Prescott Pines Inn**. It has 11 Victorian-style guest accommodations, including a two-story chalet, beautifully decorated in subdued color schemes. Some have fireplaces and others have kitchens and kitchenettes. Sumptuous full breakfasts are served on rose-patterned china. Reservations are recommended. ~ 901 White Spar Road; 928-445-7270, 800-541-5374, fax 928-778-3665; www.prescottpinesinn.com, e-mail info@prescottpinesinn.com. BUDGET TO MODERATE.

More modest rooms, all with private baths, are available at the **Hotel St. Michael**. The location couldn't be better for those who wish to enjoy the Wild West nightlife of Whiskey Row, on the same block. A full breakfast is included. ~ 205 West Gurley Street; 928-776-1999, 800-678-3757, fax 928-776-7318; www.hotelst michael.net, e-mail hsmevents@cabelone.net. MODERATE.

Prescott also has more than its share of low-priced, basic lodging from which to explore the wild canyons and forests surrounding the city. The prices can't be beat at the Mediterranean-style **American Motel**. Rooms are refurbished in adobe and terra-cotta hues, and some have wonderful old murals on the walls. ~ 1211 East Gurley Street; 928-778-4322, fax 928-778-1324. BUDGET TO MODERATE.

By making reservations well in advance, visitors can stay overnight in **Arcosanti**. Visionary architect Paulo Soleiri's futuristic village has a group of greenhouse guest rooms, each with basic furnishings including two double beds, as well as a Sky Suite with two small bedrooms, a private bath, a kitchenette, a living room and a patio. Room rates are surprisingly low, though late sleepers may find that construction noise is a drawback. ~ Route 17, Exit 262 at Cordes Junction; 928-632-7135, fax 928-632-6229; www.arcosanti.org, e-mail info@arcosanti.org. BUDGET.

Prescott's finer restaurants include the **Peacock Dining Room** in **DINING** the Hassayampa Inn. Here you'll find lunch and dinner menus of Continental and American specialties in an elegant old-time atmosphere. An etched-glass peacock adorns the front door of this art-deco dining room. Choose between seating at tables or semicircular booths. Tiffany-style lamps add to the quaint atmosphere of this high-ceilinged establishment. Breakfast, lunch and dinner served Monday through Saturday; breakfast and dinner only on Sunday. ~ 122 East Gurley Street; 928-778-9434, 800-322-1927; www.hassayampainn.com, e-mail inn1@mindspring.com. MODERATE TO DELUXE.

A century-old general merchandise store that has been transformed into a popular restaurant, **Murphy's** is a walk through history. A leaded-glass divider separates the bar and restaurant sections decorated with photos of Prescott's mining heyday. Mahogany bar booths and a burgundy carpet add to the charm of this establishment. You can also enjoy a drink in the lounge offering views of Thumb Butte. Specialties include mesquite-broiled seafood and prime rib of beef along with fresh home-baked bread. ~ 201 North Cortez Street; 928-445-4044, fax 928-778-4844. MODERATE TO DELUXE.

With a list of awards as long as my arm, **Prescott Brewing Company** claims to be the town's only brew pub. Regardless, it's a great place to nosh and people-watch simultaneously. In addition to Southwestern-tinged entrées like Angus burgers and Sonoran enchiladas you'll find some vegetarian options: the "Settler's Pot Pie" is a mish-mash of mushrooms, tomatoes, carrots, artichoke hearts, yams and fresh herbs, baked with mozzarella and parmesan cheese and served with—what else?—beer bread. ~ 130 West Gurley Street; 928-771-2795, fax 928-771-1115; www.prescott brewingcompany.com. BUDGET TO MODERATE.

◆◆

SHARLOT HALL

One of the most admired women in Arizona history was Sharlot Mabridth Hall, who arrived in Prescott in 1882. She helped manage the family ranch east of Prescott, passing time writing poetry and panning for gold. But in 1909 she became the territorial historian and the first woman in Arizona to hold a political office. In 1924, Hall was asked to go east and represent Arizona in the electoral college. Originally she turned down the offer, not having enough money for suitable clothes. But officials at the United Verde Mine saved the day, buying her a blue silk dress with a fine copper mesh coat. This "copper dress" was a hit back east and gave a free shot of publicity to the Arizona copper industry. Today, you can learn all about her in the Sharlot Hall Museum.

HIDDEN ▶   For breakfast or lunch in Prescott, a very popular place in the downtown area is the **Plaza Café**, which serves an assortment of pancakes, omelettes and homemade soups. ~ 106 West Gurley Street; 928-445-3234. BUDGET.

Also good is the **Prescott Pantry** in the Iron Springs Plaza shopping center. This bakery/deli has restaurant seating and offers ever-changing daily specials, hearty sandwiches, espresso drinks and fresh-baked pastries. Closed Sunday. ~ 1201 Iron Springs Road; 928-778-4280. BUDGET.

Elmer Young started farming 80 acres in 1946, in the heart of Consume Valley. His small farm has since grown into an Arizona tradition for families statewide. The farm complex includes a popular restaurant, **The Hungry Bear**, which serves hearty breakfasts and huge sandwiches. After your meal, you can stop by the on-site produce store and pick up fresh treats for later including pumpkins, turkeys, sweet corn, vegetables and meat, as well as more unusual pumpkin butter and Hopi Corn jelly. Crowds are especially thick during seasonal festivals when wagon rides around the farm are offered. The place has a real down-home country feel. Open for breakfast and lunch. ~ East of Prescott at the intersection of Routes 69 and 169, Dewey; 928-635-7272, fax 928-632-7975; www.youngsfarminc.com, e-mail information@youngsfarminc.com BUDGET.

SHOPPING   Because it is old as Arizona towns go, and perhaps because of Sharlot Hall's recognition that it was important to preserve the everyday objects of 19th-century Arizona, Prescott is a good place for antique shopping. As in most antique hunting areas, some items offered for sale do not come from the Prescott area but have been imported from other, less-visited parts of the country. Most, however, are the real thing, and antique buffs will find lots of great shops within walking distance of one another in the downtown area, especially along the two-block strip of Cortez Street between Gurley and Sheldon streets.

◆◆◆

COME AND GET IT

For home-style cooking in Prescott head to the **Dinner Bell Café**. It may not look like much from the outside, but give it a try and you'll find out why this is one of the most popular restaurants in central Arizona. For breakfast try the hubcap-size pancakes or three-egg omelettes. Lunch specials include sandwiches, burgers, salads and hot roast beef. Be sure to sample the homemade salsa. No dinner. ~ 321 West Gurley Street; 928-445-9888. BUDGET.

Some of the best places to browse are the indoor mini-malls where select groups of dealers and collectors display, such as the **Merchandise Mart Antique Mall**. ~ 205 North Cortez Street; 928-776-1728. **Prescott Antique & Craft Market** is another such mall. ~ 115 North Cortez Street; 928-445-7156. Nearby is the **Deja Vu Antique Mall**. ~ 134 North Cortez Street; 928-445-6732.

Inside the historic Hotel St. Michael is **Puttin' on the Hats**, which has everything from Greek fisherman's hats to cowboy hats. ~ 110 Montezuma Street; 928-776-1150.

An excellent gallery in town is **Sun West**. Arizona and local artists sell sculpture, pottery, furniture, paintings and jewelry, and there are also rugs woven by the Zapotec people. ~ 152 South Montezuma Street; 928-778-1204.

Other noteworthy galleries that exhibit and sell the works of local artists include the **Prescott Fine Arts Gallery**. ~ 208 North Marina Street; 928-445-3286. Visit **Mountain Artists Guild**. ~ 228 North Alarcon Street; 928-445-2510. There's also the **Yavapai College Gallery**. ~ In the performance hall on campus, 1100 East Sheldon Street; 928-776-2031.

NIGHTLIFE

Rock-and-roll and blues acts entertain on Friday and Saturday nights, as well as Sunday afternoon at **Piñon Pines Nite Club**. See what the musicians come up with on Wednesday's live jam night. ~ 2701 East Route 89A; 928-445-9935.

Moctezuma's occasionally has live bands on Friday and deejay tunes on Wednesday, Thursday and Saturday. ~ 144 South Montezuma Street; 928-445-1244.

Prescott has its own theater company performing year-round at the **Prescott Fine Arts Theater**. It offers both a main stage and a Family Theater for child-oriented productions. ~ 208 North Marina Street; 928-445-3286; www.pfaa.net.

The Yavapai-Prescott Indian tribe owns **Bucky's Casino** east of Prescott. Besides the usual rows upon rows of slot machines, there is a no-limit poker room featuring seven-card stud, Texas hold-'em and Omaha poker. When you need to refuel for another round of gaming, you can retreat to the **Yavapai Cantina**, a sports bar with snacks and beverages. ~ 1500 Route 69; casino: 800-756-8744; www.buckyscasino.com.

PARKS

J.S. ACKER MEMORIAL PARK 🏃 Organized by a grassroots community group that fought to protect the land from a housing development, Acker Park is an ideal spot for strolling through the summer flowers, experiencing the colors of an Arizona fall, identifying local plants or just admiring a dramatic sunset. Officials encourage visitors to appreciate a landscape left alone—no manicured sportsfields or jungle gyms here. Avid walkers will love the park's 75 acres of open space and hilltops with gorgeous views of the surrounding area. There are restrooms, a children's area and a picnic set-up. ~ Located at the end of South Virginia Street, Prescott; 928-771-1428; www.wpo.net/ackerpark.

WATSON LAKE AND PARK A labyrinth of granite rock formations along Route 89 just outside of Prescott surrounds pretty little Watson Lake, a manmade reservoir that is locally popular for boating and catfish fishing. The area used to be a stronghold for Apache Indians. More recently, from the 1920s to the 1950s, there was a major resort at Granite Dells and some artifacts survive from that era. Hiking and rock climbing are popular pursuits here. There are restrooms, showers and several picnic areas. Day-use fee, $12 per vehicle. ~ Route 98, four miles northeast of Prescott; 928-777-1564, fax 928-771-5845.

▲ There are 42 sites (no hookups); $10 per night. Camping is on a first-come, first-served basis only.

▼▼▼▼▼▼▼▼▼▼▼▼▼▼

Outdoor Adventures

North Central Arizona is a popular region for both downhill and cross-country skiing.

SKIING

FLAGSTAFF AREA   Arizona's premier downhill ski area is the **Arizona Snowbowl**, located 14 miles north of Flagstaff on the slopes of the San Francisco Peaks. The ski area has four chairlifts, ranging from the beginners' Hart Prairie Chairlift (3200 feet long with only a 650-foot vertical rise) to the steep Agassiz Chairlift (6450 feet long with a 1981-foot vertical rise to an elevation of 11,500 feet). Skis and boots, as well as snowboards, are available at the snowboard rental shop. Snowboarders can use the designated park or share the slopes with skiers. The season runs from mid-December to mid-April. ~ Seven miles off Route 180 on Snowbowl Road; 928-779-1951, 928-779-4577 (snow report), fax 928-779-3019; www.arizonasnow bowl.com, e-mail marketing@arizonasnowbowl.com. The small **Williams Ski Area**, located on Bill Williams Mountain, offers rentals and lessons for skiers and snowboarders. There's also a tubing hill. ~ Four miles south of the town of Williams; 928-635-9330.

For cross-country skiers, the **Flagstaff Nordic Center** (maintained by Arizona Snowbowl), 16 miles north of Flagstaff in Coconino National Forest, maintains an extensive system of trails from mid-November to mid-March. The center offers equipment rentals, guided tours and a ski school. Closed Monday through Wednesday. ~ Route 180; 928-779-1951; www.arizonasnow bowl.com, e-mail marketing@arizonasnowbowl.com.

BALLOON RIDES

For the most spectacular guided tour in town, sightsee from a hot-air balloon.

SEDONA AREA   Experience the Red Rock Country from the sky with **Red Rock Balloon Adventures**. All rides begin at sunrise and include a champagne picnic. ~ Sedona; 928-284-0040, 800-258-3754; www.redrockballoons.com. Also hovering above is **Northern Light Balloon Expeditions**. Balloon rides last an hour and go over Sedona or along the Mogollon Rim depending on the winds. Each operator launches one trip a day at sunrise and follows it up with a picnic breakfast. ~ P.O. Box 1695, Sedona, AZ 86339; 928-282-2274, 800-230-6222.

For Sedona visitors who wish to explore the surrounding Red **JEEP TOURS** Rock Country, the town has an extraordinary number of jeep tour services, offering everything from general sightseeing journeys to spiritual inner journeys. Trips range from one hour to all day, and are fully guided. They'll usually pick you up at any Sedona lodging.

Pink Jeep Tours runs sightseeing trips in—what else—those flashy pink jobs you see darting around town. They provide off-road backcountry tours of the Sedona red rock area, as well as trips to Indian ruins and petroglyphs, which require a little hiking as well as jeeping. The tours focus on American Indian folklore, geology and wildlife appreciation. ~ 204 North Route 89A; 928-282-5000, 800-873-3662, fax 928-282-8818; www.pinkjeep.com.

Perched 12,633 above sea level, Humphreys Peak in the San Francisco Peaks is the state's highest point.

Whether you're looking for a Wild West sightseeing tour that traverses private ranchlands, or a New Age "Vortex Tour" where you can absorb the electromagnetic energy that is said to swirl among select stones in Boynton Canyon, the cowboy-garbed guides at **Sedona Red Rock Jeep Tours** can provide it; the emphasis on these one-and-a-half to three-hour trips is educational and photographic, so whichever tour you take, you'll doubtless learn as much as you ever wanted to know about the area and take home plenty of pictures. ~ 270 North Route 89A; 928-282-6826, 800-848-7728; www.redrockjeep.com.

Earth Wisdom Jeep Tours runs two- to six-hour trips to the scenic vortex, sacred wheel, remote canyon and rim, ruins and hiking spots. Jeep/horseback combo tours are also available. ~ 293 North Route 89A; 928-282-4714, 800-482-4714; www.earthwisdomtours.com, e-mail earthwisdomtours@sedona.net.

While you might not be able to golf year-round here, most of the **GOLF** year offers excellent weather for hitting the greens.

FLAGSTAFF AREA Tee off at the 18-hole, public **Elden Hills Golf Resort**. There are clubs and golf carts for rent. Closed in winter if there's snow on the ground. ~ 2380 North Oakmont Drive, Flagstaff; 928-526-5125; www.continentalflagstaff.com.

SEDONA AREA Sedona Golf Resort's 18-hole course designed by Gary Panks is ranked third in the state among public courses.

Clubs are available for rent, and the use of a cart is included in the green fee. ~ 35 Ridge Trail Drive; 928-284-9355; www.sedonagolfresort.com. Drive a wedge at the semiprivate, 18-hole, Robert Trent Jones–designed **Oak Creek Country Club**. Carts and clubs can be rented. ~ 690 Bell Rock Boulevard, Sedona; 928-284-1660; www.oakcreekcountryclub.com. Play the greens at the semipublic **Canyon Mesa Country Club**, a nine-hole executive course with red-rock views. Clubs and carts are available for rent. ~ 500 Jacks Canyon Boulevard, Sedona; 928-284-0036. The nine-hole, par-three course at **Radisson Poco Diablo Resort** wends its way among challenging water hazards and a sand trap as well as beautiful stands of willow trees. There are clubs for rent, but no carts; it is a walking course, and metal cleats are prohibited. ~ 1752 South Route 179, Sedona; 928-282-7333, fax 928-282-2090. Go for a hole in one on either (or both) of the two 18-hole courses at the public **Antelope Hills Golf Course**. There are clubs and carts for rent. ~ 1 Perkins Drive, Prescott; 800-972-6818; www.antelopehillsgolf.com.

TENNIS　There is not a lot of tennis in this area, but you should be able to find a few open courts.

FLAGSTAFF AREA　**Thorpe Park** has four lighted public courts. ~ Thorpe Park Road. The public **Bushmaster Park** has two lighted courts. ~ Alta Vista Street. You can call the **Parks and Recreation Department** for more information. ~ 928-779-7690, fax 928-779-7693.

SEDONA AREA　Sedona has no public tennis courts. For a fee, courts are available to the public at **Poco Diablo Resort**, with four courts, two of which are lighted. Hitting assistants and a ball machine are available, and there is a tennis pro on call. ~ 1752 South Route 179; 928-282-7333.

PRESCOTT　In Prescott, six tennis courts are open to the public year-round at **Yavapai College**. ~ 1100 East Sheldon Street; 928-445-7300, or 928-778-7071. Public summer courts are also found at **Prescott High School**, which has six courts. ~ 1050 North Ruth Street; 928-445-2322. **Ken Lindley Field** has four courts open year-round. ~ East Gurley and Arizona streets; 928-777-1553.

RIDING STABLES　The equestrian will find many riding opportunities in this region.

FLAGSTAFF AREA　Year-round trips in Coconino National Forest are offered by **Flying Heart Stables**, which also has a horse motel for overnight horsekeeping. ~ 8400 North Route 89, Flagstaff; 928-526-2788.

SEDONA AREA　**Red Rock Jeep** offers one- or two-hour-long trail rides. ~ 270 North Route 89A; 928-282-6826, 800-848-

7728. For one- and two-hour rides through Coconino National Forest, contact **Trail Horse Adventures**. ~ 85 Five J Lane, Sedona; 800-723-3538.

PRESCOTT **Granite Mountain Stables** provides guided horse rides in the Granite Mountain Wilderness. ~ 2400 West Shane Drive off Williamson Valley Road; 928-771-9551.

As in the rest of the state, this region is fast becoming a mecca for biking.

BIKING

FLAGSTAFF AREA Flagstaff has about eight miles of paved trails in its **Urban Trail System and Bikeways System**, linking the Northern Arizona University campus, the downtown area and Lowell Observatory. Maps and information on the trail system are available upon request from the **Parks and Recreation Department**. ~ 211 West Aspen Avenue; 928-779-7690, fax 928-779-7693.

> Sedona Red Rock Jeep Tours' "Complete Cowboy Evening" includes sunset trail and wagon rides, outdoor steak cookouts, and Western music under a canopy of stars.

Outside Flagstaff, a popular route for all-day bike touring is the 36-mile paved loop road through **Sunset Crater and Wupatki national monuments**, starting at the turnoff from Route 89 about 20 miles northeast of town.

For mountain bikers, several unpaved primitive roads lead deeper into the San Francisco Volcano Field in **Coconino National Forest**. For more information, contact the **Peaks Ranger Station**. ~ 5075 North Route 89; 928-526-0866; www.coconinoforest.us.

SEDONA AREA The same network of unpaved back roads that makes the **Red Rock Country** around Sedona such a popular area for four-wheel-drive touring is also ideal for mountain biking. Get a map from one of the local bike shops and try the dirt roads leading from Soldier Pass Road to the Seven Sacred Pools or the Devil's Kitchen. Or follow the Broken Arrow Jeep Trail east from Route 179 to Submarine Rock. The Schnebly Hill Road climbs all the way north to Flagstaff, paralleling the Oak Creek Canyon Highway. The upper part of the road is steep, winding and very rough, but the lower part, through Bear Wallow Canyon, makes for a beautiful mountain biking excursion.

PRESCOTT AREA **Thumb Butte Trail** and **Copper Basin** are among the favorite mountain-biking areas around Prescott.

Bike Rentals In Flagstaff, you can rent mountain bikes and obtain trail information at **Absolute Bikes**. They also offer repair service. ~ 18 North San Francisco Street, Flagstaff; 928-779-5969; www.absolutebikes.net. In Sedona, you'll find trail information, bike rentals and repairs at **Mountain Bike Heaven**. ~ 1695 West Route 89A, Sedona; 928-282-1312; www.mountainbikeheaven. com. **Sedona Sports** also rents bikes. ~ Artesania Creekside Plaza,

251 Route 179, Sedona; 928-282-1317; www.sedonasports.com. You can rent a mountain bike by the hour, day or week (complete with helmet, tire pump, repair kit, water bottle, lock and map) at **Ironclad Bicycles**. Closed Sunday in winter. ~ 710 White Spar Road, Prescott; 928-776-1755; www.ironcladbicycles.com.

ROCK CLIMBING   Many areas in the canyon country of central Arizona are ideal for technical rock climbing. However, safe climbing requires training, practice and proper equipment—all of which are available at the **Vertical Relief Rock Gym** in Flagstaff. Said to be one of the finest indoor climbing facilities in the country, this gym is basically a tall, empty downtown building, its 6000 square feet of windowless interior walls set with stone hand- and footholds. Instructors give daily classes for climbers of all ages and abilities, covering such topics as knots, belaying, rappelling and teamwork. ~ 205 South San Francisco Street, Flagstaff; 928-556-9909, 877-265-5984; www.verticalrelief.com, e-mail programs@verticalrelief.com.

HIKING   Lovers of the outdoors will delight in the number and variety of hiking trails this area provides. All distances listed for hiking trails are one way unless otherwise noted.

FLAGSTAFF AREA   Just north of Flagstaff rise the San Francisco Peaks, the highest in Arizona. Numerous trails start from Mount Elden and Schultz Pass roads, which branch off Route 180 to the right a short distance past the Museum of Northern Arizona. Other trailheads are located in Flagstaff at Buffalo Park on Cedar Avenue and near the Peaks Ranger Station on Route 89. Most trails in the Flagstaff area close in winter.

North of the ranger station, off Route 180, the **Elden Lookout Trail** (3 miles) climbs by switchbacks up the east face of 9299-foot Mount Elden, with an elevation gain of 2400 feet and, waiting to reward you at the top, a spectacular view of the city and the volcano fields around Sunset Crater.

AUTHOR FAVORITE

I must confess a growing distaste for summertime crowds and parking problems. But while every visitor to Flagstaff or Sedona drives through often-crowded Oak Creek Canyon, one of central Arizona's "must-see" spots, few stop to explore the canyon's west fork, a narrow canyon with sheer walls hundreds of feet high in places, which is only accessible on foot. For more information on trails in this area, call the Red Rock Ranger Station, 928-282-4119; www.redrockcounty.org.

The **Fatman's Loop Trail** (2 miles), branching off of Elden Lookout Trail for a shorter hike with a 600-foot elevation gain, also offers a good view of Flagstaff.

From the Buffalo Park trailhead, the **Oldham Trail** (5.5 miles) ascends the west face to the top of Mount Elden. The longest trail on the mountain, this is a gentler climb. The Oldham Trail intersects Mount Elden Road three times, making it possible to take a shorter hike on only the higher part of the trail. **Pipeline Trail** (2.8 miles) links the lower parts of the Oldham and Elden Lookout trails along the northern city limit of Flagstaff, allowing either a short hike on the edge of town or a long, all-day loop trip up one side of the mountain and down the other.

Perhaps the most unusual of many hiking options in the strange volcanic landscape around the base of the San Francisco Peaks is on **Red Mountain,** 33 miles north of Flagstaff off Route 180. A gap in the base of this 1000-foot-high volcanic cone lets you follow the **Red Mountain Trail** (1 mile) from the end of the national forest access road straight into the crater without climbing. Not often visited by tourists, this is a great place to explore with older children.

◄ *HIDDEN*

For maps and detailed hiking information on these and many other trails in Coconino National Forest, contact the **Peaks Ranger Station.** ~ 5075 North Route 89; 520-526-0866; www.fs.fed.us/r3/coconino.

SEDONA AREA The trailhead for the **West Fork Trail** (14 miles) is in the parking lot (there is a parking fee) of the Call of the Canyon on the west side of Route 89A, ten miles north of Sedona. The first three miles of the trail pass through a protected "research natural area," are heavily used and easy to hike. Farther up, the trail becomes less distinct, requires repeatedly swimming through pools of water while floating your gear and leads into the Red Rock Secret Mountain Wilderness.

A very popular hiking spot in the Red Rock Country is Boynton Canyon, one of Sedona's four "Vortex" areas. According to the New Age community, Boynton Canyon is the most powerful of the vortexes, emanating an electromagnetic psychic energy that can be felt for miles around. Whether you believe or not, it is undeniably beautiful. From the trailhead on Boynton Pass Road—a continuation of Dry Creek Road, which leaves Route 89A in West Sedona—the nearly level **Boynton Canyon Trail** (2.5 miles) goes up the canyon through woods and among red-rock formations. There are several small, ancient Sinagua Indian cliff dwellings in the canyon. If you visit the ruins be aware that the dwellings are very fragile and are disappearing due to impact.

A right turn from Dry Creek Road on the way to Boynton Pass will put you on unpaved Forest Road 152, which is rough enough in spots that drivers of low-clearance vehicles may want to think twice before proceeding. One and a half miles up this road, the **Devil's Bridge Trail** (1 mile) climbs gradually through piñon and juniper country to a long red sandstone arch with a magnificent view of the surrounding canyonlands. You can walk to the top of the arch. Located three miles farther, at the end of Dry Creek Road, is the trailhead for the **Vultee Arch Trail** (1.7 miles), which follows Sterling Canyon to another natural bridge.

PRESCOTT   There are many hiking trails in the national forest around Prescott. One of the most popular is the **Thumb Butte Trail** (1.4 miles), which goes up a saddle west of town, through oak and piñon woods, offering good views of Prescott and Granite Dells. The trail starts from Thumb Butte Park. To get there, go west on Thumb Butte Road, an extension of Gurley Street.

More ambitious hikers may wish to explore the **Granite Mountain Wilderness**. Of its several trails, the one that goes to the summit of the 7125-foot mountain is **Little Granite Mountain Trail** (3.3 miles), a beautiful all-day hike with an elevation gain of 1500 feet. For information on this and other trails in the area, contact the Prescott National Forest—Bradshaw District ranger station. ~ 2230 East Route 69, just east of Prescott; 928-443-8008.

▼▼▼▼▼▼▼▼▼▼▼▼
Transportation

CAR

One hundred and thirty eight miles north of Phoenix via Route 17, Flagstaff is located on **Route 40**, the main east–west route across northern Arizona. Grand Canyon–bound travelers leaving the interstate at Flagstaff have a choice between the more direct way to Grand Canyon Village, 79 miles via **Route 180**, or the longer way, 105 miles via **Route 89** and **Route 64**, which parallels the canyon rim for 25 miles. These routes combine perfectly into a spectacular loop trip from Flagstaff.

Another scenic loop trip from Flagstaff goes south on **Route 89A**, descending through Oak Creek Canyon to Sedona in Red Rock Country, a distance of 26 slow miles. From Sedona, Route 89A continues for 58 more miles through the historic mining town of Jerome, with a steep climb over Cleopatra Hill, to Prescott, the old territorial capital. From there, a 51-mile drive on Route 89 returns travelers to interstate Route 40 at Ash Fork, about 55 miles west of Flagstaff.

AIR

America West Express flies into **Flagstaff Pulliam Airport** (928-556-1234) and **Prescott Municipal Airport** (928-777-1801).

Sedona Sky Treks (928-282-6628) provides on-demand charter service for travelers from the **Sedona Airport** (928-282-4487).

BUS

Greyhound Bus Lines (800-231-2222; www.greyhound.com) stops at the bus terminals in Flagstaff at 399 South Malpais Lane,

928-774-4573; and in Prescott at 820 East Sheldon Street, 928-445-5470.

Amtrak serves Flagstaff daily on its "Southwest Chief" route be-tween Chicago and Los Angeles. The westbound passenger train stops in Flagstaff late in the evening, so arriving passengers will want to make hotel reservations in advance, with a deposit to hold the room late. Amtrak offers a shuttle bus service to the Grand Canyon for its Flagstaff passengers. ~ 1 East Santa Fe Avenue, Flagstaff; 800-872-7245; www.amtrak.com.

TRAIN

Flagstaff has about a dozen car-rental agencies, most of them at the airport. Among the airport concessions are **Avis Rent A Car** (800-831-2847), **Budget Rent A Car** (800-527-0700) and **Hertz Rent A Car** (800-654-3131).

CAR RENTALS

Located downtown, and more convenient for those arriving by train or bus, is **Budget Rent A Car**. ~ 175 West Aspen; 800-527-0700. Also in Flagstaff is an office of **Cruise America**, a na-tionwide motorhome rental agency. ~ 824 West Route 66; 928-774-4707, 800-327-7799.

At the Sedona Airport, rentals are available from **Arizona Jeep and Car Rentals** (800-879-5337).

For rentals in Prescott try **Hertz Rent A Car** (Prescott Munici-pal Airport; 928-776-1399, 800-654-3131) or **Budget Rent A Car** (1031 Commerce Drive; 928-778-3806, 800-527-0700).

Flagstaff has more than its share of taxi companies because many public transportation travelers stop there en route to the Grand Canyon. These cabs will take you anywhere in central Arizona at any time of day or night. Sedona? Phoenix? No problem. Call **A Friendly Cab** (928-774-4444, 928-214-9000) or **Arizona Taxi and Tours** (928-779-1111). Shop and compare—rates vary.

TAXIS

Sedona's local taxi company is **Bob's Sedona Taxi** (928-282-1234). Prescott's taxi company, **Ace City Cab** (928-445-1616), offers discounted rates for senior citizens.

SEVEN

Western Arizona

Heading west, the mighty Colorado River pours out of the Grand Canyon, spreads itself into Lake Mead, proceeds through a succession of scenic lakes, resorts and riverfront coves, then rolls south until it reaches the Gulf of California. In its wake, visitors to the region will discover a number of unusual points of interest and unparalleled recreational opportunities—each one surrounded by a distinctive landscape, each one quite different from the others. Here, you'll find broad expanses of sparkling water, summer breezes whipping up whitecaps, waterskiers cutting crystal wakes, colorful sails curled above catamarans, and miles of sandy beaches—all along the Colorado River on Arizona's "West Coast."

Kingman is a good starting point for exploring Arizona's western edge. Set at the crossroads of Routes 93 and 40, the town is strategically placed for excursions to Lake Mead and Hoover Dam, Bullhead City/Laughlin and Lake Mohave, Lake Havasu and its London Bridge, and the Parker Strip and Quartzsite. Along the way, you can explore gold and silver mining ghost towns such as Oatman and Chloride, which cling to a tenuous existence amid scenic surroundings. From Kingman, there's also a steep road that leads to the alpine greenery of Hualapai Mountain Park, where you can picnic and camp.

About 80 miles north of Kingman, on Route 93, is manmade Lake Mead, which is shared by Arizona and Nevada. Created in the 1930s when the Colorado River was backed up by Hoover Dam, Lake Mead is a popular recreation area.

In the forbidding, rocky hills of western Arizona's Mojave Desert, real estate promoters used to sell lots in planned communities sight unseen to gullible people in the East. Most of these would-be towns never even came close to reality, but two "cities" set in the middle of nowhere along desolate stretches of the Colorado River have become the twin hubs of a genuine phenomenon.

Bullhead City, one of the fastest-growing cities in Arizona, is an isolated resort community with an area population of about 40,000 people. Founded as the construction camp for Davis Dam, Bullhead City has no visible reason for its existence except daily sunshine, warm weather year-round, boating and fishing access to the Colorado River—and a booming casino strip across the river in Laughlin, at the extreme southern tip of Nevada.

Even more improbable than Bullhead City is Lake Havasu City, which the *Los Angeles Times* once called "the most successful freestanding new town in the United States." Though it enjoys a great wintertime climate and a fine location on the shore of a 46-mile-long desert lake, there is really no logical explanation for Lake Havasu City—except that, in the 1960s, chainsaw tycoon Bob McCulloch and partner C. V. Wood, Jr., planner and first general manager of Disneyland, decided to build it. Since their planned community had no economic base, they concluded that what it needed was a tourist attraction. They came up with a doozie—the London Bridge. Yes, the *real* London Bridge, bought at auction and moved block by massive granite block across the Atlantic, where it was reassembled over a channel to connect to an island in Lake Havasu. The unprecedented, seemingly absurd plan actually worked, and you can see the result for yourself today.

In addition to London Bridge, Lake Havasu City has an "English Village" to complement it. Nearby, the two sections of Lake Havasu State Park are well-developed recreational areas that take advantage of the lake's 46 miles of shoreline. The Windsor Beach Unit on the upper level of the lake has boat ramps, shaded picnic areas, campsites and more primitive camping areas accessible by boat. The Cat-tail Cove Unit has similar facilities, plus a marina, restaurant, store and boat rentals.

Near Parker Dam, which impounds Lake Havasu, Buckskin Mountain State Park attracts tube floaters, boaters and waterskiers. Hiking trails into the Buckskin Mountains lead to panoramic vista points and, for some lucky hikers, sightings of desert bighorn sheep.

About halfway down the "coast," the Bill Williams River empties into the Colorado River just above Parker Dam. Upstream is Alamo Lake, a large man-made reservoir created for recreation and flood control. The lake has bass fishing, swimming, boating, canoeing and views of native wildlife, including the bald and golden eagle.

En route to these unusual Arizona communities, you'll have a chance to visit Havasu National Wildlife Refuge. Keep a sharp eye and you may glimpse a bald eagle, peregrine falcon or desert bighorn sheep, along with a wide variety of other fauna.

Downriver from Parker Dam, the town of Parker and the Colorado River Indian Reservation serve as trade centers and jumping-off points for more recreation. Farther south, the town of Quartzsite, which is more a sprawling RV park than a city, attracts several hundred thousand people late January and early February for its annual rock and mineral shows.

Kingman Area

At the crossroads of Routes 40 and 93, Kingman has earned a reputation as a comfortable stopover for travelers hurrying between Phoenix and Las Vegas or Los Angeles and Albuquerque. It is also a natural hub for leisurely trips to nearby ghost towns, Hoover Dam, Lake Mead and other recreational resorts along the Colorado River.

SIGHTS   **Kingman** was named for surveyor Lewis Kingman, who passed through the area in 1892 while charting a railroad route between Needles, California, and Albuquerque, New Mexico. The railroad camp subsequently built here took his name, but the town didn't flourish until the early 1900s, when silver and copper deposits were discovered in the surrounding hills. The mines were depleted by the 1940s, but the town survived as an important pit stop for travelers on the Santa Fe railway and old Route 66.

With more than 30 motels and 50 restaurants, modern-day Kingman continues its tradition as a key provisioning center. Most of the commercial activity has shifted to Motel Row—East Andy Devine Avenue—and suburban shopping centers, but there are a few historical gems around town worth seeing. To find out about them, stop at the **Powerhouse Visitors Center**, which dispenses maps, brochures and a listing of the area's annual events and festivals. Be sure to ask for a map of downtown's historic district tour. The center also houses the Historic Route 66 Association of Arizona, which offers information on the old transcontinental highway. ~ 120 West Andy Devine Avenue, Kingman; 928-753-6106, fax 928-753-6156; www.kingmanchamber.org, e-mail info@kingmanchamber.org.

An interesting stop is the **Mohave Museum of History and Arts**, which gives visitors a glimpse of many of the unusual aspects of northwestern Arizona. A mural and dioramas in the lobby depict the settlement of the region and show how camels used to be used as beasts of burden in these parts. Kingman is the source of much of the turquoise mined in the United States, and the museum has a fine collection of carved turquoise objects. American Indian exhibits include portrayals of the traditional ways of the Hualapai and Mohave tribes. Other rooms contain a collection of paintings of U.S. presidents and their first ladies by artist Lawrence Williams, as well as memorabilia of the town's most famous native son, the late actor Andy Devine. Closed Sunday. Admission. ~ 400 West Beale Street, Kingman; phone/fax 928-753-3195; www.mohavemuseum.org, e-mail mocohist@ctaz.com.

A drive through the older section of Kingman, away from the chain-store motels and generic coffee shops, reveals a turn-of-the-20th-century downtown area that is gradually being revitalized. For the time being, you can still admire the architectural splendor the proud buildings once enjoyed, from Victorian mansions to simple adobe shacks. Some of the sights on the chamber's historic district tour include the Spanish Colonial **Santa Fe Railroad Depot** at Andy Devine Avenue and 4th Street; the mission revival–style IOOF building at 5th and Beale streets; the classic Greek-style tufa-stone, glass-domed **Mohave County Courthouse** at Spring and 4th streets; and, just east of the museum, **Loco-**

Western Arizona

motive Park, where you'll find a 1927 Baldwin steam engine and bright red caboose as the centerpiece.

About an hour's drive east of Kingman are the **Grand Canyon Caverns**, limestone caves with selenite crystals and marine fossils dating back three million years. Guided tours begin with a 21-story elevator ride below ground to the cavern floors for a 45-minute walk along lighted trails equipped with handrails. Above ground are an information center, gift shop and restaurant. Admission. ~ Route 66, 12 miles east of Peach Springs; 928-422-4565, fax 928-422-4470; www.gcctaverns.com, e-mail gcca@tabletop telephone.com.

LODGING It seems nearly every motel chain is represented in Kingman. Most are located along East Andy Devine Avenue and West Beale Street, and provide dependable lodging. Among the nicer ones, the **Quality Inn** features modern guest rooms, equipped with microwaves and refrigerators. Fitness buffs will like its pool, sauna and workout room. Full breakfast buffet is included. ~ 1400 East Andy Devine Avenue, Kingman; 928-753-4747, 800-869-3252, fax 928-753-5175. BUDGET TO MODERATE.

In the downtown area, the **Arizona Inn** is within walking distance from the historic downtown sights. Comfortable rooms are decorated with dark-wood furniture and cool pastels. ~ 411 West Beale Street, Kingman; 928-753-5521, fax 928-753-6579. BUDGET.

In a town that seems to consist mainly of brand-name motor inns, the historic **Hotel Brunswick** is a refreshing exception. This three-story edifice was the tallest building in western Arizona when it was built in 1909. Abandoned in the 1970s, it has gone through several transformations. Now it's a European-style boutique hotel. The lobby is filled with period antiques, and the guest rooms have eclectic blends of contemporary and old-fashioned furnishings. Rooms vary greatly in size, from economical "cowboy/cowgirl" singles with shared baths to lavish suites with full kitchens. ~ 315 East Andy Devine Avenue, Kingman; 928-718-1800, fax 928-718-1801; www.hotel-brunswick.com, e-mail rsvp@hotel-brunswick.com. BUDGET TO DELUXE.

HIDDEN ▶ In the ghost town of Oatman, the old **Oatman Hotel** is the place to stay. The authentic two-story adobe, with eight guest rooms, an arched facade, and corrugated iron walls and ceilings may induce you to take a room, as it did Clark Gable and Carole Lombard on their wedding night after a surprise ceremony in Kingman. One of her dresses is displayed in the honeymoon suite. Otherwise, opt for the room inhabited by Oatie, the inn's resident ghost. Don't miss the downstairs museum of old movie posters, rusty mining equipment and period antiques. Oatman was on the main highway—Route 66—to Hollywood back then. Closed in August. ~ Route 66, Oatman; 928-768-4408, fax 928-788-2425. BUDGET.

Dozens of chain restaurants and coffee shops line East Andy Devine Avenue in Kingman, but for some local flavor try **The Kingman Deli**, where the chili is thick and flavorful, and there are over three dozen types of sandwiches. Sample the popular "Sneaky Snake" with ham, turkey, roast beef and swiss cheese, or the "Tumbleweed" with cucumber, avocado, sprouts, tomatoes and swiss cheese. No dinner. Closed Saturday and Sunday. ~ 419 East Beale Street, Kingman; 928-753-4151. BUDGET.

Ask Kingman locals where to find fine dining and they're likely to recommend **Dambar's Steakhouse**, a restaurant equally suited to family-night-out and Friday-night-date clientele. The fare is a selection of beef cuts big and juicy enough to lure the burliest trucker off the interstate. Non-meat eaters can choose a pasta dish or request a special vegetable plate. ~ 1960 East Andy Devine Avenue, Kingman; 928-753-3523, fax 928-718-3500. MODERATE TO DELUXE.

For your Mexican-food fix, visit **El Palacio** of Kingman. In addition to the usual standard items, the menu is peppered with dishes you don't usually find in your typical burrito joint. Try the simmered stew of tripe and hominy, or the *chile relleno* burrito. ~ 401 East Andy Devine Avenue, Kingman; 928-718-0018, fax 928-758-3792. BUDGET TO MODERATE.

Most of Kingman's commercial activity takes place along Stockton Hill Road and Andy Devine Avenue, two streets that intersect in the downtown area. There's not much before this intersection, but one exception is **Classy Collections**, a quaint little shop featuring Victorian-style antiques and gifts. Closed Sunday. ~ 421 Beale Street, Kingman; 928-753-5002.

NIGHTLIFE   **The Fountain,** a charming café that serves up gourmet coffee drinks, is open until 10 p.m. on Friday nights with occasional entertainment. ~ 310 East Beale Street, Kingman; 928-718-2333. Or you can catch a flick at **The Movies.** ~ 4055 Stockton Hill Road, Kingman; 928-757-7985.

Locals head to **Mulligan's Bar** at the Hotel Brunswick. Billed as a "businessman's bar," there's an understated tone to the place, and you can find international beers and cigars. ~ 315 East Andy Devine Avenue, Kingman; 928-718-1800; www.hotel-brunswick.com.

PARKS   **HUALAPAI MOUNTAIN PARK** 🏃 This island of forested slopes in the middle of the Mojave Desert is a locally popular picnicking, camping and hiking area. These mountains were once the ancestral home of the Hualapai Indians, until they were forced to relocate by the U.S. military in the 1870s. The Hualapai, whose name translates to "pine-tree folk," now live farther north on a reservation at the west end of the Grand Canyon. Managed by the Mohave County Parks Department, the park offers cool, protected habitat for wildlife including deer, elk, coyotes and occasional mountain lions. There are picnic areas, restrooms, cabins, a softball diamond and hiking trails. Day-use fee, $5. ~ Located 14 miles southeast of Kingman on the paved Hualapai Mountain Park Road; 928-757-0915, fax 928-757-5662; www.hualapai mountainpark.com.

▲ There are 70 tent sites, as well as 11 RV hookups available May to September; $10 per vehicle per night for tent sites, $17 for hookups. Besides tent and RV campgrounds, there are 15 cabins built in the 1930s as part of a Civilian Conservation Corps camp that can be rented for the night ($35 to $75 per night). Reservations are required for cabins: 928-757-0915, 877-757-0915.

▼▼▼▼▼▼▼▼▼▼▼▼

Lake Mead Area

Downriver from the Grand Canyon, the Colorado River turns into a series of manmade desert lakes formed by the dams of the Colorado River Project, which provides: electricity for Southern California, a steady supply of irrigation water for Imperial Valley agriculture, and flood control for all the communities along the once-raging river. With Nevada and California on the other side, the river and lakes form the Arizona state line.

SIGHTS   The largest of the reservoirs is 110-mile-long **Lake Mead,** about 80 miles north of Kingman on Route 93, not far from Las Vegas. Created when the Colorado River was backed up by Hoover Dam from 1935 to 1938, Lake Mead is a popular destination for boating, fishing, windsurfing, waterskiing, lying on the beach or ex-

Exploring Western Arizona

It's easy to see most of the western Arizona sights that are reachable by car in a single day. (If you had a boat here, of course, you could spend weeks exploring the areas where roads don't go.)

- Start early. From Route 40 Exit 9, a half hour south of Kingman or Bullhead City, drive south on Route 95 for 21 miles to Lake Havasu City. Walk across **London Bridge** (page 200), pondering why this improbable anachronism ranks as Arizona's second-biggest tourist attraction. Allow half an hour, or more if you take a cruise on Lake Havasu. Leave before it gets crowded and hot.

- Return to Route 40. Go west on the interstate to Exit 1, then head north on Route 95 for four miles to Oatman Road. Follow this remnant of old Route 66 to the touristy ex–ghost town of **Oatman** (page 207). In Oatman, pet a "wild" burro. Watch a Wild West shootout. Tour the funky hotel where Gable and Lombard spent a night on their honeymoon. Allow one hour.

- Continue for 27 more miles on Oatman Road, past the ghost town of Goldroad and over Sitgreave Pass, from which you'll get a great view of Kingman (where you'll be in less than half an hour).

- Stop for lunch in Kingman. (See page 187 for dining suggestions.)

- Drive north from Kingman on Route 93 for about eight miles to the marked road that turns off to the east and goes to **Chloride** (page 207). Park your car and spend half an hour strolling the streets (both of them) in this eccentric little ghost town.

- Backtrack to Kingman. Continue through town and follow Hualapai Mountain Park Road for 14 miles to **Hualapai Mountain Park** (page 188), where you'll spend the hottest part of the afternoon walking among the shady pines here. Return to Kingman, Bullhead City or Route 40 before dark.

IF YOU HAVE MORE TIME

Head north to see **Hoover Dam** (page 190) and explore **Lake Mead** (page 188). By the time you get there, you'll be just over the hill from Las Vegas, Nevada—a completely different adventure.

ploring hidden coves and inlets by houseboat. The sheer size of the lake—700 miles of shoreline and nine trillion gallons of water—and the surrounding jagged canyons and desert sand dunes are reason enough to visit the largest manmade lake in the United States.

The lake is a special favorite of anglers, who take a run at largemouth bass, rainbow, brown and cutthroat trout, catfish and black crappie. Striped bass, which can reach 50 pounds, are the most popular game fish in recent years.

A good way to learn about the lake is to stop at the **Lake Mead Visitors Center**. Located midway between Boulder City and Hoover Dam, the center's botanical garden, exhibits and short movie shown periodically throughout the day describe the area's history and attractions. There are also books for sale that can provide more in-depth information on the area's history, flora and fauna. ~ Route 93 and Lakeshore Road, Boulder City, NV; 702-293-8906, fax 702-293-8936; www.nps.gov/lame, e-mail lame_interpretation@nps.gov.

The easiest way to access Lake Mead from the isolated Arizona shore is at **Temple Bar Marina**. You'll find moderate-priced lodging, a café, gas and provisions here. This is the last outpost for supplies if you plan to boat north of Temple Bar. ~ Reached by a well-marked, paved 28-mile road that turns off Route 93 about 55 miles north of Kingman; 928-767-3211, 800-752-9669.

Hoover Dam, which impounds Lake Mead, was a tourist attraction in the area even before the first casino was built on the Las Vegas Strip. This huge dam rises 726 feet above the river and generates four billion kilowatt-hours of electricity in a year. Containing over three million cubic yards of concrete, it was completed in 1935. Its Depression-era origins are evident in the art deco motifs that decorate the top of the dam, including two huge Winged Figure of the Republic statues and a terrazzo floor patterned with mystical cosmic symbols.

Discovery Tours allows guests to explore the dam at their own pace. Staff give informal talks every 15 minutes at various stops along the self-guided tour. Purchase tickets at the **Hoover Dam Visitors Center,** which hosts a variety of exhibits and has a stunning overlook. From the center, board an elevator and head into the depths of the dam for further exploration. Admission. ~ 702-294-3524, 866-291-8687, fax 702-294-3585; www.hooverdam.usbr.gov.

Although more remote, **South Cove/Pearce Ferry** is recommended for its scenic vistas of the lake and craggy peaks of Iceberg Canyon, about 46 miles east of Hoover Dam. Take Route 93 north from Kingman about 40 miles to the Dolan Springs turnoff and drive east. After passing Dolan Springs, you'll enter a massive forest of Joshua trees and the retirement resort of Mead-view. Soon, you'll begin to catch glimpses of Lake Mead, from atop Grapevine Mesa. South Cove has only a boat ramp, a picnic area and toilets, but it offers a serene respite, accented by the deep blue waters of Lake Mead and rough-hewn mountains that frame it. The final four-mile stretch of dirt road to Pearce Ferry drops down through steep canyon walls and granite buttes. At the shoreline are primitive campsites, a picnic area, an unpaved boat ramp and plenty of peace and quiet. If the rocky granite corridors remind you of the Grand Canyon, it's because the park's western boundary is just a mile east of here.

There's also a scenic drive that runs along the Nevada side of the lake, where there are more marinas, a campground, a popular public beach and a few small resorts. Take Route 166 from Boulder City through the washes and canyons above the lake until you reach **Northshore Road** (Routes 147 and 167). You can stay on the highway that follows the shoreline all the way to the Valley of Fire State Park, or drop down to the lake at Las Vegas Bay, Callville Bay, Echo Bay or Overton Beach. You'll find food and facilities at all four resorts.

LODGING & DINING

The only lodging on the Arizona shore of Lake Mead is at Temple Bar Marina, where you can rent a room at the modern **Temple Bar Resort,** or one of the older cabins with kitchenettes. You'll also find a restaurant, cocktail lounge, campground, RV park, boat-launching ramp, fuel dock and store. This is the last outpost for supplies if you plan to boat north of Temple Bar. Limited menu

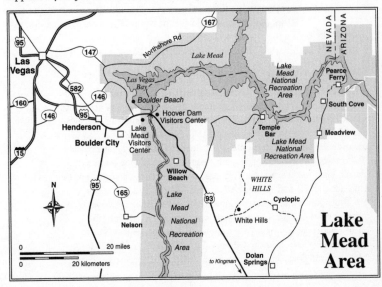

in January and February. ~ 928-767-3211, 800-752-9669, fax 928-767-3033; www.sevencrown.com. BUDGET TO MODERATE.

There's a motel on the Nevada shore of the lake at **Echo Bay Resort and Marina**. Along with a restaurant and lounge, the motel offers modern rooms, an RV village and an airstrip for light aircraft (day-use only). ~ Overton, NV; 702-394-4000, fax 702-394-4182, 800-752-9669; www.sevencrown.com. MODERATE.

Located about a half-mile north of Boulder Beach, **Lake Mead Resort and Marina** has hundreds of boat slips and a popular floating restaurant, coffee shop and cocktail lounge. The marina also operates a lodge (702-293-2074) down the road with 42 budget-priced rooms. Limited menu off-season. ~ 322 Lakeshore Road; 702-293-3484, fax 702-293-3835; www.sevencrown.com. BUDGET TO MODERATE.

You can also camp or park your RV ($10 for tents, $20 for hookups) at **Callville Bay Resort Marina**, which has a boat launch, store, snack bar and cocktail lounge. The marina rents everything from jet skis to 65-foot houseboats. ~ HCR 30, Box 100, Las Vegas, NV 89124; 702-565-8958, 702-565-8498; www.foreverresorts.com, e-mail fresorts-usa@foreverliving.com. BUDGET.

PARKS

BOULDER BEACH 🏃 🚴 🏊 🛶 ⛵ 🚤 ⚓ Most of Lake Mead's shoreline consists of rocks and gravel, but you can spread a beach towel at Boulder Beach. The two miles of beach and the clear water of Lake Mead attract year-round sunbathers. The clear water and warm temperatures attract divers, who can explore the sunken yachts *Tortuga*, near the Boulder Islands, and the *Cold Duck*, submerged in 35 feet of water. There are picnic areas, rest-

AUTHOR FAVORITE

The most awesome roadside sight on the lower Colorado River is Hoover Dam after dark, when it's floodlit all the way down into the pitch-darkness of Black Canyon. When the full moon sparkles on Lake Mead, it's better than London Bridge! Lake Mead Cruises offers a **Hoover Dam cruise** aboard a three-deck paddleboat, the *Desert Princess*. The 100-foot-long sternwheeler is the largest vessel to ply the waters of the lake, and features a snack bar, two glass-enclosed decks, an open promenade deck, an 80-seat dining room, cocktail lounge and dancefloor. The late afternoon cruise features a sunset dinner and stunning views of illuminated Hoover Dam. Cruises leave several times a day from the Lake Mead cruises landing, next to the Las Vegas Boat Harbor, 490-B Horsepower Cove, Boulder City, NV; 702-293-6180, fax 702-293-0343; www.lakemeadcruises.com, e-mail info@lakemeadcruises.com.

rooms, a restaurant and a ranger station. ~ Located two miles north of the Lake Mead Visitors Center; 702-293-8990.

▲ There are over 150 sites; $10 per night for tents and self-contained RVs. Privately owned **Lake Mead RV** (702-293-2540) offers full RV hookups from $22.

Bullhead City, 35 miles west of Kingman via Route 68, owes its prosperity to Laughlin, Nevada, on

Bullhead City/Laughlin Area

the far side of the river. The city of Laughlin is a shimmering riverfront resort that has blossomed into Nevada's third-largest gambling center. Because it has few residential and commercial areas of its own, most of the thousands of people who work there live and shop in its Arizona sister, Bullhead City. Laughlin is packed to overflowing every weekend. The rest of the week, the casinos, buffets, lounges and showrooms play host to motorhome nomads who appreciate the opportunity to avoid Las Vegas traffic and avail themselves of Laughlin's vast, free RV parking lots.

But gambling isn't the only attraction in the Bullhead City/ Laughlin area. Originally established in 1984 as a retirement town, Bullhead City has matured quickly into a community of more than 40,000—the largest in western Arizona—where residents fall into all age groups and many occupations, from hospitality workers and RV salespeople to telecommuters. The Colorado River and nearby Lake Mohave are major draws, offering year-round water sports such as swimming, boating, fishing and waterskiing. Also within short driving distance are ghost towns, historic mines, and intriguing lost canyons waiting to be explored.

Commercial boat cruises are a popular pastime. Before the bridge across the Colorado River was built in the mid-1980s, visitors used to park on the Arizona side of the river and ride **passenger ferries** across to the casinos on the Nevada shore. Now, on busy weekends when parking lots in Laughlin are full, the ferries still carry people across the river, making for a brief, fun and, best of all, free cruise. Several companies also offer longer riverboat sightseeing tours down the river from casino docks. One is **Laughlin River Tours,** which runs the *Fiesta Queen* and *Celebration* paddlewheel steamers from the Edgewater Casino dock and the Flamingo Hilton dock. Both are available for on-board weddings. Closed Sunday. ~ P.O. Box 29279, Laughlin, NV 89028; 702-298-1047, 800-228-9825, fax 702-298-8259.

SIGHTS

Bullhead City was incorporated in 1984, but it was founded in 1945 when it was the construction camp for Davis Dam, three miles upstream. The town, named for a rock formation now submerged by Lake Mohave, is a collection of lowrise housing tracts, shopping centers and mobile home parks. New housing developments and retirement communities along the Colorado River—Riviera, Fort Mohave and Golden Shores—have extended Bullhead City's outskirts as far south as Topock, at the junction of Route 40.

The best time to visit Bullhead City/Laughlin is in the winter and spring months, when the daytime temperatures range from 65 to 80°. Temperatures in July and August can reach an astounding 120° or more, making this area the hottest spot in the nation.

There's not much to see or do in Bullhead City, unless pre-fab homes and tilt-up shopping centers are your idea of excitement. So it's no surprise that the most-visited attraction in the area is the strip of casinos across the water on the river's western shore. Unlike their larger cousins on the famed Las Vegas Strip, the Laughlin hotel/casinos are close together and are easily accessible by a concrete strand that follows the river. The best is the **Colorado Belle**, a 600-foot replica of a Mississippi steamboat, complete with three decks and four black smokestacks. In the evening, the paddlewheel "turns" by timed neon light. Inside, the decor is turn-of-the-20th-century New Orleans, with lots of plush red carpeting, glass-globe lamps, brass railings and wrought-iron fixtures. The cluster of shops on the mezzanine level has several restaurants and an old-fashioned candy store. ~ 2100 South Casino Drive, Laughlin; 702-298-4000, 866-352-3553, fax 702-299-4129; www.colo radobelle.com.

For a bit of Dodge City by the river try the **Pioneer Hotel and Gambling Hall** next door. The two-story hotel looks like a U-shaped fort, finished with weathered wood panels. The facade of the casino entrance suggests a Wild West boarding house. Swinging doors and a wooden porch lead into a hectic casino. On the river side of the hotel is a waving neon cowboy, River Rick. Laughlin's version of Vegas Vic. The grounds facing the river include a lush flower garden, green grass and shade trees. ~ 2200 South Casino Drive, Laughlin; 702-298-2442, fax 702-298-7462, 800-634-3469; www.pioneerlaughlin.com.

Also worth visiting is the **Don Laughlin's Riverside Resort Hotel & Casino**. Be sure to stop in at the antiques shop just off the casino. The small but interesting collection consists of slot machines, jukeboxes, vintage radios, antique cars and a variety of old neon signs. On display, but not for sale, are antique slots from Don Laughlin's personal collection, including a 1938 vest pocket slot machine and a 1931 slot that paid off in golf balls. The resort also has a 34-lane bowling center. ~ 1650 South Casino Drive, Laughlin; 702-298-2535, 800-227-3849, fax 702-298-2612; www.riversideresort.com.

The **Davis Dam and Powerplant** was built in 1953 to produce hydroelectric power and regulate water delivery to Mexico. Along with Hoover Dam to the north and Parker Dam, about 80 miles downstream, these three dams comprise the Lower Colorado River Dams project. They also divert river water to form three lakes: Lake Mead, Lake Mohave and Lake Havasu. Another six large dams in Colorado, Utah and New Mexico also control the waters of the mighty Colorado. The powerplant, downstream from the dam embankment on the Arizona side of the river, is no longer open to the public, but you can walk across the top of the dam for a scenic view of the Colorado River and the Bullhead City–Laughlin area downstream. ~ About three miles north of Bullhead City on Route 68; 928-754-3628, fax 928-754-3620; www.lc.usbr.gov.

Behind the dam lies **Lake Mohave** (part of the Lake Mead National Recreation Area), which extends 67 miles upstream to Hoover Dam. The long, narrow lake (four miles across at its widest point) provides a multitude of recreational opportunities, including fishing, boating, waterskiing and windsurfing. Most of Lake Mohave's shoreline cannot be reached by road because it is flanked by steep cliffs. For boaters, popular destinations include a number of hot springs—including hot waterfalls—along the riverbanks and in side canyons, especially in the Willow Beach area.

Lake Mohave is accessible at only two points in Arizona: Willow Beach, off Route 93 about 60 miles north of Kingman, and Katherine Landing, six miles north of Bullhead City and Laughlin. Canoers can launch below Hoover Dam and paddle down spectacular Black Canyon to Willow Beach, a distance of about 12 miles. (It is not possible to go farther down the lake by canoe because the distance is too great to transport enough drinking water.) **Lake Mohave Resort**, six miles north of Bullhead City, rents houseboats, bass boats and other craft for use on Lake Mohave. ~ Katherine Landing; 928-754-3245, 800-752-9669; www.sevencrown.com. **Willow Beach Harbor** also provides small boat rentals. ~ 928-767-4747.

On the Nevada shore of Lake Mohave is **Cottonwood Cove Resort**. Facilities include a marina, a motel, boat rentals, a campground and a small RV park. ~ 702-297-1464; www.foreverresorts.com.

TICKET TO RIDE

Casino hopping requires time and energy some would consider better spent at the tables rather than getting to them. Laughlin's Silver Rider operates two daily bus routes for $1.50 a ride. For a more scenic trip, water taxis on the Colorado River transport gamblers to the casinos of their choice at $2 for a one-way ticket, and $3 for roundtrip. May Lady Luck be with you!

LODGING   On Sunday through Thursday nights, rooms cost significantly less in the casino hotels of Laughlin, Nevada, than they do in Bullhead City on the Arizona side of the Colorado River. In fact, on week-nights, you can rent a spacious, modern room with a king-size bed, remote control television, and designer wallpaper in Laughlin for about the same rate as a plain, somewhat threadbare room in an aging mom-and-pop motel by the interstate in Kingman.

Although there are 10,000 hotel rooms in Laughlin, busy week-ends often attract up to 50,000 visitors. You don't need a calcu-lator to figure the result: Reservations are a must.

For most visitors to the Bullhead City/Laughlin area, there is probably not much point to staying on the Arizona side of the river. Most of the motels in Bullhead City are clean and modern but unexceptional, and room rates tend to run higher than in the Laughlin casino hotels. Most tend toward weekly or monthly accommodations. They seem to thrive on weekend and peak-season overflows.

For half the year, Bullhead City, AZ, is one hour ahead of Laughlin, NV, which is in another time zone. The rest of the time Nevada switches to daylight-saving time and you won't need to adjust your watch each time you cross the Colorado River.

It's hard to believe that many people with aversions to the gambling scene would go out of their way to stay in Bullhead City when they could as easily proceed south to the more family-oriented Lake Havasu City. But if they did, they'd find good noncasino lodging in Bullhead City at the **Bullhead River Lodge**. It is an all-suite motel that rents by the week or month, ideal for families, with a boat and fishing dock available for use at no charge. ~ 455 Moser Avenue, Bullhead City; 928-754-2250; e-mail gentry@ctaz.com. BUDGET.

Operated by the same folks who run Bullhead River Lodge, **Hilltop Hotel** has 57 rooms and suites. Laundry facilities are available, as well as beach dock, fishing and boating privileges at Bullhead River Lodge. ~ 2037 Route 95, Bullhead City; 928-758-6620, fax 928-758-6612; e-mail gentry@ctaz.com. BUDGET.

Just a stone's throw from the Colorado River, **Gretchen's Inn** is a small but modern hostelry, with a Southwest motif. The rooms, some with river views, are exceptionally large and tastefully dec-orated. Suites and kitchenettes are available. ~ 1081 Route 95, Bullhead City; 928-754-2440, 800-643-6723, fax 928-754-2526. BUDGET TO MODERATE.

Set on a prime lakefront location, the **Lake Mohave Resort** features a private boat launch and landscaped grounds for spot-ting quail, roadrunners and jackrabbits. Accommodations, which are basic motel-style rooms decorated with blue fabrics and desert artwork, all face the lake. ~ 2690 East Katherine Spur Road; 928-754-3245, 800-752-9669, fax 928-754-1125; www.sevencrown.com. MODERATE.

Top of the line, and the closest to the bridge across the river from Bullhead City, is **Don Laughlin's Riverside Resort Hotel & Casino**. The resort's owner conceived the idea of promoting a casino strip here, founded the town that is named after him, and in 1966 converted the old Riverside Bait Shop on this site into Laughlin's first casino. There is also a 26-story hotel tower, swimming pools and a nonsmoking casino. ~ 1650 South Casino Drive, Laughlin; 702-298-2535, 800-227-3849, fax 702-298-2612; www.riversideresort.com. BUDGET.

It's not quite the Reading, but you can ride the rails on a mini-passenger train at the **Ramada Express**. The narrow-gauge railroad shuttles you on a 15-minute ride from the parking lot to the casino, decorated like a Victorian railroad station. Guest rooms in the 1501-room towers behind the casino feature deep green carpets with burgundy walls and dark wood furniture. ~ 2121 South Casino Drive, Laughlin; 702-298-4200, 800-243-6846, fax 702-298-6403; www.ramadaexpress.com, e-mail info@ramada express.com. BUDGET TO MODERATE.

Some of the other hotels are famous-name spinoffs from well-known Las Vegas and Reno establishments, such as the **Flamingo Laughlin**, which is the town's largest with 2000 rooms. ~ 1900 South Casino Drive; 702-298-5111, 800-352-6464, fax 702-298-5177; www.laughlinflamingo.com. MODERATE. Or try the 300-room **Golden Nugget**. ~ 2300 South Casino Drive; 702-298-7111, 800-950-7700, fax 702-298-7279; www.gnlaughlin.com. Another option is **Harrah's Laughlin**, a very nice hotel over a hill from the others at the south end of Casino Row. ~ 2900 South Casino Drive; 702-298-4600, 800-427-7247, fax 702-298-6896. BUDGET TO DE-LUXE. The **Colorado Belle**, a showy casino hotel shaped like a giant riverboat midway down the strip, was created by the same company that owns Circus Circus and the Excalibur in Las Vegas. ~ 2100 South Casino Drive; 702-298-4000, 800-477-4837, 702-298-0671; www.coloradobelle.com. BUDGET TO MODERATE.

The covered terrace and pool area at **River Palms Resort and Casino** with its palm trees, green lawns and river view is a great spot for lounging. Inside, the 1000 rooms are bright and airy with plush carpeting, smoked-glass tables and velour-upholstered chairs. Be sure to check out the casino with its high ceilings and tropical decor. ~ 2700 South Casino Drive, Laughlin; 702-298-2242, 800-835-7904; www.rvrpalm.com. BUDGET TO MODERATE.

There is also the 26-story **Edgewater Hotel**, a 1421-unit highrise. ~ 2020 South Casino Drive; 702-298-2453, 800-677-4837, fax 702-298-8165; www.edgewater-casino.com. BUDGET TO ULTRA-DELUXE.

Along with a nice view of Lake Mohave, Lake Mohave Resort's restaurant **Tail of the Whale** serves a tasty grilled catfish and other

DINING

seafood dishes, plus steaks and chops. ~ Katherine Landing just above Davis Dam; 928-754-3245, fax 928-754-1125. MODERATE.

Each casino also has a full-service 24-hour coffee shop, many of them featuring $1.99 breakfast specials. Notable among the 24-hour casual places is **Flamingo Diner**, a classic '50s-style diner and coffee shop. ~ Flamingo Laughlin, 1900 South Casino Drive; 702-298-5111, 800-352-6464, fax 702-298-5177; www.laughlin flamingo.com. BUDGET TO MODERATE.

Many, though not all, casinos also have slightly more upscale fine-dining restaurants. **Harrah's Laughlin** offers an intimate atmosphere and a riverside view at the Range Steakhouse. Reservations suggested. Closed Sunday. ~ 2900 South Casino Drive; 702-298-4600, 800-427-7247, fax 702-298-6896. DELUXE.

Another option is the **Prime Rib Room**, where you can supervise the carving at your table. ~ Riverside Resort, 1650 South Casino Drive, Laughlin; 702-298-2535. BUDGET TO MODERATE. Yet another choice is the **Alta Villa** for Continental-style cuisine. ~ Flamingo Laughlin, 1900 South Casino Drive, Laughlin; 702-298-5111. MODERATE TO DELUXE.

In the **Colorado Belle**, you can order a steak, seafood or pasta in the casually classy Orleans Room. Dinner only. Next door, the **Mississippi Lounge** is the only fresh seafood bar in Laughlin. ~ 2100 South Casino Drive; 702-298-4000, 800-477-4837, fax 702-298-0671; www.coloradobelle.com. MODERATE TO ULTRA-DELUXE.

River Palms serves fine American and Continental selections in The Lodge, designed in a hunting lodge theme with wood-beamed ceiling and big stone fireplace, all so convincing that you may forget that you're in a casino. Reservations suggested. Dinner only. ~ 2700 Casino Drive; 702-298-2242; www.rvrpalm. com, e-mail info@rvrpalm.com. MODERATE TO ULTRA-DELUXE.

Country cooking is never out of reach at the **Boarding House Restaurant** at the Pioneer Hotel, where you can feast on a din-

AUTHOR FAVORITE

In Laughlin, I hit the casinos for inexpensive feasts. Just about every hotel on Casino Row has an all-you-can-eat buffet featuring 40 or more items, in the budget range for dinner and almost absurdly affordable—no more than you'd spend at a franchise hamburger joint—for breakfast and lunch. To sweeten the deal even more, two-for-one buffet coupons are included in free "fun books" widely distributed in visitors centers and truck stops in Kingman and elsewhere along Route 40. The largest buffet in town is located at the **Edgewater Hotel**. ~ 2020 South Casino Drive; 702-298-2453; www.edgewater-casino.com, e-mail jcarey@mrgmail.com. BUDGET.

ner of fried chicken, barbecued ribs, prime rib or baked ham. These entrées are also available during their daily buffet. Go easy on the cornbread and save room for homemade strawberry shortcake. Open 24 hours. ~ 2200 South Casino Drive, Laughlin; 702-298-2442. BUDGET TO MODERATE.

Shoppers will delight in the bargains found at **Horizon Outlet Center**, which brings together more than 50 shops offering everything from clothing, shoes and jewelry to perfumes and luggage. Among them are **Gap Outlet, Reebok/Rockport, Maidenform, Mikasa, Levi's Outlet** and **Van Heusen**. ~ 1955 South Casino Drive, Laughlin; 702-298-3003. **SHOPPING**

Nightlife on the river all happens in Laughlin, where each of the casinos has at least one, often two, cocktail lounges that don't charge for watching musical acts that perform here while practicing for Las Vegas. Only one of the casinos has a showroom where name acts appear: **Don's Celebrity Theatre** has hosted such performers as Roy Clark, the Smothers Brothers, the Oakridge Boys and Vicki Lawrence. Cover. ~ Don Laughlin's Riverside Resort Hotel & Casino, 1650 South Casino Drive; 702-298-2535, 800-227-3849, fax 702-298-2612; www.riversideresort.com. The resort also has a lounge and rock-and-roll danceclub (known as the "Loser's Lounge"), as well as six movie theaters. **NIGHTLIFE**

Also at the Riverside, the **Lightning Strikes Ballroom** features a deejay and dancing to country music. Every Sunday afternoon there's also a tea dance in the ballroom.

The town's only production show is staged at the **Club Flamingo** in the Flamingo Hilton. Past acts have included top comedians and a Broadway-style revue. **Flamingo Spring and Fall Concert Series** at the Flamingo's outdoor amphitheater usually features nostalgic acts the likes of Wynonna, the Four Tops and the Beach Boys. Cover at both facilities. ~ 1900 South Casino Drive, Laughlin; 702-298-5111, 800-435-8469.

The **Colorado River** and **Lake Mohave** provide a multitude of recreational activities, including boating, fishing, waterskiing, scuba diving and windsurfing. Landlubbing hikers will love the desert and canyons surrounding Bullhead City/Laughlin. Lake Mohave above Davis Dam actually resembles the river below the dam—the lake stretches for 67 miles through jagged canyons and rocky mountains. At its widest point, it is only four miles from shore to shore. **PARKS**

KATHERINE LANDING Located just 640 feet above sea level along Lake Mohave, Katherine Landing's flora and fauna is representative of the surrounding Mojave Desert. Short hikes into the area reveal desert shrubs, cacti and roadrunners, as well as views of the Black and Newberry mountains in the distance. There's striped bass, bluegill and channel catfish for anglers, and there's good swimming at South Telephone Cove. There are restrooms, pay showers, laundry facilities, a picnic area, a full-service marina with boat rentals, fishing tackle and waterski rentals, a motel, a restaurant, a grocery store and a visitors center. ~ Located just north of Bullhead City off Route 68; 928-754-3272, fax 928-754-5614; www.nps.gov/lame.

▲ There are 167 campsites, each with a barbecue grill and a picnic table; the campground has running water; $10 per night.

DAVIS CAMP COUNTY PARK Here at the only public beach on the Colorado River you'll find a stretch of sandy beach where you can swim, fish or launch a jet ski. You can angle here for striped bass, catfish and trout, and there's a marked off swimming area good for children. At the south end of the park is a marsh that's home to variety of birds and other small wildlife. There are restrooms, showers, laundry facilities, barbecue grills and ramadas with picnic tables. Day-use fee, $5. ~ Located about one mile north of Laughlin on the Arizona side of the river; 928-754-7250, fax 928-754-7253; www.daviscamp.com, e-mail info@daviscamp.com.

▲ There are 141 sites with full hookups ($17 per night), partial hookups ($14 per night) and an open area for tent camping ($10 per night).

WILLOW BEACH Nearby, you can take a self-guided tour of the Willow Beach National Fish Hatchery (928-767-3456) that keeps Lake Mohave stocked. Bait, tackle and fishing licenses are available at the dock; try for trout and striped bass. There are restrooms, picnic grounds, barbecue grills, boat rentals, fuel and a grocery store. ~ On Lake Mohave, about 14 miles south of Hoover Dam off of Route 93; 928-767-4747, fax 928-767-3736.

▼▼▼▼▼▼▼▼▼▼▼▼

Lake Havasu Area

About 20 miles upstream from Parker Dam, Lake Havasu may be the prettiest dammed lake along the Colorado River. Cool and bright blue in the heart of the desert, this 46-mile-long lake has become a very popular recreation area.

SIGHTS   Lake Havasu's main claim to fame is **London Bridge** in Lake Havasu City; except for the Grand Canyon, the bridge is the most visited tourist attraction in Arizona. The audacity and monumental pointlessness of the city fathers' moving the bridge here when the city of London decided to replace it draws curiosity seekers in droves. To believe it, you have to see it.

Originally built in 1825 to replace a still older London Bridge that had lasted 625 years, this bridge was sold at auction in

1968. Lake Havasu City's promoters bought it for $2,460,000. The 10,000 tons of granite facing were disassembled into blocks weighing from 1000 to 17,000 pounds each, shipped and trucked 10,000 miles to this site and reconstructed on the shore of Lake Havasu when the city was practically nonexistent. Then a canal was dug to let water flow under the bridge. It is 49 feet wide and 928 feet long, and you can drive or walk across it. Every year, millions do. Is it worth seeing? Absolutely! It's a giant object lesson in the fine line between madness and genius—and one of the strangest sights in Arizona.

> Blessed (or cursed, depending on your perspective) with 300 days of sunshine a year, Lake Havasu City once reached 128 degrees on a sweltering June day.

Nevertheless, the stately London Bridge is an impressive sight with its sweeping arches of chiseled granite. A great time to see it is at night, when it glows against the cobalt sky.

To add more British atmosphere, the developers built an English-style village nearby. Here, you'll find a double-decker bus, a London cab, a bright-red wooden phone booth and a somewhat authentic Liverpool pub—the City of London Arms. In recent years, however, the "shoppes" in the English village have begun to look more like Coney Island than Piccadilly Circus, with a slew of T-shirt and ashtray souvenir stores, fast-food stands that dispense flavorless fish-and-chips, even a Wild West gift shop.

Stretching alongside the city is its namesake—**Lake Havasu.** Fed primarily by the Colorado River, this broad, blue body of water is nestled among stark, rocky desert hills. It offers 450 miles of shoreline and loads of gorgeous scenery.

For more information about the bridge and the surrounding area head for the **Lake Havasu Chamber of Commerce.** ~ 314 London Bridge Road; 928-855-4115, fax 928-680-0010; www. havasuchamber.com, e-mail info@havasuchamber.com.

In **Lake Havasu City,** a number of boats offer sightseeing tours from London Bridge, including the large Mississippi riverboat replica *Dixie Belle.* ~ 928-453-6776. **BlueWater Jetboat Tours** runs daily boat excursions from London Bridge to Topock Gorge and the Havasu National Wildlife Refuge from May to September. ~ 928-855-7171, 888-855-7171; e-mail jetboat@earthlink.net.

In the little town of **Topock,** located midway between Bullhead City and Lake Havasu City at the junction of Route 40 and Route 95S, Jerkwater Canoe & Kayak Co. rents canoes and kayaks to explore otherwise inaccessible areas of the **Havasu National Wildlife Refuge.** The company can also provide directions to the beautiful **Topock Gorge,** ancient petroglyph sites and the **Topock Maze,** where Mohave Indians used to go to cleanse their spirits after long journeys. ~ Jerkwater Canoe & Kayak Co.; 928-768-7753, fax 928-768-8162; www.jerkwater.com, e-mail jerk water@jerkwater.com.

◀ *HIDDEN*

LODGING   Across the bridge from the Olde English Village, on the island, the **Nautical Inn Resort & Conference Center** has a golf course, as well as a private dock with waterskiing, kayaking, boating and jet-skiing equipment for guest rental. All the rooms are on the waterfront. Each carpeted unit comes with two queen-sized beds, a patio and direct access to the lawn and beach. The suites include refrigerators and microwaves. ~ 1000 McCulloch Boulevard, Lake Havasu City; 928-855-2141, 800-892-2141, fax 928-453-5808; www.nauticalinn.com, e-mail resort@nauticalinn.com. MODERATE TO ULTRA-DELUXE.

Within a half-mile of the bridge, 64 standard motel rooms are available at the **Windsor Inn**, which has a pool and a spa. ~ 451 London Bridge Road, Lake Havasu City; 928-855-4135, 800-245-4135, fax 928-855-3583; www.windsorinnmotel.com, e-mail jkmi @hotmail.com. BUDGET. The **Days Inn** also has similar accommodations, with a pool. ~ 2190 McCulloch Boulevard, Lake Havasu City; 928-855-4157, 800-982-3622, fax 928-453-1514. BUDGET TO MODERATE.

Spacious one- and two-bedroom suites are available at the **Sands Vacation Resort**. Each carpeted suite includes a living room, dining area and full kitchen. A heated pool, sauna, jacuzzi and fitness center are on the premises. ~ 2040 Mesquite Avenue, Lake Havasu City; 928-855-1388, 800-521-0360, fax 928-453-1802; www.sands-resort.com, e-mail reservations@sands-resort.com. MODERATE.

For an economical lodging choice in Lake Havasu City, try **El Aztec All Suites Inn**, located about a mile from the lake and London Bridge. Each of the suites has one bedroom, one bath and a separate living/dining room area, all with plain white walls, as well as a full kitchen with all cooking utensils, dishes and appliances. A queen-size bed and a fold-out sofa make the inn ideal for families. ~ 2078 Swanson Avenue, Lake Havasu City; 928-453-7172, fax 928-855-1685; www.aztecinn.com. BUDGET.

DINING   Lake Havasu City, oddly, has virtually no high-priced haute cuisine, but it does have a good selection of pleasant, affordable restaurants. A good place for salads, steaks and seafood is **Shugrue's** in back of the Island Fashion Mall, which has an unbeatable view of London Bridge from the island side through tall wraparound windows. Fresh bakery goods are the specialty. ~ 1425 McCulloch Boulevard, Lake Havasu City; 928-453-1400, fax 928-453-3577. DELUXE TO ULTRA-DELUXE.

Next door to Shugrue's, **Barley Brothers** microbrewery cooks pizzas in a wood-burning oven and also serves salads, pasta, rotisserie chicken, ribs and sandwiches. ~ 1425 McCulloch Boulevard, Lake Havasu City; 928-505-7837; www.barleybrothers. com, e-mail brewmaster@barleybrothers.com. MODERATE.

Lake Havasu and Parker Dam Area

Also on the island, the **Captain's Table**, in the Nautical Inn, serves seafood and traditional American menu selections with a lakeside view. ~ 1000 McCulloch Boulevard, Lake Havasu City; 928-855-2141. MODERATE TO DELUXE.

Away from the water, a local favorite is **Krystal's**, featuring specialties such as Alaskan king crab legs, lobster tails and mahi-mahi. Dinner only. ~ 460 El Camino Drive, Lake Havasu City; 928-453-2999. BUDGET TO MODERATE.

Another longtime local favorite is **Chili Charlie's**, serving homemade Mexican and American favorites. ~ 790 Lake Havasu Avenue North, Lake Havasu City; 928-435-5055. BUDGET.

In the English Village on the mainland side of the bridge, there's the usually busy **Mermaid Inn**, serving fish and chips, clam strips and hamburgers. ~ 401 English Village, Lake Havasu City; 928-855-3234. BUDGET.

SHOPPING   Arizona's "West Coast" holds a number of enticements for visitors, but shopping isn't one of them. The most interesting shopping district in the area is the **Olde English Village**, located on the mainland side of London Bridge in Lake Havasu. The cute Olde English buildings housing the shops and snack bars remind us that Lake Havasu City and the bridge were the brainchild of the retired general manager of Disneyland. The Olde English Village has about two dozen theme gift shops such as the Golden Unicorn, and the London Bridge Candle Factory, which claims to be the world's largest candle shop. ~ 928-855-0888, fax 928-855-9209.

At the other end of the bridge, the **Island Fashion Mall** houses a dozen shops selling sportswear, women's fashions and fine jewelry. ~ 1425 McCulloch Boulevard, Lake Havasu City.

NIGHTLIFE   In addition to Lake Havasu City's hotels cocktail lounges, a nice spot for an intimate encounter is **London Arms Pub and Restaurant**, a pub and dinner theater that looks transplanted from Walpole Street. It has a used-brick facade, a "Big Ben" clock tower, two outdoor patios (one a replica of Hyde Park), a wrought-iron fence and stately carriage lamps. Closed Monday and Tuesday. ~ 422 English Village, Lake Havasu City; 928-855-8782, fax 928-855-3828; www.londonarmspub.com.

Grab a "desert martini" (a beer with an olive in it) or settle for standard beer and wine at the **Desert Martini**. This pool hall also features darts, shuffleboard and five TVs. ~ 2120 McCulloch Boulevard, Lake Havasu City; 928-855-1818.

PARKS   **LAKE HAVASU STATE PARK** 🏃 🛶 ⛵ 🎣 🚤 ⚓ ⛴ This shoreline park area in and around Lake Havasu City encompasses most of the Arizona shore of this broad blue lake nestled among stark, rocky desert hills. The park has a campground and rocky swimming beach—Windsor Beach (with boat ramps), north of the center of town. Fish for largemouth bass, striped bass and catfish. There are picnic areas, restrooms, showers and nature trails. Day-use fee, $8. ~ The main automobile-accessible area is at Windsor Beach. Other areas of the park, which includes most of the east shore of Lake Havasu, are only accessible by boat; 928-855-2784, fax 928-855-2647.

Lake Havasu State Park's Arroyo-Camino Interpretive Garden is a great place to spot desert critters like birds, lizards and cottontail rabbits. There's also a native foodstuff garden in winter and early spring.

▲ The 46 first-come, first-served sites at Windsor Beach (928-855-2784) cost $14 per night. The Aubrey Hills Natural Area, south of Lake Havasu City and operated by the BLM (928-505-1200), has 125 primitive boat-in sites (also first-come, first-served) along the shore. Some have vault toilets, picnic tables and shade structures; $10 per night per boat.

CATTAIL COVE STATE PARK About 15 miles south of Lake Havasu City, Cattail Cove is a 2000-acre lakeside park with ample recreational opportunities. Fishing yields crappie, bluegill and striped and largemouth bass. Nearby, Sandpoint Marina and RV Park (928-855-0549; www.lakehavasu. com/sandpoint) has a restaurant, groceries, laundry facilities and boat rentals. Facilities include picnic areas, restrooms, showers and concessions. Day-use fee, $8. ~ Off Route 95, 15 miles south of Lake Havasu City; 928-855-1223.

▲ There are 173 RV campsites with full hookups; $30 to $38 per night.

HAVASU NATIONAL WILDLIFE REFUGE Nature buffs will enjoy this wildlife refuge, which straddles the Colorado River from Topock, 20 miles north of Lake Havasu City, to Mesquite Bay, just north of the city. Hikers through the marshy trails are often rewarded with views of a bald eagle, peregrine falcon, or a number of winter visitors: snow and Canada geese and other waterfowl. There are restrooms at Catfish Paradise and Mesquite Bay; showers and laundry facilities are available at 5-Mile Landing. ~ The refuge headquarters is located at 317 Mesquite Avenue, Needles, CA. To get to the park from Lake Havasu, drive north on Route 95 to Route 40, then drive nine miles west to the exit marked Havasu National Wildlife Refuge (Mohave County 227); 760-326-3853, fax 760-326-5745.

▲ There are 74 hookups and 45 dry sites at 5-Mile Landing on Topock Marsh; $7 per night; information, 928-768-2350.

▼▼▼▼▼▼▼▼▼▼▼▼
Parker Dam Area

Downstream from Parker Dam, which impounds Lake Havasu, the Colorado River flows through the Colorado River Indian Reservation to Parker, a nondescript trade center about 35 miles south of Lake Havasu City. Just two miles north of Parker, Headgate Rock Dam impedes the Colorado to form Lake Moovalya, an 11-mile stretch of water recreation better known as "The Parker Strip."

SIGHTS

Parker was nothing more than a postal stop until the railroad came through in 1908. Most of the town's development, however, occurred after the river was dammed and tourists began flocking to the lakes upstream. Recreation remains Parker's main reason for existing, along with a moderate climate that attracts several thousand snowbirds, mostly retirees, each winter.

The town itself has little to offer; many of its 3000 citizens live in wall-to-wall RV parks scattered across the scrub-brush hillsides, dotted with an occasional red-tile-roof home. Despite Parker's lackluster appeal, the area is besieged by visitors who enjoy year-round boating, waterskiing and inner-tubing (there's even an annual seven-mile inner-tube race) along the scenic Parker Strip.

The city's main attraction is the **Colorado River Indian Tribes Museum**, a storehouse of prehistoric American Indian artifacts from the Anasazi, Hohokam and other tribes, as well as dioramas of pueblos and other dwellings, crafts and folk art of the more modern Mohave, Chemehuevi, Navajo and Hopi people. Visit the gift shop before leaving; it has a good assortment of American Indian publications, baskets, beadwork and other crafts. Closed weekends. ~ 2nd Avenue and Mohave Road, Parker; 928-669-9211, fax 928-669-8262.

About 15 miles upstream sits **Parker Dam**, a virtual twin to Davis Dam. One significant difference is that you can see only one-third of Parker Dam; the bedrock foundation is 235 feet below the riverbed. The inner workings of the dam are off-limits to the public; you can, however, walk across the top and enjoy views of the river and reservoir. ~ 760-663-3712, fax 760-663-3212.

If you'd like a change of pace, drive 34 miles south on Route 95 to the town of **Quartzsite**, the site of one of the strangest reunions in Arizona, and possibly the world. Although the dusty scrub-brush town—if you can call it that—consists of just a few motels, restaurants, and RV parks, each winter its population swells from several thousand to about a million. The reason? The **Quartzsite Gemborees**, shows resembling Bedouin bazaars for rock-swappers and gem collectors. Mostly held in late January and early February, the festivals attract droves of rock and gem aficionados for a metallurgical freakout. In addition to the hundreds of booths, where you can buy everything from healing crys-

In the Land of Gold & Ghosts

Western Arizona's ghost towns come in all shapes and sizes. Some have been completely and irrevocably abandoned to the ravages of time; others have risen into new life thanks to tourism. Good examples of both can be found in the barren, rocky hills around Kingman.

Oatman, about 25 miles southwest of Kingman, has gone from rags to riches several times since it was founded in 1900. Its mines produced more than $3 million worth of gold before they played out. After the mines closed, the town survived as a refreshment stop along old Route 66 until 1946, when the highway was rerouted. Almost all Oatman residents moved away, but the town had such a well-preserved Old West look that it was used as a location for many Westerns, including *How the West Was Won*. Oatman's popularity as a tourist destination has made it livelier than ever. With daily staged shootouts on the main street and wild burros that have learned to panhandle food from sightseers, it has become a Disneyesque version of itself.

Just two miles away, near the summit of 3500-foot Sitgreaves Pass, **Gold Road** was founded about the same time as Oatman and grew to about a quarter of the size. Its mine produced more than twice as much gold yet all that remains today are crumbled stone and adobe walls. Why the difference? Landowners in Gold Road destroyed their buildings to reduce their property-tax assessments. Despite their actions, this forlorn ruin of a town is staging a modest comeback as groups of visitors take the **Gold Road Mine Tour** into a shaft that produced 140,000 ounces of pure gold in five years. Admission. ~ 928-768-1600, fax 928-768-9588; www.goldroadmine.com, e-mail goldrd@ctaz.com.

A less touristy example of an Arizona ghost town is **Chloride**, about 23 miles northwest of Kingman via Route 93. Named for the salt deposits in the surrounding hills, this 1860s mining town never quite died because Tiffany's of New York opened a large turquoise mine there after the silver mines closed down. Today, buildings around town have been spruced up by a new wave of residents who seem a little on the eccentric side, judging from the number of homes that display outlandish desert landscaping and exterior decor consisting of road signs and old license plates. There are several cluttered but clearly authentic antique shops, a general store, and an antique gas station. If you want to prolong your ghost-town experience, check into the old gray 12-room **Shep's Miners Inn**, next door to **Shep's Mining Camp Café**. (Look for the "God Bless John Wayne" sign in the café window.) ~ 9827 2nd Street, Chloride; 928-565-4251, 877-565-4251, fax 928-565-3996; www.sheps minersinn.com, e-mail miners4251@aol.com. BUDGET.

tals to 5000-pound slabs of quartz, the festivals feature flea markets, antique and collectibles shows, camel and ostrich races, country music, an auto show—all choreographed in the tradition of Hunter Thompson. Started in 1964 by a rag-tag group of rock hounds, the original event has grown into a number of shows, becoming Quartzsite's main reason for existence. Be forewarned: If a stone looks too perfect, it may not be the real thing. For further details about the Quartzsite Gemborees, contact Quartzsite Chamber of Commerce; 928-927-5600, fax 928-927-7438; www.quartz sitechamber.com, e-mail info@quartzsitechamber.com.

LODGING   You won't find a bellhop in this part of the country, but there are clean rooms at **El Rancho Motel**, along with a few kitchenettes, microwave ovens, refrigerators, a pool and in-room coffee. ~ 709 California Avenue, Parker; 928-669-2231. BUDGET.

Traveling families will like the **Stardust Motel** because of its oversized rooms and mini-suites, all with refrigerators and microwave ovens, all clean and well-maintained. The motel also has a pool. ~ 700 California Avenue, Parker; 928-669-2278. BUDGET TO MODERATE.

DINING   For home-cooked American dishes, consider the **Paradise Cafe**, a formica-topped, family-run eatery that caters to regular locals who
HIDDEN ►   feast on the barbecued chicken, pork ribs, fish and chips, and homemade pies. ~ Route 95 at Riverside Drive, Parker; 928-667-2404. BUDGET TO DELUXE.

PARKS   **LA PAZ COUNTY PARK** 🏖️ 🏕️ 🚤 🛥️ ⛵   You can spread a beach towel or picnic blanket at this grassy recreational area. Located along a one-mile stretch of the Colorado River, the park is perfect for a relaxed family outing. Common catches for anglers are bass, catfish, bluegill, striper, flathead and perch. Swimming is good at the sandy beach. There are covered ramadas, barbecue grills, picnic tables, restrooms, showers, tennis courts, a baseball field and a playground. Day-use fee, $2 per person. ~ Route 95, about eight miles north of Parker; 928-667-2069, fax 928-667-2757.

At Quartzsite's flea markets, dinosaur bones, fossils and petrified wood have been known to make appearances among the hundreds of quirky offerings. Happy digging!

▲ About a third of the county park is open to tent camping; $11 per night. There are also 35 ramada sites ($13 per night) and 114 RV sites with water and electricity hookups ($16 per night). All camping fees are for two people; there's a $2 charge for each additional person.

BUCKSKIN MOUNTAIN STATE PARK 🚶 🏖️ 🏕️ 🚤 🛥️ ⛵   This state park located near Parker Dam caters to tube floaters, boaters and waterskiers. But you can also hike the nature trails in the mountains that surround the eastern edge of the park. In addition to panoramic vistas of the Colorado River, hikers can sometimes catch a glimpse of desert bighorn sheep that roam the area. Fish for bass, bluegill and catfish. There are restrooms, a picnic ground, a gas dock, inner-tube rentals and a snack bar. Day-use fee, $7. ~ Buckskin Mountain is on Route 95, about 11 miles north of Parker. The River Island unit is another one and a half miles north of Buckskin Mountain; 928-667-3231, fax 928-667-3387.

▲ Buckskin Mountain has 68 sites (water and electric hookups, $19 to $22 per night; cabañas, $22 per night). River Island offers 37 sites (water and electricity hookups; all sites are $19 per night). Restrooms and showers are available at both campgrounds.

ALAMO LAKE STATE PARK 🚶 🏇 ⚓ 🛶 🚤 ⛴ ⚓ The main draw at this 5642-acre park is the fishing. The 3000-acre Alamo Lake offers up bass, bluegill, crappie and catfish; get your fishing license from the park concessions stand. Water activities such as waterskiing are other popular pastimes. Facilities include a playground, picnic areas, a concession stand, gasoline, restrooms and showers. Day-use fee, $5. ~ Located about 100 miles from Parker. Take Route 95 from Parker, continue on Route 72 to Route 60. It's about 40 miles from Wenden; 928-669-2088.

▲ There are 200 sites: $19 per night for hookups; $12 per night for developed sites; $10 per weeknight for undeveloped sites.

This region offers some of Arizona's best fishing. It's open season on all fish year-round at Lake Mead and the abundant Colorado River.

Outdoor Adventures

FISHING

LAKE MEAD AREA There's plenty of catfish, bluegill, crappie and striped bass, often tipping the scales at 30 pounds, at **Lake Mead**. Spring and fall are the best seasons. One of the best spots for bass is near the Las Vegas Boat Harbor because of the wastewater nutrients that dump from the Las Vegas Wash. Also worth trying are Calico Basin, Hemenway Harbour the Meadows, Stewarts Point and Meat Hole. For tips on other spots, ask any park ranger or try any of the marinas, which also sell licenses, bait and tackle. For example, **Lake Mead Marina** rents fishing boats and fishing poles and sells bait and other fishing gear at the marina store. ~ 322 Lakeshore Road; 702-293-3484; www.sevencrown.com. Also on the lake is the **Las Vegas Bay Marina**. ~ Lake Mead Drive; 702-565-9111; www.boatinglakemead.com. **Callville Bay Resort & Marina** has licenses, bait and tackle. ~ HCR 30, Box 100, off Northshore Scenic Drive; 702-565-8958; www.foreverresorts.com. **Echo Bay Resort and Marina** is a good spot to fulfill your fishing and boating needs. ~ North Shore Road; 702-394-4000. **Temple Bar Marina** also sells bait. ~ 1 Maine Street; 928-767-3211.

BULLHEAD CITY/LAUGHLIN AREA Fishing is also excellent along the **Colorado River** near the Bullhead City/Laughlin area. Anglers can fill their creels with striped bass, rainbow trout, bass, catfish, bluegill and crappie. A good spot is the cold water below Davis Dam. There's also good fishing above the dam on **Lake Mohave**, noted for its rainbow trout and bass.

BOATING & WATER-SKIING

This is one of the wettest parts of the state and opportunities for water sports abound.

LAKE MEAD AREA On Arizona's West Coast, you can skip across Lake Mead in a power or ski boat, or simply relax under sail or on the deck of a houseboat. For rentals in the Lake Mead area, try the **Callville Bay Resort & Marina**. ~ HCR 30, Box 100, off Northshore Road; 702-565-8958; www.foreverresorts.com. **Lake Mead Marina** also has rentals. ~ 322 Lakeshore Road; 702-293-3484; www.sevencrown.com. Another place to rent boats at the north end of Lake Mead is **Echo Bay Resort and Marina**. ~ North Shore Road; 702-394-4000.

BULLHEAD CITY/LAUGHLIN AREA In the Bullhead City/Laughlin area, waterskiing is permitted along the Colorado River from Davis Dam to Needles. The sparsely populated area just below Bullhead City is the best choice. You can also waterski on Lake Mohave north of Davis Dam. For boat rentals and equipment, check out **Lake Mohave Resort**. ~ Katherine Landing; 928-754-3245.

LAKE HAVASU AREA The lower Colorado River and Lake Havasu are a mecca for watersport enthusiasts, and craft of all kinds are available for rent. **Havasu Springs Resort** rents fishing boats, pontoons and runabouts. ~ Route 95, Parker; 928-667-3361; www.havasusprings.com. **Bluewater Boat Rentals** has pontoon boats for fishing and waterskiing. They also provide charter boat tours of Topock Gorge. ~ 501 English Village; 928-453-9613, 888-855-7171; www.coloradoriverjetboattours.com. Fifteen miles south of Lake Havasu City, **Sandpoint Marina** rents fishing boats, pontoon boats and houseboats. ~ 928-855-0549; www.sandpointresort.com.

RIVER RUNNING

The 11-mile stretch of Colorado River from Hoover Dam to Willow Beach is open year-round to rafts, canoes and kayaks, but the best time is spring and fall. Expect to see birds and other desert wildlife in this steep-walled wilderness canyon. It's smooth water all the way, with no rapids, and there are hot springs along the river bank. River running requires a permit from the **Hoover Dam Canoe Launch**. Only 30 permits are issued a day; advance reservations are required. ~ 702-293-8204. It's not exactly white-knuckle rafting, but you can float down the Colorado River from Hoover

Dam to Willow Beach and see waterfalls, hot springs and geological formations. After securing a permit, find an outfitter with rentals. **Boulder City Outfitters** offers kayaks and canoes. ~ 1631 Industrial Boulevard, Boulder City, NV; 702-293-1190. **Jerkwater Range and Kayaks** has the same. ~ P.O. Box 800, Topock AZ 86436; 928-768-7753.

KINGMAN AREA   Kingman visitors won't be disappointed with the semiprivate 18-hole golf course and driving range at **Valley Vista Country Club**, which boasts some of the best greens in Arizona. Clubs and cart rentals are available. ~ 9686 Concho Drive; 928-757-8744, fax 928-757-3094. The 18-hole **Cerbat Cliffs Golf Course** is a high desert course with a few challenging water hazards and sand traps. Soft spikes are required. You can rent cart and clubs. ~ 1001 East Gates Road; 928-753-6593, fax 928-753-8361.

LAKE MEAD AREA   Serving the Lake Mead and Hoover Dam area is the 18-hole **Boulder City Municipal Golf Course**, one of the prettier courses in the greater Las Vegas area, with shade trees and bright green greens. Green fees include a cart, and club rentals are available. ~ 1 Clubhouse Drive, Boulder City, NV; 702-293-9236, fax 702-293-9237.

BULLHEAD CITY/LAUGHLIN AREA   In Laughlin, tee off at the 18-hole **Emerald River Golf Course**, a target desert course with narrow fairways and small greens. The USGA rates it the second most-challenging course in Nevada. There are clubs for rent, and the green fee includes the use of a cart. ~ 1155 West Casino Drive, Laughlin; 702-298-0061. In Bullhead City play the greens at the nine-hole, par-three **Riverview Golf Course**, which features lots of water hazards. There are rental carts and clubs. ~ 2000 East Ramar Road; 928-763-1818. Also in Bullhead City is the nine-hole, semiprivate **Chaparral Country Club**. Club and cart rentals are available. ~ 1260 East Mohave Drive; 928-758-3939. The 18-hole **Desert Lakes Golf Course** is about 12 miles south of the Laughlin/Bullhead City bridge. Club rentals are available and carts are included in the green fee. ~ 5835 Desert Lakes Drive, Bullhead City, AZ; 928-768-1000.

The largest freshwater striped bass caught in Arizona—weighing in at 59 lbs., 12 oz.—was at Bullhead City's Lake Mohave.

LAKE HAVASU AREA   Golfers can choose from two excellent courses around Lake Havasu. The first is the **Bridgewater Links**, a nine-hole, par-three executive course with cart and club rentals. ~ 1477 Queen's Bay Road; 928-855-4777. You'll hope your score is falling down, falling down at the semiprivate **London Bridge Golf Club**. It has two 18-hole desert courses lined with palm trees. There are carts and clubs for rent. ~ 2400 Clubhouse Drive; 928-

855-9096. Tee off amid magnificent surroundings at the 18-hole, par-72 championship **Emerald Canyon Golf Course**. A putting green, driving range and pro shop are on the premises. Clubs, carts and lessons are available. ~ 72 Emerald Canyon Drive, Parker; 928-667-3366.

TENNIS   Courts are fairly easy to come by if you want to rally away the endlessly sunny days.

BULLHEAD CITY/LAUGHLIN AREA   In Laughlin, guests can use the **Flamingo Laughlin's** three lighted courts. ~ 1900 South Casino Drive, Laughlin; 702-298-5111. The **Riverview RV Resort** has two lighted courts for the exclusive use of campers staying at the resort; no fee. A tennis pro is on call. ~ 2000 East Ramar Road, Bullhead City; 928-763-5800.

Personal watercrafts are available for rent at all Laughlin hotels and at some in Bullhead City.

LAKE HAVASU AREA   Tennis courts are open to the public for a fee in Lake Havasu City at **London Bridge Racquet and Fitness Center**. There are six courts, of which four are lighted. The center has a tennis pro. ~ 1407 Mc-Culloch Boulevard; 928-855-6274, fax 928-855-9382.

HIKING   Hikers will be happy with all the forest and canyons this area has to offer. All distances listed for hiking trails are one way unless otherwise noted.

KINGMAN AREA   **Hualapai Mountain Park**, 14 miles southeast of Kingman, has an extensive network of hiking trails through piñon, oak, aspen and ponderosa forest teeming with bird and animal life. Six interconnecting trails totaling six miles, starting from the **Aspen Springs Trail** (1 mile), allow you to custom-design your own hike. Aspen Springs Trail connects with the **Potato Patch Loop** (4-mile loop) and from that trail various spur trails take off—the short and easy **Stonestep Lookout Trail** (.04 mile), and the slightly more ambitious **Aspen Peak Trail** (.7 mile), **Hayden Peak South Trail** (.8 mile) and **Hayden Peak West Trail** (.6 mile).

BULLHEAD CITY/LAUGHLIN AREA   A wonderful, little-known wintertime hike is **Grapevine Canyon** (1 mile). There is no clearly defined trail, but you will have no trouble tracing the tracks of other hikers up the wash along the canyon floor. Some rock scrambling is involved. At the mouth of the canyon are many American Indian petroglyphs dating back 1200 years. Farther up the canyon, a thin waterfall flows year-round. The presence of water in the Grapevine Canyon attracts nocturnal wildlife, and you may see tracks of badgers, skunks, desert bighorn sheep and even mountain lions. The wild grapes that grow here give the canyon its name. Grapevine Canyon is in Nevada, 13 miles west of the Laughlin/Bullhead City bridge on Route 163 and one and a half

HIDDEN ►

miles in on the clearly marked, unpaved road to Christmas Tree Pass. There is a parking area near the mouth of the canyon.

LAKE HAVASU AREA   The Mohave Sunset Walking Trail in Lake Havasu State Park begins at Windsor Beach and winds for two miles through a variety of terrains from lowlands dense with salt cedar to ridgelines commanding beautiful views of the lake. Signs along the sometimes hilly trail identify common Mojave Desert plant life.

Transportation

On Arizona's "West Coast" along the lower Colorado River, the Bullhead City/Laughlin area is reached by exiting **Route 40** at Kingman and driving 26 miles on **Route 68** through the most starkly stunning scenery in the Mohave Desert, or by exiting Route 40 at Topock, 12 miles east of Needles, California, and driving 35 miles north on **Route 95**. The other major Colorado River resort, Lake Havasu City, is 21 miles south of Route 40 on Route 95. A fascinating backroad route connecting Route 95 with Route 40 at Kingman goes through the historic town of Oatman on its steep climb over Sitgreaves Pass, a drive challenging enough to evoke amazement at the fact that this numberless road used to be part of Old Route 66, the main highway across the Southwest to Los Angeles in the days before the interstate was built.

CAR

The **Bullhead City–Laughlin Airport** (928-754-2134) is serviced by Air Laughlin; the **Kingman Airport** (928-757-2134) in Kingman and the **Lake Havasu City Airport** are serviced by America West.

AIR

Greyhound Bus Lines (800-231-2222; www.greyhound.com) stops at the bus terminals in Kingman at 3264 East Andy Devine Road, 928-757-8400; and in Lake Havasu City at 1940 Mesquite Avenue.

BUS

Amtrak (800-872-7245; www.amtrak.com) provides service to Kingman (4th and Andy Devine streets) and Needles, CA (900 Front Street), which is close to Lake Havasu.

TRAIN

Car-rental agencies at the Bullhead City–Laughlin Airport are **Avis Rent A Car** (800-331-1212) and **Hertz Rent A Car** (800-654-3131). Hertz also has rental cars at the Kingman Airport.

CAR RENTALS

EIGHT

South Central Arizona

If your image of Arizona is cowboys, ranches and hitching posts, think again, partner. For while the flavor of the West is very much evident in the central band of the state, the trappings of the modern age are everywhere—indeed, flourishing and growing apace. Head to its major cities—including Phoenix, Scottsdale, Tempe and Mesa—and you'll find a vibrant arts community, professional sports galore, shopping centers and stores as far as the eye can see, a fine college campus, intriguing architecture, enough golf, tennis and other activities to satisfy anyone and everyone. But if you're hankering for a glimpse of the frontier or a taste of the outdoor life, well, they're here, too: miles of virgin desert, rivers to swim and sail, towns more in the past than the present, trails to roam. So saddle up, friend.

Phoenix takes its name from the legendary phoenix bird, and with good reason: The biggest metropolis between southern Texas and California and the ninth largest in the country, Phoenix is a city taking flight. The population of Phoenix proper is 1,321,000, which balloons to 3,000,000 when you include the 23 satellite towns that blend seamlessly along the valley of the Salt River. Some thousand families a month set up homes in the broad river valley as subdivisions and shopping centers mushroom.

Phoenix today is a far cry from the era of the Hohokam Indians. The Hohokam, meaning "those who vanished," built a network of irrigation ditches to obtain water from the Salt River, part of which is still in use today. Then, as now, irrigation was vital to Phoenix. So much water is piped in to soak fields, groves and little kids' toes that the desert air is actually humid—uncomfortably so through much of the summer. Lettuce, melons, alfalfa, cotton, vegetables, oranges, grapefruit, lemons and olives are grown in abundance in the irrigated fields and groves, lending a touch of green to the otherwise brown landscape. Boating, waterskiing, swimming and even surfing—in a gigantic, mechanically activated pool—are splendid byproducts. Did we mention sports? Whatever your game may be, this is sports heaven. In professional competition, Phoenix has baseball (the Arizona Diamondbacks), hockey (the Phoenix Coyotes), football (the Cardinals) and basketball (the Suns). Plus, the Arizona State University Sun Devils play football, basketball and baseball. Still other spectator sports include rodeos and horse racing. For the active set, there are 125 golf courses and hundreds of tennis courts, as well as bike, jogging and horse-riding trails, and opportunities for all kinds of other pursuits.

The action here isn't all on the field. The city has completed a $1.1 billion re-development of the downtown that began in 1988. Testimony to the effort are the glitzy Arizona Center, the Mexican-themed Mercado and the 18,000-seat America West Arena next to the Civic Center Plaza.

Metropolitan Phoenix, or the Valley of the Sun, originated in 1850 on the banks of the Salt River and became the capital of the Arizona Territory in 1889. At one time, nearly 25,000 Indians were the exclusive inhabitants of Arizona. The earliest were the Hohokam, who thrived from A.D. 30 until about A.D. 1450. Signs of their settlements remain intact to this day. Two other major tribal groups followed: the Anasazi in the state's northern plateau highlands, and the Mogollon People, in the northeastern and eastern mountain belt. Today there are 23 reservations in Arizona, more than any other state, with an estimated 190,091 Indians from 21 different tribes living in sad testimony to the white settlers' land grabs. Some 150 miles east of Phoenix in the White Mountain region of northern Arizona is the Fort Apache Indian Reservation with a million and a half acres of land. Bordering it, with another two million acres, is the San Carlos Apache Indian Reservation. The largest Indian reservation in North America, Navajoland, home to 174,000 Navajos, begins 76 miles north of Flagstaff and extends into northwestern New Mexico and southeastern Utah. Located almost in the center of the Navajo Indian Reservation is the Hopi Indian Reservation, 11,210 members strong, who have lived on the same site without interruption for more than 1000 years, retaining more of their ancient traditions and cultures than any other Indian group.

In the mid-1500s, the conquistadors arrived, carrying the banner of Spain. They were looking for gold and seeking souls to save. They found more souls than gold and in the process introduced the Indians to cattle, horse raising and new farming methods, augmenting their crops of beans, squash and maize with new grains, fruits and vegetables. The Spanish-Mexican influence is still strongly evident throughout the Southwest. And the gold prospector eventually became the very symbol of the Old West—an old man with a white beard, alone with his trusted burro, looking to strike it rich. You only have to go 30 miles east of Phoenix into the Superstition Mountains to find the lore and the legend and the lure of gold still very much alive today.

Until about the mid-1880s, the Indians accepted the few white miners, traders and farmers who came West, but as the number of settlers grew, friction arose and fighting resulted. The cavalry was called in and one of the most brutal chapters in the history of the Southwest followed. Black troops of the Tenth Cavalry, known as Buffalo Soldiers because of their dark skin and curly black hair, came in large numbers to protect citizens of the Arizona land where Geronimo, Cochise, Mangus, Alchise and other chieftains had dotted the cactus-covered hills and canyons with the graves of thousands of emigrants, settlers and prospectors. Numerous sites throughout the entire state bring those days of conflict into vivid focus—Cochise Stronghold in the Dragoon Mountains south of Willcox, hideout of the notorious

Apache chief; Fort Bowie National Historic Site, an adobe ruin that was a key military outpost during the Indian wars, and nearby Fort Huachuca, an important territorial outpost that's still in operation today as a communications base for the U.S. Army; and Fort Verde State Historic Park, located in Camp Verde on Route 17 between Phoenix and Flagstaff, yet another military base that played a key role in subduing the Apaches in the 1870s.

With the construction of the first railroad in 1887, fast-paced expansion took hold as Phoenix drew settlers from all over the United States. In 1889 it was named the capital of the Arizona Territory, and statehood was declared in 1912.

Once hailed as the agricultural center of Arizona, Phoenix by 1920 was already highly urbanized. Its horse-drawn carriages represented the state's first public transportation. Its population reached 29,053 and the surrounding communities of Tempe, Mesa, Glendale, Chandler and Scottsdale added 8636 to the count.

As farmers and ranchers were slowly being squeezed out, these years of Phoenix's development saw a rugged frontier town trying to emulate as best it could famous cities back East. It had a Boston store, a New York store, three New England–style tea parlors and a number of gourmet shops selling everything from smoked herring to Delaware cream cheese. The region's dry desert air also began to attract scores of "health-seekers." The advent of scheduled airline service and the proliferation of dude ranches, resorts and other tourist attractions changed the character of the city still further.

Today, high-tech industry forms the economic core of Phoenix, while tourism remains the state's number-two job producer. Not surprisingly, construction is the city's third major industry. But Phoenix retains a strong community flavor. Its downtown area isn't saturated with block after block of highrises and apartment houses. The city and all its suburbs form an orderly, 800-square-mile pattern of streets and avenues running north and south and east and west, with periphery access gained by soaring Los Angeles–style freeways. Beyond are the mountains and desert, which offer an escape from city living, with camping, hiking and other recreational facilities.

If the desert isn't your scene, neighboring Scottsdale just might be. Billing itself as "The West's Most Western Town," Scottsdale is about as "Western" as Beverly Hills.

Scottsdale's population of over 200,000 appears to be made up primarily of "snow birds" who came to stay: rich retirees from other parts of the United States who enjoy the sun, the golf courses, the swimming pools, the mountains, the bolo ties and the almost endless selection of handicraft shops, boutiques and over 120 art galleries. Actually, retired persons account for only 20 percent of this fast-growing city, whose median adult age is 41. There are far more yuppies than grandmas.

Scottsdale was only desert land in 1888 when U.S. Army Chaplain Winfield Scott bought a parcel of land located near the Arizona Canal at the base of Camelback Mountain. Before long, much of the cactus and greasewood trees here had been replaced by 80 acres of barley, a 20-acre vineyard and 50 orange trees. Scottsdale remained a small agricultural and ranching community until after World War II. Motorola opened a plant in Scottsdale in 1945, becoming the first of many electronics manufacturing firms to locate in the valley.

Less than a quarter-mile square in size when it was incorporated in 1951, Scottsdale now spreads over 150 square miles. Its unparalleled growth would appear never-ending except that the city is now braced up against the 50,000-acre Salt River Indian Reservation, established in 1879 and home of the Pima and Maricopa people who haven't let their juxtaposition with one of the nation's wealthiest communities go unrewarded. The reservation boasts one of the largest shopping areas in the Southwest, a junior college, thousands of acres of productive farmland and future hotel sites.

The network of satellite communities that surrounds the Phoenix–Scottsdale area, like random pieces of a jigsaw puzzle, is primarily made up of bedroom communities. Tempe to the south is home of Arizona State University. Burgeoning Glendale, to the northwest, was originally founded as a "temperance colony," where the sale of intoxicants was forever forbidden. Mesa, to the east, covering over 100 square miles, is Arizona's third-largest city. Carefree and Cave Creek, to the north, are two communities sheltered by the Sonoran Desert foothills and surrounded by mountains. Carefree was planned for those who enjoy fun-in-the-sun activities like tennis, golf and horseback riding. Cave Creek, a booming ranching and mining center back in 1873, thrives on its strong Western flavor. A bit hokey, but fun. Like

South Central Arizona

fallout from a starburst, these and other neighboring communities all revolve around the tempo, pace and heartbeat of the Phoenix–Scottsdale core.

Beyond the urban centers, you can pull up to a gas station that's the last one from anywhere, visit honky-tonk saloons, skinny-dip in a mountain lake, pan for gold, meet dreamers and drifters. The best way to see the West is to be part of it, to feel the currents of its rivers or the steepness of its hills underfoot. South central Arizona certainly offers ample opportunity.

▼▼▼▼▼▼▼▼▼▼
Phoenix

The history of south central Arizona unravels in smooth, easy chapters through Phoenix's museums and attractions, particularly highlighting its Indian heritage. But this is by no means all you'll find here. The city is also a bustling art mecca, evident from the moment visitors arrive at Sky Harbor Airport, with its array of contemporary and Western artworks on display. The airport's program of changing art exhibits, in conjunction with the Phoenix Art Commission, is a model for similar programs at airports throughout the country. You'll also find art everywhere in the city. Along Piestewa Peak Freeway, a ten-mile stretch that connects downtown Phoenix with the city's northern suburbs, you may think you're seeing things, and you are. The freeway is lined with 35 giant three- and four-foot sculptures—vases, cups, Indian-style pots and other utensils, all part of the city's public arts project "to make people feel more at home with the freeway." Not everyone in Phoenix loves the idea. Detractors have dubbed the freeway art project "Chamber Pots of the Gods."

Surely the last of the rugged Marlboro men can still be seen astride handsome, well-groomed horses in Phoenix, but they're not riding off into the sunset, never to be seen again. Chances are they're heading into the vast expanse of desert land that still surrounds the city proper to recharge their motors. Long considered a scourge of man, arid and untamable, the desert with its raw awesome beauty is now considered by many as the last vestige of America's wilderness. Numerous tour operators offer guided jeep and horseback tours into the desert, but as any Arizonian will tell you, the desert is best appreciated alone. Southwestern Indians have long known the secrets of the desert. Now the settler man comes to turn his face skyward into the pale desert sun. (Arizona's broad central band stretches across the state in what visiting English author J. B. Priestley once described as "geology by day and astronomy by night.")

But whether the city proper or its environs are your scene, trying to take in all the sights and sounds in one trip is a bit like counting the grains of sand in a desert. We suppose it can be done, but who on earth has the time? To help you on your quest, here are some of this city's highlights.

Phoenix's once lackluster downtown is starting to reap the benefits of some $1.1 billion worth of cultural and architectural enhancements in progress since the late 1980s. A focal point of the **Phoenix Municipal Government Center**, which includes a new city hall, is one of the city's oldest landmarks—the **Orpheum Theatre**, a magnificent 1929 Spanish baroque revival building that was once considered the most luxurious playhouse west of the Mississippi River. The theater gives free public tours of the exterior and is a showcase for performing arts, community and civic events, ballet, children's theater, film festivals and other special events. Tours are conducted on Monday between noon and 1 p.m. if there are no productions then; call ahead. ~ 203 West Adams Street; 602-262-7272.

Phoenix was named after the legendary Egyptian symbol of rebirth because the city was built upon the ruins of the Hohokam civilization.

Other improvements are making downtown more pedestrian-friendly, such as the **Margaret T. Hance Park**, a 29-acre greenbelt stretching from 3rd Street to 3rd Avenue, with wooded areas, fountains and a Japanese garden (admission; open Saturday only) symbolizing Phoenix's ties to sister city Hemeji, Japan. ~ 602-256-3204, fax 602-534-2635.

Southwestern anthropology and primitive arts are showcased at the **Heard Museum**. The ten exhibition galleries on three levels include a Hopi kachina collection, Cochi storyteller figures, pottery by Maria Martinez, silver and turquoise jewelry, basketry, blankets and other American Indian crafts. The museum also includes an education pavilion, a working artist studio, a café and a gift shop and bookstore. Admission. ~ 2301 North Central Avenue; 602-252-8848, fax 602-252-9757; www.heard.org.

The **Phoenix Art Museum**, which features exhibits on Western, Asian, Latin American, European, contemporary and decorative arts, has an outstanding fashion design collection that includes accessories and textiles. The museum also presents temporary exhibitions on tour from other major museums. In addition, children can engage in hands-on fun at ArtWorks, an interactive gallery. Call for specific exhibition information. Closed Monday. Admission. ~ 1625 North Central Avenue; 602-257-1222, fax 602-253-8662; www.phxart.org, e-mail info@phxart.org.

The **Arizona Capitol** was built in 1900 to serve as the Territorial Capitol. The building has been restored to the 1912 era when Arizona won statehood. Its roof contains the amount of copper equivalent to 4,800,000 pennies. That's $48,000 (which doesn't seem so outrageous now, considering the costs of major construction projects).

Housed within the building is the **Arizona Capitol Museum**, which provides guided tours of exhibits in the Senate and House Chambers, the Governor's Suite and the Rotunda. A wax figure of the state's first governor, George Hunt, is seated at his partnership desk surrounded by period furnishings. Major artifacts include the original silver service taken from the USS *Arizona* before the battleship was sunk at Pearl Harbor and the roughrider flag carried up Cuba's San Juan Hill during the Spanish-American War, which is brought out for special events. The museum is closed Sunday from January through May, closed weekends the rest of the year. ~ 1700 West Washington Street; 602-542-4675, fax 602-542-4690; www.lib.az.us/museum/capitol. htm, e-mail capmus@lib.az.us.

Minerals, ores and mining equipment from Arizona and the rest of the world are displayed at the **Arizona Mining and Mineral Museum,** one of the finest of its kind in the Southwest. Closed Sunday. ~ 1502 West Washington Street; 602-255-3791, 800-446-4259, fax 602-255-3777; www.admmr.state.az.us.

Over at the **Arizona's Women Hall of Fame,** you will find a small exhibit dedicated to the women who made Arizona what it is today. Closed weekends. ~ 1101 West Washington Street; 602-255-2110; www.lib.az.us/museum/hof.htm.

Museo Chicano features changing exhibits ranging from local to international focus. Latino culture, arts and history are exhibited, as well as the work of well-known and emerging artists. In addition, the museum offers a popular series of cultural programs and performing-arts events, such as the Mexican Ballet Folklorico with live mariachi bands, and an annual Day of the Dead festival in November. The museum store features Latino fine and folk art, bilingual books and hundreds of posters; it also hosts author readings and book signings. Closed Sunday and Monday. Admission. ~ 147 East Adams Street; 602-257-5536, fax 602-257-5539; e-mail museochicano@juno.com.

Heritage Square is a Southwestern time warp featuring four turn-of-the-20th-century homes: the **Arizona Doll & Toy Museum;** the **Rosson House,** an 1895 Eastlake Victorian that contains an exquisite collection of period furniture; the **Silva House,** a Victorian-style bungalow; and the **Stevens-Haustgen House.** There is an admission charge at the Rosson House and the Arizona Doll & Toy Museum. The Silva and Stevens-Haustgen houses are currently closed to the public, but are still worth a walk-by. Closed August to Labor Day, and Monday and Tuesday. ~ Heritage Square, 115 North 6th Street; 602-262-5071, fax 602-534-1786; www.rosson housemuseum.org.

The **Phoenix Museum of History,** located in the Heritage and Science Park next to Heritage Square, focuses on the territorial history of Phoenix from prehistoric to the 1930s and beyond. Many displays are interactive and involve personal stories and historical figures; others include an impressive printing press exhibit and one

Central Phoenix

Northern   Ave

Phoenix Mountains Park & Recreation Area

Glendale   Ave

Lincoln   Dr

McDonald   Dr

17

Bethany Home   Rd

Camelback
Mtn

Scottsdale   Blvd

Ave   19th   7th   St   16th   St   24th   St   32nd   St

Camelback   Rd

Camelback   Rd

Indian School   Rd

Indian   School   Rd

51

Central   Ave

40th   St   44th   St   48th   St   56th   St   64th   St

Grand   Ave

60

Thomas   Rd

Thomas   Rd

I

N

McDowell   Rd   Central   Rd

McDowell   Rd

K

10

202

Papago Park

E

Galvin Pkwy

O

L

Van Buren St

A   **B** **G**   **F**   **J** **D**

10

Washington St

H

Jefferson   St

P

River

Curry   Rd

Buckeye   Rd

Sky Harbor Blvd

202

17

Sky Harbor International Airport

143

University   Dr

10

Salt

C

Apache   Blvd

Broadway   Rd

Priest   Dr

Ave   19th   Ave   7th   St   Central   Ave   7th   St   16th   St   24th   St   32nd   St   40th   St   48th   St

Southern   Ave

Southern   Ave   Rural Rd

60

Baseline   Rd

Dobbins   Rd

Pima Canyon Rd

M

San Juan Rd   Telegraph   Pass   Rd   South   Mountain   Park

N

0   3 miles

0   3 kilometers

POINTS OF INTEREST

- **A** Arizona Capitol Museum
- **B** Arizona Mining and Mineral Museum
- **C** Arizona State University
- **D** Civic Plaza
- **E** Desert Botanical Garden
- **F** Government Center
- **G** Arizona Women's Hall of Fame
- **H** Hall of Flame Fire Museum
- **I** Heard Museum
- **J** Heritage Square
- **K** Margaret T. Hance Park
- **L** The Mercado
- **M** Mystery Castle
- **N** Phoenix Art Museum
- **O** Phoenix Zoo
- **P** Pueblo Grande Museum

Downtown Phoenix

While recent skyscraper construction has replaced most of Phoenix's original downtown buildings, a few—often protected by National Historic Landmark status—remain to show the kaleidoscope of architectural exuberance that characterized the city's early years. These structures can be seen on a two-mile walk from Heritage Square.

FRY BUILDING   The Fry Building is the oldest surviving commercial building in Phoenix, dating back to 1885, just five years after the city was founded. The storefront was remodeled in 1950. ~ Located at the northwest corner of 2nd and Washington streets.

HANNY'S BUILDING   The construction in 1947 of the contemporary-style Hanny's Building inspired a major facelift of the downtown area and the destruction or renovation of most historic architecture. ~ 44 North 1st Street.

PROFESSIONAL BUILDING   The Professional Building gave Phoenix its first centrally located medical offices. Built in 1931, this limestone-sheathed building exemplifies the Art Deco/Moderne style. ~ 137 North Central Avenue.

HOTEL SAN CARLOS   The Hotel San Carlos was built in 1927 in the Renaissance revival style. A gathering place for Hollywood stars, it was one of the first hotels to have steam heat, elevators and air-cooling. It has recently undergone a multimillion-dollar restoration. ~ 202 North Central Avenue.

of the state's oldest mining locomotives. There is a library for research and browsing, as well as a gift shop. Closed Sunday and Monday. Admission. ~ 105 North 5th Street; 602-253-2734, fax 602-253-2348; www.pmoh.org, e-mail info@pmoh.org.

Also next to Heritage Square is the **Arizona Science Center,** which is outfitted with a planetarium, a giant-screen theater and over 300 hands-on exhibits. Admission. ~ 600 East Washington Street; 602-716-2000, fax 602-716-2099; www.azscience.org, e-mail info@azscience.org.

For a glimpse into the Hohokam culture's past, visit the **Pueblo Grande Museum.** The exhibits include a prehistoric Hohokam ruin, a permanent display on this legendary tribe and a changing gallery featuring Southwestern Indian arts, crafts and archaeology.

SECURITY BUILDING   Also typifying the Renaissance revival style is the Security Building, built down the block from the Hotel San Carlos in 1928. ~ 234 North Central Avenue.

TITLE AND TRUST BUILDING   The Moderne-style Title and Trust Building was the largest office building in Arizona when it was built in 1931. It still has the original travertine and marble floors and etched glass. ~ 114 West Adams Street.

ORPHEUM THEATRE   The 1929 Spanish Baroque revival–style Orpheum Theatre is Phoenix's largest and most architecturally intact theater. A major restoration in 1997 has given it new life as a center for the performing arts. ~ 203 West Adams Street.

WALKER BUILDING   The Walker Building was built entirely of poured concrete in neoclassic revival style in 1920. Originally the location of JC Penney's department store, it later became the headquarters of Central Arizona Light and Power. ~ 302 West Washington Street.

HISTORIC CITY HALL/MARICOPA COUNTY COURTHOUSE   Built in 1928, the Historic City Hall/Maricopa County Courthouse combines elements of most architectural styles that were in vogue in 1920s Phoenix, including Art Deco, Moderne, Spanish Baroque revival and Renaissance revival. ~ 125 West Washington Street. City government moved to the new 20-story City Hall at 200 West Washington Street in 1992.

LUHRS BUILDING AND TOWER   The Luhrs Building (c. 1923), 45 West Jefferson Street, and Luhrs Tower (c. 1929), 13 West Jefferson Street, were each the tallest building in Arizona in the year they were built.

Of special interest is an outdoor trail that leads visitors to the top of a Hohokam platform mound and through full-sized replicas of Hohokam houses. There is also an interactive exhibit for children. Admission. ~ 4619 East Washington Street; 602-495-0901, fax 602-495-5645; www.pueblogrande.com, e-mail pueblo.grande. museum.pks@phoenix.gov.

Located not far from the central Phoenix museums is the **Desert Botanical Garden,** where more than 50,000 plants from desert lands around the world are displayed. You can see this beautiful garden via a self-guided nature walk or a group tour. Featured is a 40-acre showcase of native Sonoran desert plants, a saguaro forest, a mesquite thicket, a desert stream and an upland chaparral habitat, complete with historic American Indian dwellings. The botanical garden has trail exhibits and interactive displays as well as "islands" of shade that offer relief from the often brutal afternoon sun. Admission. ~ 1201 North Galvin Parkway; 480-941-1225, fax 480-481-8124; www.dbg.org, e-mail media@dbg.org.

Nearby is the **Phoenix Zoo**, which uses natural settings, including a four-acre African Savanna, to showcase over 1300 mammals, birds and reptiles. Phoenix newcomers are frequently startled to find themselves driving along busy Van Buren alongside a family of trumpeting elephants. For a convenient zoo overview take the Safari Train. Popular highlights are the World Herd of Arabian Oryx, a rare Sumatran tiger exhibit and the Baboon Kingdom. Children will especially enjoy the hands-on participatory exhibits. Be sure to visit the one-acre tropical rainforest, home to 15 bird and animal species adopted from around the world. Admission. ~ 455 North Galvin Parkway; 602-273-1341, fax 602-273-7078; www.phoenixzoo.org, e-mail zooqna@thephxzoo.com.

Home of the Fiesta Bowl, Arizona State University has the largest enrollment of any school in the Southwest.

The largest firefighting museum in the world is the **Hall of Flame Fire Museum**. On display are more than 90 restored hand-drawn, horse-drawn and motorized fire engines and hundreds of artifacts. Special games, exhibits and programs, all stressing fire safety, are offered for children. You'll also find a theater where videos are shown. Admission. ~ 6101 East Van Buren Street; 602-275-3473, fax 602-275-0896; www.hallofflame.org, e-mail webmaster@hallofflame.org.

Tucked away in the foothills of South Mountain Park, the **Mystery Castle** is an 18-room extravaganza fashioned from native stone, sand, cement, water, goat's milk and Stutz Bearcat wire-rim wheels. Warmed by 13 fireplaces, the parapeted castle has a cantilevered stairway, chapel and dozens of nooks and crannies and is furnished with Southwestern antiques. It's known as the "mystery" castle because the builder, Boyce Luther Gulley, thinking he was about to die from tuberculosis, ran away from his Seattle home in a Stutz Bearcat and devoted 15 years to the construction project. It was only after his death in 1945 that the missing builder's family learned of his whereabouts and inherited the castle. Closed Monday through Wednesday from October through June; closed July through September. Admission. ~ End of South 7th Street; 602-268-1581.

Pioneer Arizona Living History Museum re-creates an Old West town using mostly original buildings—a church, schoolhouse, printing shop and blacksmith shop—and featuring costumed interpreters. Living-history exhibitions include cooking, gardening and sewing. At the opera house you'll see melodramas and historic performances all themed to the territorial period, 1858 to 1912. You can also enjoy the picnic area and a restaurant. Closed Monday and

Tuesday. Admission. ~ 3901 West Pioneer Road (Pioneer Road exit off of Route 17); 623-465-1052, fax 623-465-0683; www.pio neer-arizona.com.

For a midday break from sightseeing—one the kids will thank you for—stop at **Encanto Park**. The picnic tables and landscaped grounds provide a cool place to lunch or doze, and the on-site Enchanted Island Amusement Park (admission; closed Monday and Tuesday; 602-254-2020) has rides and bumper boats if you can muster the energy. ~ 2606 North 15th Avenue; 602-261-8991.

West of Phoenix, the **Bead Museum** displays a phenomenal collection of beads, jewelry and other adornments from around the world and explains their uses as trade goods, currency, religious items and status symbols. Visitors to this one-of-a-kind nonprofit museum discover that there's more to beads than they ever suspected. ~ 5754 West Glenn Drive, Glendale; 623-931-2737, fax 623-930-8561; www.beadmuseumaz.org.

LODGING

As a major resort and convention center, the Valley of the Sun features some of the most spectacular hotel resorts in the country. It has had the rare distinction of having more *Mobil Travel Guide* Five Star resorts (three of the twelve top-rated resorts nationwide) than any other city in the United States (see "Spoil Yourself" in this chapter). Yet it's not without its share of budget- and moderate-priced hotels and motels, and proliferating bed and breakfasts.

An elegant scene of the past is mirrored in the glossy facade of the present with the rebirth of the **Hotel San Carlos** in the heart of downtown. Built in 1928, the seven-story San Carlos has undergone a multimillion-dollar restoration while keeping its charm intact—a crystal chandelier and period furnishing in the lobby, original bathtubs, basins and furniture in the 109 guest rooms and 12 suites. There's also a rooftop swimming pool. The San Carlos is one of the largest hotels listed in the National Register of Historic Places. ~ 202 North Central Avenue; 602-253-4121, 866-253-4121, fax 602-253-6668; www.hotelsancarlos.com, e-mail info@ hotelsancarlos.com. MODERATE TO ULTRA-DELUXE.

The 24-story **Hyatt Regency Phoenix** is across from Civic Plaza downtown. With 712 rooms, it's the city's largest hotel. It has a heated swimming pool, exercise equipment, a café, lounges and a revolving rooftop dining room. Rooms are smallish but tastefully furnished in a light, Southwest style. ~ 2nd and Adams streets; 602-252-1234, 800-233-1234, fax 602-254-9472; www.hyatt.com. DELUXE TO ULTRA-DELUXE.

The **Pointe Hilton Squaw Peak Resort** is an all-suite resort on 180 acres near the Phoenix Mountain Preserve. The architecture and ambience here are a cross between Southwestern and Mediterranean. The 563 suites have desks, marble bathroom countertops and fully stocked mini-bars. There are also 78 one- and two-bedroom villas. Amenities include the use of a nearby 18-hole golf course, tennis courts, a fitness center, swimming pools, miniature golf and the Coyote Camp to keep the kids occupied. ~ 7677 North 16th Street; 602-997-2626, 800-876-4683, fax 602-997-2391; www.pointehilton.com. ULTRA-DELUXE.

You may want to spend several nights in hostels if it allows splurging on the luxurious accommodations of **Embassy Suites Biltmore**. Walk through the doors and your first sight is a huge atrium complete with palm trees, tropical plants and waterways shimmering with goldfish. With the price tag comes a complimentary cooked-to-order breakfast. The 232 modern two-room suites each offer a microwave oven, wet bar, refrigerator and dining area. ~ 2630 East Camelback Road; 602-955-3992, 800-362-2779, fax 602-955-6479; www.phoenixbiltmore.embassy suites.com. ULTRA-DELUXE.

A find, price-wise, is the **Pyramid Inn**, a two-story brick inn with 30 large rooms and a swimming pool and free airport shuttle service. The neighborhood isn't great, but you can't beat the price. ~ 3307 East Van Buren Street; 602-275-3691, fax 602-267-0448; www.pyramidinn.com, e-mail pyramidinn@att.net. BUDGET.

For those interested in meeting fellow budget travelers, try the **Hostel Metcalf House**. Here's what you get: two dormitory-style rooms (men's and women's) with bunk beds for ten in each. Guests may use the kitchen and community room. Closed during the day and in August. ~ 1026 North 9th Street; 602-254-9803. BUDGET.

The YMCA has 139 rooms in an seven-story downtown building. It's good old Y-style, nothing fancy, but it's clean. For $2 extra, full use of the gym facilities and swimming pool is included. ~ 350 North 1st Avenue; 602-253-6181. BUDGET.

If you want to stay in shape while you're away, try the **Hilton Garden Inn Phoenix/Midtown**, a hotel with 156 rooms, a restaurant and a lounge along with a full-scale athletic club facility including basketball and racquetball courts, sauna and pool. Rooms have contemporary decor, and the workout's great. ~ 4000 North Central Avenue; 602-279-9811, fax 602-285-2932; www.hiltongardeninn.com, e-mail phxmd-salesadm@hilton.com. MODERATE TO DELUXE.

The **Hawthorn Hotel Inn & Suites** offers 93 suites with modern furnishings. There's a swimming pool as well as a free shuttle to and from downtown and the airport. ~ 3422 East Elwood Street; 602-470-0500, 800-527-1133, fax 602-470-0200; www.phoenixairport.garden.com. MODERATE.

HIDDEN ►

The **Maricopa Manor** is a Spanish-style bed and breakfast situated in a garden-like setting of palm trees and flowers in the heart of north central Phoenix. Built in 1928, the inn has seven individually decorated suites, all with private baths. Typical is the Library Suite with its king-size iron bed, private deck entrance, handsome collection of leather-bound books and an antique work desk. The Manor Suite has a double whirlpool tub and a three-sided fireplace. Guests may also use the inn's formal living, dining, music rooms, patio, pool and gazebo spa. Expanded continental breakfast included. ~ 15 West Pasadena Avenue; 602-274-6302, 800-292-6403, fax 602-266-3904; www.maricopamanor.com, e-mail res@maricopamanor.com. DELUXE TO ULTRA-DELUXE.

DINING

Looking for a quick snack? Go to the **Arizona Center**, take the elevator or stairs to the second floor and *voilà!* Here you'll find a whole array of attractive fast-food restaurants all sharing a mutual sit-down dining—**Copper Square Grill, Mi Amigo, My Pal Joey's Pizzeria** and more. ~ Van Buren between 3rd and 5th streets; 602-271-4000, fax 602-271-4417; www.arizonacenter.com. BUDGET.

At **Sam's Cafe** in the Arizona Center, a large patio set amidst fountains is one draw; good Southwestern cuisine is another. Start with *poblano* chicken chowder, then have Hannah's roasted chicken with jalapeño-garlic marinade, or the blackened salmon caesar salad. If the weather is inclement (which it rarely is), indoor dining is also nice, with more fountains and terra-cotta colored walls. ~ 455 North 3rd Street; 602-252-3545, fax 602-252-0334. MODERATE TO DELUXE.

With a dozen aquariums scattered around the lobby and dining room, the **Golden Phoenix** appears to have the largest tropical fish population of any Arizona restaurant. While the decor of this stucco-style establishment offers few Asian touches, the kitchen does wonders with Mandarin dishes like *kung pao* shrimp and hot sizzling beef. ~ 1534 West Camelback Road; 602-279-4447, fax 602-279-0158. BUDGET TO MODERATE.

AUTHOR FAVORITE

When money's no object, a stay at the **Royal Palms & Casitas** is akin to stepping onto the grounds of a Spanish-Mediterranean estate. Built in 1929 by a wealthy world traveler, it served double duty as inn and favorite winter haven for such luminaries as Groucho Marx and Helena Rubinstein. Today, this luxurious hostelry offers 117 *casitas* and guest rooms set among lush desert gardens. All are appointed with vibrantly colored Southwestern decor and boast contemplative desert views. Amenities include a fitness area and spa, sparkling pool and cabanas, and a championship golf course nearby. ~ 2500 East Camelback Road, Phoenix; 602-840-3610, 800-672-6011, fax 602-840-6927; www.royalpalmshotel.com, e-mail reservations@destinationhotels.com. ULTRA-DELUXE.

Christo's specializes in Northern Italian cuisine, which means less pasta in favor of meatier fare—chicken *zingarella*, osso buco veal, rack of lamb—and fish dishes such as halibut topped with feta cheese, olive oil, garlic and sliced tomatoes. Sparkling stemware, crisp peach-and-white tablecloths and table flowers add a festive note. No lunch on Saturday. Closed Sunday. ~ 6327 North 7th Street; 602-264-1784, fax 602-230-8953. MODERATE TO DELUXE.

If you're looking for a large, festive, family-oriented Mexican restaurant, **Carlos O'Brien's** fits the bill. Exposed ductwork, hanging plants and modern artwork supply the ambience for chowing down on fajitas, enchiladas and chimichangas. ~ 1133 East Northern Avenue; 602-274-5881, fax 602-997-7201. BUDGET TO MODERATE.

HIDDEN ▶   A popular neighborhood restaurant, **Texaz Grill** really looks like it was transferred over from Dallas with its neon beer signs, glowing jukebox and antique wall memorabilia (old Texas license plates and the like). Steaks come in a variety of sizes, from an 8-ounce filet to an 18-ounce T-bone, but the biggest seller of all is the chicken-fried steak served with heaps of mashed potatoes and buttermilk biscuits, just like in Texas. No lunch on Sunday. ~ 6003 North 16th Street; phone/fax 602-248-7827; www.texazgrill.com, e-mail texaz@texazgrill.com. MODERATE.

What it lacks in decor, **Ham's** makes up for in great cooking. Specials change daily and include beef tips and noodles, fried chicken, barbecued beef and meatloaf, all served with heaps of mashed potatoes, veggies and biscuits. ~ 3302 North 24th Street; 602-954-8775. BUDGET TO MODERATE.

Comfort is not a problem at **Richardson's**, where lots of plump pillows adorn pale brown faux adobe booths. This New Mexico–style eatery is irreverent (political commentary often livens up the chalkboards), intimate and lively, with lots of music and talk competing at loud decibels. Favorites here include the garlic pasta with shrimp and the Santa Fe chicken with jalapeño hollandaise. ~ 1582 East Bethany Home Road; 602-265-5886, fax 602-241-3354. MODERATE TO ULTRA-DELUXE.

For a stylish escape from the often awful heat of downtown Phoenix, pamper yourself with high tea at the elegantly Victorian **Spicery**. Located in the Catlin Court Historical District, an area where historic homes have been preserved, this eatery is in a charming 1895 Victorian house. It makes food the way mother used to—homemade soups, salads, chubby sandwiches, fresh-baked bread and pies. The Spicery offers high tea Tuesday through Saturday (by reservation only). Closed Sunday in summer and winter. ~ 7141 North 59th Avenue, Glendale; 623-937-6534; www.thespicery.com. BUDGET.

At **Ayako of Tokyo**, teppanyaki chefs grill chicken, scallops, shrimp, filet mignon and lobster at your table. Each entrée comes with soup, salad, rice and vegetables. Rice paper screens add a Japanese touch to the decor of this restaurant graced with oriental paintings and panels. There are also a sushi bar and a lounge. Keep in mind, however, that we've received reports indicating that the restaurant's not living up to its reputation and is often overcrowded and noisy. No lunch on Sunday. ~ 2564 East Camelback Road, Biltmore Fashion Park; 602-955-7007. MODERATE TO ULTRA-DELUXE.

Wright's is an open, airy dining room at the Arizona Biltmore with a menu featuring New American cuisine. There is raisin and pistachio french toast with warm fruit compote as well as snazzy egg dishes for Sunday brunch. The dinner and Sunday brunch menus are filled with seafood and meat dishes served with intriguing sauces. For dinner, start with an appetizer such as *foie gras* with a currant compote, and then try an entrée such as pan-roasted scallops with Swiss chard or lamb loin with a mushroom ragout. Save room for one of their fabulous desserts. Dinner and Sunday brunch only. Hours vary in summer; call ahead. ~ 2400 East Missouri Avenue; 602-954-2507, fax 602-381-7600; www.arizonabiltmore.com, e-mail reservations@arizonabiltmore.com. ULTRA-DELUXE.

Ever try duck tamales? Mix Southwest and French cuisine, as they do at **Vincent Guerithault**, and that's the result. You'll find a country French atmosphere, complete with floral seat cushions and dried floral table centerpieces, while diners enjoy chimichanga of lobster and the like. Top it off with crème brûlée in, what else, a sweet "taco" shell. Valet parking is available in this establishment. ~ 3930 East Camelback Road; 602-224-0225, fax 602-956-5400. ULTRA-DELUXE.

Havana Cafe offers the not-too-spicy cuisine of South America, Spain and Cuba in an atmosphere that's more a small, cozy café than in the style of Hemingway's Havana. *Chicharitas*, an appetizer

AUTHOR FAVORITE

Christopher's Fermier Brasserie ("Farmers' Tavern") features chef-owner Christopher Gross' gourmet fare prepared with fresh local produce. The French-inspired cuisine includes specialties such as truffle-infused smoked sirloin and house-smoked salmon. The menu matches a wine with each entrée and provides a rotating selection of 100 vintages available by the glass. The adjacent wine bar offers cheese and seafood platters and after-meal (or late-night) cigars. Reservations recommended. ~ In Biltmore Fashion Park, 2584 East Camelback Road; 602-522-2344, fax 602-468-0314; www.fermier.com. DELUXE TO ULTRA-DELUXE.

of fried green plantain chips, will get the juices flowing. In addition, you'll find Cuban chicken marinated in orange juice, lime juice and garlic, and paella (for two), the house specialty; sausage; *sopa de ajo* (garlic soup); *escabeche*; *picadillo* and more. No lunch on Sunday. ~ 4225 East Camelback Road; 602-952-1991, fax 480-991-0535; e-mail havanacafe@prodigy.net. MODERATE.

HIDDEN ►

A spot popular with the downtown office workers eager for a touch of home cooking, **Mrs. White's Golden Rule Cafe** offers pork chops, chicken, cornbread and cobbler. Get there early for a table. No dinner. Closed weekends. ~ 808 East Jefferson Street; 602-262-9256. MODERATE.

SHOPPING

Western wear would seem a natural when hitting the Phoenix shopping scene—and you're right. There's a herd of places selling boots, shirts, buckles and whatever else you might want.

If you're in the market for Western clothes, just to look the part or to get ready for your next rodeo appearance, you might start with **Aztex Hats**, which offers the largest selection of Western hats in Arizona. Closed Sunday. ~ 15044 North Cave Creek; 602-971-9090. **Saba's Western Store**, in business since 1927, included Barry Goldwater among its clientele. There are branches of the store dotted around Arizona. Check their website for locations. ~ 2901 West Bell Road, 602-993-5948; and 7611 West Thomas Road, 623-873-0753; www.sabaswesternwear.com. **Sheplers** is part of the world's largest Western-wear chain. ~ 9201 North 29th Avenue; 602-870-8085; www.sheplers.com.

If you like malls and shopping complexes, get ready. Phoenix has them in great abundance. One entertainment complex that has helped revitalize the downtown Phoenix area is the **Arizona Center**, with dozens of restaurants, bars and shops on two levels. People come here to dine, meander through the three-acre garden area, browse in the shops or listen to occasional live entertainment in the evenings. ~ 455 North 3rd Street; 602-271-4000, fax 602-271-4417; www.arizonacenter.com.

Town & Country Shopping Center showcases more than 70 shops, restaurants and services. Red brick sidewalks, fountains and soft music set the tone at this outdoor shopping center. Highlights include **Jutenhoops** (602-957-8006) with a whimsical, funky blend of gifts, cards and jewelry. **Bookstar** (602-957-2001) offers a huge selection of new books. ~ 2021 East Camelback Road; 602-955-6850.

Located just blocks from the Town & Country Shopping Center, but infinitely more exclusive, is **Biltmore Fashion Park**. Stroll along brick-paved walkways lined with green trees and shrubs, and peek into the expensive galleries, restaurants, jewelry stores and clothing stores. For women's clothing, names include **Ann Taylor** (602-468-3339) and **Escada** (602-224-0336). Larger stores featured here include **Saks Fifth Avenue** (602-955-8000) and **Macy's** (602-468-2100). ~ Camelback Road and 24th Street; 602-955-8400.

You can also shop at old standbys. The **Green Woodpecker** (602-266-7381), a large novelty gift shop, can be found at **Park Central**, which also has several restaurants. ~ 3110 North Central Avenue; 602-264-5575. **Metrocenter** is an enclosed double-deck mall that includes **Robinson's-May**, **Dillard's** and **Macy's**. ~ 9617 North Metro Parkway West; 602-997-2641.

For designer merchandise at legendary low prices, head for **Loehmann's**. ~ 3135 East Lincoln Drive; 602-957-8691.

Museum gift shops offer unique finds for selective shoppers. For instance, the **Phoenix Art Museum** carries books, posters, catalogs and art-replica gifts, as well as a special section for kids. Closed Monday. ~ 1625 North Central Avenue; 602-257-2182; www.phxart.org.

> Phoenix averages 211 days of sunshine per year. An all-time-high temperature of 122 degrees was recorded on June 26, 1990.

The **Desert Botanical Garden** has a gift shop offering foods, spices and jellies made from desert plants, as well as plants, nature books and Southwestern souvenirs and crafts. ~ 1201 North Galvin Parkway; 480-941-1225.

Don't drop just yet. Because after all those malls and other stores, we come to the farmer's markets! Every Thursday from 10 a.m. to 2 p.m., October through April, farmers from around the community sell their freshest produce at decent prices in the courtyard at **Wesley Bolin Park**. ~ 15th and 17th avenues off Washington Street; 623-848-1234.

For a kicker, **Phoenix Park 'N Swap** is the largest open-air flea market in the Southwest, with over 2000 dealers selling or swapping everything from used office furniture and rare antiques to Indian jewelry and rare one-of-a-kind photos of Marilyn Monroe. You can shop to the sounds of live music on weekend mornings. Readers warn there's been an increase of crime at the swap; be sure not to leave anything valuable in your car, and to park as close to the action as possible. Open Wednesday, Friday and weekends. Admission. ~ 3801 East Washington Street; 602-273-1258, fax 602-273-7375; www.americanparknswap.com.

◄ HIDDEN

A small town south of Phoenix is the setting for the **Guadalupe Farmer's Market**. You will find fresh vegetables, exotic fruits and dried chile peppers. Closed Wednesday. ~ 9210 South Avenida del Yaqui, Guadalupe; 480-730-1945. A few blocks north is **Mercado Mexico**, where Mexican pottery and ceramics are sold. ~ 8212 South Avenida del Yaqui, Guadalupe; 480-831-5925.

Nightlife in south central Arizona is as diverse and far-reaching as the area itself, from twanging guitars of country-and-western bands

NIGHTLIFE

to symphony strings. There are Indian ceremonials and sophisticated jazz as well. To find out what's happening, check the entertainment pages of the *Arizona Republic* and the *Phoenix Gazette*.

If you feel adventurous, you might try **Rodeo**, where deejays spin country-and-western and Top-40 dance music. Live country-and-western bands perform some nights. Closed Monday through Wednesday. Cover. ~ 4029 North 33rd Avenue; 602-279-3800; www.rodeonightsphx.com.

A major sports and entertainment center for downtown Phoenix is the 20,000-seat **America West Arena**, a venue for Phoenix Suns basketball games, concerts, ice shows and other special events. ~ 201 East Jefferson Street; 602-379-7800, 602-379-2000; www.americawestarena.com.

A valley institution for the two-step crowd, **Mr. Lucky's** has live country music. Closed Sunday through Tuesday. Weekend cover. ~ 3660 West Grand Avenue; 602-246-0686; www.mrluckys.com.

The **Rhythm Room** is a sophisticated blues nightclub. Framed black-and-white photographs of blues greats hang on gray wood walls in this clean, uncluttered bar. Live bands play nightly, and a good-sized dancefloor in front of the stage invites audience participation. Cover. ~ 1019 East Indian School Road; 602-265-4842; www.rhythmroom.com.

Char's Has the Blues has live rhythm-and-blues nightly. Inside this old house, intimate burgundy curtains cover the windows and people dance on worn wooden floors. Wall sconces and tiny Christmas lights provide the soft lighting. ~ 4631 North 7th Avenue; 602-230-0205; www.charshastheblues.com, e-mail info@charshastheblues.com.

The Herberger Theater Center features noon performances from March through August, Tuesday through Thursday. The audience can purchase sandwiches to enjoy during the performance (tickets and sandwiches are $5 each).

Nightlife here isn't restricted to the bar and two-step scene. A more refined look at the arts flourishes here as well. **The Herberger Theater Center** is an ultramodern theater complex housing two separate theaters, **Center Stage** and **Stage West**, where professional theater performances take place. The Center features the **Actors' Theater of Phoenix** and **Child's Play** and is home to the **Arizona Theater Company**, which has performed in Phoenix for more than 25 years. ~ 222 East Monroe Street; 602-254-7399, fax 602-258-9521; www.herbergertheater.org, e-mail info@herbergertheater.org.

The **Phoenix Civic Plaza and Symphony Hall** houses the Phoenix Symphony and stages entertainment ranging from opera and ballet to Broadway shows and top-name concert performers. ~ 3rd Street between Monroe and Jefferson streets; 602-262-7272.

The nationally acclaimed **Arizona Opera Company** presents five operas per season, with classic such as Verdi's *Don Carlo* and Mozart's *Cosí Fan Tutte*. ~ The box office is located at 4600 North 12th Street; 602-266-7464.

SOUTH MOUNTAIN PARK 🚶 🚲 🐎 With 16,500 acres, this is the largest municipal park in the world, a vast rugged mountain range that was once American Indian hunting ground. A spectacular view of Phoenix can be seen from Dobbins Lookout, one of four scenic overlooks located 2300 feet above the desert floor. The park offers over 50 miles of well-marked hiking and riding trails. Its steep canyons reveal evidence of ancient American Indian artifacts and petroglyphs. Facilities include picnic areas, restrooms and a sunken concrete stage for park ranger lectures or impromptu sing-alongs. The South Mountain Environmental Education Center (closed Monday; 602-534-6324) has displays on the people, history, flora and fauna of the park. Park rangers are also available for questions. ~ 10919 South Central Avenue; 602-495-0222, fax 602-534-6330.

PARKS

PAPAGO PARK 🚶 🚲 ⚓ A part of the Phoenix parks network since 1959, Papago is a neat blend of hilly desert terrain, quiet lagoons and glistening streams. The former American Indian townsite now offers golf, picnic sites, ballfields and fishing. Three lagoons are stocked with bass, catfish, bluegill and trout in winter. (It's free for kids 13 and under but an urban fishing license is required for all others.) Also within its boundaries are the Phoenix Zoo, the Desert Botanical Garden, and the Phoenix Municipal Stadium, where the Oakland A's hold their spring training. You'll also find firepits, restrooms, an archery range, a wheelchair-accessible trail, bike paths and running courses. ~ 625 North Galvin Parkway; 602-262-4837, fax 602-534-5517.

PHOENIX MOUNTAINS PARK & RECREATION AREA 🚶 🚲 One of Phoenix's most familiar landmarks with its craggy, easily identifiable pinnacle, Piestewa Peak is primarily known for its hiking trails. However, the rocky terrain has been moderately developed for other recreational pursuits as well, whether picnicking or curling up in the shade of a towering saguaro with an Edward Abbey tome on the evils of overdevelopment. The picnic ramadas have electricity. Other amenities include drinking water, firepits, tables, benches and restrooms. ~ 2701 East Piestewa Peak Drive; 602-262-7901, fax 602-262-7901.

ESTRELLA MOUNTAIN REGIONAL PARK 🚶 🚲 🐎 With 19,840 acres, Estrella offers abundant vegetation and spectacular mountain views, with peaks within the Sierra Estrella Mountains reaching 3650 feet. The park offers excellent areas for hiking and riding, a rodeo arena and a golf course. Horse and hiking trails abound. There's an amphitheater for lectures and gatherings. Picnic areas and restrooms are located in the park. Day-use fee, $5 per vehicle. ~ Route 10, 16 miles southwest of Phoenix. Take Exit 126 onto Estrella Parkway and follow it five miles south to the park; 623-932-3811, fax 623-932-7718.

▲ There is "primitive" RV camping (no hookups); $5 per night.

WHITE TANK MOUNTAIN REGIONAL PARK 🏃 🚴 🐎 Covering 29,572 acres of desert, canyons and mountains, White Tank is the largest park in the Maricopa County Park System. Elevations range from 1402 feet at the entrance to 4083 feet at the park's highest point. White Tank contains an excellent hiking, mountain bike and horse trail system, a seasonal flowing waterfall (reached by a mile-long self-guided hiker's trail) and American Indian petroglyphs scattered throughout. Two wheelchair-accessible trails allow visitors with disabilities to view some of the park's petroglyphs. Facilities include a visitors center, picnic sites, restrooms and showers. Day-use fee, $5. ~ Dunlap Avenue (which turns into Olive Avenue before reaching the park), 15 miles west of Glendale; 623-935-2505, fax 623-535-4291.

▲ There are 36 sites; $10 per night. Backpack camping is $5 per night.

Phoenix Gay Scene

While gay and lesbian activities are found throughout Phoenix, the highest concentration centers around the blocks between Camelback and Indian School roads and between 7th Avenue and 7th Street. This area is home to an array of gay lodging, cafés, bars, shops and nightclubs.

LODGING
Larry's Bed & Breakfast, a European-style lodging, is centrally located and features three comfortable guest rooms. Folks may watch movies and play cards in the spacious living room, or lounge in the clothing-optional outdoor pool and jacuzzi. Women are welcome, but this is primarily a spot for gay men. A full breakfast is served. ~ 502 West Claremont Avenue; 602-249-2974; e-mail kenezz1@cox.net. BUDGET.

You can stay for a week or a month at the gay-owned **Arizona Royal Villa Apartments**. Hotel rooms, junior suites and one-bedroom apartments are available here. All accommodations face the courtyard. The private grounds, located within a walled complex with keyed entry, include a clothing-optional swimming pool, jacuzzi and sunbathing area. Men only. ~ 1110 East Turney Avenue; 602-266-6883, 888-266-6884, fax 602-279-7437; www.royal villa.com, e-mail rvilla@royalvilla.com. MODERATE.

The men-only **Arizona Sunburst Inn** is an L-shaped ranch house with five large, comfortable rooms furnished in contemporary designs; some rooms have private baths while others share. The outdoor heated pool and jacuzzi are clothing optional. Continental breakfast is served. ~ 6245 North 12th Place; 602-274-1474, 800-974-1474; www.azsunburst.com, e-mail sunbrstinn@aol.com. MODERATE.

Dine on all-American food in an art-deco atmosphere at the popular gay-owned **Pookie's Café**. This lively spot adorned with colorful stained-glass windows features a piano bar lounge plus more than 30 television screens playing music videos. Choose from a menu offering sandwiches, burgers, quesadillas, buffalo wings and dinner specials such as steak and pasta. Dinner and Sunday brunch are served. ~ 4540 North 7th Street; 602-277-2121; www.pookies cafe.com. BUDGET TO MODERATE.

DINING

Plaster parrots greet you as you enter **Arriba Mexican Grill** for a festive meal of New Mexican fare generously spiced with Hatch green chile. Dine on delectable shrimp fajitas, *carnitas* flavored with orange and lime, New Mexican enchiladas and fiery Taos tacos amid colorful handpainted murals, a fireplace and a fountain. Wash down your meal, if you're inclined, with some of the 22 brands of tequila. ~ 1812 East Camelback Road; 602-265-9112, fax 602-265-9182; www.arribamexicangrill.com. BUDGET TO MODERATE.

Gay-owned **Root Seller Gallery** offers gay and lesbian book titles, gifts and cards, clothes and flashy clubwear. ~ 1605 North 7th Avenue; 602-712-9338.

SHOPPING

Unique on Central is a gay-owned shop offering a large selection of cards, gifts, music, videos, travel books and magazines. ~ 4700 North Central Avenue, Suite 105; 602-279-9691; www. uniqueoncentral.com.

WEATHER OR NOT? WHILE SOME LIKE IT HOT . . .

All of south central Arizona gets hot, despite the seemingly innocuous average annual temperature of 72°F. Winter is cool and clear, in the 60s; spring is breezy and warm, in the 90s; summer is torrid, often topping 100, and that's when the monsoons come, the swift summer rainstorms that usually arrive late in the day with spectacular flashes of lightning and deep, rolling rumbles of thunder; autumn is marvelously dry and clear, in the 80s. Depending on your weather preference, choose your time to visit accordingly.

NIGHTLIFE   Perhaps the most popular gay bar in the city is **Charlie's**, where you can take two-step and line-dancing lessons two nights a week and dance to good ol' country-and-western music nightly. You can play volleyball outside on Sunday. The scene is mostly men, from 21 to 81 years of age, but all are welcome. ~ 727 West Camelback Road; 602-265-0224, fax 602-264-1065; www. charliesphoenix.com.

At **Harley's Club 155 West** you'll find a mixed crowd dancing to Top-40 and deejay music every night of the week. Cover on weekends. ~ 155 West Camelback Road; 602-274-8505; www.harleysclub155.biz.

For nightly live entertainment from drag shows to karaoke, head to **Wink's Cabaret**, a neighborhood bar. ~ 5707 North 7th Street; 602-265-9002.

Join gay and lesbian sports enthusiasts at **Roscoe's on 7th**, a popular sports bar boasting 12 monitors. Daily drink specials include Sunday's do-it-yourself bloody Mary bar. ~ 4531 North 7th Street; 602-285-0833; www. roscoeson7.com.

For a comprehensive listing of all things gay and lesbian in Phoenix, visit the Gay and Lesbian Yellow Pages at www.glyp.com.

For a women's sports club that caters mostly to lesbians, head to **Misty's**. A large dancefloor and a lively game room are the attractions. ~ 4301 North 7th Avenue; 602-265-3233.

Expect a sophisticated (if flamboyant) night out at **Eddie Matney's**. Also known as an excellent Lebanese-inspired restaurant, Eddie's bar is where Phoenix's gay elite meet. Gleaming wood and Southwestern decor, comfortable seating and scrumptious appetizers all accompanied by live jazz (on weekends) make this place *the* place. ~ 2398 East Camelback Road; 602-957-3214; www. eddiematneys.com.

Once voted the best cruise/leather bar, **The Padlock** is the place to see and be seen for the denim and leather crowd. ~ 998 East Indian School Road; 602-266-5640; www.padlockaz.com.

Ain't Nobody's Bizness is a very pink women's bar (although gay men are welcome) with R&B and Top-40 dance music most evenings. Standup comedy is featured occasionally and Monday is karaoke night. ~ 3031 East Indian School Road; 602-224-9977.

A sports bar with eight large music video screens, plus pool tables, darts, video games, foosball and shuffleboard, **Nasty's** attracts a mix of lesbians and gay patrons. There's karaoke on Wednesday and Friday nights. ~ 3108 East McDowell Road; 602-267-8707.

The dancing crowd works up a sweat on **Boom Nightclub's** large dancefloor, with state-of-the-art light and sound, Thursday through Saturday nights, when deejays spin high-energy tunes. Cover on Friday and Saturday. ~ 1724 East McDowell Road; 602-254-0231.

Over by the airport stands Phoenix's oldest gay bar, **Nu–Towne Saloon**. Sunday and Tuesday drink specials ensure a convivial bunch at this popular hangout. ~ 5002 East Van Buren Street; 602-267-9959; www.nu-towne.com.

▼▼▼▼▼▼▼▼▼
Scottsdale

Like neighboring Phoenix, Scottsdale is proud of its frontier heritage, which can be traced at a number of locations in and near the town. In the Old Scottsdale section, where only 35 years ago Lulu Belle's and the Pink Pony were the only two watering holes for miles around, the buildings all have false fronts, handcrafted signs and hitching posts, and horses still have the right of way. Many restaurants feature waiters and waitresses in period dress. The women have teased hairdos, and the men are all called Slim, Ace, Tex, Shorty and Stretch.

But that's about as Western as it gets. Otherwise, Scottsdale is chic, elegant and expensive. Amid its ties to the past, Scottsdale is a showplace of innovative architecture. The Frank Lloyd Wright Foundation is located here (at Taliesin West), as is the Cosanti Foundation, design headquarters for the controversial prototype town of Arcosanti, some 30 miles from Prescott, where building and nature are being fused.

SIGHTS

Don't miss **Rawhide Wild West Town** with its colorful variety of rides and attractions, shops, a steakhouse and a saloon—all mostly located along a rickety Main Street where visitors dodge authentic-looking cowboys and -girls on horseback. Western shootouts, fiddlers, a gypsy fortuneteller, stunt shows, a covered-wagon circle and Old West artifacts are all part of the fun. ~ 23023 North Scottsdale Road; 480-502-1880, fax 480-502-1301; www.raw hide.com.

Taliesin West/Frank Lloyd Wright Foundation, a National Historic Landmark owned by the Frank Lloyd Wright Foundation, was the architect's Arizona home and studio. Situated on 600 acres of rugged Sonoran Desert, this remarkable set of buildings still astounds architectural critics with its beauty and unusual forms. A variety of guided tours are offered. Closed Tuesday and Wednesday from July to September. Admission. ~ 12621 North Frank Lloyd Wright Boulevard; 480-860-2700, fax 480-451-8989; www.franklloydwright.org, e-mail bevhart@franklloyd wright.org.

The **Scottsdale Museum of Contemporary Art** is housed, appropriately, in an ultramodern concrete-and-steel building complete with understated neon lettering. The collection focuses on the contemporary, with a rotating series of exhibits. An example includes James Turrell's celebrated "skyspaces." It's a good (air-conditioned) place to wander and, if needed, take a break from the more Southwestern-themed art of other local museums. Closed

Monday. Admission (free on Thursday). ~ 7374 East 2nd Street; 480-994-2787, fax 480-874-4655; www.smoca.org, e-mail smoca @sccarts.org.

LODGING   The **James Hotel** is located in the heart of "Old Town," close to everything. Its 195 rooms have a colorful and modern motif. You'll find a lounge, a restaurant and a swimming pool. ~ 7353 East Indian School Road; 480-994-9203, 800-505-2637, fax 480-308-1200; www.jameshotel.com. DELUXE TO ULTRA-DELUXE.

Plunging down a waterslide might seem like a silly thing for a grown-up to do, but when the temperature tops 100° in the shade, you'll understand its charm. But why go to a water park when the **Hyatt Regency Scottsdale Resort at Gainey Ranch** is around? Lounge on the sand beach, take a dip in the jacuzzi beneath a Greek water temple, or swim in the ten pools connected by a network of fountains, waterfalls, and a three-story waterslide. The 490 rooms, suites and *casitas* are modern with Sonoran Desert tones. Amenities here include a health spa, four restaurants, golfing, tennis and an American Indian seed garden and environmental learning center. ~ 7500 East Doubletree Ranch Road; 480-991-3388, 800-554-9288, fax 480-483-5550; www. scottsdale.hyatt.com. ULTRA-DELUXE.

The **Scottsdale Plaza Resort** is a true find. Set within 40 acres, with 404 rooms, 180 of them suites, the resort features Spanish Mediterranean–style villas throughout, accented with courtyard swimming pools. The rooms are large and styled with Southwestern furnishing and art. Fountains, palm trees, earth-tone tiles, mauve carpeting, acres of fresh-cut flowers and potted greens add cooling touches. There are swimming pools, outdoor spas, tennis courts, indoor racquetball courts, a pro shop, a gym and a putting green. ~ 7200 North Scottsdale Road; 480-948-5000, 800-832-2025, fax 480-998-5971; www.scottsdaleplaza.com, e-mail info@ scottsdaleplaza.com. DELUXE TO ULTRA-DELUXE.

If you're looking for a gem of a mini-resort, try the 56-room **Best Western Papago Inn & Resort**. Amenities include a heated pool, sauna, lounge and dining room. Guest rooms all overlook a treed and flowered interior courtyard and swimming pool. Environmental "green" rooms—nonsmoking rooms with air and water filter systems—are available for a charge. ~ 7017 East McDowell Road; 480-947-7335, 800-528-1234, fax 480-994-0692; www.papagoinn.com, e-mail papago@interwrx.com. BUDGET TO DELUXE.

Holiday Inn–Sunspree Resort, located on 16 lushly landscaped acres in the heart of Scottsdale, has 200 guest rooms (including 17 one- and two-bedroom suites). All are decorated in contemporary, upscale style. Recreational facilities include tennis courts, a pool, on-site golf, jogging trails and horseback riding. ~ 7601 East Indian Bend Road; 480-991-2400, 800-852-5205, fax 480-998-2261; www.arizonaguide.com/sunspree, e-mail srs@quik.com. DELUXE.

Ramada Scottsdale on Fifth Avenue, a secluded retreat in the heart of Scottsdale's premier shopping district, sprawls out around a central courtyard with a large heated swimming pool. Its 92 rooms feature desert colors, king and double queen beds, and separate dressing areas. Rates includes continental breakfast. ~ 6935 5th Avenue; 480-994-9461, 800-553-2666, fax 480-947-1695; www.econolodge.com. DELUXE.

The **Best Western Scottsdale Airport Suites** is a four-story, all-suite hotel designed in a courtyard setting with a heated pool and spa and a restaurant on the premises. Each of the hotel's two-room suites is styled in desert mauve and teals with light Southwestern contemporary furnishings. ~ 7515 East Butherus Drive; 480-951-4000, fax 480-483-9046; www.scottsdalebest western.com. DELUXE.

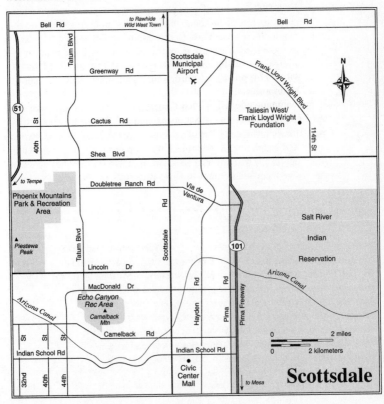

DINING

In the heart of the Scottsdale shopping district is **Jacqueline's Marketplace & Cafe**, an upscale, whimsical café/shop with lots of Southwestern gifts and bright coyote paintings and cards by artist Holly Haas. For dining, choices include table service or self-service, selecting from the wide variety of pastas, salads and sandwiches. The outdoor patio with its plants, brick walls and Southwestern tiles are a favorite in warm weather. Breakfast and lunch only. ~ 7303 East Indian School Road; 480-947-8777. BUDGET.

Julio G's, established in 1934, somehow manages to combine a '30s art deco, Santa Fe and Mexican truck-stop decor—ceiling fans, black-tile walls and framed vintage-Mexican advertisements—into a trendy contemporary look. The food is much more clearly defined: *pollo magnifico*, beef tacos, bean tostadas, steaming bowls of rice and beans, chili con carne and tortillas. The staff is friendly and attentive. ~ 7633 East Indian School Road; 480-423-0058, fax 480-874-1193. BUDGET TO MODERATE.

For burgers, chicken and appetizers in a trendy eatery, stop by **AZ88**. The furnishings are made of glass, wood and steel and there are lots of climbing vines and floor-to-ceiling windows that overlook the green Civic Center Mall. Fresh flowers dot tabletops and contemporary urban music plays in the background for a lively meal. No lunch on weekends. ~ 7353 Scottsdale Mall; 480-994-5576; www.az88.com, e-mail paulaz88@quest.net. BUDGET TO MODERATE.

Malee's on Main Thai Gourmet is a charming little spot with a bar in one corner, tables inside and a patio, weather permitting, for dining outside. Attractive tableware is set against sandalwood- and eggplant-colored tablecloths. Popular with the art crowd (in Scottsdale that covers a wide swath), the restaurant has an extensive menu that comes in various degrees of spiciness. No lunch

AUTHOR FAVORITE

A courtyard—complete with a lagoon, two pools (one with a sand beach and a waterslide) and a jacuzzi—is the center of attention at **SunBurst Resort**. Decked out in contemporary Southwestern decor, the 204 rooms and suites feature French doors and private balconies and are equipped with satellite TV, coffeemakers, minibars and double phone lines. With a restaurant/lounge and a fitness room on-site, you won't have to abandon this modern oasis. ~ 4925 North Scottsdale Road; 480-945-7666, 800-528-7867, fax 480-946-4056; www.sunburstresort.com, e-mail mperdue@sunburstresort.com. DELUXE TO ULTRA-DELUXE.

on Sunday. ~ 7131 East Main Street; 480-947-6042, fax 480-994-3474; www.maleesonmain.com. MODERATE TO DELUXE.

One of the oldest Mexican restaurants in Scottsdale (also considered the finest by many) is **Los Olivos**. The restaurant was founded in 1945, but the adobe building in which it's located was built in 1928 and is officially listed as one of Scottsdale's historic landmarks. Large and rambling, with viga ceilings, it has several individual dining rooms inside and patio dining outside. The Mexican cuisine served is primarily Sonoran—enchiladas, seasonal green corn tamales, chimichangas, *chiles rellenos* and steak *picado*. The decor is festive (clay pots, flowers and piñatas) and there's live music and dancing on weekends. Aficionados rate its margaritas among the best in the state. ~ Two locations: 7328 East 2nd Street, 480-946-2256; and 15544 North Pima Road, 480-596-9787; www.azeats.com/losolivos. BUDGET TO MODERATE.

Located in the Phoenician resort, **Mary Elaine's** is classically elegant, decorated in soft shades of beige, gray and peach, with lavish touches such as 18th-century Italian oil paintings, German crystal stemware and romantic outdoor patios. The restaurant's menu offers modern French cuisine, with such specialties as cream of lobster soup with porcini mushrooms, herb-crusted rack of lamb and pan-roasted wild fresh turbot. Dinner only. Closed Sunday and Monday. ~ 6000 East Camelback Road; 480-423-2530. DELUXE TO ULTRA-DELUXE.

A traditional breakfast spot is **The Original Pancake House**, serving up steaming stacks of golden flapjacks, topped with melted butter, honey, maple syrup, berries or whatever's your pleasure. The restaurant is small—eleven tables and ten booths. The decor is Southwestern with light green and tan colors dominating. Large picture windows in front keep it bright and cheerful. ~ 6840 East Camelback Road; 480-946-4902; www.originalpancakehouse.com, e-mail info@originalpancakehouse.com. BUDGET.

Dark hardwood tables and white limestone walls add to the Southwestern ambience at the bi-level **Z'Tejas Grill**. Try the voodoo tuna blackened with a spicy soy mustard and black pepper vinaigrette, followed by ancho chile fudge pie. The Southwestern cuisine is also laced with flavors from Louisiana. ~ 7014 East Camelback Road; 480-946-4171, fax 480-946-0079. MODERATE.

Voltaire is a bastion of French gastronomy, all candlelight and crystal. Chicken provençal, rack of lamb and sweetbreads sautéed in lemon butter and capers highlight the extensive menu. Dinner only. Closed Sunday and from August to mid-September. ~ 8340 East McDonald Drive; 480-948-1005. DELUXE.

Ristorante Sandolo is an Italian café known for its singing gondoliers. The restaurant dishes out Venetian-style entrées, followed by complimentary *sandolo* (similar to gondola) rides on the wa-

Text continued on page 244.

Spoil
Yourself

The American West is big and grand—how inconsistent it would be if its great resort hotels were not just a reach beyond all expectation. And Central Arizona is home to some of the biggest and grandest around.

Inspired by Frank Lloyd Wright and designed by Albert Chase McArthur, the refurbished **Arizona Biltmore** has maintained an aura of ease and luxury since its opening in 1929. From its palm-lined drive, elaborate high portico and immense lobby to its bright, handsomely furnished guest rooms, the 730-room Biltmore is as dramatic and visually exciting as it is comfortable. The "Jewel of the Desert" provides a full range of activities: golf courses, tennis courts, pools, a children's playground, a water slide and a spa, salon and fitness center. ~ 2400 East Missouri Avenue, Phoenix; 602-955-6600, 800-950-0086, fax 602-954-2548; www.arizonabiltmore.com, e-mail azbres@arizonabiltmore.com. ULTRA-DELUXE.

Another ultra-deluxe establishment in Phoenix, to say the least, is **The Phoenician**, the most prestigious and talked-about resort in the Valley of the Sun. Sprawled over 250 acres along the sun-dappled flanks of Camelback Mountain, it's set within a tiered oasis of waterfalls and pools, the largest of which is tiled entirely with mother-of-pearl. Its 654 guest rooms are large and lavish, with most situated in the main hotel. There are also 119 *casita* units with parlor suites that have hand-carved travertine fireplaces. If you really want to make a night of it, there are 4 presidential and 71 luxury suites, and 7 villas. Recreational facilities run the gamut—a 27-hole golf course, lighted tennis courts, tournament croquet and a health and fitness spa. ~ 6000 East Camelback Road, Scottsdale; 480-941-8200, 800-888-8234, fax 480-947-4311; www.thephoenician.com, e-mail info@thephoenician.com. ULTRA-DELUXE.

The Fairmont Scottsdale Princess Resort, an ultra-luxury resort set against the dramatic backdrop of the McDowell

Mountains, has 650 rooms. It's one of the Valley's largest hotels. Set on 450 elaborately landscaped acres with a central courtyard, waterfall, five swimming pools and 18th-century Spanish Colonial architecture, the Princess is one of the most visually arresting of its kind. The rooms are large, decorated in Southwestern furnishing, with a hint of Santa Fe. The grounds include seven tennis courts, a fitness center, a spa and two championship golf courses. ~ 7575 East Princess Drive, Scottsdale; 480-585-4848, 800-344-4758, fax 480-585-0086; www.fairmont.com. ULTRA-DELUXE.

With 453 rooms, **Camelback Inn, A JW Marriott Resort & Spa** outside Scottsdale is yet another glorious world-class retreat dramatically nestled in the foothills between the Camelback and Mummy mountains, where landscaped paths wind through gardens of cactus and desert palms. Its Southwestern pueblo architecture and adobe-style *casitas* blend harmoniously into the stunning desert background. For the sportsminded there are championship golf and tennis, swimming, trail rides, a spa, weekly cookouts and fitness facilities. ~ 5402 East Lincoln Drive, Paradise Valley; 480-948-1700, 800-242-2635, fax 480-951-8469; www.camelbackinn.com. ULTRA-DELUXE.

Who says the West is wild? The **Wigwam** west of Phoenix is an upper-upper-scale resort on 75 acres of what was originally virgin desert. The design is pueblo-style, with 331 desert-brown adobe *casitas* set in a lavish golf and country-club setting—towering palms, green lawns, cascading flowers and fragrant orange trees. Through the use of building materials native to the Southwest, architecture blends with nature. Slate, stone and wood surfaces are accented with Indian themes and desert colors. Championship golf courses, nearby riding, tennis, swimming and other activities keep the body occupied while the mind relaxes. ~ 300 Wigwam Boulevard, Litchfield Park; 623-935-3811, 800-327-0396, fax 623-935-3737; www.wigwamresort.com. ULTRA-DELUXE.

terway winding through the Hyatt Regency Scottsdale. Dinner only. ~ 7500 East Doubletree Ranch Road; 480-991-3388, fax 482-443-1278. MODERATE TO DELUXE.

Although chain restaurants are generally frowned on in the travel-writing business, **Roy's of Scottsdale** is an exception. Pacific-rim influenced, the Asian food is tinged with a touch of the French and a bit of the Hawaiian, and always delicately and deliciously prepared. Dinner only. ~ 7001 North Scottsdale Road; 480-905-1155. DELUXE TO ULTRA-DELUXE.

House of Yang is small, only a few tables and chairs, and it appears to do a large takeout business. But whether you eat in or take out, the House of Yang is a course in Chinese cuisine, serving Szechwan, Hunan, Mandarin and Cantonese. Shrimp with lobster sauce—shrimp, onions and peppers, stir-fried and topped with a black bean sauce—comes with rice, wontons and an egg roll. Mongolian beef is thinly sliced beef served with egg roll, fried rice and wontons. ~ 13802 North Scottsdale Road; 480-443-0188. BUDGET TO MODERATE.

Rawhide Steakhouse and Saloon is the place to belly up to the bar in Scottsdale's popular Old West frontier town. There's good things to eat, too—mesquite-grilled steaks, prime rib, barbecued chicken, baby back ribs and even fried rattlesnake. The saloon section has an antique bar and live country music nightly. Dinner nightly; lunch served on weekends and seasonally only. ~ 23023 North Scottsdale Road; 480-563-5600, 800-527-1880; www.rawhide.com, e-mail info@rawhide.com. MODERATE TO DELUXE.

Heavily used in Southwestern cuisine, the mighty chile pepper serves double duty as a flavor enhancer and a body temperature regulator. Arizonans have long known that spicy foods trigger sweating, which is the body's natural cooling mechanism.

Greasewood Flats is a hot dog, chili and beer kind of place housed in an old graffiti-covered wooden shack in what appears to be a Western junkyard, with discarded school desks, wooden wagons, saddle frames, wagon wheels and egg crates all around it. But folks line up to get in. Live music Wednesday through Sunday. ~ 27000 North Alma School Road; 480-585-9430. BUDGET.

The **Marquesa** is one of the top restaurants in the valley. Even people who normally avoid hotel dining rooms flock to this one in the Fairmont Scottsdale Princess to soak up all of its Old World Spanish ambience and nibble on *tapas* before settling down to more serious pursuits—Marseille bouillabaisse, for instance, or steaming Mediterranean-style paella for two. The Marquesa is also known for its excellent wine list. Dinner Wednesday through Saturday, plus Sunday brunch. ~ 7575 East Princess Drive; 480-585-4848; www.fairmont.com, e-mail scottsdale@fairmont.com. ULTRA-DELUXE.

Don't wear a necktie if you're going to the **Pinnacle Peak Patio** because they'll snip it off and hang it from the rafters. In fact, over the last 40 years, more than a million customers have lost their ties to the butcher knife. That's part of the appeal of this highly informal Western-style steakhouse where 16-ounce mesquite-broiled steaks, with all the beans and fixin's, top the menu and the walls reverberate with the sounds of live country bands nightly. No lunch Monday through Saturday. ~ 10426 East Jomax Road; 480-585-1599; www.pinnaclepeakpatio.com, e-mail info@pppatio.com. MODERATE TO ULTRA-DELUXE.

SHOPPING

The **Borgata of Scottsdale** may just be a harbinger of a striking new trend in shopping—mini-theme-park shopping malls—this one, a 14th-century-style village with medieval courtyards. International fashions, fine jewelry, unusual gifts and a spate of art galleries await. ~ 6166 North Scottsdale Road; 480-812-0152, fax 480-998-7581; www.westcor.com.

Despite the trendy intrusions, **Scottsdale Fashion Square** remains the city's most fashionable shopping complex. It features top-quality stores like **Neiman Marcus** (480-990-2100), **Dillard's** (480-949-5869) and **Robinson's-May** (480-941-0066). There's even a shop for the kiddies—**The Disney Store** (480-994-9616). ~ 7014 East Camelback Road; 480-990-7800.

Fifth Avenue Shops comprise the landmark shopping area in the heart of downtown Scottsdale, a sprawl of specialty shops, boutiques, bookstores, galleries, jewelry stores, American Indian crafts shops and restaurants, over 200 in all by latest count. ~ 7121 East 5th Avenue; 480-946-7566. Among them is **Sewell's Indian Arts** with American Indian jewelry, kachinas, Pueblo pottery and Navajo sand paintings. ~ 7087 5th Avenue; 480-945-0962.

Kactus Jock has casual apparel and active wear, as well as Southwestern gifts. ~ 7121 5th Avenue, #7; 480-946-7566.

Arizona Sun Products has fun gift items, but specializes in a wonderful moisturizer containing native plants such as aloe vera, jojoba, wild roses and cacti. The desert scene on the front makes it a good souvenir, too. ~ 7136 East 5th Avenue; 480-941-9067.

Mystery lovers should seek out **The Poisoned Pen**, a mystery bookstore specializing in crime, detective and suspense books from American and British publishers. ~ 4014 North Goldwater Boulevard; 480-947-2974; www.poisonedpen.com.

For you cowpokes, **Porters** is one of the oldest names in Scottsdale cowboy gear and features top-of-the-line name brands. ~ 3944 North Brown Avenue; 480-945-0868.

After New York City and Santa Fe, Scottsdale is the busiest art center in the country, with more than 200 galleries. They offer contemporary works, Indian art, Western and Old Masters.

If you're interested in the local art scene, the **Scottsdale Gallery Association** conducts an ArtWalk every Thursday from 7 to 9 p.m., visiting many of the leading galleries. ~ 480-990-3939; www.scottsdalegalleries.com.

Bursting with upscale boutiques and art galleries, Scottsdale is more akin to Rodeo Drive than to a rodeo, despite its Western roots.

Arizona West Galleries specializes in Western and Indian War relics and American 19th- and 20th-century Western art, including works by Frederic Remington, Charlie Russell and Maynard Dixon. Closed Sunday. ~ 7149 East Main Street; 480-994-3752.

The **Biltmore Galleries** also has 19th- and 20th-century art, including works by early New Mexico master Nicolai Fechin, Joseph Sharp and Ernest Blumenschein. Closed Sunday. ~ 7113 Main Street; 480-947-5975.

At **King Galleries of Scottsdale** you'll find a selection of Pueblo pottery with an emphasis on the traditional that never cancels out the innovative. Stone-polished, hand-painted and hand-fired, the pieces are some of the most gorgeous around. Closed Sunday. ~ 7171 Main Street #1, Scottsdale; 480-481-0187, 800-394-1843; www.kinggalleries.com.

Packaged gift items featuring one of Arizona's most flavorful products are available at the **Sphinx Date Ranch**. ~ 3039 North Scottsdale Road; 480-941-2261.

A unique assortment of boutiques and gift shops can be found at **El Pedregal Festival Marketplace**. **Blue Sage Gallery** (480-488-1292) features contemporary American Indian and Western ceramic art, jewelry, kachinas and paintings. ~ 34505 North Scottsdale Road; www.elpedregal.com.

Glenn Green Galleries uses the elegant grounds of the posh Phoenician Resort (the gallery is in the hotel's retail corridor) to display the mammoth bronze and stone sculptures of famed Indian artist Allan Houser, as well as sculptors Melanie Yazzie and Eduardo Oropeza. ~ 6000 East Camelback Road; 480-990-9110; www.glenngreengalleries.com, e-mail glenngreengalleries@glenngreengalleries.com.

J. F. Fine Arts handles serigraphs, lithographs, oils and sculpture, including those by top contemporary painters Jean Richardson and Earl Biss. Closed Sunday. ~ 4151 North Marshall Way; 480-945-7856.

Contemporary American Indian art is the focus of **Lovena Ohl Gallery** where there are sculptures by Larry Yazzie, paintings by David Johns and Tony Da, and pottery, jewelry and Kachina dolls by a variety of artists. Closed Sunday. ~ 7144 East Main Street; 480-946-6764.

To get your practical shopping done in one convenient stop, drive to **Scottsdale Pavilions**, a 1.2-million-square-foot complex that includes a pharmacy, clothing stores, fast-food stops, a bookstore and a home improvement store. ~ Corner of Pima and Indian Bend roads; 480-991-6007.

Simic Contemporary handles wallhangings, sculptures, oils and lithographs from top contemporary artists. Closed Sunday. ~ 4151 North Marshall Way; 480-945-7856; www.simic.com.

For starters, get an eyeful of the beautiful, Spanish Mediterranean-style **Bar at T. Cook's**. The walls are hand-painted, enhanced by fireplaces and antiques. Daily piano music sets the mood for drinks and conversation. There's also a well-ventilated cigar room. ~ Royal Palms Resort and Spa Inn, 5200 East Camelback Road; 602-840-3610, fax 602-808-3116.

NIGHTLIFE

At the spirited **Handlebar J**, live country-and-western bands perform nightly. Cover on the weekend. ~ 7116 East Becker Lane; 480-948-0110.

The **Lobby Bar** features live music—flamenco Wednesday through Saturday and Caribbean steel drums Sunday through Tuesday. ~ Hyatt Regency Scottsdale, 7500 East Doubletree Ranch Road; 480-991-3388.

J. Chew & Company is an intimate, European-style pub with French doors leading to two outdoor patios with fireplaces. During the winter, the schedule varies so call ahead. ~ 7320 Scottsdale Mall; 480-946-2733.

Buzz Funbar offers high-energy deejay-spun tunes on Friday and Saturday nights. ~ 10345 North Scottsdale Road; 480-991-3866.

Scottsdale Center for the Arts, located in the beautifully sculptured Scottsdale Mall, hosts a variety of events, including the Scottsdale Symphony, guest performing artists, concerts, lectures, classic cinema and art exhibitions. During the summer, music lovers flock to the concerts held outside on the grassy lawn at the mall's east end. ~ 7380 East 2nd Street. For a schedule, call 480-994-2787; www.scottsdalearts.org, e-mail info@sccarts.org.

There's dueling honky tonkin' pianos on Friday and Saturday nights at the **Satisfied Frog**. Wednesday night is open mike. ~ 6245 East Cave Creek Road; 480-488-3317.

Immediately east of Phoenix are the communities of Tempe and Mesa. Continuing out over the desert that stretches on to New Mexico are Apache Junction and Globe. It's as though, heading east, all the big-city sheen dissolves in degrees into the West of the Old West, the pace slows down and you can almost reach up and feel the sky in your hands.

▼▼▼▼▼▼▼▼▼▼▼▼
Tempe/Mesa Area

Bordered by Scottsdale, Mesa, Phoenix and Chandler, **Tempe** was founded in 1872 by Charles Turnbell Hayden, who established

SIGHTS

the Hayden Flour Mill that year, now the oldest continuously operating business in Arizona. **Old Town Tempe** is where Tempe was originally founded, set up around the old Hayden Flour Mill. Today many of the early homes and buildings have been renovated and serve as restaurants, shops, offices and galleries. ~ North of University Street along Mill Avenue.

Stop by the **Tempe Convention and Visitors Bureau** for maps and information. Closed weekends. ~ 51 West 3rd Street, Suite 105; 480-894-8158, 800-283-6734, fax 480-968-8004; www. tempecvb.com, e-mail info@tempecvb.com.

Forming the character of Tempe is **Arizona State University** (480-965-9011, fax 480-965-2159; www.asu.edu, e-mail information@asu.edu), located in the heart of the city. With its 450-acre main campus, where strikingly modern buildings rise from a setting of palm trees and subtropical plants, Arizona State provides the chiefly residential city with its main industry. A number of outstanding museums dot the campus and are open to the public. **Arizona State University Art Museum** has an extensive collection of American paintings, prints and crafts as well as artworks from Latin America. Closed Sunday and Monday. ~ 480-965-2787; www.asuartmuseum.asu.edu. The **Museum of Anthropology** includes archaeological, physical and sociocultural anthropology exhibits. Closed weekends. ~ 480-965-6224. Highlight exhibits at the **Museum of Geology** focus on rare geologic specimens, seismographs and mammoth bones. Closed weekends and sporadically throughout the week; call ahead. ~ 480-965-7065.

For a trip back in time, visit the outstanding **Tempe Historical Museum**, which covers the history of Tempe from early Indian days to the present. Two changing galleries offer historic exhibits on the area. There are also hands-on displays for children. Closed Friday. ~ 809 East Southern Avenue; 480-350-5100, fax 480-350-5150; www.tempe.gov/museum.

Just east of Tempe, you'll come to the town of **Mesa**. Situated on a plateau, Mesa in Spanish means "table." The town was founded by Mormons in 1883 and was long a farming community. Irrigation canals built by the Hohokam Indians were still used in Mesa until fairly recent times. For information on sights and services in Mesa, stop by the **Mesa Convention and Visitors Bureau**. Closed weekends. ~ 120 North Center Street, Mesa; 480-827-4700, 800-283-6372, fax 480-827-4704; www.mesacvb. com, e-mail info@mesacvb.com.

Mesa Southwest Museum covers the history of the Southwest from the time of the dinosaurs to the settlement of the West, with hands-on exhibits inside. Closed Monday. Admission. ~ 53 North MacDonald Street, Mesa; 480-644-2230; www.mesasouthwest museum.com.

Twenty minutes north of Mesa is the **Out of Africa Wildlife Park**, where lions, tigers, bears, wolves and reptiles do their things. There are shows, natural habitat viewing, cub-petting and a playground for the kids. There's also a gift shop and restaurant. Closed Monday, and Monday and Tuesday in summer. Admission. ~ 9736 North Fort McDowell Road, Fountain Hills; 480-837-7779, fax 480-837-7379; www.outofafricapark.com.

LODGING

Located in the heart of downtown Tempe is the **Tempe Mission Palms Hotel**, with 303 Southwestern-style rooms and a lobby that has a wonderful wooden registration desk with a granite top and intricate millwork. Nice touches in the rooms include paintings of pottery on the walls, pastel bedspreads, bathrooms with marbleized sinks and a small makeup bureau. Most rooms overlook the lush, palm tree–dotted courtyard with fountains. Other amenities include a restaurant, a sauna, a rooftop swimming pool, whirlpool, exercise room and tennis courts. ~ 60 East 5th Street, Tempe; 480-894-1400, 800-547-8705, fax 480-968-7677; www.missionpalms.com. DELUXE TO ULTRA-DELUXE.

Sprawling across 33 acres, the **Fiesta Inn Resort** offers 270 Southwestern-style guest rooms. All have refrigerators and several are mini-suites. The fitness-minded will find a swimming pool, jacuzzi, tennis courts and an exercise room. There's also a restaurant on the premises. ~ 2100 South Priest Drive, Tempe; 480-967-1441, 800-528-6481, fax 480-967-0224; www.fiestainnresort.com. ULTRA-DELUXE.

Tempe/Mesa Area

The **Wyndham Buttes Resort** is a dramatic 353-room, four-story resort built into the mountainsides, with Southwestern styling and art throughout. All guest rooms feature a Southwestern decor or rose and earth tones, cactus and wood furnishings. It has two restaurants, a nightclub, pools, tennis courts and all of the modern trim and trappings associated with luxury resort living in the valley, including cascading waterfalls and four romantic mountainside whirlpools. ~ 2000 Westcourt Way, Tempe; 602-225-9000, 800-996-3426, fax 602-431-2422; www.wyndhambuttes.com. MODERATE TO ULTRA-DELUXE.

Cornerstone of downtown Mesa, the **Phoenix Marriott Mesa** has 273 rooms, contemporary furnishings, a lounge, a restaurant, a swimming pool and an elegant lobby. ~ 200 North Centennial Way, Mesa; 480-898-8300, 888-236-2427, fax 480-964-9279; www.phoenixmarriottmesa.com, e-mail info@phxmarriottmesa.com. ULTRA-DELUXE.

Buckhorn Mineral Wells is an unusual combination of a motel and natural history museum. The museum displays 400 species of Arizona wildlife, while the motel has 14 rooms decorated in contemporary Southwest decor. ~ 5900 East Main Street, Mesa; 480-832-1111. BUDGET.

DINING

Housed in the Old Tempe train station, **Macayo's Depot Cantina** is charmingly decorated with historic photographs and train memorabilia. The menu is Southwest/Mexican, particularly good for mesquite broiled meats and seafood. ~ 300 South Ash Avenue, Tempe; 480-966-6677, fax 480-894-9196; www.depotcantina.com, e-mail depot_cantina@macayo.com. BUDGET TO MODERATE.

Casa Reynoso is one of the better Mexican restaurants in town, despite its modest appearance—vinyl booths and wrought iron. Try the *gollo burro* or *chiles rellenos*. Closed Monday. ~

AUTHOR FAVORITE

Since I love digging into the past, the **Mesa Historical Museum** was a real find. Anything and everything that has been involved with Mesa's development is in the collection: old citrus crates and labels from when fruit was a major industry, hundreds of photos and local records, memorabilia, vintage clothing, a life-size replica of Mesa's first schoolhouse (1882), and aerial photography chronicling Mesa's growth into Arizona's third largest city. All of the artifacts are donated by descendants of Mesa's pioneer families. The enthusiastic docents are happy to narrate a tour. Closed Sunday and Monday. ~ 2345 North Horne Street, Mesa; 408-835-7358; www.mesaaz.org, e-mail mesamuseum@netzero.net.

3138 South Mill Avenue, Tempe; 480-966-0776, fax 480-966-3005. BUDGET.

The Coffee Plantation is a Caribbean-style coffeehouse and retail store in a plantation house. There's indoor and outdoor seating where espresso, cappuccino and specialty coffees are served, along with pastries and desserts, light lunch and dinner. ~ 680 South Mill Avenue, Suite 101, Tempe; 480-829-7878, fax 480-804-1494. BUDGET.

For Italian Continental cuisine, try **John Henry's**. Duck, lamb, steak, seafood and pasta are some of the favorites you can enjoy in this elegant, upscale dining room. Live music Tuesday through Sunday. No lunch on weekends. ~ 909 East Elliot Road, Tempe; 480-730-9009, fax 480-831-2487; www.johnhenrysrestaurant. com, e-mail johnhenrys1@qwest.net. MODERATE TO DELUXE.

Though the decor is plain and simple, the food is anything but at **Char's Thai Restaurant**, where an exotic touch of the East comes to Tempe with such offerings as chicken soup with coconut milk, smoked beef salad, curried duck and seafood combinations in peanut sauce. There's also a good selection of Asian beers. ~ 927 East University Drive, Tempe; 480-967-6013. BUDGET TO MODERATE.

For a good solid breakfast or lunch, they don't come much better than the **Ripe Tomato Cafe**, where it's always wall-to-wall people. It's a great find for breakfast, and the steak, sandwiches and Mexican specialty lunches aren't bad, either. No dinner. ~ 745 West Baseline Road, Mesa; 480-892-4340. BUDGET.

SHOPPING

Historic **Old Town Tempe** exudes ambiance with its old-fashioned red-brick sidewalks and planters, tree-lined streets and quaint street lamps. Walk the area and you'll find dozens of shops and restaurants. For clothing, gifts and accessories from around the world, try **Mazar Bazaar**. ~ 520 South Mill Avenue, Suite 201, Tempe; 480-966-9090.

Those Were the Days! has one of the largest selections of books on antiques and collecting in the Southwest, with more than 13,000 new titles, as well as 5000 used, out-of-print and rare titles on antiques. As an added bonus, you can buy antiques and kitsch here as folk music constantly plays in the background. ~ 516 South Mill Avenue, Tempe; 480-967-4729; www.twtdbooks. com, e-mail askus@twtdbooks.com.

If you have teenagers in tow, or if you just feel like revisiting your past, stop by **Plush Living**. The store's a favorite with hip college students but fairly undiscovered by the rest of the area. Two floors of vintage clothing await your sifting—coolness is only a cheap pair of leather pants away. ~ 2115 West University Drive, Tempe; 480-967-9200; www.plushliving.com.

In addition to the usual mall lineup of anchor stores and chain specialty shops, **Superstition Springs Center** has a full-size carousel for the kids, a desert botanical garden with more than 100 plants, a playground with a 15-foot-tall Gila Monster slide, several short hiking trails and a stage for free concerts. ~ Intersection of Power Road and the Superstition Freeway, Mesa; 480-396-2570, fax 480-830-7693.

East Side Art in Mesa offers modern paintings, posters and prints, as well as art supplies, classes and framing services. Closed Sunday. ~ 9919 East Apache Trail, Mesa; 480-986-5450. **Mesa Contemporary Arts** features contemporary art from around the country. Closed Sunday. ~ 155 North Center Street, Mesa; 480-644-2056.

NIGHTLIFE   **Grady Gammage Memorial Auditorium**, at the Arizona State University campus in Tempe, is a 3000-seat auditorium designed by Frank Lloyd Wright. Its entertainment features range from Broadway productions to symphony orchestra concerts and ballet. Free guided tours of the center are offered on Monday. ~ Tour information: 480-965-4050. Gammage Auditorium box office: corner of Mill Avenue and Apache Street; 480-965-3434; www.asupublicevents.com.

Serving dinner, drinks and laughs, the **Tempe Improv** is a restaurant/comedy club that has a changing lineup of stand-up comics. No shows Monday through Wednesday. Cover. ~ 930 East University Drive, Tempe; 480-921-9877.

The Wyndham Buttes Resort's swinging **Top of the Rock Bar**, with its 24-foot video screen and live entertainment on weekends, is one of the hottest spots in town. ~ 2000 Westcourt Way, Tempe; 602-225-9000.

Satisfy your urge to jump, jive and wail at **Club Bash**, where throngs of college kids take to the dancefloor to shake their moneymakers. Cover. ~ 230 West 5th Street, Tempe; 480-966-8200.

OSTRICH MANIA

A small, nondescript town bordering the Gila River Indian Reservation, Chandler certainly knows how to get attention. If you're in the area in mid-March, stop by for its annual **Chandler Ostrich Festival**, a three-day event hailed by some as one of the top 10 unique festivals in the United States. Brimming with quirkiness, the cornerstone of this family festival are hour-long ostrich races (camels and zebras also make an appearance) held throughout the day, but there's also music, food, arts and crafts, a carnival, and a parade that winds through town. ~ www.ostrichfestival.com.

Rula Bula Irish Pub & Restaurant offers live music Tuesday through Saturday, and a cold pint of Guinness. Weekend cover. ~ 401 South Mill Avenue; 480-929-9506; www.rulabula.com.

Chandler Center for the Arts has three stages hosting musical, dance and theater performances by local and national performers. Artwork is displayed in the foyer and exhibit hall. Admission. ~ 250 North Arizona Avenue, Chandler; 480-782-2680; www.chandlercenter.org, e-mail info@chandlercenter.org

MCDOWELL MOUNTAIN REGIONAL PARK 🚶 🚵 🐎 This **PARKS**
21,099-acre wilderness expanse 15 miles northeast of Scottsdale is one of the region's most scenic parks with an abundance of vegetation and majestic mountain views. Elevation ranges from 1600 feet at the southeast corner to 2000 feet along the western boundary. The area is ideal for camping, picnicking, horseback riding, hiking and mountain bike riding. Facilities include picnic areas, restrooms and showers. Day-use fee, $5 per vehicle. ~ Located via McDowell Mountain Road, four miles northeast of Fountain Hills; 480-471-0173, fax 480-471-3523.

▲ There are 76 sites (all with RV hookups), first-come, first-served; $18 per night.

From cactus flowers to remote mountain lakes, here is a region rich in scenic wonders. Best known for **North of Phoenix** its dude-ranch resorts, mining towns, cool forests and desert playgrounds, this recreational paradise includes the Wild West town of Wickenburg—the Dude Ranch Capital of the World—the three-million-acre Tonto National Forest and some of the Southwest's better ghost towns.

Established in 1950, **Carefree** is a planned community set in the **SIGHTS** scenic foothills of the Arizona desert. To the north and east stretches the immense Tonto National Forest. Next door is the old-time town of **Cave Creek**. Once a booming mining camp in the 1880s (gold and silver), Cave Creek wasn't incorporated until a hundred years later. Sheep and cattle were raised here as well. Today Cave Creek leans heavily on its past, boasting a Frontier Town re-creation and annual spring rodeo. For more information contact **Carefree/Cave Creek Chamber of Commerce.** Closed weekends. ~ P.O. Box 734, Carefree, AZ 85377; 480-488-3381, fax 480-488-0328; www.carefree-cavecreek.com, e-mail chamber@carefree-cavecreek.com.

Cave Creek Museum offers exhibits of the desert foothills region, with a restored 1920s tuberculous cabin and a 1950s church, as well as displays of pioneer living, ranching, mining and American Indian artifacts. Closed Monday and Tuesday, and from

June through October. ~ 6140 East Skyline Drive, Cave Creek; 480-488-2764, fax 480-595-0838.

To the northwest, on Route 89, you will come to the site of the richest gold strike in Arizona. Named after the Austrian settler Henry Wickenburg, who discovered it, **Wickenburg** is primarily known today as a winter resort.

Frontier Street preserves Wickenburg's early-20th-century character with its old-time train depot now housing the **Wickenburg Chamber of Commerce**, and a number of vintage wood and brick buildings. One, the Hassayampa, was once the town's leading hotel. Maps for a self-guided historic walking tour are available at the chamber office. ~ 216 North Frontier Street, Wickenburg; 928-684-5479, 800-942-5242, fax 928-684-5470; www.wicken burgchamber.com, e-mail info@wickenburgchamber.com.

Before the town jail was built, the nearby **Jail Tree** was used to chain criminals. Friends and relatives brought them picnic lunches. Today the tree is on the property of the Chaparral Ice Cream Parlor, and tykes eat their ice cream cones there now, probably none the wiser. ~ Tegner Street and Wickenburg Way, Wickenburg.

Venture over to the **Desert Caballeros Western Museum**, which covers the history of Wickenburg and the surrounding area with major exhibits divided into various rooms. "Period" rooms include the Hall of History and a Street Scene representing Wickenburg at the turn of the 20th century. Others focus on 19th- and early-20th-century lifestyles. Its art gallery features American Indian art and Western masters of the past and present. There's a special display of cowboy gear. The Museum Park outside offers unique desert landscaping and plants. Admission. ~ 21 North Frontier Street, Wickenburg; 928-684-2272, fax 928-684-5794; www.westernmuseum.org, e-mail info@westernmuseum.org.

Robson's Mining World is an old mining town that supposedly has the world's largest collection of antique mining equipment. Along with seeing the thousands of pieces of equipment, you can stroll through a mineral and gemstone museum, a print shop, a trading post and several other buildings. There is also an ice cream parlor and a moderately priced bed and breakfast on the premises. Closed May through September. Admission. ~ Take Route 60 24 miles west of Wickenburg to Route 71, then go four miles north to Milepost 90; 928-685-2609, fax 928-685-4393; www.robsons miningworld.com.

To the northeast of Phoenix lies **Payson**, district headquarters for the Tonto National Forest. Payson provides a base camp for numerous scenic attractions within the forest primeval. Founded over a century ago as a tiny mining and ranching community, it now thrives on its recreation industry. **Payson Chamber of Commerce** offers information on the area. ~ 100 West Main Street, Payson; 928-474-4515, fax 928-474-8812; www.rimcountrychamber.com.

Prolific writer Zane Grey famously captured the West in his writings about the region. The author had a cabin in Payson, and reportedly enjoyed fishing the local lakes and finding inspiration in his environs. The **Rim Country Museum** will tell you all you want to know about him, as well as the town's history, culture, geology and everything else both fascinating and not. Closed Monday and Tuesday. Admission. ~ 700 Green Valley Parkway, Payson; 928-474-3483; www.rimcountrymuseum.org.

A state historic monument, **Strawberry Schoolhouse** is the oldest standing schoolhouse in Arizona. Built in 1885, its last class was held in 1916. The small mountain village at 6000 feet was named for the many wild strawberries that covered the area when pioneers first arrived. Closed weekdays and October through April. ~ Village of Strawberry; 520-476-3095.

LODGING

Located just northeast of Scottsdale, **The Boulders Resort and Golden Door Spa** is built directly against a stunning backdrop of 12-million-year-old granite boulder formations that soar hundreds of feet against the desert sky. Situated on 1300 acres, the resort consists of a main lodge and 160 adobe-style *casitas*, each individually designed to fit the sculptured contours of the desert and the rocks. The hotel is designed in broad architectural sweeps and makes dramatic use of American Indian and regional art and artifacts—Navajo blankets, weavings, pottery, ceramics, paintings, stone sculptures and basketry. Guest rooms feature earthtone furnishings, hand-hewn, viga ceilings, fireplaces, wet bars,

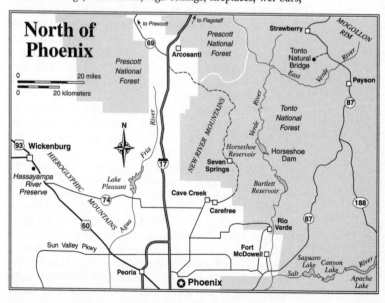

ceiling fans and oversized windows for broad desert vistas. ~ 34631 North Tom Darlington Drive, Carefree; 480-488-9009, 800-553-1717, fax 480-488-4118; www.wyndhamluxury.com. ULTRA-DELUXE.

Carefree Resort & Villas offers 405 spacious rooms, suites and *casitas*. If you need even more space, head up to The Village, where 160 fully equipped condos are available. Located near 20 premier golf courses, this resort boasts plenty of outdoor activities. Guests can explore the surrounding terrain by hot-air balloon, bike or jeep. Those content to stay on-site will find multiple tennis courts, swimming pools and a full spa. ~ 37220 Mule Train Road, Carefree; 480-488-5300, 888-488-9034, fax 480-595-3777; www.carefree-resort.com. DELUXE.

At the peak of the gold rush, Wickenburg had more than 80 mines, with the town growing into what was Arizona's third-largest city at the time.

Nestled within the Sonoran Desert, the Spanish-style **Full Circle Ranch Bed & Breakfast** offers a secluded getaway. Two guest rooms and two *casitas*—each with private patio and jacuzzi—are all outfitted in a Southwestern ranch theme. Spend your day horseback riding nearby or stable your horse in the three-stall mare motel on the premises. You can also hike or just lounge around the lavish pool and spa. An indoor activity room features a pool table, bar and TV. Full breakfast included. ~ 40205 North 26th Street, Cave Creek; 623-465-7570, 877-465-7570, fax 623-465-7579; www.fullcircleranch.com, e-mail jlangan@fullcircleranch.com. ULTRA-DELUXE.

Tumbleweed Hotel is a small downtown Cave Creek hotel made of white slumpstone brick, with 16 rooms in the main building and eight *casita*-style guest suites, all with modern Western-style furnishings and decor. The hotel has a swimming pool. ~ 6333 East Cave Creek Road, Cave Creek; 480-488-3668, fax 480-488-2936; www.tumbleweedhotel.com, e-mail tumblehotel@aol.com. MODERATE TO DELUXE.

Spread across 20,000 acres, the **Rancho de los Caballeros** resort/guest ranch has a homey feel, having been owned by the same family since it opened in 1947. Out here, boredom is impossible. There's golfing on a championship 18-hole course, horseback riding and horsemanship clinics, a skeet and trap range, tennis courts, a swimming pool and programs for the kids. The 79 rooms and suites are Southwestern in style, with private patios and indoor sitting areas. The ranch is on the full American plan. Closed from Mother's Day to early October. ~ 1551 South Vulture Mine Road, Wickenburg; 928-684-5484, 800-684-5030, fax 928-684-2267; www.sunc.com, e-mail home@sunc.com. ULTRA-DELUXE.

HIDDEN ►

Flying E Ranch is a working cattle ranch—and guest ranch—complete with trail rides, hay rides and chuckwagon cookout dinners on its 20,000-acre spread. There are 17 rooms, plus a heated

pool, sauna and spa, and exercise room, along with tennis, volleyball, basketball and shuffleboard. Rates are on the American
Plan—all meals included. Closed May through October. ~ 2801
West Wickenburg Way, Wickenburg; 928-684-2690, 888-684-
2650, fax 928-684-5304; www.flyingeranch.com, e-mail vaca
tion@flyingeranch.com. ULTRA-DELUXE.

Another top-notch dude ranch in Wickenburg (this one's listed
in the National Historic Register), the **Kay El Bar Ranch** has room
for 24 guests in hacienda-style adobe buildings beneath huge salt
cedar trees. The living room has a stone fireplace, and outside
there's a heated pool for soaking after those long hours in the saddle. There is also a spa here. All meals and horseback riding are
included. Closed May to mid-October. ~ Off Rincon Road,
Wickenburg; 928-684-7593, 800-684-7583, fax 928-684-4497;
www.kayelbar.com, e-mail info@kayelbar.com. ULTRA-DELUXE.

The 76-room **Best Western Rancho Grande Motel** offers guests
a pool, whirlpool, playground and restaurant. Rooms are furnished in a contemporary Southwest motif. ~ 293 East Wickenburg Way, Wickenburg; 928-684-5445, 800-854-7235; www.bw
ranchogrande.com, e-mail info@bwranchogrande.com. MODER-
ATE TO DELUXE.

Best Western Payson Inn is a handsome two-story hotel with
Southwestern flavor in the midst of a European-style village of
shops and restaurants. Its 99 rooms are well-kept and some have
fireplaces. A spa, swimming pool and conference center are on the
premises. Rates include a continental breakfast. ~ Route 87, Payson; 928-474-3241, 800-247-9477, fax 928-472-6564; www.best
westernpaysoninn.com. MODERATE TO DELUXE.

A landmark around these parts for years, **Kohl's Ranch Lodge**
sits on the banks of Tonto Creek 17 miles east of Payson. Many of
the 66 rooms and cabins overlook the creek and are equipped with
outdoor grills and patios. Cabins have stone fireplaces, vaulted ceilings and kitchenettes, and rustic furnishings. Amenities here include
a restaurant, lounges, a pool and horseback riding. ~ Route 260
East, Payson; 520-478-4211, 800-331-5645, fax 520-478-0353;
www.ilxresorts.com. MODERATE TO DELUXE.

Crazy Ed's Satisfied Frog Restaurant and Goatsucker Saloon captures a bit of the Old West with wood tables, sawdust on the floor
and weird things on the walls—posters and old farm tools. The
house specialty is mesquite-smoked barbecue. The Frog has its
own microbrewery and produces seven house brands including
Ed's famous chili beer. ~ 6245 East Cave Creek Road, Cave
Creek; 480-488-3317; www.satisfiedfrog.com, e-mail info@satis
fiedfrog.com. MODERATE TO DELUXE.

DINING

Another amphibian-named eatery, **The Horny Toad** is a rustic, informal restaurant with wooden tables and booths, seating

about 100 for lunch and dinner. Specialties include fried chicken and barbecued ribs. ~ 6738 East Cave Creek Road, Cave Creek; 480-488-9542; www.thehornytoad.com, e-mail info@thehorny toad.com. MODERATE TO DELUXE.

Don't be fooled by the delicate peach tablecloths and soft country and easy listening music. At **Charley's Steak House**, bring your appetite to chow down on thick steaks served with salad, baked potato, cowboy beans and dessert. Dinner only. Closed Sunday and Monday. ~ 1187 West Wickenburg Way, Wickenburg; 928-684-2413. BUDGET TO DELUXE.

The **Mandarin House** offers Chinese fare, including a large dinner buffet. ~ 1200 South Beeline Highway, Payson; 928-474-1342. BUDGET TO MODERATE.

A Western theme dominates in the Kohl's Ranch Lodge's **Zane Grey Steakhouse**, where painted cowboys cook over a campfire on one wall and a replica of an 1884 hotel, complete with stained-glass windows, covers another wall. Beneath the glow of a wagon-wheel chandelier, diners can enjoy mounds of barbecued ribs, chicken, steaks and seafood. ~ Route 260 East, Payson; 928-478-4211, fax 928-478-0353. MODERATE TO DELUXE.

SHOPPING   Wickenburg has several Southwestern gift shops and art galleries. The **Old Livery Mercantile** is a 5000-square-foot store filled with Southwestern-themed gifts. Choose from jewelry, home accents and even kids' toys. ~ 104 North Tegner Street, Wickenburg; 928-684-3298.

Just up the street is **The Refried Bean**, where you'll find home furnishings and jewelry with a Mexican flair. ~ 144 North Tegner Street, Wickenburg; 928-684-5977.

It's hard to miss **Ben's Saddlery & Shoe Repair**, with a life-sized horse on top of the building. The owner is a roper, and even if you're not in the market for authentic Western gear, it's fun to breathe in the heady smell of leather and saddle soap while walking down aisles stocked with spurs, saddles and boots. Closed Sunday. ~ 174 North Tegner Street, Wickenburg; 928-684-2683, fax 928-684-1328.

The **Gold Nugget Art Gallery** is housed in an adobe building built in 1863 that was once Old Fort Wickenburg, a U.S. Cavalry base. Inside these historic walls are original Southwestern wood-carvings, pottery, paintings, sculptures and designer jewelry. ~ 274 East Wickenburg Way, Wickenburg; 928-684-5849; www.gold nuggetartgallery.com, e-mail cindy@goldnuggetartgallery.com.

Antique lovers have several options in Payson, with the majority of shops off the Beeline Highway. **Payson Antiques** houses dolls, furniture and primitives by a variety of dealers. ~ 1001 South Beeline Highway, Payson; 928-474-8988.

Cozy booths, a pool table and darts draw people to the **Zane Grey** **NIGHTLIFE**
Saloon at Kohl's Ranch Lodge, a rustic log building that has been
around for years. On seasonal weekends, dance to live music. ~
Route 260 East, Payson; 928-478-4211.

TONTO NATIONAL FOREST 🚶 🚲 🐎 ⛵ ⛷ 🎣 ♨ 🚤 🛥   **PARKS**
Ranging from Sonoran Desert to sprawling forests of ponderosa pine, this national forest covers nearly 2.9 million acres.
The Payson and Cave Creek districts are outdoor playgrounds for
area residents who can enjoy tubing, rafting and fishing on the
Verde River. Bartlett and Horseshoe reservoirs serve as watersheds,
wildlife habitats and recreational sites for camping, swimming,
fishing and boating. **Tonto Natural Bridge**, the largest natural
travertine bridge in the world, is a popular attraction, as was
Zane Grey's cabin until it burned down in 1990. (The Zane Grey
Society has plans for its restoration.) Facilities in
the national forest include picnic areas, restrooms,
showers, a marina, boat rentals, snack stands, a
restaurant, and hiking and riding trails. Parking fee,
$4. ~ There is access to the forest via Route 87 north
from Phoenix to the town of Payson, in the heart of
Tonto National Forest. To reach Horseshoe and Bartlett
reservoirs take the Cave Creek Road east from Carefree
to the entrance of the forest. From here Forest Service
Road 24 takes you north to Seven Springs Campground. Horseshoe Dam Road continues east seven and a half miles until it
forks. Forest Service Road 19 (the right fork) takes you to Bartlett Reservoir; Forest Service Road 265 (the left fork) takes you
to Horseshoe Reservoir. Cave Creek Ranger district: 480-488-
3441, fax 480-595-3346. Payson Ranger district: 928-474-7900;
www.fs.fed.us/r3/tonto.

> Cutting down a saguaro
> cactus in Arizona is a
> serious felony that
> may land you in
> prison for up to 25
> years.

▲ The Payson district's Houston-Mesa Campground is con-
veniently located two miles from Payson. There are 75 tent/RV
sites; $15 per night. Seven Springs Campground in the Cave Creek
district is on a remote spring and has good access to hiking trails.
There are 23 tent/RV sites; no fee.

HASSAYAMPA RIVER PRESERVE 🚶 A green desert oasis, this riparian area along the Hassayampa River features a cottonwood-
willow forest and other vital Sonoran Desert habitats that are
being protected by the nonprofit Nature Conservancy. Sit by the
banks of spring-fed Palm Lake, a four-acre pond and marsh habitat, and you might spot a great blue heron or snowy egret. Birdwatchers also gather at the preserve to see the more than 280
species of birds that pass through this migration corridor. Naturalists offer guided walks (on the last Saturday of the month)
along paths ranging from desert areas with cacti to lusher stretches

along the river. Tours start at the visitors center; call ahead for schedule. Facilities here include restrooms and picnic areas. Closed Monday and Tuesday; closed Monday through Thursday in summer. ~ Route 60, three miles southeast of Wickenburg near Mile Marker 114; 928-684-2772, fax 623-544-6843; www.nature.org.

▼▼▼▼▼▼▼▼▼▼▼▼
South of Phoenix

Out beyond the metropolis, where the bright lights give way to American Indian archaeological sites, you'll find the homeland of the Pima and Maricopa Indians, the site of Arizona's only Civil War battlefield and cotton fields that stretch for miles. Also, mountain peaks, great fishing and, for the born-to-shop crowd, factory-outlet malls. It is an intriguing blend of old and new Arizona.

SIGHTS

Gila Indian Center in the Gila River Indian Reservation has an Indian museum, gift shop and restaurant featuring authentic Indian fry bread and Southwestern food. Here, too, is **Gila Heritage Park**, featuring about half a dozen mini Indian villages. The museum is free; there are no tours, but it's interesting just to wander around on your own. ~ Casa Blanca Road, off Route 10 via Route 387, Exit 175; 520-315-3411, fax 520-315-3968; www.gila indiancenter.com.

Farther south is **Casa Grande**, named for the ancient Indian dwellings northeast of town. Casa Grande is known primarily for cotton-growing, industry and a name-brand factory-outlet store that has thrived there in recent years. For additional information, contact **Greater Casa Grande Chamber of Commerce**. Closed Sunday. ~ 575 North Marshall Street, Casa Grande; 520-836-2125, 800-916-1515, fax 520-836-6233; www.casagrandechamber.org, e-mail chamber@ cgmailbox.com.

There is much speculation about the disappearance of the Hohokam Indians, or "those who vanished." General scholarly consensus, however, rules that they may have been driven away by an extensive drought.

Casa Grande Ruins National Monument was built by the Hohokam Indians in the early 1300s; the village was abandoned by 1450. Four stories high, and covered by a large protective roof, the main structure is the only one of its size and kind in this area. (The monument grounds contain about 60 prehistoric sites.) The structure is easily viewed via a short path on a self-guided tour. There's a visitors center and museum where ranger talks are presented. Admission. ~ State Route 87, about 20 miles east of Casa Grande; 520-723-3172, fax 520-723-7209; www.nps.gov/cagr.

For cowboy fans, the **Tom Mix Monument** honors the silent-movie cowboy star near the spot where he died in a bizarre car accident in 1940: a suitcase flew off the rear shelf of his roadster, crushing his head. "In memory of Tom Mix whose spirit left his body on this spot and whose characterizations and portrayals in life served to better fix memories of the Old West in the minds of living men," reads the inscription. For information, call the Florence Chamber of Commerce. ~ Pinal Pioneer Parkway, 18 miles south of Florence; 520-868-9433; www.florenceaz.org, e-mail info@florenceaz.org.

Francisco Grande Resort and Golf Club is where it's all at in Casa Grande. Originally built by the former owner of the San Francisco Giants, Horace Stoneham, the place has a distinctive baseball theme. The hotel's tower building contains most of its 106 rooms, while other motel-type rooms are located around the courtyard. Furnishings are Southwestern-style throughout, including paintings of cowboys and Western landscapes on the walls. The hotel has a restaurant, lounge (with seasonal entertainment), a swimming pool and wading pool (in the shape of a baseball bat and ball) and golf. ~ 26000 Gila Bend Highway, Casa Grande; 520-836-6444, 800-237-4238, fax 520-381-8222; www.franciscogrande.com. MODERATE TO DELUXE.

LODGING

Holiday Inn in Casa Grande, a four-story, Spanish-style stucco building, has 176 rooms in contemporary style, an outdoor pool and spa, restaurant and lounge. ~ 777 North Pinal Avenue, Casa Grande; 520-426-3500, 800-858-4499, fax 520-836-4728. MODERATE.

Beautifully set in a 1930s adobe guest ranch surrounded by saguaro cacti, the **Inn at Rancho Sonora** offers six rooms with private baths and entrances plus three fully equipped cottages. Stroll through the enclosed brick courtyard, where a fountain spurts merrily, or take a dip in the outdoor pool and waterfall spa. Continental breakfast included. ~ 9198 North Route 79, Florence; phone/fax 520-868-8000, 800-205-6817; www.ranchosonora.com, e-mail rancho@c2i2.com. MODERATE TO DELUXE.

Gila River Arts and Crafts Restaurant features Indian fry bread along with burritos, tacos, hamburgers, homemade pies and coffee. No dinner. ~ Gila River Indian Reservation; 520-315-3411. BUDGET.

DINING

Mi Amigo Ricardo offers up hot and spicy Mexican specialties —chimichangas, enchiladas, *frijoles*, tamales, *flautas* and *posole*— with beer and wine to soothe the flames. The decor is Mexican, of course, and quite attractive. ~ 821 East Florence Boulevard, Casa Grande; 520-836-3858. BUDGET.

Bedillon's is a restaurant and museum in two separate historic buildings. The museum features Indian artifacts and Western memorabilia. There is also a cactus garden dating from 1917. The menu offers a full range of Southwestern/American cuisine. No lunch on Saturday. Closed Sunday and Monday. ~ 800 North

Park Avenue, Casa Grande; 520-836-2045, fax 520-836-6030. MODERATE TO DELUXE.

A small, downtown Casa Grande bakery and café, the **Cook E Jar** serves up breakfast and lunch, as well as take-out bakery goods (even wedding cakes) and sandwiches. Closed Sunday. ~ 100 West 2nd Street, Casa Grande; 520-836-9294. BUDGET.

SHOPPING   **Gila Indian Center** has a shop selling traditional American Indian crafts, silver and turquoise jewelry, sand paintings, kachinas and baskets. ~ Gila River Indian Reservation; 520-315-3411.

Casa Grande, the main town along Route 10 between Phoenix and Tucson, is the site of about 30 factory-owned **outlet stores** in Arizona, mainly located in a sprawling commercial mall off Route 10 (take Exit 198). More than a million shoppers a year come to Casa Grande seeking bargains from such major firms as **Liz Claiborne, Samsonite, Levi's, The Gap** and **Reebok.** For information, call the Outlet at Casa Grande at 520-836-9663, fax 520-836-9580.

▼▼▼▼▼▼▼▼▼▼▼▼▼▼

Outdoor Adventures

Arizona's climate is ideal for recreational pursuits—most of the time. But in the summer, dry heat can be deceiving and you may think it's cooler than it actually is. Keep summer exertion to a minimum and play indoors, where there's air conditioning, if you can.

RIVER RUNNING   Three main rivers in south central Arizona—the Verde, the Salt and the Gila, all east of Phoenix—offer a wealth of recreational activities year-round. A number of companies provide a variety of rafting and tubing expeditions, with pickups, meals and guides included.

SCOTTSDALE   **Cimarron River Co.** has guided two-hour scenic float trips for groups of ten or more on the lower Salt River. The gentle trips, which involve no whitewater, glide through Sonoran Desert landscapes with towering cliffs and stately saguaros. ~ 7902 East Pierce Street; 480-994-1199, fax 480-990-0205. **Desert Voyagers Guided Rafting Tours** offers a variety of half-day trips on the Verde and Salt rivers. ~ P.O. Box 9053, Scottsdale, AZ 85252; 480-998-7238; www.desertvoyagers.com.

TEMPE/MESA AREA   In Mesa, **Salt River Tubing & Recreation** rents large inner tubes and operates a shuttle to carry you up the Salt River so you can tube back down through easy whitewater. They also rent ice chests made especially for tubes, so you can float and picnic. Closed October to May. ~ 1320 North Bush Highway; 480-984-3305; www.saltrivertubing.com.

JOGGING   The Valley's extensive network of canals provides ideal, often shaded tracks.

PHOENIX If you want to jog during the hot summers stick to cooler early-morning hours. Phoenix's **Encanto Park**, three miles north of the Civic Plaza, is an excellent jogging trail.

SCOTTSDALE **Indian Bend Wash Greenbelt** is a dream trail for joggers. It runs north and south for the entire length of Scottsdale, including 13 winding miles of jogging and bike paths within the Greenbelt's scenic system of parks, lakes and golf courses.

Swimming pools are plentiful and popular in south central Arizona; you shouldn't have a problem finding a place for a dip.

SWIMMING

PHOENIX Many public pools are available, about 30 in Phoenix alone. For starters, there's **Cactus Pool**. ~ 3801 West Cactus Road; 602-262-6680. You can also dive into **Grant Pool**. ~ 714 South 2nd Avenue; 602-261-8728. Make a splash at **Starlight Pool**. ~ 7810 West Osborn Road; 602-495-2412. **Washington Pool** will also cool you down. ~ 6655 North 23rd Avenue; 602-262-7198. For more information and listings, call 602-534-7946. The pools are open only in summer.

There are so many swimming pools in south central Arizona that gathering rain clouds, so it's said, are often colored green from all the chlorine.

Telephone Pioneer Pool is exclusively for people with disabilities, their families and friends. Closed Friday and Sunday and in December and January. ~ 1946 West Morningside Drive; 602-495-2404.

The **Adobe Dam Recreation Area** is home to **Water World Safari** (623-581-1947; www.golfland.com), which features a wave pool, waterslides and a 1100-foot-long Zambezi River complete with little rapids. Open Memorial Day through Labor Day. Admission. ~ Recreation area: Northwest of Adobe Dam, on Pinnacle Peak Road and North 43rd Avenue, Phoenix; 602-506-2930.

TEMPE/MESA AREA In Tempe, **Big Surf Waterpark** includes, among other watercentric attractions, a 300-foot surf slide and raft-riding in a gigantic, mechanically activated fresh-water pool. Open Memorial Day through Labor Day. Admission. ~ 1500 North McClintock Road; 480-947-7873; www.golfland.com.

For ballooning enthusiasts, the surrounding mountains provide the perfect setting to let it all hang out. Dozens of firms will be happy to take you up, up and away.

BALLOON RIDES & HANG GLIDING

PHOENIX Float through the air with **Cloud Chasers Balloon Company**, which offers sunrise flights over the Sonoran Desert, followed by a champagne breakfast. ~ 1716 West Butler Drive; 602-944-4080. You can soar in the skies over the north Phoenix area and Sonoran Desert with **Adventures Aloft**. ~ 6716 East Malcomb Drive; 480-951-2650. **Hot Air Expeditions** has year-round sunrise and candlelit sunset flights from November through March. ~ 2243 East Rose Garden Loop; 602-788-5555.

For hang gliding, contact the **Sky Masters School of Hang Gliding** for aero-tours and tandem instruction. They also provide equipment rentals, sales and service. ~ Grand Valley Airport; 602-867-6770.

SCOTTSDALE   View desert wildlife and vegetation as you drift through the sky with **Adventures Out West**. Sunrise and sunset excursions conclude with champagne and treats. Summer only. ~ P.O. Box 12009-266, Scottsdale, AZ 85267; 602-996-6100, 800-755-0935.

Try **Sky Masters School of Hang Gliding** for aero-tours and tandem instruction. Equipment rentals, sales and service are available. ~ 1902 East Behrend Drive; 602-867-6770.

The **Unicorn Balloon Co.** will take you on flights that ascend to heights of 3000 feet and, at other times, glide just above the treetops to spot deer, javalinas, coyotes and other desert wildlife. The trip finishes with a champagne award ceremony in which passengers receive their "First Flight Certificate." ~ 15001 North 74th Street; 480-991-3666, 800-468-2478; www.unicornballoon. com, e-mail support@unicornballoon.com.

RIDING STABLES

Dozens of stables, dude ranches and equestrian outfitters are available for saddling up and heading off into desert wilderness for a few hours or a few days under the supervision of a crusty trail boss. If ever there was a place for horsing around, this is it.

PHOENIX   Saddle up in Phoenix at **All Western Stables**. Guided horseback tours ranging in length from an hour to all day go through Phoenix's 18,000-acre Desert Park. ~ 10220 South Central Avenue; 602-276-5862.

SCOTTSDALE   **MacDonald's Ranch** takes riders through their 1300 acres of high desert terrain. ~ 26540 North Scottsdale Road; 480-585-0239; www.macdonaldsranch.com.

TEMPE/MESA AREA   **Papago Riding Stables** offers one- and two-hour wrangler-guided trips into the desert foothills of Papago Park, where knolls afford spectacular views of the greater Phoenix area. ~ 400 North Scottsdale Road, Tempe; 480-966-9793.

GOLF

More than half of Arizona's 205 golf courses are located in south central Arizona, making Phoenix and environs the undisputed Golf Capital of the Southwest. Some of the country's finest courses can be found among its resorts, parks and country clubs. Cart and club rentals are generally available.

PHOENIX   One of the most spectacular is the **Wigwam Golf & Country Club** in Litchfield Park just west of Phoenix. The club has three separate 18-hole courses with mature landscaping. ~ 451 Old Litchfield Road; 623-935-9414; www.wigwamresort.com.

Among Phoenix's top public links is **Encanto Golf Course**, an 18-hole course with club rentals and a golf pro in residence. ~ 2775 North 15th Avenue; 602-253-3963. The 18-hole public **Papago Golf Course** has shade trees and challenging water hazards. There is a pro shop. ~ 5595 East Moreland Street; 602-275-8428. The nine-hole **Palo Verde Golf Course** is a third public course in Phoenix. ~ 6215 North 15th Avenue; 602-249-9930.

SCOTTSDALE   Top public courses include the 18-hole **Continental Golf Course**. ~ 7920 East Osborn Road; 480-941-1585. Also open for duffers is the nine-hole public **Coronado Golf Course**, which has a driving range. Eight teaching pros are available. ~ 2829 North Miller Road; 480-947-8364. The **Tournament Players Club of Scottsdale** welcomes the public to its greens. The 18-hole stadium course, built specifically to host the PGA Tour FBR Open, features a unique island green. The club also has two 18-hole desert courses. A pro is available for lessons. ~ 17020 North Hayden Road; 480-585-3600, fax 480-585-3151.

TEMPE/MESA AREA   The nine-hole **Pepperwood Golf Course** in Tempe has a golf pro available for lessons. ~ 647 West Baseline Road; 480-831-9457. Or you can bring your clubs to the **Tempe Rolling Hills Golf Course**, where you'll find an 18-hole course in the hilly terrain of the Papago Buttes; there are cart and club rentals, as well as a pro shop, a bar and a restaurant. ~ 1415 North Mill Avenue; 480-350-5275. A "hidden" golfers' option, the **Karsten Golf Course** on the campus of Arizona State University is open to the public. Designed by Pete Dye, the 18-hole championship course has some of the most challenging water hazards and mounds anywhere. It hosts several major tournaments each year. ~ 1125 East Rio Salado Parkway; 480-921-8070.

EDEN FOR EQUESTRIANS

The heart and soul of the Southwest, horses are taken seriously around these parts. Nowhere is this more reflected or celebrated than at the 1500-acre **Arizona Horse Lovers Park**. Four equestrian arenas allow you to watch aspiring local cowboys and their mounts practice their roping, team penning, barrel racing and cutting skills. Managed by the Phoenix Parks and Recreation Department, there are also all sorts of seasonal horse-oriented activities, including horsemanship workshops and classes, hayrides, kid rodeos and trail rides. Riding lessons are also offered. ~ 19224 North Tatum Boulevard, Phoenix; 602-534-4656, 602-534-1968 (information line).

TENNIS   Almost all of the parks in the valley's vast network have a tennis court; for information, call the **Parks and Recreation Department**. ~ Phoenix: 602-262-6861; Scottsdale: 480-312-2722.

PHOENIX   The **Phoenix Tennis Center** is a large facility with 22 lighted public courts. A fee is charged and tennis pros are available. ~ 6330 North 21st Avenue; 602-249-3712. The **Mountain View Tennis Center** is also in the Phoenix area, with 11 lighted public courts. Closed Sunday. Fee. ~ 1104 East Grovers Avenue; 602-534-2500.

SCOTTSDALE   The city of Scottsdale has no fewer than 40 public courts. Most are hard-surfaced and lighted for evening play. Look for them at **Indian School Park**, where there are 13 courts. ~ 4289 North Hayden Road; 480-312-2740. Or try **Chestnut Park**, 2 courts. ~ 4565 North Granite Reef Road; 480-312-2771. **Mountain View Park**, 4 courts, is another option. ~ 8625 East Mountain View; 480-312-2584.

TEMPE/MESA AREA   Outstanding is the City of Tempe's **Kiwanis Park Recreation Center**. There are 15 "cushioned"-surface, lighted courts available by reservation. ~ 6111 South All-American Way; 480-350-5201.

BIKING   Biking is popular as both recreation and transportation in the valley and outlying areas.

PHOENIX   *The Bikeways Map*, which shows the Phoenix Bikeway System, is available for free at most bike shops, or call the Parks, Recreation and Library Department. ~ 602-262-6861. For bicycling events call 602-261-8765. Also for special-event biking activities, check out the **Greater Arizona Bicycle Association**. ~ www.bikegaba.org. Phoenix's **South Mountain Park** (10919 South Central Avenue), **Cave Creek** and **Carefree**, located 30 miles northeast of town, offer great biking conditions. Also popular is **Papago Loop Bicycle Path**, which wends through the rolling hills that border the canal edging Papago Park.

A basic bikeway system was set up for Phoenix in 1987, and since then more than 100 miles of paths have been added. Unfortunately, there's a lot of traffic, so be careful.

SCOTTSDALE   Scottsdale's **Indian Bend Wash Greenbelt** has miles of excellent bike paths.

Bike Rentals   Need to rent a bike or get one repaired? Try **Try Me Bicycle Shop** for both mountain bikes and road-touring bikes. Closed Sunday. ~ 1514 West Hatcher Road, Phoenix; 602-943-1785. **Arizona Outback Adventures** has just the bike for you, whether you're looking to rent a mountain bike, road bike, hybrid or children's tandem. Repairs are available. ~ 16447 North 91st Street, Suite 101, Scottsdale; 480-945-2881. **Tempe Bicycle Shop** has a variety of bikes to rent. Repairs are also available. ~ 330 West University Drive, Tempe; 480-966-6896.

With all that elbow room and knockout scenery, south central **HIKING**
Arizona is a hiker's paradise. Visitors, in fact, have been known
to park their cars on the highway and impulsively hike up the
side of a mountain. *Note:* Be sure to take water with you, and
allow plenty of time to get there and back. All distances listed for
hiking trails are one way unless otherwise noted.

PHOENIX AREA   One of the best park trails in Phoenix's South
Mountain Park is the **Mormon Loop/Hidden Valley Loop National Trail** (6 miles) that begins at the Pima Canyon parking lot
near 48th Street and Guadalupe Road and ends at the Buena
Vista parking area. At the parking lot, a dirt road rambles for a
quarter mile to the trailhead where you'll find a sign for Hidden
Valley. The trail passes stands of saguaro, but the highlights are
The Tunnel—a naturally formed rock tunnel, 50 to 60 feet long,
that leads into Hidden Valley—and Fat Man's Pass, a tight
squeeze between huge boulders where it is cool year-round. Here
children can take turns on Slide Rock, a large, naturally polished,
sleek boulder that's as smooth as a playground slide.

The **Phoenix Mountain Preserve** has 50 miles of trails and
almost pristine areas virtually in the center of Phoenix. It
stretches from Lincoln Drive in Paradise Valley north to
Greenway Boulevard, bordered on the west by 19th Avenue and
on the east by Tatum Boulevard.

Its most popular trail is the **Piestewa Peak Summit Trail** (1.2
miles) that wraps its way up Piestewa Peak, offering good lookout points along the way, and from its 2608-foot summit, a dramatic view of the city. (The only drawback is the number of fellow hikers you'll meet along the way.)

Camelback Mountain is the valley's best known landmark,
and serious hikers truly haven't hiked Arizona until they've conquered it. Part of the Echo Canyon Recreation Area (off McDonald Drive east of Tatum Boulevard; 602-262-4599), Camelback
offers sheer red cliffs that in some places rise 200 feet straight up
its side. An interpretive ramada near the parking area offers information about the various trails.

A relatively easy climb (.8 mile) goes from the ramada to
Bobby's Rock, a landmark formation of rocks set aside from the
cliff and perfect for rock climbers.

Also beginning at the ramada, the **Camelback Mountain Trail**
(1.2 miles) is steep and very rocky, becoming progressively difficult the higher you climb, with a 1300-foot gain in elevation. The
view from the top of Camelback Mountain, 2704 feet above sea
level, is spectacular, but expect a crowd on weekends.

NORTH OF PHOENIX   A favorite at North Mountain Recreation
Area is the **North Mountain National Trail** (1.6 miles), just off

7th Street north of Peoria. The moderate to difficult paved trail climbs from 1490 feet to 2104 feet with scenic views along the way. It ends at the AK-CHIN picnic area.

The historic, 51-mile-long **Highline Trail** in the Tonto National Forest was established in the late 1800s to link various homesteads and ranches under the Mogollon Rim. In 1979, it was designated a National Recreation Trail. With 23 trailheads and spur trails, hikers can explore it in segments and loops. But a word of caution—most of the trails from the highline to the top of the rim are steep, rocky and rugged.

The main trail begins at the Pine Trailhead 15 miles north of Payson off Route 87 and ends at Two-Sixty Trailhead on Route 260. Shorter jaunts include **East Webber Trail** (3 miles), a difficult, little-used stretch that follows Webber Creek before ending at a spring. The most popular is **Horton Creek Trail** (4 miles), which starts at the Upper Tonto Creek Campground.

For the *Highline Trails Guide*, contact the Payson Ranger Station. ~ 1009 East Route 260; 928-474-7900, fax 928-474-7966.

Transportation

CAR

Visitors driving to Phoenix by car are in for a treat. Arizona's highways are among the best in the country, gas is traditionally cheaper and the scenery in any direction is spectacular—lofty saguaros, magnificent mountains, a cowboy here, a pickup truck there, beer signs blinking faintly in the purple glow of evening. Along the way, small Western towns unfold like storybook pop-ups. Route 10 traverses the city from the east (El Paso) and west (Los Angeles). From the northwest, Route 40, once the legendary Route 66, enters Arizona near Kingman; Route 93 continues on from there to Phoenix. Route 17 brings you to Phoenix from the Preston or Flagstaff area.

AIR

Sky Harbor International Airport (602-273-3300; www.phxsky harbor.com) is located four miles from downtown Phoenix and is served by Alaska Airlines, America West Airlines, American Airlines, American Trans Air, Continental Airlines, Delta Air Lines,

THE RIGHT TO A GLASS OF WATER

With summertime temperatures known to reach 120 degrees in Arizona, state law makes it illegal to refuse a person a glass of water. Drafted and passed with the homeless and others who may not afford to pay for water in mind, it's a law that is very much enforced. Businesses are routinely reported and heavily fined for this infraction. If you find yourself in dire need of water, head for the nearest convenience store, where this law is diligently upheld.

Frontier, Northwest Airlines, Scenic Airlines, Southwest Airlines, United Airlines and US Airways.

A variety of ground transportation options are available from Sky Harbor International Airport. **SuperShuttle** offers airport-to-door service 24 hours a day. ~ 602-244-9000, 800-258-3826. **Courier Transportation** also provides transportation to the airport. ~ 602-232-2222. **Arizona Shuttle Service** has service to and from Tucson and Phoenix. ~ 520-795-6771, 800-888-2749; www.arizonashuttle.com.

Greyhound Bus Lines has service to Phoenix from all around the country. Other stations are found in Mesa and Tempe. ~ 800-229-9424; www.greyhound.com. Phoenix: 2115 East Buckeye Road; 602-389-4200. Mesa: 1423 South Country Club Drive; 480-834-3360. There's a pick-up stop in Tempe at 6th Street and College Avenue.

BUS

Rental companies with counters at the airport include **Advantage Rent A Car** (800-777-5500), **Alamo Rent A Car** (800-327-9633), **Avis Rent A Car** (800-831-2847), **Budget Rent A Car** (800-527-0700), **Dollar Rent A Car** (800-800-4000), **Hertz Rent A Car** (800-654-3131) and **National Car Rental** (800-227-7368). Agencies with pick-up service are **Enterprise Leasing and Rent A Car** (800-736-8222) and **Thrifty Car Rental** (800-847-4389).

CAR RENTALS

Valley Metro covers Phoenix and Scottsdale and provides express service to and from other districts within the Valley. It also serves the Phoenix airport. Express buses access Phoenix from Mesa, Tempe and other suburbs. ~ 602-253-5000; www.valleymetro.maricopa.gov. **Ollie the Trolley** offers a free rubber-tire trolley shuttle within the downtown shopping area mid-November through May, every day except Sunday. ~ 480-970-8130. **Downtown Dash** serves the downtown Phoenix area with free shuttles that depart every six to twelve minutes and loop the downtown area between the ball park, America West Arena, Dodge Theatre, the Arizona Center and Collier Center. ~ 602-254-8696; www.coppersquare.com.

PUBLIC TRANSIT

Taxis are expensive in Phoenix since the city sprawls out in all directions. Going from Point A to Point B, at times, may seem like you're crossing the entire state. Some of the major companies in south central Arizona are **Statewide Sedan, Van and Limo Service** (602-252-1277), **Courier Cab** (602-232-2222), **Discount Cab** (602-266-1110) and **Yellow Cab** (602-252-5252).

TAXIS

NINE

Eastern Arizona

Perhaps no other region of the state is as geographically diverse as eastern Arizona. The seemingly endless urban sprawl of Phoenix, Tempe and Mesa quickly gives way to breathtaking scenery in the form of desert gardens, jagged river canyons, rolling grasslands and deep pine forests. Venture here and you will find a wide variety of recreational opportunities, everything from fishing and hunting to hiking and skiing. There's also plenty of history—prehistoric Indian ruins and old mining towns—to be discovered along the way.

The strip of eastern Arizona stretching 203 miles east of Phoenix along Routes 89, 60 and 70 to the New Mexico state line is known as the Old West Highway. Rich in frontier history, it travels a route of the notorious—from Coronado to Geronimo to Billy the Kid.

Anchored on the west by Apache Junction, a growing suburb of the Phoenix metropolitan area and a winter retreat for thousands of snowbirds, the Old West Highway is also the starting point for a scenic detour along the Apache Trail (Route 88). Today's adventurers can wend their way along the trail through the Superstition Mountains, to the reconstructed Goldfield Ghost Town, a series of lakes originating from the Salt River, colorful Tortilla Flat, the Lost Dutchman's Mine and finally Theodore Roosevelt Dam and Lake.

Continue east on the Old West Highway and you'll come to Globe, a quiet town that retains the flavor of the late 1800s. The Old West Highway flattens out east of Globe, and the countryside becomes more arid as you descend into the lower desert. The Mescal Mountains to the south escort you into the Gila River Valley, where the mesas and buttes of the San Carlos Apache Indian Reservation stand out against the sky.

Route 70 branches off Route 60 east of Globe and crosses the southern tip of the 1.8 million-acre San Carlos Apache Indian Reservation, which stretches from the White Mountains to within two miles of Globe, north to the Mogollon Rim and south to Coronado National Forest. An estimated 12,000 Apache live on the reservation, much of it wooded forests that are home to elk, mule deer, wild turkeys, black bear and mountain lions.

On the southern horizon stands Mount Graham, at 10,720 feet one of Arizona's highest peaks. In addition to being a popular fishing, camping and hiking area, the mountain is the site of the Mount Graham International Observatory.

Route 70 continues on to the town of Safford, an important trade center for the Gila River Valley's numerous cotton farmers. From Safford, the Old West Highway cuts through the pastoral Duncan Valley, with its green alfalfa fields, grazing horses and trickling creeks at the eastern edge of Arizona. Duncan, the birthplace of Supreme Court Justice Sandra Day O'Connor, is a fertile source of fire agate, a relatively rare semiprecious stone, which can be picked up right off the ground in designated Bureau of Land Management areas.

North of Duncan on Route 191 is the historic mining town of Clifton, the southern anchor of the Coronado Trail, which climbs through the Apache-Sitgreaves National Forest on its 105-mile journey to Alpine, in the heart of Arizona's Alps.

The Coronado Trail, named for the Spanish explorer who sought the Seven Cities of Gold nearly 500 years ago, practically brushes the Arizona–New Mexico border. The trail runs north–south as Route 191 from St. Johns to Clifton via a winding and twisting paved highway, cutting through rugged mountains and magnificent forests—some of the Southwest's most spectacular scenery.

The White Mountains offer high, cool country dotted with fishing lakes and blanketed in ponderosa pine, spruce, aspen and Douglas fir. At the heart of this area are Pinetop–Lakeside, Show Low and Greer. The main reason folks venture to this part of eastern Arizona is to enjoy the outdoors, whether by fishing, skiing, hiking or simply sitting on a rock with a picnic lunch, breathing in the scent of pine and watching the breeze ripple across a lake. These towns all abound with rustic lodges, inexpensive eateries and plenty of scenic beauty.

Apache Junction Area

▼ ▼ ▼ ▼ ▼ ▼ ▼ ▼ ▼ ▼ ▼ ▼ ▼ ▼

At the meeting point of Routes 60, 88 and 89, Apache Junction is in an area of rough lowlands about 30 miles east of Phoenix. Once a sunburned babble of bars, motels and filling stations, it has blossomed into a rustic bedroom community for the Valley of the Sun and a popular snowbird retreat that attracts about 55,000 people each winter, causing local dude ranch operators to complain that there's no range left to ride. A metal impression in the center of the town honors the man believed to have discovered the elusive Lost Dutchman Gold Mine, who died with the secret of its location unspoken. Apache Junction is also the starting point for the 48-mile Apache Trail, Route 88, which slices its way through the Superstition Mountains.

SIGHTS

Apache Junction was unofficially founded in 1922, when a traveling salesman named George Cleveland Curtis put up a tent and sold sandwiches and water to travelers along the highway. A year later he filed a homestead claim and built the Apache Junction Inn.

Others soon followed and by 1950 there were enough residents to form a town. They chose the name Superstition City, but because it was a historical site, the Apache Junction name could not be changed.

Learn about the area's history and sights at the **Apache Junction Chamber of Commerce**, which dispenses maps and brochures. They also operate as a visitors booth, an excellent resource for local information. ~ 567 West Apache Trail, Apache Junction; 480-982-3141, 800-252-3141, fax 480-982-3234; www.apache junctioncoc.com, e-mail info@apachejunctioncoc.com.

For a taste of the Old West, stop at **Goldfield Ghost Town**, which saw its heyday in the 1890s when gold was discovered at the base of the Superstitions. The weathered-wood buildings that house a restaurant, museum and antique shops look original, but they are actually re-creations, constructed in 1988. The old mining and railroad equipment scattered about are authentic, as are the museum's geology and mining exhibits and the underground mine, which you can tour. Other activities available are jeep tours, carriage rides and gold panning. ~ Route 88, four miles north of Apache Junction; 480-983-0333, fax 480-834-7947; www.gold fieldghosttown.com.

Canyon Lake wends its way ten and a half miles upstream through one continuous deep canyon. There are boat facilities, beaches, picnic sites, a snack bar and campsites. Recreational activities include fishing (bass and walleye) and waterskiing. There's also a replica of a double-deck sternwheeler that plies the waters with its cargo of tourists and photographers. ~ Canyon Lake Marina, Route 88; 480-288-9233, www.canyonlakemarina.com, e-mail azcanyonlake@yahoo.com.

The **Theodore Roosevelt Dam**, completed in 1911 and constructed entirely of quarry stone, is the world's tallest masonry dam. A recent concrete addition, covering the original construction, raised the dam's height to 357 feet. A quarter mile upstream from the dam, a 1000-foot steel arch bridge spans a portion of the reservoir, Roosevelt Lake. ~ Route 88, 45 miles east of Apache Junction (note: half this distance is unpaved).

The **Tonto National Monument** contains the remains of the apartment-style dwellings of the Salado people and is one of the state's better-preserved prehistoric archaeological sites. At the visitors center, you can see Salado crafts and tools and an audiovisual program. A highlight of the park itself is a paved but steep, half-mile self-guiding trail that climbs 350 feet up to the 19-room **Lower Cliff Dwelling**. The 40-room **Upper Cliff Dwelling** is open for tours from November through April (reservations are required). Admission. ~ Route 188, Roosevelt; 928-467-2241.

Back on Route 60, about 25 miles east of Apache Junction near the tiny mining camp of Superior, is the **Boyce Thompson Ar-**

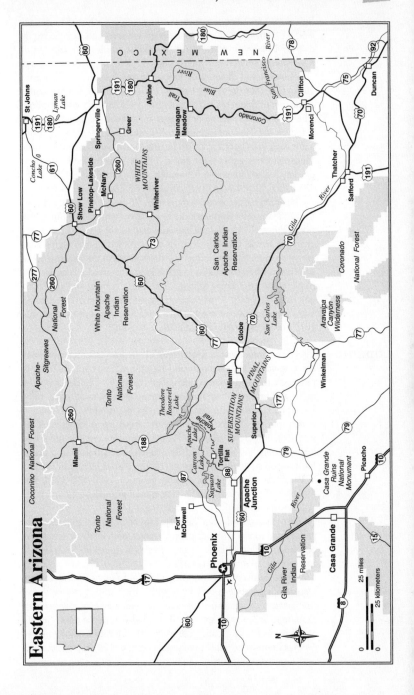

Eastern Arizona

boretum. This Eden-like preserve boasts over 1500 specimens, including cacti, succulents and water-efficient trees and shrubs. Home to over 200 kinds of birds and 40 wildlife species, the arboretum has walking trails that wind through 35 acres of outdoor displays and historic buildings. One long-time resident here, a red gum eucalyptus that rises more than a hundred feet and boasts a trunk eight feet in diameter, was planted in 1929 as a six-foot sapling. The interpretive center is located in a 1920s cut-stone house listed on the National Register of Historical Places. In addition, a gift store sells books, cacti and various succulents. The **Clevenger House**, a stone cabin built into a hillside surrounded by an herb garden, is also of interest. Admission. ~ 37615 Route 60; 520-689-2811, fax 520-689-5858; ag.arizona.edu/bta.

Heading east from the arboretum, Route 60 gradually climbs through Gonzales Pass until the desert gives way to the Tonto National Forest. The two-lane highway cautiously winds through enchanting **Devils Canyon**, an eerie though picturesque region that seems to change its mood as the day's sunlight progresses. Near sundown, when the shadows grow long, the granite rock formations take on the shape of giant trolls and gnomes, and appear to be crouching, as if to pounce on passing motorists. The canyon and highway are narrow, but there are ample pullouts to photograph or simply enjoy the scenery.

LODGING The 121-room **Grande Hotel and Conference Center** stands at the gateway to the Superstition Mountains. The main building is red-brick tile and white stucco. The rooms, coolly decorated in teals and grays, have modern furnishings. Many have fully equipped kitchens and can be rented by the month. The lobby is contemporary, the bar Western with copper appointments. A favorite of film crews shooting Westerns in the area, the hotel has hosted John Wayne, Ronald Reagan, Richard Boone and other Hollywood stalwarts. Rooms where they stayed bear their names. ~ 201 West Apache Trail, Apache Junction; 480-982-3500, fax 480-983-7963; www.grand1.com, e-mail grand@neta.com. BUDGET TO MODERATE.

The small, family-run **Palm Springs Motel** has 12 clean, well-maintained rooms with refrigerators, some with kitchenettes. ~ 950 South Royal Palm Road, Apache Junction; 480-982-7055; e-mail azplmsprmotel@msn.com. BUDGET.

In the Superstition foothills, the **Gold Canyon Golf Resort** features chalet-style guest rooms with dark-wood furniture, stone fireplaces, private patios and impressive views of the nearby mountain. Some boast spa tubs. There's also a heated pool. ~ 6100 South Kings Ranch Road, Gold Canyon; 480-982-9090, 800-624-6445, fax 480-830-5211; www.gcgr.com, e-mail stay@gcgr.com. ULTRA-DELUXE.

DINING

Lake Shore Restaurant is a rustic, casual dining facility on Saguaro Lake with a deck where you can enjoy lunch with a lake view. Shaded by a giant awning, this outdoor eatery is cooled by a mist system and ceiling fans or warmed by outdoor heaters, depending on the season. Start with a strawberry daiquiri and then order from the menu featuring burgers, salads, sandwiches and fried fish (all you can eat on Wednesday and Friday). No dinner on Monday and Tuesday. ~ 14011 North Bush Highway, Tonto National Forest; 480-984-5311, fax 480-986-1210; www.saguarolake.net. BUDGET TO MODERATE.

Down Apache Junction way, **Mining Camp Restaurant and Trading Post** is almost as famous as the Lost Dutchman Gold Mine—and it's easier to find. The long wooden tables, planked floors, tin trays and cups, and family-style, all-you-can-eat dining— chicken, beef and barbecued ribs—make it worth looking for. No lunch Monday through Saturday. Closed July through September. ~ Route 88, Apache Junction; 480-982-3181, fax 480-982-5428; www.miningcamprestaurant.com, e-mail miningcamp@hotmail.com. DELUXE.

There's no shortage of charm at **Tortilla Flat Restaurant**, whose weathered-wood exterior suggests a Wild West saloon. Inside, the natural-wood walls are covered with mining and cowboy artifacts, as well as business cards and currency from around the world. Home-cooked specials include oversized burgers, spicy hot chili and a full Mexican menu. In the saloon section, you can belly up to the solid-wood bar, plant yourself on a barstool topped with a leather saddle and pretend you're in Dodge City. The Judds on the Wurlitzer jukebox will bring you back to reality. Breakfast, lunch and

Apache Trail

The **Apache Trail** (Route 88) follows the route originally used by Apache Indians as a shortcut through the Superstition Mountains. It runs about 56 miles one-way from Apache Junction to Theodore Roosevelt Lake, with about 20 unpaved miles above Tortilla Flat. En route are pull-offs for hiking, picnicking or just plain staring at the beautiful scenery.

SUPERSTITION MOUNTAINS   Once past the outskirts of Apache Junction, the road enters the dacite cones of the Superstition Mountains, formed 20 million years ago when cataclysmic earthquakes and widespread volcanic eruptions pushed land masses thousands of feet into the air and left a depression 20 miles wide. Magma from below the earth's surface flowed in and the mountains resulted. The triangular-shaped peak east of the Superstitions is Weaver's Needle, which treasure hunters say is a landmark for the Lost Dutchman Mine.

CANYON LAKE   Continuing north, you'll find a chain of lakes originating out of the Salt River. They include Saguaro, Canyon and Apache lakes. The most accessible is Canyon Lake (page 272). As you proceed upstream, you'll pass geodes embedded in sheer rock walls, deposited by eruptions millions of years ago, on your way to **Tortilla Flat**, which

dinner are served. ~ Route 88, 18 miles northeast of Apache Junction; 480-984-1776; www.tortillaflataz.com. BUDGET TO MODERATE.

Barleen's Arizona Opry presents a Grand Ole Opry–style country music show. Served at the table are hearty dinners of slow-cooked roast beef, mashed potatoes, vegetables and chocolate cake. Dinner only. Closed Sunday. ~ 2275 Old West Highway, two miles east of Apache Junction; 480-982-7991, fax 480-982-7991; www.azopry.com, e-mail arizonaopry@msn.com. DELUXE.

SHOPPING   If you plan to go looking for the Lost Dutchman Gold Mine, or even if you don't, **Pro Mack South** sells mining equipment, gold pans, lanterns, picks, rope, boots, supplies and just about everything else but the treasure map. Closed Sunday. ~ 940 West Apache Trail, Apache Junction; 480-983-3484; www.promackminingsupsouth.com, e-mail promack@quik.com.

NIGHTLIFE   From Christmas to Easter, **Tortilla Flat Restaurant** features live bluegrass and country music on an outdoor barbeque patio. ~ Route 88, 18 miles north of Apache Junction; 480-984-1776.

boasts a population of six people. One of the last remnants of the Old West, the town was once a stagecoach stop, complete with a school, general store, restaurant/saloon, hotel and post office, and was home to about 125 people. Today only the general store, post office and restaurant remain.

FISH CREEK HILL & THEODORE ROOSEVELT DAM   About five miles east of Tortilla Flat, the paved road surrenders to dirt and gravel as it climbs to the top of Fish Creek Hill, which provides spectacular views of the canyon below. Descending the hill, the road twists through a narrow chasm along Apache Lake and finally arrives at Theodore Roosevelt Dam (page 272).

TONTO NATIONAL MONUMENT   From Roosevelt Dam you can return to Apache Junction the way you came, but it's almost as fast to return by the 83-mile paved southern route through the old mining camp of Superior. To do this, continue on Route 88 (which becomes paved again at the dam). Soon you will come to Tonto National Monument. After visiting the visitors center and ruins, continue south for about 26 more miles to the intersection with Route 60 near Globe. Turn west (right) and follow Route 60 all the way back to Apache Junction. Along the way, you will come to **Boyce Thompson Arboretum** (page 272), where a stop to enjoy the cacti, birds and wildlife rounds out a perfect day-long adventure.

Join the Barleen Family Band at their 500-seat **Barleen's Arizona Opry** for Grand Ole Opry–style entertainment after you indulge in a gut-busting meal. Closed May through October. ~ 2275 Old West Highway, two miles east of Apache Junction; 480-982-7991, fax 480-982-7991; www.azopry.com, e-mail arizonaopry@msn.com.

USERY MOUNTAIN RECREATION AREA 🚶 🚵 🐎 This 3324-acre recreational area is just northwest of the Superstition Mountains. It has extensive hiking, mountain biking and horseback riding trails. Throughout the park you will find restrooms, showers and horse-staging areas. Day-use fee, $5 per vehicle. ~ Located east of Phoenix via Apache Boulevard or Superstition Freeway (Route 60). Head east to Ellsworth Road and turn north. At McKellips Road, Ellsworth becomes Usery Pass Road. Continue north to the entrance.

PARKS

▲ There are 70 campsites, all have RV hookups; $15 per night. Tent sites are also available here; $10 per night. ~ 480-984-0032.

LOST DUTCHMAN STATE PARK 🏃 Located in the foothills of the Superstition Mountains, this 292-acre park features eight miles of hiking trails through saguaro, palo verde and other desert flora. Interpretive tours by park rangers are conducted October through April. Facilities include a visitors center, restrooms, showers, picnic tables, drinking water and barbecue grills. Day-use fee, $6 per vehicle. ~ 6109 North Apache Trail, about five miles north of Apache Junction; phone/fax 480-982-4485.

▲ There are 70 sites (35 with hookups); $20 per night. There is a dump station.

TONTO NATIONAL FOREST 🏃 🚵 🏇 ⚓ 🛶 🎣 ⛵ 🚤 🚣
🛶 To explore the national forest northeast of Apache Junction, travel the famed Apache Trail (Route 88), which eventually leads to the Salt River chain of lakes—Saguaro, Canyon, Apache and Roosevelt lakes. The lakes have been developed for fishing, boating, picnicking, hiking, biking and camping. Day-use fee, $4 per vehicle ($2 per watercraft) at Butcher Jones Beach on Saguaro Lake. The Salt River itself is a favorite spot for tubing.

There are several privately run marinas in the forest offering a variety of services. The **Saguaro Lake Marina** has boat rentals (weekends only), storage, fuel, tours and a restaurant. There are primitive campsites around the lake, accessible by boat only. ~ Located off Bush Highway; 480-986-5546. The **Apache Lake Marina** offers boat rentals, storage and gas. Three motels, a restaurant, a lounge and a grocery store are also located here. There are RV sites, and tent-camping is allowed all around the lake. ~ Route 88; 928-467-2511. A full-service marina with a restaurant, a gift shop and camping facilities, the **Canyon Lake Marina** is situated 15 miles northeast of Apache Junction. Boat tours are available. ~ Route 88; 602-944-6504.

Throughout the forest you'll find picnic areas, restrooms and hiking and riding trails. ~ The main access road from Apache Junction is Route 88 (Apache Trail). Tortilla Campground is on Route 88 about 11 miles from Apache Junction. Cholla Campground is on Route 188, eight miles north of Roosevelt Dam in Roosevelt. Tonto Basin Ranger District, 928-467-3200, fax 928-467-3239; www.fs.fed.us/r3/tonto.

▲ There are 36 campgrounds; free to $17 per night. Primitive backcountry camping is also allowed. Reservations are only needed for group sites; call USF Reservations, 800-280-2267. Located near Canyon Lake, Tortilla Campground has 77 tent/RV sites ($10 per night) and is open from October through March. Located on the south side of Roosevelt Lake, **Cholla Campground** has 188 tent/RV sites ($11 to $17 per night, no hookups), and **Windy Hill** has 348 tent/RV sites ($11 to $17 per night, no hookups).

The Lost Dutchman Gold Mine

With blunted peaks reaching nearly 6000 feet and razor-edged canyons plunging earthward, the Superstition Mountains comprise an area 40 miles long and 15 miles wide—some of the roughest, rockiest, most treacherous territory in the United States. It was in this rugged territory that Dutchman Jacob Waltz was believed to have discovered the Lost Dutchman Gold Mine.

Waltz supposedly found an old Spanish mine in the Superstitions near what is now Apache Junction. He was vigilant about keeping its whereabouts secret, and died in 1891 without revealing the location. For a while people looked for the mine, then it was forgotten for about 30 years.

In the 1930s, Dr. Adolph Ruth came to the area claiming to have a map of the mine. One hot summer day he went into the area to search, and was never seen again. A few months later his skull was found with what looked like a bullet hole in it. Once again, interest in the mine was sparked and people resumed the search. To this day, the treasure has never been found, but prospectors are still looking. Today in Apache Junction, a statue of Jacob Waltz in the center of the town honors the man believed to have discovered an elusive gold treasure.

To learn more about this local legend, head to the **Superstition Mountain/Lost Dutchman Museum**, which displays historical artifacts pertaining to the story of the Lost Dutchman Gold Mine. You'll also find exhibits of folk art, prehistoric Indian artifacts, Spanish and Mexican crafts and documents, pottery and relics of early cowboys, prospectors and miners. Admission. ~ Route 88, Goldfield Ghost Town, four miles north of Apache Junction; 480-983-4888; e-mail smgold@uswest.com.

If you'd like to try your luck in finding the legendary Lost Dutchman Gold Mine, there are a number of companies that offer three- to seven-day—or longer—treks into the Superstitions. With the help of experienced guides, you will lash your gear to packhorses and mount up for a trip where you can pan for gold or simply ride the wilderness trails, camp, cook, bathe in icy streams and sleep out under the stars. For information, try the **O.K. Corral, Inc.** ~ P.O. Box 528, Apache Junction, AZ 85217; 480-982-4040; www.okcorrals.com.

THEODORE ROOSEVELT LAKE

Fed by Tonto Creek from the north and the Salt River from the southeast, Theodore Roosevelt Lake has more than 100 miles of shoreline, and hundreds of coves that provide excellent bass and crappie fishing, as well as hideaways for campers and picnickers. There are picnic tables, restrooms, showers and playgrounds. Roosevelt Lake Marina has a boat launch and rentals, a small grocery store (928-467-2245), a snack bar, restrooms and picnic tables. ~ Route 88 near Theodore Roosevelt Dam; 928-467-3200, fax 928-467-3239.

▲ There are numerous camping opportunities here. The two most developed campgrounds are Cholla and Windy Hill. Cholla Campground offers 206 sites with drinking water, showers and toilets; $10 to $15 per night. Windy Hill features 347 sites with drinking water, showers, toilets and grills; $10 to $15 per night.

Globe

East of Devils Canyon, the Pinal Mountains rise to dominate the horizon, until the historic old copper-mining town of Globe wrests control of the horizon. This quiet old copper town, with its many Victorian homes dotting the hillsides, retains the flavor of the late 1800s with an early-20th-century main street, complete with an old-fashioned F. W. Woolworth store. Here, you'll find one of the finest American Indian archaeological sites in the state.

Globe began as a mining town in the 1860s after silver was discovered on the Apache reservation. Located at the eastern end of the Apache Trail, the town was originally called "Besh-Ba-Gowah" by the Apache, meaning "place of metal" or "metal camp." Today, it is named for a spherical silver nugget with markings that resemble the continents. After the silver mines were depleted, copper was discovered, but those mines, too, were shut down by the Great Depression. The town has been dozing in the sun ever since.

SIGHTS

On your drive into **Globe** (if arriving from the west), you'll notice massive manmade hills of bleached-out dirt, a byproduct of the copper mining operations here. The white mesas, which stretch for a couple of miles, are what's left after the ore has been bleached, crushed and smelted. Attempts to grow vegetation in the miniature moonscape have been all but futile, so the mountains of residue remain, perhaps to be recycled as new mining techniques allow extraction of more copper from them.

For local information, visit the **Globe–Miami Regional Chamber of Commerce and Economic Development Corporation.** Be sure to ask for the walking tour of downtown Globe, and directions to the nearby archaeological sites. Closed on weekends. ~ 1360 North Broad Street; 928-425-4495, 800-804-

5623, fax 928-425-3410; www.globemiamichamber.com, e-mail gmr@cableone.net.

Set among modern homes and paved streets, **Besh-Ba-Gowah Museum and Archaeological Park** is a prehistoric pueblo village built from rounded river cobblestone and mud walls, which surround rooms and plazas. Here, you can climb a rough wooden ladder and examine rooms with pottery and utensils that were used 600 years ago. There's also a pot over a firepit, manos and metates. A nearby museum displays artwork and utensils of the Salado, an advanced band of hunters and gatherers who lived here from A.D. 1100 to 1400. The Salado built a pueblo of more than 200 rooms (146 on the ground floor and 61 second-story rooms) around three central plazas, which housed an estimated 300 to 400 people during its peak. There is also a botanical garden that demonstrates how the Salado utilized the surrounding vegetation. Admission. ~ 1100 Jess Hayes Road, one mile southwest of town at the Globe Community Center; 928-425-0320, fax 928-402-1071; e-mail beshbagowah@theriver.com.

After leaving the archaeological park, you can get an eagle's-eye view of the area by making a right turn on Jess Hayes Road

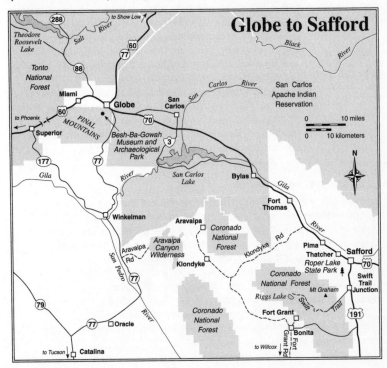

then driving to Ice House Canyon Road and Kellner Canyon, where you will circle up through the beautiful Pinal Mountains for 15 miles. At the 7850-foot level you'll pass through ponderosa pine, ferns and thick foliage. Pull out anywhere and the overlooks will give you sweeping views of Globe and Miami below.

In town, the rip-roaring days of the early miners come to life at the **Gila County Historical Museum** with exhibits of early artifacts, mining equipment and Salado Indian relics dating back to A.D. 1400. The museum is housed in the former Globe–Miami Dominion Mine Rescue and First Aid Station. Closed Sunday. ~ Route 60; 928-425-7385.

The **Old Dominion Mine**, across from the museum on Broad Street, is what's left of what was once the world's richest copper mine. In the 1930s, the depressed price of copper, coupled with increasing water seepage into the mine shafts, forced the closure of the mine. Today the mine belongs to BHP Copper Company and is a valuable source of water, which is vital to the company's other operations in the area.

In downtown Globe stands the **Historic Gila County Courthouse**, built in 1906. This stately stone structure now houses the Cobre Valley Center for the Arts and a small theater. Climb the 26 stone steps and enter the wooden doors to find finished hardwood floors, arched passways, grand rooms with high ceilings and tall windows, and a staircase accented with copper banisters and overhead skylight. ~ 101 North Broad Street; 928-425-0884, fax 928-425-6154; e-mail cvca@theriver.com.

Also worth visiting is the **Globe Elks Lodge**, the world's tallest three-story building, built in 1910. ~ 155 West Mesquite Avenue; 928-425-2161. You can also check out the old **Gila County Jail** (behind the Historic Gila County Courthouse), constructed of reinforced concrete in 1909, with cell blocks transported from the

GLOBAL ARCHITECTURE

History buffs will enjoy Globe's **Historic Home and Building Tour and Antique Show**, held in February. Many of the structures were built by the same stonemasons who worked on nearby Roosevelt Dam. The tour usually consists of six to eight buildings. A recent one included a 1911 home built from dacite stones, a material quarried locally; a church that was hand-built by Episcopalian priests between 1900 and 1908; and a plantation-style mansion built in the late 1800s, complete with upper and lower verandas. For more information call the Globe–Miami Regional Chamber of Commerce and Economic Development Corporation. ~ 928-425-4495, 800-804-5623, fax 928-425-3410; www.globemiamichamber.com, e-mail gmr@cableone.net.

Yuma Territorial Prison. The **Gila Valley Bank and Trust Building**, with its white terra-cotta facade, is an unusual example of the beaux-arts neoclassical style of 1909. The building was the pioneer branch of the former Valley National Bank. ~ Mesquite Avenue and Broad Street.

The art deco–style **Globe Theater** was built in 1918 and features copper-covered pillars under the movie marquee. ~ 141 North Broad Street. Nearby is old **Engine No. 1774**, one of only seven remaining steam locomotives in existence. Originally, 355 were built between 1899 and 1901. ~ Pine and Oak streets.

Globe is the commercial gateway to the **San Carlos Apache Indian Reservation**, the 1.8-million-acre expanse that's home to nearly 12,000 Apache Indians. Rambling and remote, lush and rustic, the land is a natural habitat for javelina, elk, bear, mountain lions, bighorn sheep, antelope, waterfowl, grouse, quail, rabbits and a variety of freshwater fish. Camping, hunting and fishing are permitted, with licenses. A recreation permit is required for off-road hiking. Tribal lakes offer boating and waterskiing. Contact the Recreation and Wildlife Department. ~ 928-475-2343, fax 928-475-2701.

In Globe you'll find the **Super 8**, a 40-unit, two-story motel with contemporary furnishing, a pool and an all-night café. ~ 637 East Ash Street; 928-425-7124. BUDGET.   **LODGING**

The Globe **Motel 6** offers ultra-clean guest rooms decorated in cool pastels, some with refrigerators and spa tubs. There is a pool and a jacuzzi. ~ 1699 East Ash Street; 928-425-5741, fax 928-402-8466; www.motel6az.com. BUDGET.

Globe has a small but growing number of bed-and-breakfast inns. One of the most distinctive is **Noftger Hill Inn**, located in a former schoolhouse dating from 1907. Six large suites include five of the original classrooms, each with a fireplace, school desk and the original blackboard. No smoking. ~ 425 North Street; 928-425-2260, 877-780-2479, fax 928-402-8235; www.noftsger hillinn.com, e-mail info@noftsgerhillinn.com. MODERATE.

Built in 1903 for a family of 12, **Cedar Hill** is a spacious historic house with high ceilings, a backyard and a porch with swings. Its two cozy rooms share a bath and are individually decorated; each is outfitted with a queen brass bed and one has antique furniture straight from the proprietress' grandmother's dowry. Two ground-floor apartments are fully furnished and available on a weekly basis. Breakfast is made to order. ~ 175 East Cedar Street; 928-425-7530; www.cedarhill.biz, e-mail reserve@ cedarhill.biz. BUDGET.

Most locals agree some of the best food in town is at 24-hour **Jerry's Restaurant**, a fast-paced, coffee shop–style eatery that   **DINING** dishes up hearty portions of steaks, chops, meatloaf, fish and other American standbys. ~ 699 East Ash Street; 928-425-5282, fax 928-425-6703. BUDGET TO MODERATE.

Family-owned and -operated since 1969, **Chalo's Casa Reynoso** is a traditional Mexican restaurant, with entrées ranging from burritos to green chile to *rellenos* to enchiladas. If you've OD'd on spicy foods, they also have your basic hamburger-type offerings. ~ 902 East Ash Street; 928-425-0515; www.chalos.com. BUDGET.

Don't let the decor at **La Luz Del Día** fool you. Despite the old-fashioned counter, mushroom stools and vinyl booths, this isn't a 1950s burger joint; it's a Mexican bakery and coffee shop with a tasty selection of Mexican sweet rolls, buns and quesadillas. Breakfast and lunch only. Closed Sunday. ~ 304 North Broad Street; 928-425-8400. BUDGET.

> Although Globe's copper was depleted in the 1930s, mining operations in nearby Miami have kept this historic hamlet going.

SHOPPING　The **Cobre Valley Center for the Arts**, located in the Historic Gila County Courthouse, houses arts and crafts produced by local members of the Cobre Valley Fine Arts Guild (*cobre* is Spanish for copper). Media represented include stained glass, ceramics, weaving, painting (oil, acrylic, watercolors), sculpture (stone, metal, wood, plastic), photography, jewelry (silver, stone, beaded) and mixed media. There are also prints, batik silk scarfs and gift items. ~ 101 North Broad Street; 928-425-0884; e-mail cvca@theriver.com.

Bacon's Boots and Saddles represents the last of the great saddle makers. The store's owner, Ed Bacon, has been hand-crafting saddles for more than 50 years. A full range of Western wear is also featured. Closed Sunday. ~ 290 North Broad Street; phone/fax 928-425-2681.

West of Globe on Route 60, **Pastime Antiques** is filled with antique furniture, paintings, Western memorabilia, historic photos, old magazines, postcards, posters and other relics and remnants of the past. ~ 150 West Mesquite Street, Miami; 928-425-2220.

NIGHTLIFE　Not much happens after dark, but you can see current movies at the **Globe Theater**. ~ 141 North Broad Street; 928-425-5581. Or if you prefer an evening nightcap, go to **Under the Palms Cocktails**. ~ 230 North Broad Street; 928-425-2823.

PARKS　**TONTO NATIONAL FOREST** 🏃 🚲 🏇 🛶 🎣　The Globe district, located in the southeast corner of Tonto National Forest, is a popular escape from the desert heat. The Upper Salt River boasts some of the country's best whitewater, as well as fishing and swimming at the calmer stretches. The Pinal Mountains offer endless opportunities for hiking, biking and horseback riding. The forest has picnic areas, restrooms and hiking and riding trails. ~

Main access to the Globe district is Route 60. To reach Upper and Lower Pinal campgrounds from Globe, turn south on Jess Hayes Road and follow signs to the campgrounds. Oak Flat Campground is located right off of Route 60, four miles east of Superior; 928-402-6200, fax 928-402-6292.

▲ There are 86 campgrounds in Tonto National Forest; free to $17 per night. Primitive camping is allowed. Reservations are only needed for group sites in fee areas; call USFS Reservations, 800-280-2267. At a cool 7500 feet, Upper Pinal Campground and Lower Pinal Campground (19 tent sites total; no fee) are popular in the summer. At a lower elevation, Oak Flat Campground (16 tent/RV sites; no fee) is five and a half miles east of Superior.

SAN CARLOS LAKE 🏃 🚤 🎣 The lake, created by the construction of the Coolidge Dam, has 158 miles of shoreline when full. The fishing is good for catfish, bass and crappie. There's a general store providing bait and other items. The only other facilities are pit toilets. Day-use fee, $7. ~ Located 30 miles east of Globe.

▲ There are 11 RV sites, some with hookups; $10 per night for RVs needing hookups, otherwise wilderness camping is included with a two-day fishing license, but not with the one-day license, which expires at midnight. For fishing licenses, hiking permits, camping and any other information, call the Recreation and Wildlife Department. ~ 928-475-2343, 928-475-2653.

Lying low in the fertile Gila River Valley is Safford, a trade center for the valley's numerous cotton farmers, and jumping-off point for outdoor recreation in the Coronado National Forest. Just west of town are the adjoining communities of Thatcher and Pima. Named to commemorate a Christmas visit by Mormon apostle Moses Thatcher, the town is home to Eastern Arizona College; nearby Pima is the site of the Eastern Arizona Museum.

Safford Area

Safford's main highway is lined with modern shopping centers, but the downtown district, with its wood-frame and mason buildings, suggests a Midwestern borough. Despite the arid climate, the valley is irrigated by the Gila River and cotton is king here. The **Safford Valley Cotton Growers** have one of a handful of gins in the area that you can tour during season, typically October through January and on Friday afternoons. Call for reservations. ~ Route 191 and 9th Street, Safford; 928-428-0714.

SIGHTS

◄ HIDDEN

Underground hot springs are another natural resource in Safford. To take a dip, stop by **Kachina Mineral Springs Spa**, where you can soak in springs funneled into tiled, Roman-styled tubs. Other amenities include massages, sweat wraps and reflexology (therapeutic foot massage). The baths are wonderful and the tubs

◄ HIDDEN

are clean; two large tubs are available for private groups. There's a charge for services. Closed Monday and Tuesday in summer; open by appointment only. ~ 1155 West Cactus Road just off Route 191, Safford; 928-428-7212, fax 928-348-0217; e-mail kachina@zekes.com.

A good first stop is the **Graham County Chamber of Commerce** for brochures and maps. You can also view historical dioramas and exhibits on gems and minerals. Closed Sunday. ~ 1111 Thatcher Boulevard, Safford; 928-428-2511, 888-837-1841, fax 928-428-0744; www.graham-chamber.com, e-mail director@graham-chamber.com.

One of Safford's main landmarks is the **Safford Courthouse**, a neocolonial brick building with white pillars built in 1916. ~ 8th Avenue at Main Street. Nearby, Safford's 1898-vintage city hall was the town's original schoolhouse. ~ 717 Main Street, Safford.

Just outside of town, the quiet residential neighborhoods are dotted with elegant old homes. One of them is the **Olney House**, built in 1890 for George Olney, a former sheriff of Graham County. The two-story home features a plantation-style upper and lower front veranda. It is currently a bed-and-breakfast inn (see "Lodging" for more information). ~ 1104 Central Avenue, Safford.

For a glimpse at the area's past, visit the **Graham County Historical Society Museum**, which contains a photo gallery, printed materials and displays of Graham County. Open Monday, Tuesday and Saturday or by appointment. ~ 3430 West Route 70, Thatcher; 928-348-0470.

The **Eastern Arizona Museum** has an interesting collection of pioneer and Indian relics in a turn-of-the-20th-century building. There are also an extensive rock and mineral display and a reading room filled with historic documents. ~ Route 70 at Main Street, Pima; 928-485-9400.

If you feel like getting spaced out in Safford, stop by **Discovery Park**. This complex contains exhibits on the origins of the universe, the history and science of astronomy and radio astronomy, as well as a multimedia room where family activities are held. There is also a 20-inch telescope for daytime and nighttime observations and, perhaps most exciting of all, a full-motion flight simulator. Open to the public Friday from 6 to 10 p.m. and Saturday from 4 to 10 p.m. only. Admission. ~ 1651 West Discovery Park Boulevard, Safford; 928-428-6260, fax 928-428-8081; www.discoverypark.com, e-mail discover@discoverypark.com.

Nearby 10,720-foot **Mount Graham** makes for good scenic drives, and its unique ecosphere provides a succession of climate zones, each with its own ecology. The main access road to the mountain is Swift Trail, which at first passes through stands of prickly pear, mesquite, creosote and ocotillo in the lower foothills. As you rise in elevation, the dominant trees are various types of

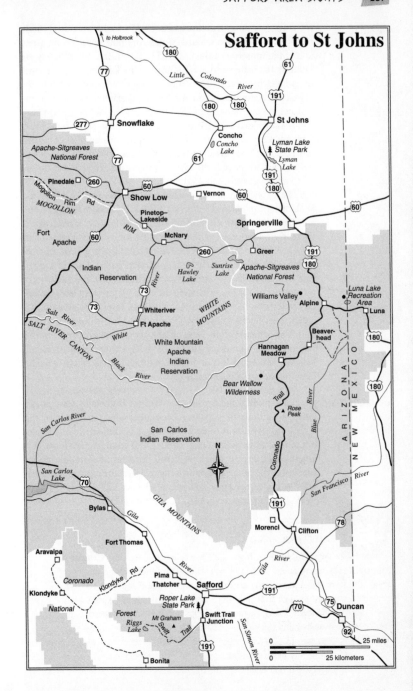

Safford to St Johns

oak, alligator juniper and piñon pine. At a higher elevation (8000 feet) you'll find a profusion of ponderosa pine, Douglas fir, aspen and white fir, some of them dating to A.D. 1200. Botanists say the Douglas firs have survived because the rocky cliffs of the mountains have protected them from the harsh environment. On the drive up the mountain is an apple orchard maintained under a special use permit from the U.S. Forest Service. While the orchard survived the extensive April 1996 fires, 6000 acres on Mount Graham were not as lucky; you'll pass through a number of burned out areas on your trek up the Swift Trail. The first 24 miles of Swift Trail are paved, the last 13 are gravel. The road is closed from mid-November to May.

The **Mount Graham International Observatory** on Emerald Peak outside of Safford features a 1.8-meter Lennon Telescope and a Submillimeter telescope. An 8-millimeter binocular telescope is currently under construction (it will be the world's largest of its type and the most powerful, able to see deeper into space than the Hubble telescope, when completed in 2005). Further expansion of the facility is continuing and will result in the addition of four other telescopes, including an eight-meter class infrared/optical telescope. All-day tours of the observatory, including a box lunch, are offered to the public from late May to mid-November by advance reservation. The observatory is closed to the public the rest of the year. Admission. ~ 1651 West Discovery Park Road, Safford; 928-428-6260, fax 928-428-8081; mgpc3.as.arizona.edu, e-mail mgi.mail@as.arizona.edu.

LODGING

HIDDEN ►

Olney House Bed and Breakfast, a Western Colonial Revival home, has three antique-filled guest rooms, all of which share a bath and a parlor. In addition to rooms in the main house, there's a one-bedroom cottage and a circa-1890 studio cottage; both have TVs. Guests start the morning with a full breakfast. Before leaving, be sure to see the pecan tree, which they claim is the tallest in Arizona. ~ 1104 Central Avenue, Safford; phone/fax 928-428-5118, 800-814-5118; www.olneyhouse.com. MODERATE.

AUTHOR FAVORITE

Across the street from the Quality Inn & Suites, the **Country Manor Restaurant** opens early and stays open late (well, late for this area). Old farm implements hang on the walls and you're likely to see a table of old timers in here shooting the breeze and eating home-cooked meals such as Mexican dishes, homemade soups and pies, chicken-fried steak, liver and onions and meatloaf. ~ 420 East Route 70, Safford; 928-428-7148. BUDGET TO MODERATE.

The rest of Safford's lodgings are mostly chain motels. You won't be disappointed with the **Days Inn**, which features rooms with refrigerators and microwaves, a pool and a hot tub. There's a restaurant across the street. ~ 520 East Route 70, Safford; 928-428-5000, 800-329-7466, fax 928-428-7510. BUDGET.

The best restaurant in town is **El Coronado**, a friendly place with blue-vinyl booths, ceiling fans and a deep narrow dining room. The tasty Mexican specialties include green chile chimichangas and quesadillas stuffed with green chile, meat, chicken, chorizo and chopped green chile. American dishes include chicken-fried steak, shrimp and sandwiches. Closed Tuesday. ~ 409 Main Street, Safford; 928-428-7755. BUDGET.

DINING

El Charro Restaurant is a local hangout with formica tables and local artwork on the wall. Mexican specialties include cheese crisps with green chile *con carne*, green or red chile burritos and Sonora enchiladas. Closed Sunday. ~ 601 Main Street, Safford; 928-428-4134. BUDGET.

The **Branding Iron Restaurant** is a ranch-style building flanked by large trees. They serve Western broiled steaks, chicken, seafood, barbecued ribs in a dining room that overlooks the Gila Valley. Dollar tacos served on Monday. Closed Sunday. ~ 2346 North Branding Iron Lane, Safford; 928-428-7427. MODERATE.

The small shops on downtown's Main Street are fun to explore. In addition to thrift shops, jewelry stores and Western-wear boutiques, you'll find **Trophies n' Tees**, which has a selection of Arizona souvenirs, caps, sweatshirts and T-shirts. Closed Saturday and Sunday. ~ 513 Main Street, Safford; 928-428-0906.

SHOPPING

Brown's Turquoise Shop Inc. has rough and cut natural Morenci turquoise and handmade American Indian jewelry. Closed Sunday. ~ 2248 South 1st Avenue, Safford; 928-428-6433.

You can't miss **Pollock's Western Outfitters** with its distressed-wood exterior and horse statue on the roof. Inside, there are the latest Western fashions and accessories. Suppliers include Levi, Rocky Mountain, Justin, Tony Lama, Wrangler, Stetson and Resistol. You'll also find Classic ropes. ~ 610 5th Street, Safford; 928-428-0093, fax 928-348-9102. Behind Pollock's Western Outfitters, **Pollock's Outback Outlet** offers merchandise at discounted prices.

In late summer and early fall you can purchase fruit at **roadside stands** around the Mount Graham area.

Locals converge on **Tuttie's American Club**. Occasional live music, but the jukebox always cooks! ~ 503 Main Street, Safford; 928-428-2727.

NIGHTLIFE

PARKS

MOUNT GRAHAM 🚶 🚴 🐎 🛷 ⛵ The highest peak of the Pinaleño Mountains at 10,720 feet is Mount Graham. Drive the 37-mile-long Swift Trail and you'll leave the cactus and mesquites at the base and travel to a forest of ponderosa pine, aspen and white fir, punctuated by charred areas consumed by the April 1996 forest fire. Near the end of the road is 11-acre Riggs Lake, which is stocked with trout (license plus trout stamp required) and also available for boating (electric motors only). The forest's facilities are limited to restrooms and picnic areas. ~ Go south from Safford for seven miles on Route 191 and turn west at the Swift Trail sign. The first 24 miles of the Swift Trail are paved; the last 14 are graded dirt. Swift Trail is closed at the end of the pavement from at least November 15 to April 15. Safford Ranger District: 928-428-4150, fax 928-428-2393.

▲ There are eight developed campgrounds; $10 per night. Primitive camping is allowed free below 9800 feet. (Above 9800 feet is closed to all entry.)

ROPER LAKE STATE PARK 🏊 🎣 🛶 🚤 ⛵ In addition to swimming in a 30-acre lake with a beach, you can soak outside in a rock tub filled with water from nearby hot springs. You can fish for catfish, bass, bluegill, trout and crappie from a shady dock. Only boats with electric motors are allowed. For meals, sit out on the peninsula's grassy picnic area under a grove of shade trees. You'll find restrooms and showers. Day-use fee, $6 per vehicle. ~ Off Route 191, six miles south of Safford; 928-428-6760, fax 928-428-7879.

▲ There are 95 sites, 40 with RV hookups; $12 per night for standard sites and $19 per night for hookups.

Dankworth Pond 🚶 🎣 🚤 ⛵ Part of Roper Lake State Park, this day-use-only area features 15-acre Dankworth Pond. Along the west side of the lake are picnic ramadas and restrooms. A trail here leads to a prehistoric Indian village. Fish you're likely to net include catfish, bass, bluegill, trout and crappie. ~ Route 191, three miles south of Roper Lake State Park (ask rangers at Roper Lake for directions); 928-428-6760, fax 928-428-7879.

ARAVAIPA CANYON WILDERNESS 🚶 Aravaipa Creek flows through an 11-mile-long canyon bordered by spectacular cliffs. Lining the creek are large sycamore, ash, cottonwood and willow trees, making it a colorful stop in fall. You may spot javelina, coyotes, mountain lions and desert bighorn sheep, as well as nearly every type of desert songbird and more than 200 other bird species. There are no facilities whatsoever. ~ To get to the West Trailhead, drive on Route 77 about 11 miles south of Winkelman. Go east on Aravaipa Road; it's 12 miles to the trailhead. To get to the East Trailhead from Globe, drive on Route 70 to Klondyke

Road (8 miles east of Fort Thomas). Take this graded dirt road 45 miles. Or take Route 10 to Willcox. Take Exit 340 to Fort Grant Road, then follow the signs. It's advisable to check on road conditions with the Safford Field Office before setting out; high-clearance vehicles are a good idea.

When hiking through the Aravaipa Canyon Wilderness, keep in mind that several species of rattlesnakes call it home.

▲ Primitive camping allowed; $5 per person, per day. The maximum stay is three days/two nights. Permits are required and can be obtained from the Bureau of Land Management's Safford Field Office. Closed weekends. ~ 711 14th Avenue, Safford; 928-348-4400, fax 928-348-4450; safford.az.blm.gov.

CLUFF RANCH WILDLIFE AREA ↲ This area contains 1300 acres of wildlife sanctuary and recreational areas. Streams from Mount Graham feed four ponds that provide year-round fishing for trout, catfish, largemouth bass and bluegill. Birding is also excellent here. ~ Located about nine miles northwest of Safford; 520-485-9430.

Clifton–Morenci Area

To begin the 44-mile drive from Safford to Clifton, continue east out of Safford on Route 70. The road passes along the edge of Roper Lake State Park and parallels the Gila River for a few miles. Soon after the river parts ways with the road, take a left turn onto 191 North—otherwise, you'll promptly end up in New Mexico. The route is scenic, traveling between the Gila Mountains to the north and the Whitlocks to the south. As you pass the appropriately named Thumb Butte on your right, you'll cross from Graham County into Greenlee County; finally, the road rejoins and crosses over the Gila River, and takes you into Clifton.

The Clifton–Morenci area is a region shaped by its mining past. Today, the continent's second-largest copper mine operates in Morenci, while the copper industry's heyday is preserved along Clifton's historic Chase Creek Street.

SIGHTS

Route 191 follows the San Francisco River, much the way Francisco de Coronado and his conquistadors did, around the bend and into the historic little mining town of **Clifton**, built along the banks of the river.

All around Clifton, the red sandstone cliffs paint a brilliant contrast to the grays and tans of the shale and the tin-and-brick buildings that are reminiscent of the town's golden days at the turn of the 20th century, when copper was king.

The town was founded around 1865, but didn't prosper until copper deposits were discovered in 1872. At first, copper ore had to be shipped to Swansea, Wales, for smelting. Then miners built their own crude adobe smelters along Chase Creek Street and set up a narrow-gauge railroad to transport the ore from the mines on the surrounding hillsides.

Many of the remnants of early mining operations remain, along with dozens of old buildings—47 are on the National Register of Historical Places—in early-20th-century architecture. You will find most of them along **Chase Creek Street**, which was once the town's main thoroughfare, lined on both sides with stores, saloons, brothels, churches and even an opera house. Today, the four-block-long street, plus a few narrow alleys, parallels Coronado Boulevard (Route 191), separated by a rudimentary brick wall. But you can still walk among the buildings, many of which have been restored or are in the process of being restored. Most retain their architectural splendor.

For instance, the **Catholic Church**, which was rebuilt in 1917 after being destroyed by flood and fire, has leaded and stained-glass windows, a marble altar and porcelain figures imported from Italy. Down the street is Clifton's first **Town Jail**, which is carved into the side of a granite cliff. Next door is the **Copper Head**, a 19th-century locomotive that once carried ore to the smelters. Across the river, the **Carmichael House** is now headquarters for mine officials. It was built in 1913 for mine president James Carmichael, who once had to flee through the home's storm sewer system to escape a mob of angry strikers. The **Greenlee County Chamber of Commerce**, which has its offices in the old Southern Pacific train depot, dispenses maps and information about the sights and history of the area. Be sure to ask for the walking-tour map of historic Chase Creek. ~ 100 North Coronado Boulevard, Clifton; phone/fax 928-865-3313.

At the Greenlee County Historical Museum are a baby chair and doll that once belonged to Supreme Court Justice Sandra Day O'Connor, who was born in nearby Duncan.

You'll notice a few caves in the mountain above the south side of Chase Creek. These were built by merchants to store valuables such as whiskey, meat and vegetables. They often had rugged steel doors and sometimes were vented with a vertical shaft.

The renovated **Greenlee County Historical Museum** on the west end of Chase Creek has assembled an impressive collection of early Clifton memorabilia, including recollections of Geronimo's birth near the Gila River about four miles from downtown. The photo gallery displays images of the region's history and paintings by Ted De Grazia, one of Arizona's most famous artists and a native of Morenci. Open Tuesday, Thursday and Saturday afternoons. ~ 315 Chase Creek, Clifton; 928-865-3115.

Phelps Dodge Corporation became a major player in Clifton's development at the turn of the 20th century, when it took over most of the local mining operations, about four miles north of town. The original mining camp was called Joy's Camp, but was later renamed **Morenci**, after a town in Michigan. Over the next 50 years, Phelps Dodge, or "PD" as the locals call it (often confused with "Petey"), became one of the largest producers of copper in the world.

Today's Morenci was built by Phelps Dodge in 1969. It consists of a motel/restaurant, a school, a library, two shopping centers, a bowling alley and a supermarket. Phelps Dodge operates the open-pit copper mine here, the second largest in North America.

The **Phelps Dodge Morenci, Inc.** mine is an awesome sight from the viewpoints along Route 191. Most impressive are the earth moving equipment with tires so huge they dwarf a man, the scoop shovels that can unearth 85 cubic tons of ore with one bite, and the futuristic dump trucks with wedge-shaped bays that haul 320 tons of ore. ~ 4521 Route 191, Morenci; 928-865-4521, fax 928-865-2723.

Continuing north, the highway ascends a series of switchbacks into a high-desert climate zone, with juniper trees seemingly growing from the red-rock formations.

About halfway to Alpine, you can stop at **Rose Peak**, which offers panoramic vistas of the Escudilla Mountains. For even better views, you can hike to the forest lookout tower, about a half-mile off the highway.

Each town has its own motel. **Rode Inn Motel** is in the traditional motel style. Rooms are well-kept and offer in-room coffee, microwaves, refrigerators and color cable television. ~ 186 South Coronado Boulevard, Clifton; 928-865-4536, fax 928-865-2654; www.rodeinn.com. BUDGET.

LODGING

The more modern **Morenci Motel** sits on a hill overlooking Clifton and features an adobe brick exterior, wrought-iron fixtures, an adobe-tiled lobby, a restaurant, a lounge and a gift shop. The large rooms are decorated with pastels and Southwestern-style furnishings. ~ Route 191, Morenci; 928-865-4111, fax 928-865-5525. BUDGET.

PJ's Restaurant, a storefront hole-in-the-wall near the old section of town, is popular with locals who feast on hamburgers or Mexican entrées like chile cheese crisps and green chile plates or red enchiladas. Seating is at the counter or formica dinettes, but the food is tasty and plentiful. No dinner on Saturday or Sunday. ~ 307 South Coronado Boulevard, Clifton; 928-865-3328. BUDGET TO MODERATE.

DINING

The best place in town to eat is the **Copperoom Restaurant and Sportspage Lounge**, a somewhat plain but cavernous dining room with ceiling fans, wooden tables, captain chairs and a brick fireplace used during the winter. The house specialties include steaks, prime rib, chicken, liver and onions, halibut and several Mexican dishes. ~ Morenci Motel, Route 191, Morenci; 928-865-4111, fax 928-865-5525. BUDGET TO MODERATE.

SHOPPING   There's not much here, but if you run out of toothpaste try **Bascha's**, a grocery store. ~ Morenci Plant Site shopping center, Morenci; 928-865-1820.

NIGHTLIFE   For contemporary surroundings, try the **Copperoom Restaurant and Sportspage Lounge**, a small but surprisingly active bar with a handful of wooden tables and big-screen TVs. ~ Morenci Motel, Route 191, Morenci; 928-865-4111.

▼▼▼▼▼▼▼▼▼▼
Alpine Area

The long and winding road from Clifton up to Alpine is a beautiful one—just make sure you have plenty of gas and supplies before you begin because there are no facilities along the 105-mile stretch. Starting from Clifton, you'll first need to make the 1300-foot climb to Morenci, then bid civilization farewell as you continue the ascent into Apache-Sitgreaves National Forest. Your progress through the Blue Range toward Alpine will be marked by the increasing height of the peaks you pass: Mitchell Peak at just under 8000 feet, Rose Peak at almost 8900 feet and Sawed Off Mountain at 9346 feet.

Be aware that this road is subject to closure during winter snow storms. If the road is closed by snow or mudslides, you can drive to Alpine via Routes 78 and 180 through western New Mexico. The detour adds only 20 miles to the trip.

SIGHTS   Twenty-two miles before you reach Alpine is **Hannagan Meadow**, a grassy clearing framed by stately ponderosa pine and blue spruce forests. In addition to excellent hiking trails, there's a rustic mountain lodge and, in winter, cross-country skiing and snowmobiling. ~ Route 191.

The mountain village of **Alpine** is located in the heart of the Apache-Sitgreaves National Forest, or the "Arizona Alps," as it is called locally. The town was founded in 1879 by Mormon settlers who originally named it Frisco, after the San Francisco River. The name was later changed to Alpine because residents thought the area resembled the Alps. The Arizona Alps don't attract the large number of tourists who flock to the Grand Canyon, the Colorado River or other state attractions, but nature buffs will love the region's abundance of outdoor activities—hiking, camping, hunting, fishing and cross-country skiing.

Alpine has no traffic lights or video stores, just a handful of year-round residents and even fewer commercial attractions. Actually it's nothing more than an intersection of Routes 191 and 180, but there are dependable services and lodging. More important, within a 30-mile radius there are 200 miles of trout streams, 11 lakes and numerous campgrounds, plus a country club and golf course.

The region is also a favorite with hunters because it is home to nine of Arizona's ten big-game species, including mule deer, elk, black bear, bighorn sheep and mountain lion. Small-game hunters stalk blue grouse, wild turkey, Gambel's quail and a host of waterfowl.

Founded during a period of strife between pioneers and American Indians, Alpine was a small fort before evolving into a commercial hub for settlers and ranchers.

From Alpine, you can strike out in any direction and discover unspoiled forests of tall pines and shimmering aspens, trickling streams, wildflower meadows and clear blue lakes. For detailed maps and descriptions of the area, stop at the **U.S. Forest Service**, where rangers can also advise on current road conditions. The office lobby is now open 24 hours, with an interactive video display giving out tourist information when rangers aren't available. ~ At the junction of Routes 180 and 191; 928-339-4384, fax 928-339-4323; www.fs.fed.us/r3/asnf.

A picturesque spot is the pristine **Williams Valley**, located seven miles northwest of Alpine via Route 191 and Forest Road 249. Here you can explore 15 miles of hiking trails through wooded forests. Beyond Williams Valley you can drop a line in tiny Lake Sierra Blanca, which is stocked with rainbow and brook trout.

A nice scenic drive from Alpine is the **Blue River–Red Hill Loop**. Drive east three miles from Alpine on Route 180 to Forest Road 281 (the Blue Road turnoff). As you make this turnoff, you will see the western tip of **Luna Lake**, 80 acres of crystal-clear waters surrounded by green meadows and pine forests. Facilities at the lake include a boat dock, campground and small store.

From Route 180, Blue Road winds south through ten miles of rugged hills until it descends past a few horse ranches into Box Canyon, where the road follows the **Blue River**. Continue downstream past jagged Maness Peak nine miles to the junction with Forest Route 567 (Red Hill Road). Along the way are tributaries, such as Centerfire Creek, which are home to small schools of rainbow and brook trout. Drive west on Red Hill Road, which twists and climbs out of the valley, often following ridges with panoramic vistas back to Route 191, about 14 miles south of Alpine.

The wood-paneled **Tal-wi-wi Lodge** offers clean, comfortable rooms featuring rustic furnishings, some with woodburning stoves and spa tubs. The seasonal restaurant serves breakfast and dinner (weekends only), and the lounge often has live music or karaoke. ~ Route 191, four miles north of Alpine; 928-339-4319, 800-476-2695, fax 928-339-1962; www.talwiwilodge.com, e-mail talwiwi@cybertrails.com. MODERATE.

LODGING

If you came to the mountains seeking a cozy retreat, try the **Alpine Cabins**, which feature kitchenettes and cable TV. Closed December through March. ~ On Route 180, one-half block east of the intersection with Route 191, Alpine; 928-339-4440. BUDGET.

Surrounded by pine forests, the **Coronado Trail Cabins and RV Park** offers a few cozy single-room cabins fully furnished with kitchenettes and bed covers. Barbecue and picnic areas are outside the units. RV sites have full hookups. ~ 25304 Route 191, Alpine; 928-339-4772, fax 928-339-4516; www.ctcrv.com, e-mail ctcrv@cyber trails.com. BUDGET.

A pair of Alpine motels offer clean, well-maintained rooms—some with kitchenettes—at reasonable prices. One is the **Mountain Hi Lodge**. ~ 42698 Route 180; 928-339-4311. BUDGET. Your other choice is the **Sportsman's Lodge**. They have some units with kitchens. ~ 42627 Route 191, Alpine; 928-339-4576, 888-202-1033. BUDGET.

About 22 miles south of Alpine, **Hannagan Meadow Lodge** rents ten rustic cabins with fireplaces and antique furnishings, and eight rooms in the main lodge, which also has a dining room. One of the oldest inns in the state, the lodge also has a general store. ~ Route 191 at Hannagan Meadow; 928-428-2225, fax 928-428-1012; www.hannaganmeadow.com, e-mail info@hanna ganmeadow.com. MODERATE TO DELUXE.

The unofficial community of Blue—made up of a post office and a few ranches—lies at the bottom of the Blue River Canyon.

DINING

You'll find home cooking and a casual, friendly atmosphere at the **Bear Wallow Cafe**. Traditional favorites here include T-bone steak, chicken-fried steak, homemade bread and pies. ~ 42650 Route 180, Alpine; 928-339-4310. MODERATE.

SHOPPING

One-stop shopping is the specialty at **The Tackle Shop**, where you can fill your tank, restring your crossbow or eat lunch. ~ Routes 180 and 191, Alpine; 928-339-4338.

If you crave satisfaction for your sweet tooth, head for the **Lollipop Shoppe** for a decent selection of all things sinful. ~ 24680 Route 180, Alpine; 928-339-4966.

Pinetop–Lakeside Area

Where Route 60 intersects with Route 191 and the Coronado Trail, you'll come to the town of Springerville, where you can make a detour and head west to the recreation and ski area of Pinetop–Lakeside, a winter resort popular with Phoenix residents.

SIGHTS

In the Springerville area, there are two places of interest worth stopping for. Situated on a rim of volcanic rock overlooking the Little Colorado River's Round Valley is **Casa Malpais Pueblo**.

Tours originate at the museum in Springerville. Here, you'll learn that the Mogollon people abandoned the pueblo in A.D. 1400, and now the archaeological dig is open to the public. For the best pueblo views, take the guided tour up a steep basalt staircase to the top of the mesa. A tour highlight is the **Great Kiva** made of volcanic rock. Admission. ~ 318 Main Street, Springerville; 928-333-5375, fax 928-333-3512; www.springerville.com/area.html, e-mail sitetour@springerville.com.

Follow a dusty, bumpy road for several miles and the unlikely reward is the **Little House Museum** on the X Diamond Ranch. Inside the two-story building are exhibits relating to the area's history, including ranching and horse show memorabilia. Beside it are two restored cabins more than 100 years old. One contains antique musical instruments ranging from a player piano to a Wurlitzer circus organ. Another building houses the expanding instrument collection as well as an exhibit on John Wayne, who had a ranch next door. Reservations are required and include a substantial tour. Admission. ~ Located just over three miles south of Route 260 on South Fork Road, near Springerville; 928-333-2286, fax 928-333-5009; www.xdiamondranch.com, e-mail info @diamondranch.com.

Climbing the steep incline of the Mogollon Rim leads to Show Low, Pinetop and Lakeside, forested hamlets of cabins, motels, resorts and campgrounds in a pine woods setting. Most of the commercial activity takes place in Show Low along Route 60.

The population of **Show Low** swells from about 8500 year-round residents to more than 13,000 during the summer, when the big attractions are excellent trout fishing and big-game hunting in the Mogollon Rim country and White Mountains. Also popular are hiking, horseback riding, golf and scenic drives. Many Arizonans also keep summer homes at the 6400-foot-elevation town to escape the blistering summer temperatures in Phoenix and other "flatlander" communities. During winter, the Sunrise ski resort on the White Mountain Apache Reservation is famous for its downhill runs and cross-country trails.

Southeast of Show Low lie the mountain resort twins of **Pinetop** and **Lakeside**, and beyond, the Indian towns of Whiteriver and Fort Apache. Lakeside is a starting point for hiking, fishing, camping and backpacking in and near the three resort communities, which are connected by a highway lined with motels, restaurants, gas stations and small businesses.

A nice alternative to camping out is staying at the **Lake of the Woods Resort**. Thirty-three log cabins are scattered amidst pine trees beside a private lake. All of the cabins have fireplaces, TVs, microwaves, kitchen and dining areas and outdoor barbecues. Although some cabins are geared toward honeymooners, most

LODGING

are more family oriented. Amenities include shuffleboard, horseshoes, spas, a sauna, playground, ping-pong, pool tables and boats for rent. ~ 2244 West White Mountain Boulevard, Pinetop–Lakeside; 928-368-5353; www.privatelake.com. BUDGET TO MODERATE.

Located on Sunrise Lake near the ski resort four miles south of Route 260 is **Sunrise Park Resort**, owned and operated by the White Mountain Apache Tribe. Guests come to fish in summer and ski in winter, staying at one of the 94 modern, nicely furnished hotel rooms. Amenities include a heated indoor pool, indoor and outdoor spas and restaurant and lounge. Closed April to mid-May. ~ Route 273, 20 miles east of McNary; 928-735-7669, 800-772-7669, fax 928-735-7315; www.sunriseskipark.com, e-mail sunrise@cybertrails.com. MODERATE TO DELUXE.

A beautiful setting amidst pine, spruce and aspen trees, rather than luxurious accommodations, are what you pay for at **Hawley Lake Resort**. The resort is remote—12 long, winding miles off Route 260—and situated on a lake in one of the highest points in the White Mountains. In the summer, this area is 40° cooler than the flatlands of Phoenix. The resort has eleven motel rooms and seven cabins overlooking the lake. If you get lucky fishing, the cabins have kitchenettes. The resort is located on the White Mountain Apache Indian Reservation. Amenities include a café, boat rentals, gas and a store. Closed December through April. ~ Route 473, 19 miles east of McNary; 928-335-7511, fax 928-335-7434. MODERATE.

Pastoral is the only word for the setting at **Greer Lodge**, located on the Little Colorado River with a view of meadows and mountains. To many, it is *the* place to stay. Built by hand as a church retreat in 1948 out of ponderosa pine and aspen, it now is a charming getaway with eleven rooms in the main lodge and five cabins. The lounge/restaurant area has comfy couches, a huge fireplace, vaulted ceilings and almost floor-to-ceiling windows where guests can look out at the snow falling in winter. Country furnishings warm up the rooms; on-site spa available. There's fly-fishing in stocked ponds in summer. ~ Route 373, Greer; 928-

AUTHOR FAVORITE

Nicknamed the miniature Grand Canyon, the **Salt River Canyon** is a spectacular sight that you can drive right through on Route 60 about 50 miles south of Show Low. There's a bridge where Route 60 crosses the Salt River, which carved the canyon millions of years ago. Seven miles downstream from the bridge via a paved road are fascinating salt banks sacred to the Apache and colored with green, red and orange minerals and algae.

735-7216, 888-475-6343, fax 928-735-7720; www.greerlodge az.com. DELUXE TO ULTRA-DELUXE.

Molly Butler Lodge is the oldest lodge in Arizona, established in 1910. Guest rooms are small and very basic, but prices are inexpensive. A nice touch are the plaques on each door with the name and information about a local pioneer. There is a restaurant on the premises. ~ 109 Main Street, Greer; 928-735-7226, 866-288-3167, fax 928-735-7538; www.mollybutlerlodge.com, e-mail itsgreer@cybertrails.com. BUDGET TO MODERATE.

Snowy Mountain Inn is a sprawling resort nestled in the forest near a trout-stocked pond. Accommodations consist of seven separate log cabins, six of which have private spas and all with fireplaces (gas-log) in the living room, housekeeping kitchens and lofts with queen beds and a sitting area. There are also four three-bedroom, two-bath private homes, all with fireplaces and spas. The restaurant/bar has a high vaulted ceiling and a large rock fireplace. Hiking trails can be accessed from the property, which borders on National Forest land. ~ 38721 Route 373, Greer; 928-735-7576, 888-766-9971, fax 928-735-7705; www. snowymountaininn.com, e-mail info@snowymountaininn.com. DELUXE TO ULTRA-DELUXE.

DINING

Charlie Clark's Steak House has been around since 1938. A Western theme predominates, with stuffed deer and wildlife paintings. Prime rib, steak and seafood are the primary offerings. ~ 1701 East White Mountain Boulevard, Pinetop; 928-367-4900, 888-333-0259, fax 928-367-6025; www.charlieclarks.com, e-mail char clks2002@yahoo.com. DELUXE TO ULTRA-DELUXE.

Fine dining is available in eastern Arizona. With spot-lighting, a stone fireplace and a cigar bar, **Phineas T's** serves up a variety of dishes from baked halibut to Australian rack of lamb. Vegetarians might opt for one of their pasta dishes. ~ 1450 East White Mountain Boulevard, Pinetop; 928-367-7400; www.phi neasts.com. ULTRA-DELUXE.

Open year-round despite its name, **The Christmas Tree** serves up elegant versions of comfort food. You can start with fried mozzarella sticks (if cholesterol is not a concern), or opt for the potato skins, dripping with cheese and bacon. Chicken dumplings, a mug of soup, beef stroganoff, lamb chops, fresh fish and lasagna top the entrée list, while the kids will be happy with hot cocoa and chicken nuggets. Closed Monday and Tuesday. ~ 455 North Woodland Road, Pinetop; 928-367-3107; www.christmas treerestaurant.com, e-mail christmastree@cybertrails.com. BUDGET TO DELUXE.

For dining with a sports theme, try the **Scoreboard Restaurant & Sports Bar** at the Snowy Mountain Resort. Cuisine includes "dug out dogs," a "tailgate sausage" sandwich and the real splurge: bread mozzarella triangles. Save room, if humanly possible, for the peanut butter pie. Open Friday and Saturday evenings. ~ 38721 Route 373, Greer; 928-735-7576; www.snowymoun taininn.com, e-mail info@snowymountaininn.com. BUDGET.

Located in rustic Cattle Kate's Lodge, **Cattle Kate's Restaurant** offers casual dining in its massive log dining room. Diners feast on steak, chicken and fish (including fresh-caught trout from nearby ponds) under an antler chandelier. ~ 80 North Main Street, Greer; 928-735-7744, fax 928-735-7386. MODERATE.

SHOPPING   Antiquing is popular in this area. Choices include **The Orchard Antiques** with quality furniture, Nippon china, vintage clothing and primitives; the shop is located in an old house. Closed in winter. ~ 1664 West White Mountain Boulevard, Lakeside; 928-368-6563.

Diamond Creek Jewelry & Antiques has gold and silver estate jewelry, Depression ware, glass and furniture. Closed Sunday. ~ Route 260, Ponderosa Plaza, Pinetop–Lakeside; 928-367-5184.

Primitives, pine and oak furniture, quilts, gifts and gourmet coffee beans are what you'll find at **Country Pine Antiques**. ~ 103 West Yaeger Lane, Pinetop–Lakeside; 928-367-1709.

NIGHTLIFE   **Mor Mor Custom Coffee** has live local music on Friday evenings. ~ 1450 East White Mountain Boulevard, Pinetop; 928-367-5456.

PARKS   **WOODLAND LAKE PARK** 🚶 🚲 🐎 ⛵ 🚤 ⛴ ⛏ This 580-acre scenic park, located in the middle of Pinetop–Lakeside, offers hiking, equestrian and mountain biking trails, volleyball courts, softball fields, boating and playgrounds. People can fish for trout from the shore and piers, one of which is wheelchair accessible. Tall, thin pine trees surround the lake and a one-mile paved loop trail encircles it. The park is also connected with the White Mountain Trailsystem (see "Hiking" at the end of the chapter). Other facilities are restrooms, picnic tables, barbecues and ramadas. Restrooms are closed in winter. ~ Off Woodland Lake Road, a quartermile south of Route 260; 928-368-6700, fax 928-368-8528.

▼▼▼▼▼▼▼▼▼▼
St. Johns Area

From Show Low, head east on Route 60 and northeast on Route 61 to arrive at St. Johns. Built along the banks of the Little Colorado River, St. Johns, with a population of about 3500, serves as the Apache County seat. The Coronado Trail (Route 180/191), named after the Spanish explorer who first sojourned here, begins innocently enough in the high desert area near St. Johns.

SIGHTS   St. Johns has few sights, except for the **St. Johns Equestrian Center**, which is rapidly becoming one of the premier equestrian facilities in the Southwest, attracting horses and riders from New Mexico, Colorado and Utah, as well as throughout Arizona. Surrounded by rolling hills and juniper-studded deserts, amenities include an 80-acre cross-country course, a rodeo arena, show and dressage rings, a six-furlong race track, stables and RV sites. In spring and summer, the center hosts local and regional events, both Western and English, rodeos and other horse competitions. ~ Adjacent to St. Johns Airport; call St. Johns Parks & Recreation at 928-337-4517, fax 928-337-2195.

You can find out about the area's history at the **Apache County Historical Society Museum,** which houses displays that include pioneer memorabilia and a log cabin, as well as a set of prehistoric woolly mammoth tusks and a camel's leg bone, both estimated to be about 24,000 years old. Closed weekends. ~ 180 West Cleveland Avenue, St. Johns; 928-337-4737, fax 928-337-2020.

For more information, contact **St. Johns Regional Chamber of Commerce.** Closed Saturday and Sunday. ~ P.O. Box 929, St. Johns, AZ 85936; 928-337-2000, fax 928-337-2020; www.stjohnschamber.com, e-mail office@stjohnschamber.com.

The northern part of the **Coronado Trail** meanders through a region of juniper-dotted hillsides, alfalfa pastures, grazing cattle and a few sandy-topped buttes about 44 miles southeast of Petrified Forest National Park. The trail then heads south through Apache-Sitgreaves National Forest to Clifton. It is rumored to be the least-traveled federal highway in the U.S. Cars on this road are spaced an average of 19 minutes apart—even during rush hour.

When driving along the infrequently traveled Coronado Trail, you may catch a glimpse of some Mexican wolves that were reintroduced between Clifton and Alpine. About the size of a German shepherd, they are larger and heavier than a coyote.

Apache-Sitgreaves National Forest is habitat for a wide variety of rare and endangered birds, including the Mexican spotted owl, bald eagle and peregrine falcon.

As the Coronado Trail climbs on its journey south, chaparral gives way to pine and aspen, and you pass **Nelson Reservoir,** a 60-acre lake stocked with rainbow, brown and brook trout. If you're ready for a break, there are picnic grounds, restrooms and a boat ramp, but no overnight camping.

South of the reservoir are the rolling **Escudilla Mountains,** a 5000-acre wilderness area with forests of spruce, fir, pine and aspen, and nature trails where hikers are often rewarded with raspberries, elderberries and gooseberries, and glimpses of elk and deer in their natural habitat.

St. Johns' lodging scene is unexceptional and almost non-existent, but you'll find well-maintained rooms at **Days Inn,** a trailer-court type of motel with old-fashioned casement windows and adobe-

LODGING

like walls. A lounge adjoins the motel. ~ 125 East Commercial Street, St. Johns; 928-337-4422, fax 928-337-4126. BUDGET.

DINING   For an eclectic menu, stop by the **Rhino's Horn**, which orchestrates a good rendition of several Italian dishes including lasagna, pizza and calzones. You can also feast on frisbee-sized hamburgers, a slab of barbecue ribs or fresh catfish. Closed Sunday. ~ 855 West Cleveland Street, St. Johns; 928-337-2223. BUDGET TO MODERATE.

If you're craving something spicier, **El Camino** has a traditional Mexican menu of tacos, enchiladas and tostadas. Closed Sunday. ~ 277 White Mountain Drive, St. Johns; 928-337-4700. BUDGET.

PARKS   **CONCHO LAKE** This lake, stocked with rainbow and brook trout, is a peaceful spot to drop a line. Nonmotorized boating is allowed. Or you may choose to play a round of golf at the neighboring public course. The only facilities in the park are restrooms and a picnic area. ~ Off Route 61, ten miles west of St. Johns.

▲ There's an RV park nearby.

LYMAN LAKE STATE PARK A 1500-acre lake lures both fishing and boating enthusiasts. In fact, it is the only lake in the White Mountains where powerboating is allowed, so waterskiers and jetskiers flock to Lyman Lake. This is also a good place to swim as there's a cove especially marked off for swimming. Anglers fish offshore for catfish, walleye and largemouth bass. The lake was formed by damming the Little Colorado River and is fed by snowmelt from the slopes of Mount Baldy and Escudilla Mountain. Other attractions include hiking the three trails, which range from a half a mile to one mile in length, and are dotted with Indian petroglyphs. On weekends from May through September, guided tours take hikers to petroglyph sites and a pueblo ruin. This 1180-acre park was the first recreational state park in Arizona and sits at an elevation of 6000 feet. Facilities include restrooms, a store, a gas station and hot showers. Day-use fee, $5 per vehicle. ~ Off Route 180/191, 11 miles south of St. Johns; 928-337-4441, fax 928-337-4649.

▲ There are 55 RV sites with electrical and water hookups and 25 developed sites for tents, complete with picnic tables and barbecue grills; there are also four cabins and four yurts. Beach and wilderness camping are allowed. Fees are $12 per night for tents, $19 per night for RV hookups, $50 per night for cabins, and $35 per night for yurts.

Eastern Arizona is an angler's paradise with numerous lakes dotting the region around Pinetop-Lakeside and Greer. Anglers will also find plenty of challenge—and game fish—along the Old West Highway.

Outdoor Adventures

FISHING

APACHE JUNCTION AREA Saguaro, Canyon, Apache and Roosevelt lakes are popular year-round fishing meccas.

GLOBE San Carlos Lake near Globe is the biggest fishing draw in this area.

SAFFORD AREA Roper Lake in Safford attracts anglers from all over Arizona.

ALPINE AREA In the Alpine area, **Bear Wallow Creek**, a tributary of the Black River, is famous for native Apache trout. Also on the **Black River** at different stops you can try for rainbow trout, while trout and catfish can be found in **Eagle Creek**. East of Alpine and dropping off into the Blue Primitive Area, rainbow trout can be found in **Luna Lake** and the ruggedly remote **Blue River**. North of Alpine you'll find rainbow, brown and brook trout in **Nelson Reservoir**. More casual anglers can seek catfish in the **San Francisco River** near Clifton. You can buy bait, tackle and a license at **The Tackle Shop**. ~ At the intersection of Routes 180 and 191, Alpine; 928-339-4338.

A top fishing destination, the Apache-Sitgreaves National Forest contains over 450 miles of streams, and nearly 2000 surface acres of water, thanks to its eight cold-water lakes.

PINETOP–LAKESIDE AREA To fish at the lakes on the White Mountain Apache Indian Reservation, which are stocked with rainbow and brown trout, contact the **Game and Fish Department**. ~ South Route 73, Whiteriver; 928-338-4385. For general fishing information in the White Mountains, stop by the **Arizona Game and Fish Department**. ~ 2878 East White Mountain Boulevard, Pinetop; 928-367-4281.

For private catch-and-release flyfishing, try **X Diamond Ranch**. ~ South Fork; 928-333-2286; www.xdiamondranch.com. There are quality waters with rainbow, brown and Apache trout as well as boat rentals and camping May through November at **Hawley Lake**. ~ Route 473, 19 miles from McNary; 928-335-7511. For fishing and camping supplies or a license, check with **Western United Drug**. ~ 105 East Main Street, Springerville; 928-333-4321.

ST. JOHNS AREA The 60-acre **Concho Lake** is a good spot for rainbow and brook trout (shore fishing only). **Lyman Lake State Park** has a lake stocked with catfish, walleye and largemouth bass. ~ Located off Route 180/191, 11 miles south of St. Johns; 928-337-4441.

RIVER RUNNING   During the spring runoff, the Upper Salt River offers some of the country's best whitewater rafting opportunities. **Far Flung Adventures** runs single and multiday whitewater paddle trips from March through May through the spectacular canyons of the Upper Salt River. ~ P.O. Box 2804, Globe, AZ 85502; 800-231-7238; www. farflung.com/az.

WINTER SPORTS   Eastern Arizona increasingly attracts recreationally minded tourists, and not just in the summer. Locals are somewhat stunned by the growing number of winter visitors here in recent years.

ALPINE AREA   Cross-country skiing, sledding and snowmobiling are popular at **Hannagan Meadow**, 22 miles south of Alpine on Route 191, where there are over 11 miles of machine-packed trails that are serviced after each storm. The snowmobiles in the area are prohibited from designated ski trails. Another good spot for cross-country skiers is **Williams Valley**, which features twelve miles of groomed ski trails, plus additional miles of marked trails. From Alpine, drive one and a half miles north on Route 191 to the Williams Valley turnoff, Forest Road 249, and continue for five miles.

Swimming is ideal at Canyon, Apache and Roosevelt lakes.

PINETOP–LAKESIDE AREA   **Sunrise Park Resort** on the White Mountain Apache Reservation has 800 acres of skiable area on three mountains and ten lifts. There's a base elevation of 9200 and a vertical drop of 1800 feet. Facilities include a snowboard park and a kids' ski school, as well as groomed cross-country trails. ~ Route 273, 20 miles east of McNary ; 928-735-7669, 800-772-7669; www.sunriseskipark.com, e-mail sunrise@cybertrails.com.

GOLF   If you feel the need to tee off in the mountains, greens are scattered throughout the region. Most are nine-hole courses; keep in mind that many are closed in the winter. Cart and club rentals are generally available.

APACHE JUNCTION AREA   In Apache Junction, try one of the two 18-hole courses at the public **Gold Canyon Golf Club**. ~ 6210 South Kings Ranch Road; 480-982-9449.

GLOBE   **Cobre Valley Country Club** has a nine-hole course with lush greens, subtle breaks and slopes, a bar and a pro shop. ~ Route 88 north of Globe; 928-473-2542.

SAFFORD AREA   In the Safford area, the **Mount Graham Country Club** offers an 18-hole course for year-round play, a pro shop and a lounge. ~ Two miles south of Safford at Daley Estates; 928-348-3140.

ALPINE AREA   You can tee off at the semiprivate **Alpine Country Club**, which features an 18-hole course, a restaurant and a lounge. Closed in winter. ~ 58 North County Road 2122; 928-339-4944.

PINETOP–LAKESIDE AREA The Pinetop–Lakeside area offers
Silver Creek Golf Club, an 18-hole course with club rentals, a
clubhouse and a pro shop. ~ 2051 Silver Lake Boulevard, White
Mountain Lake; 928-537-2744. Also in the area is the 18-hole
Pinetop Lakes Golf & Country Club. Closed in winter. ~ 4643
Bucksprings Road; 928-369-4531. North of Pinetop–Lakeside,
the **Show Low Golf Club** offers a dramatic contrast between the
back nine holes, lined with ponderosa pines, and the front nine
in open high-desert terrain. ~ 860 North 36th Drive, Show Low;
928-537-4564.

This is the real Wild West; there's no better place to saddle up
and take to the hills. If you're lucky, you may even find the legendary Lost Dutchman Mine and strike it rich—but if you don't,
a ride in this beautiful backcountry is its own reward. Giddyup!

RIDING STABLES

APACHE JUNCTION AREA Don Donnelly Horseback Vacations
& Stables takes you on two- to three-hour and multiday rides to
the foot of the Superstition Mountains and through the Sonoran
Desert. ~ 5580 South Kings Ranch Road #3, Gold Canyon; 602-
810-7029; www.dondonnelly.com. For trips into the Superstition
Mountains, contact **O.K. Corral, Inc**. They offer half-day, full-day
(lunch is provided) and longer rides into the wilderness. On longer
trips, all gear and food are provided (except for sleeping bags). ~
P.O. Box 528, Apache Junction, AZ 85217; 480-982-4040; www.
okcorrals.com, e-mail info@okcorrals.com.

PINETOP–LAKESIDE AREA Between Pinetop and Greer at the
Sunrise Ski Resort Park on the White Mountain Apache Reservation, you can saddle up at **Blue Sky Stables** for one-hour to
overnight trips through the White Mountains, one of the most
scenic areas in Arizona. Wagon and sleigh rides are offered in
summer and winter, respectively. ~ P.O. Box 315, Eagar, AZ
85927; 928-735-7454.

If you don't get a chance to go horseback riding, at least take the
opportunity to hoof it along some of Eastern Arizona's wilderness trails. Bird and animal enthusiasts should keep an eye peeled
for samples of western wildlife; everyone should keep an eye on
the panoramic views. All distances listed for hiking trails are one
way unless otherwise noted.

HIKING

APACHE JUNCTION AREA Usery Mountain Recreation Area
offers the well-maintained **Wind Cave Trail** (1.5 mile), which is
moderately challenging and popular with local climbers. The
moderate-to-difficult **Pass Mountain Trail** (7 miles) takes about
four hours to complete.

SAFFORD AREA Arcadia Trail (5.1 miles), located in the Pinaleño
Mountains, passes through a forest of Douglas fir, aspen and pine

trees, along with wild raspberry vines. As the highest range in southern Arizona, hikers will see a panoramic view of the area.

ALPINE AREA The 450,000-acre Apache-Sitgreaves National Forest is a hiker's paradise, with terrain ranging from piñon and juniper woodlands to high-elevation forests of spruce and fir, meadows and alpine lakes.

About 14 miles south of Alpine, hikers can explore the **Red Hill Trail No. 56** (9.7 miles), a trek along a dirt road that leads into the Blue Range Primitive Area. From the upper trailhead at the Right Fork of Foote Creek, just off Forest Route 567 a mile east of Route 191, the trail traces the ridges of the Red Hill mountains, then descends along Bush Creek on its way to the Blue River. About seven and a half miles from the upper trailhead, the trail joins the Tutt Creek Trail (#105) for the last two miles of the journey. The lower trailhead is at Tutt Creek near Blue Crossing Campground off Forest Road 567 (Red Hill Road). If you like to do your hiking by horseback, corrals have recently been built at the upper and lower trailheads.

In the **Blue Range Primitive Area,** you'll find spectacular rock formations with steep escarpments, along with thick forests of spruce, fir and ponderosa pine. Keep a sharp watch for black bear, Rocky Mountain elk, bighorn sheep, javelina, mule deer, mountain lions and bobcats. The area is excellent for birdwatching; keep your binoculars trained for the Arizona woodpecker, American peregrine falcon and southern bald eagle.

West of the Coronado Trail (Route 191), the **Bear Wallow Wilderness** contains 11,000 acres including one of the largest stands of virgin ponderosa pine in the Southwest. **Bear Wallow Trail No. 63** (7.6 miles), which begins off of Forest Road 25, traces Bear Wallow Creek downstream from the trailhead (about 31 miles south of Alpine) through jagged canyons of spruce, fir, ponderosa pine and aspen, west to the San Carlos Apache Indian Reservation's eastern boundary. Two shorter trails connect with the main trail and creek from the north: the moderate **Reno Trail No. 62** (1.9 miles) and the very strenuous **Gobbler Point Trail No. 59** (2.7 miles).

There's excellent hiking in the **Escudilla Wilderness Area,** an alpine forest with peaks over 10,000 feet, ten miles north of Alpine. The **Escudilla National Recreation Trail** (3 miles) from Terry Flat takes you to the summit of Escudilla Mountain through aspen groves, pine forests and grassy meadows. The trailhead is along Forest Route 56, four and a half miles east of Route 191. Rangers at the **U.S. Forest Service** (intersection of Routes 191 and 180, Alpine; 928-339-4384) will provide detailed trail maps and advice on current conditions.

There area many guides and outfitters in the Alpine area. Operating out of Alpine is the **Neal Reidhead Alpine Guide Service.**

Hikes through Blue River Unit 27 and Unit 1 offer ample opportunities to view bear, elk and bald eagles. ~ P.O. Box 596, Alpine, AZ 85920; 928-339-1936. For a complete list of outfitters, call the **Alpine Ranger District**. ~ 928-339-4384.

PINETOP–LAKESIDE AREA   The White Mountains Trailsystem contains about 180 miles of trails from Vernon in the east to Pinedale in the west. For a map of trails, stop by the **Lakeside Ranger Station**. ~ 2202 East White Mountain Boulevard (Route 260); 928-368-5111, fax 928-368-6476. The Trailsystem consists of ten loop trails, with several more trails and connectors being added. Some highlights are **Blue Ridge Trail** (8.7 miles roundtrip) in Pinetop–Lakeside, which is easy to moderate. It passes Billy Creek and climbs through tall pines to the top of Blue Ridge with vistas along the way. The **Ghost-of-the-Coyote Trail** (16 miles roundtrip) begins near Pinedale. The fairly flat trail winds through juniper and pine forests.

A far cry from the arid desert landscape that springs to mind when Arizona comes up in a conversation, Eastern Arizona's White Mountains offer 2000 square miles of forested peaks, babbling brooks and placid lakes.

The **Mogollon Rim Overlook** (1 mile roundtrip) is an easy hike with interpretive placards along the way and beautiful views of the valley below the Mogollon Rim. It's two miles north of Pinetop–Lakeside off Route 260.

ST. JOHNS AREA   There are a couple of short trails that pass by ancient petroglyphs in **Lyman Lake State Park**. Along the way, you'll be able to enjoy views of the lake below.

Transportation

CAR

The western anchor of the Old West Highway, Apache Junction, is about 30 miles east of Phoenix via **Route 60**. On its eastern end you can join the Highway at Safford via **Routes 191** from Clifton, or **Route 70**, which crosses to Lordsburg, New Mexico. **Route 180/191** links the Coronado Trail towns of St. Johns, Alpine and Clifton. You can get to the Pinetop–Lakeside area from the west via Route 60, turning onto **Route 260** at Show Low. From the east, Route 260 connects to Route 180 at Springerville.

BUS

The closest **Greyhound Bus Lines** (800-231-2222; www.greyhound.com) terminal to Coronado Trail towns is in Safford about 30 miles southwest of Clifton. ~ 1123 West Thatcher Boulevard; 928-428-2150.

CAR RENTALS

Along the Old West Highway, you can get a rental car at **Hatch Brothers Auto Center**. ~ 1623 Thatcher Boulevard, Safford; 928-428-6000.

TEN

Southern Arizona

Southern Arizona is a vast region of grasslands and desert punctuated by some of the state's most beautiful mountains. Four ranges have peaks higher than 9000 feet—the Santa Catalinas, Santa Ritas, Huachucas and Chiricahuas. At the heart of the region is Tucson, an urban metropolis rising out of the Sonoran Desert. A rich cultural tradition ranging from the Pima tribe to the Jesuits reflects this community's close ties to neighboring Mexico.

Scattered east of Tucson are portions of the Coronado National Forest. To the southeast, the rolling grasslands and woodland hills around Patagonia are some of the state's best cattle and horse ranchland, while the Elgin area has acres of green vineyards where local wines are produced. Farther east is Sierra Vista, whose claim to fame is Fort Huachuca, a historic military base whose troops defeated Apache leader Geronimo. Some 11,400 soldiers and civilians are still based here. Nearby Tombstone and Bisbee are old mining towns. Tombstone, the town "too tough to die," survives by selling its history. There are museums and exhibits on every corner—each, of course, charging for the pleasure of your company. Visitors flock here to relive the rowdy life of the Old West, from the shootout at O.K. Corral to the gambling at Birdcage Theater. Bisbee has become a quiet artists' colony with a more bohemian flavor. Here, visitors can shop in historic buildings along Main Street, tour old mines and walk along the narrow, hilly streets dotted with Victorian architecture. Up around Willcox are orchards teeming with fruit and vegetables. In autumn, you can pick your own or stop at one of the many roadside stands.

South of Tucson is the most populated portion of southern Arizona. Off Route 19 is Tubac, an artists' community with about 100 studios and galleries. Farther south is the border town of Nogales, where you can bargain for Mexican crafts and sample authentic cuisine. Southwest of Tucson is a large, scarcely populated area containing the Tohono O'odham Indian Reservation, Cabeza Prieta National Wildlife Refuge and Organ Pipe Cactus National Monument. In the westernmost corner of the state is Yuma, a historic town on the Colorado River that attracts residents with its lush, subtropical climate, farmlands fertile with vegetables, citrus trees and groves of date palms.

Although Tucson and southern Arizona abound with history, the real reason people visit is for the natural beauty—for the meditative solitude of a desert that seemingly rolls on endlessly, creating vast spaces for the imagination.

Tucson

The ultimate insult to a Tucson resident is to say his town is just like Phoenix. Like bickering siblings, the two cities have never gotten along well and each is proud of its unique personality. While Phoenix is a vast, sprawling city that welcomes booming development, Tucson would just as soon stay the same size and keep developers out—especially those who would alter the environment. Phoenix thrives on a fast pace; Tucson is informal, easygoing and in no great rush to get anywhere.

Surrounded by five mountain ranges and sitting in a cactus-roughened desert, Tucson is an arid, starkly beautiful place with wide-open skies and night silences broken only by the howling of coyotes. The highest mountains are powdered with snow in winter; the desert is ablaze with cactus blooms in spring.

Most of Tucson's 12 inches of annual precipitation arrives during the late summer monsoon season when afternoon thunderstorms roll through the desert with high winds and dramatic lightning shows. During summer, the average high temperature hovers around 98°. In winter, average highs are about 65°, making the city a popular spot for winter visitors, who come to golf and relax in the balmy weather.

Basically, Tucson is an affable, unpretentious town that feels comfortable with itself. There's no need to impress anyone here with high fashion—blue jeans are good enough for most places. Nor do wealth and conspicuous consumption have a large following. Most Tucsonans don't come here to make lots of money, but rather to live in a beautiful, natural area that's within driving distance of more of the same.

The cultural heritage of Tucson is a mix of Spanish, Mexican and American Indian. The city is only 60 miles from Nogales and the Mexican border, but you don't have to go that far to find Mexican food, artwork and culture. The red-tiled adobe homes spread across the valley reflect the residents' love of Spanish and American Indian architecture.

The Hohokam people were the first in the area. Father Eusebio Francisco Kino, a Jesuit priest, came to work with them and established a chain of missions, including Tucson's famous Mission San Xavier del Bac.

Later, the Spanish flag flew over the city, as did the Mexican, Confederate and United States flags. In 1867, Tucson was the capital of the Arizona Territory. But when the capital moved north, disgruntled Tucson was given the University of Arizona as compensation. This increased the population, and it jumped again just before World War II when nearby Davis-Monthan Air Force Base began training pilots to fly B-17 bombers. Today 503,000 people call Tucson home and live within the metro area's 500 square miles. The university has grown to 35,000 students, and Davis-Monthan is still an active military base with more than 8800 military personnel and civilians.

SIGHTS   Nine miles southwest of Tucson is the **Mission San Xavier del Bac** on the Tohono O'odham Indian Reservation. Known as the White Dove of the Desert, this stunning white adobe church rises from the open desert floor and is picturesquely framed by blue sky and the mountains beyond. Although the Jesuits founded the mission in the 1600s, the present building was built between 1783 and 1797. It is a combination of Spanish, Byzantine and Moorish architecture. Visitors can walk in through weathered mesquite doors, sit on the worn wooden pews, and feast their eyes on the ornate statues, carvings, painted designs and frescoes. In addition to touring the facility, you can attend mass Tuesday through Friday (open to the public), or visit during one of the celebrations. ~ Signs appear as you drive south on Route 19; 520-294-2624, fax 520-294-3538.

> Southern Arizona enjoys sunny skies 85 percent of the time, considerably more than Florida or even Hawaii.

Across the square in the **San Xavier Plaza**, American Indians sell fry bread and crafts.

Drive north to Speedway Boulevard, turn left and you'll reach Gates Pass, where the road begins to twist and you'll have splendid panoramic views of Tucson and the saguaro-dotted landscape of Tucson Mountain Park. This is where you'll find **Old Tucson Studios**, a re-creation of an old Western frontier town. Columbia Pictures created Old Tucson Studios in 1939 as a movie location for the film *Arizona*, and since then more than 300 films and television episodes have been shot here including *Tombstone*, *The Quick and the Dead*, *Gunfight at the O.K. Corral* and *El Dorado*. If a film crew is in town, you can watch them film. Otherwise, ride the narrow-gauge railroad, watch shootouts and stunt shows on the wide dirt streets, enter the adobe and slatboard buildings and listen to dance-hall music, or indulge in shopping. There are concerts held here as well, with headliners such as Pat Benatar and Bo Diddley. Admission. ~ 201 South Kinney Road; 520-883-0100; www.oldtucson.com, e-mail afriend@oldtucson.com.

Just a few minutes down Kinney Road, the **Arizona-Sonora Desert Museum** is part zoo, part natural-history museum and part botanical garden with more than 300 different animals and 1200 plant species indigenous to the Sonoran Desert. Visitors can inspect the aquatic exhibits and the animals in their desert habitats,

Southern Arizona

or walk inside an aviary and a re-created limestone cave (all exhibits are wheelchair accessible). Definitely worth a visit. Admission. ~ 2021 North Kinney Road; 520-883-1380, fax 520-883-2500; www.desertmuseum.org, e-mail info@desertmuseum.org.

For a panoramic view of Tucson from 3100 feet, drive to the top of **A Mountain**. Settlers of territorial days used it as a lookout for Apache raiders. The latest raiders are students from the University of Arizona, who have been whitewashing the A on it before the first football game of the season since 1915. ~ Take Congress Street exit west off Route 10 to Cuesta Street, then go south onto Sentinel Peak Road.

The El Presidio District's **Historic Block**, running from Church Avenue to Alameda Street, was once the Presidio of San Agustín del Tucson, which the Spanish army enclosed with a 12-foot-high adobe wall in 1783. Today, the main attraction in El Presidio is the **Tucson Museum of Art**, a complex specializing in pre-Columbian, modern American and Southwestern art, along with several historic houses and the Plaza of the Pioneers—a showplace for the museum's sculpture collection. Closed Monday in summer. Admission (free on Sunday). ~ 140 North Main Avenue; 520-624-2333, fax 520-624-7202; www.tucsonarts.com, e-mail info@tucsonarts.com.

Arizona's oldest historical museum, the **Arizona Historical Society Museum** has everything from a full-scale reproduction of an underground mine tunnel to an exhibit on the history of transportation. One special feature is "Life on the Edge: History of Medicine in Arizona." Closed Sunday. Admission. ~ 949 East 2nd Street; 520-628-5774, fax 520-629-8966; www.arizonahistoricalsociety.org, e-mail ahsref@vms.arizona.edu.

A big part of Tucson is the **University of Arizona**, a 352-acre campus dotted with red-brick buildings. If you decide to explore the campus, there are a few worthwhile stops. ~ 520-621-2211; www.arizona.edu.

One definite stop is **Flandrau Science Center & Planetarium**, with a science store, public observatory with a 16-inch telescope available for public use and science exhibits such as a walk-through model asteroid and night skies exhibit. The facility also houses the state's largest mineral museum. Closed Monday. Admission. ~ Corner of University Boulevard and Cherry Avenue; 520-621-7827, fax 520-621-8451; www.flandrau.org, e-mail fsc@u.arizona.edu.

The **Center for Creative Photography** has a collection of more than 50,000 photographs in addition to galleries, a library and research facilities. Photography exhibitions from the permanent collection and traveling exhibitions are displayed in the galleries. ~ 1030 North Olive Road; 520-621-7968, fax 520-621-9444; www.creativephotography.org, e-mail oncenter@ccp.arizona.edu.

The **University of Arizona Museum of Art** has Renaissance and later European and American art, including works by Rembrandt, Dalí, Rothko and O'Keeffe. The collection features more than 3000 paintings, sculptures, drawings and prints. Closed Monday. ~ Southeast corner of Park Avenue and Speedway Boulevard; 520-621-7567, fax 520-621-8770; artmuseum.arizona.edu, e-mail azs@u.arizona.edu.

Tucson Botanical Gardens contains a small field of American Indian crops, a cactus and succulent garden, a tropical greenhouse, an herb garden, a sensory garden, a backyard bird garden and a xeriscape (arid landscaping) demonstration garden. Perhaps most unusual is the historic garden—lush foliage and flowers that surround and reflect the era of the 1920s Porter House. Admission. ~ 2150 North Alvernon Way; 520-326-9686, fax 520-324-0166; www.tucsonbotanical.org, e-mail tbg@tucsonbotanical.org.

Fort Lowell Museum is a reconstructed commanding officers' quarters from the days when it was a key military post during the

Apache Indian wars of the 1870s and 1880s. Life on a military post in frontier Arizona is revealed through furnishings, artifacts and displays of military equipment. Closed Sunday through Tuesday. ~ 2900 North Craycroft Road; 520-885-3832.

The late Ted De Grazia gained fame painting impressionistic-style portrayals of the Southwest and its people. Today his home and galleries, the **De Grazia Gallery in the Sun**, are open to the public. Skylights in the adobe structures bathe his paintings in light. Walking through, you pass underneath brick archways and go through landscaped courtyards that he so lovingly tended when he lived here. The unusual architecture, including an iron gate inspired by the historic Yuma Prison, is worth a visit in itself. ~ 6300 North Swan Road; 520-299-9191, 800-545-2185, fax 520-299-1381; www.degrazia.org, e-mail admin@degrazia.org.

Pima Air & Space Museum contains one of the largest collections of historic aircraft in the world. Among the 250 aircraft are the Boeing B-29 Superfortress, the type of plane that dropped the first atomic bomb on Japan, and the SR-71 Blackbird, the world's fastest aircraft. Admission. ~ 6000 East Valencia Road; 520-574-0462, fax 520-574-9238; www.pimaair.org, e-mail admin assistant@pimaair.org.

For a truly unusual experience, stop by **Columbia University's Biosphere 2 Center**, a controversial three-acre miniature replica of the earth with a tropical rainforest, savannah, marsh and desert. There are small greenhouses where different ecosystems are displayed. Research focus has shifted from sustainable agriculture to global climate changes. On the hourly tours (offered daily), you are taken along paths through the airtight structure and on forays to the living quarters and the command room. You can also see the outside of this high-tech, space-age glass and steel monolith, look through its glass walls and stop by the visitors center. Admission. ~ Route 77 Mile Marker 96.5, Oracle; 520-896-6200, fax 520-896-6209; www.bio2.edu, e-mail sales@bio2.columbia.edu.

In 2000, then-president Bill Clinton created 129,000-acre **Ironwood Forest National Monument,** which contains 200 sites from the prehistoric Hohokam period and remnants of an old mission, among other treasures. Ironwood trees live up to 800 years and attract hawks, owls, bighorn sheep, tortoises and white-winged doves. Of the 674 species that thrive here, several are listed as threatened or endangered. The BLM warns visitors to beware of unmarked roads, abandoned mine shafts, poisonous reptiles and insects, extreme heat and flash floods. If this hasn't completely terrified you, it's a beautiful and uncharted landscape to explore. ~ Route 10 at Avra Valley Road, about 25 miles northwest of Tucson; 520-258-7242, fax 520-258-7238; www.az.blm.gov.

Although Tucson is known for its upscale, full-service resorts— **LODGING** a haven for those escaping cold winters elsewhere—it also has a number of budget and mid-range accommodations.

Located across the street from the train and bus stations, the **Hotel Congress** is a piece of Tucson's history. This block-long classical brick and marble structure was built in 1919 to serve Southern Pacific railroad passengers, and John Dillinger's gang were among its guests. Geometric Indian designs add character to the lobby, which also provides seating for the Cup Cafe and overflow from the nightclubs. The renovated hotel rooms are decorated with black-and-white-tile bathrooms, black headboards and salmon-colored walls. Of the hotel's 40 rooms, four are hostels with bunk beds and private baths (a hostel card is mandatory; reservations are not accepted for hostel rooms). None of the rooms have televisions, but they *do* have a rarity nowadays— windows that open. Gay-friendly. ~ 311 East Congress Street; 520-622-8848, 800-722-8848, fax 520-792-6366; www.hotcong.com, e-mail hotel@hotcong.com. BUDGET.

Although it's in the middle of town, the **Arizona Inn**, built in the 1930s, feels like a lush oasis with 14 acres of lawns and gardens thick with orange trees, native cypress and date palms. No two of the resort's 86 rooms are alike, but all are decorated in the manner of the 1930s period and some have antiques. The inn also has a swimming pool, tennis courts, a fitness room, a restaurant and a cocktail lounge decorated with 19th-century Audubons. ~ 2200 East Elm Street; 520-325-1541, 800-933-1093, fax 520-881-5830; www.arizonainn.com, e-mail reservations@arizona inn.com. ULTRA-DELUXE.

Originally built as a market in the 1920s, **Elysian Grove Market Bed & Breakfast Inn** now stands as a stunning abode with high ceilings, hardwood floors and two fireplaces. Folk art, rugs

---

TED DE GRAZIA

One of Arizona's most renowned artists was Ted De Grazia, who depicted the Southwest in paintings, prints, bronzes and collector's plates. His distinctive, impressionistic-style works, with their signature bright colors and featureless faces, hang in Tucson's De Grazia Gallery in the Sun. Born in Morenci, Arizona, in 1909, De Grazia spent his life traveling through Mexico and the Southwest, learning the lore of the Apache, Navajo, Yaqui and Papago tribes and collecting three art degrees. One of his most surprising moves came in 1976. To protest the severe taxes on heirs of artists, he burned 150 of his paintings—valued at $1.5 million. He was irate that his wife would have to sell most of these paintings to pay the inheritance tax on their value whenever he died. In 1982, De Grazia died of cancer.

and antiques enliven both the house and its four colorful rooms. Two of the rooms were converted from wine cellars; two others have French doors that open onto a garden teeming with cactus, flowers and mesquite trees. Continental breakfast is included and features Mexican pastries. ~ 400 West Simpson Street; 520-628-1522; www.elysiangrove.com. MODERATE.

The **Sheraton Tucson**'s 216 suites and rooms are Southwestern in style, but lean toward darker shades rather than pastels. The suites feature a couch, table, coffeemaker, fridge, a television in an armoire, and a tiny balcony. The rooms have all of the above except the couch, armoire and balcony. Amenities include a swimming pool, restaurant, jacuzzi and exercise room. Guests have access to a nearby fitness center. ~ 5151 East Grant Road; 520-323-6262, 800-257-7275, fax 520-325-2989; www.sheraton.com. ULTRA-DELUXE.

For an assortment of affordably priced motels, drive down Miracle Mile, once the main thoroughfare through the city. The **Ghost Ranch Lodge** has 83 rooms housed in brick buildings surrounded by grassy lawns, palm trees and cactus gardens. The theme here is Western, with a cow skull over the lobby fireplace and Western memorabilia throughout. There's also a pool and whirlpool. Continental breakfast included. ~ 801 West Miracle Mile; 520-791-7565, 800-456-7565, fax 520-791-3898; www.ghostranchlodge.com, e-mail ghstranch@aol.com. MODERATE TO DELUXE.

For quiet lodging amid terraced gardens, stay at **Catalina Park Inn Bed & Breakfast**, a dignified 1927 gem of an inn. Elegantly decorated, yet steering clear of clutter, the six guest rooms are comfortable and lovely. You're within blocks of the University, although you'd never know it from the peaceful sur-

AUTHOR FAVORITE

When I want to stay in the thick of things yet still enjoy peace and quiet, I head for the **Adobe Rose Inn**, located just two blocks from U of A. Built in 1933, the rooms are appointed with '30s-era New Mexican antiques and furnishings; some have kiva fireplaces, mahogany floors, stained-glass windows and skylights that flood the rooms with that legendary Arizona light. The inn's six rooms are split between the main house, a *casita* and a second house. Relax poolside in the courtyard surrounded by desert foliage and encased within thick adobe walls. A gourmet breakfast is served. No children under ten. ~ 910 North Olsen Avenue, Tucson; 520-318-4644, 800-328-4122; www.aroseinn.com, e-mail innkeeper@aroseinn.com. MODERATE TO DELUXE.

roundings. Breakfast might include lemon ricotta pancakes or papaya and lime scones. Closed for a month in the summer (usually mid-July to early August). ~ 309 East 1st Street; 520-792-4541, 800-792-4885; www.catalinaparkinn.com, e-mail info@catalina parkinn.com. DELUXE.

Bed and breakfasts are proliferating in Tucson. Built in 1905, the **Peppertrees Bed and Breakfast Inn** is a red-brick Territorial home. There are two Southwest-style two-room guesthouses, a one-bedroom Mexican *casita*, and three main rooms furnished with period pieces from England. French doors lead outside to a beautifully landscaped patio. Full breakfast included. ~ 724 East University Boulevard; 520-622-7167, 800-348-5763; www.pepper treesinn.com, e-mail pepperinn@cox.net. DELUXE.

La Posada del Valle, a stucco-and-adobe inn built in 1929, serves afternoon tea in a living room furnished with art-deco antiques from the '20s and '30s. The 1920s theme carries over to the five guest rooms, and each is named after famous women of that era. Sophie's Room is a favorite with an 1818 king-size Victorian bedroom set. Karin's Cottage, separate from the main house, is an early 1900s suite with an African motif. Full breakfast included. Closed in July. ~ 1640 North Campbell Avenue; 520-795-3840, 888-404-7113, fax 520-795-3840; www.bbhost. com/laposadadelvalle. MODERATE TO DELUXE.

The Lodge on the Desert is a garden resort hotel with 35 adobe rooms grouped around patios that open to lawns and gardens. Rooms have beamed ceilings, handpainted Mexican tile accents and Monterey furniture, and many have gas-burning beehive fireplaces. Other amenities include a restaurant and a pool with mountain views. ~ 306 North Alvernon Way; 520-325-3366, 800-456-5634, fax 520-327-5834; www.lodgeonthedesert. com, e-mail inquiry@lodgeonthedesert.com. ULTRA-DELUXE.

Comfort Suites/Sabino Canyon, is a hacienda-style inn with rooms and suites, overlooks a lush courtyard dotted with Mexican fountains. The 90 guest rooms are clean and comfortable; many have kitchenettes. There is a pool and complimentary breakfast. ~ 7007 East Tanque Verde Road; 520-298-2300, 800-424-6423, fax 520-298-6756; www.comfortsuitestucson.com, e-mail tanqueverde@aol.com. BUDGET TO DELUXE.

The resorts are expensive during winter high season, but most slash prices during the hot summer months. Among the best resorts is the **Westin La Paloma Resort & Spa**. The 487 Southwest-style rooms have private balconies or patios, a sitting area, oversized closet and a stocked fridge. Many of the suites have wood-burning fireplaces and sunken spa tubs. There are three swimming pools (including one with swim-up bar), a Jack Nicklaus golf course, tennis and racquetball courts, a health center, a spa and, for tired

Text continued on page 320.

Calling All City Slickers!

Fueled by romantic images of Western heroes and desert sunsets and indulging in the fantasy of an escape to simpler times, more people than ever are opting to hang their saddles at dude ranches. In Southern Arizona, cowpokes have more than their fair share of choices. Guest ranches here range from resorts where you're more likely to overheat in the jacuzzi than the saddle, to working ranches where wranglers round 'em up and dine on beans and burgers. Whatever the orientation, most have horseback riding, a whole range of outdoor activities, and a casual, secluded atmosphere. Some are closed during the hot summer months, so call ahead.

One of the most luxurious getaways is **Tanque Verde Guest Ranch**, which has been around since the 1860s. It comes complete with indoor and outdoor swimming pools, tennis courts, an exercise room, guided nature walks, a supervised children's program and, of course, horseback riding. Guests stay in one of 70 *casitas* and patio lodges, some with beehive fireplaces, antiques and Indian bedspreads. Sliding glass doors offer stunning desert views. To relax, cozy up in the lobby with a good Western novel by the stone fireplace. ~ 14301 East Speedway Boulevard, Tucson; 520-296-6275, 800-234-3833, fax 520-721-9426; www.tanqueverderanch.com. e-mail dude@tvgr.com. ULTRA-DELUXE.

White Stallion Ranch sprawls across 3000 acres—grazing land for their herd of Longhorn. Guests take breakfast rides, watch rodeos every Saturday afternoon, and pet miniature horses, donkeys, pot-bellied pigs, pygmy goats and a llama at the on-site zoo. Rooms at this ranch are rustic with Western decor. Rates include all meals and activities. Closed June through August. ~ 9251 West Twin Peaks Road, Tucson; 520-297-0252, 888-977-2624, fax 520-744-2786; www.wsranch.com, e-mail info@wsranch.com. ULTRA-DELUXE.

Don't look for TVs or phones inside the 25-room **Lazy K Bar Guest Ranch** because here you're meant to leave the outside world behind. Ranch-style meals are served in a dining room, and Tuesday and Saturday nights are set aside for cookouts beside a waterfall. Afterward, you can relax in the comfortable library with wood paneling and beams, bookshelves, a fireplace and a card table. Rooms are comfortable, carpeted and decorated in a South-western motif. Rates include all meals and activities. ~ 8401 North Scenic Drive, Tucson; 520-744-3050, 800-321-7018, fax 520-744-7628; www.lazykbar.com, e-mail info@lazykbar.com. ULTRA-DELUXE.

Price Canyon Ranch in the Chiricahua Mountains is a working cattle ranch with a family cabin and one- and two-room bunk houses with baths. Meals are served in the 120-year-old main ranch house, and outdoor barbecues are held in the summer. Visitors can hike or ride horses in the surrounding national forest, or cool off in the swimming pool. Rates include meals, horseback riding and other ranch activities. A three-day minimum stay is required ~ Off Route 80 between the 400- and 401-mile markers. Turn onto Price Canyon Road and drive seven miles, Douglas; 520-558-2383, 800-727-0065; www.pricecanyon.com, e-mail pcranch@vtc.net. DELUXE.

Grapevine Canyon Ranch offers accommodations in guest rooms with country-ranch furnishings and American Indian touches. Visitors also lounge in the sitting room, a cozy place with a wood-beamed ceiling, Indian-design rugs and steer horns over the fireplace. At this working cattle ranch, horseback riding is the main attraction. Three meals are included. ~ Highland Road, Pearce; 520-826-3185, 800-245-9202, fax 520-826-3636; www.arizona guestranch.com, e-mail info@gcranch.com. DELUXE.

Circle Z Ranch in the foothills of the Santa Rita Mountains is a colorful, unpretentious place built in the mid-1920s. It accommodates no more than 45 people at a time. The ranch's adobe cottages are decorated with brightly painted wicker furniture and Mexican crafts, but don't have TVs or telephones (although a single phone in the lodge is available for use). Instead, recreation centers around horseback riding. There is also a heated pool and a tennis court. The lodge has a massive stone fireplace and bookshelves filled with classics, including Zane Grey titles. Rates include all meals and activities. The ranch has a three-night minimum, and is open from November 1 through May 15. ~ P.O. Box 194, Patagonia, AZ 85624; 520-394-2525, 888-854-2525; www.circlez.com, e-mail info@circlez.com. ULTRA-DELUXE.

Sitting in the foothills of Baboquivari Peak on the Mexican border, **Rancho De La Osa** is a centuries-old Territorial-style ranch. Constructed with handmade adobe block, the 19 guest rooms have fireplaces and Mexican antique furnishings. Activities include horseback riding, biking, hiking and swimming, or sampling cocktails in the Cantina, an old Spanish/Indian mission. The hacienda dining room features gourmet Southwestern cooking. All meals included. Closed in August. ~ 28201 West La Osa Ranch Road, Sasabe; 520-823-4257, 800-872-6240, fax 520-823-4238; www.ranchodelaosa.com, e-mail osagal@aol.com. ULTRA-DELUXE.

Another ranch of note is **Triangle T Guest Ranch**, with 11 cabins, a restaurant, a saloon, nature trails and horseback riding (none during the summer). ~ Route 10, Exit 318, Dragoon Road, Dragoon; phone/fax 520-586-7533; www.triangletguestranch.com, e-mail trianglet@theriver.com. BUDGET TO MODERATE. The 30-room **Rex Resort Ranch** is also worth checking out. Along with horseback riding, biking and hiking, you can enjoy the outdoor spa and junior Olympic–size pool. ~ 131 East Mado Montoso Road, Amado; 520-398-2914, 800-547-2696, fax 520-398-8229; www.rexranch.com, e-mail info@rexranch.com. DELUXE TO ULTRA-DELUXE.

parents, day care for the small fry! ~ 3800 East Sunrise Drive; 520-742-6000, 800-677-6338, fax 520-577-5877; www.westinla palomaresort.com. ULTRA-DELUXE.

Spread on 80 acres in the foothills of the Santa Catalina Mountains, the **Westward Look Resort** is a scenic getaway. The 244 rooms here are actually worth spending time in with their beamed ceilings, couches, refrigerator and wet bar, balconies and Mexican tile trim on the extra-long bathroom sinks. If you ever leave the room, check out the tennis courts, fitness center, pools, spas, restaurant or lounge. ~ 245 East Ina Road; 520-297-1151, 800-722-2500, fax 520-297-9023; www.westwardlook.com, e-mail reservations@westwardlook.com. ULTRA-DELUXE.

Located in the foothills of the Santa Catalina Mountains, **Loews Ventana Canyon** is a 93-acre, luxury resort. Highlights are an 80-foot waterfall cascading down into a pond, and secluded paths lined with mesquite, squawbush and blue palo verde. Many of the resort's 398 Southwest-style rooms have original artwork, burnished-pine furnishings, private balconies and bathrooms with marble floors. Amenities include five restaurants and lounges, tennis, golf, fitness trails, pools, a health club and shops. ~ 7000 North Resort Drive; 520-299-2020, 800-234-5117, fax 520-299-6832; www.loewshotels.com. DELUXE TO ULTRA-DELUXE.

Looking for a little pampering? Then check out the **Omni Tucson National Golf Resort & Spa**, where you can relax in the European spa with a massage, facial, herbal wrap and other treatments. Located on the northwest edge of town, away from the city's hustle and bustle, the resort offers quiet and mountain views. The 167 suites and rooms have wet bars and refrigerators, and most have private patios overlooking the championship 27-hole golf course. Other amenities include a gift shop, restaurant, beauty salon, pool, tennis and volleyball. ~ 2727 West Club Drive; 520-297-2271, 800-528-4856, fax 520-297-7544; www.tucsonnational.com. ULTRA-DELUXE.

Located on five acres of Sonoran desert, surrounded by saguaro cacti, is **Casa Tierra Adobe Bed and Breakfast Inn**. With a central courtyard and fountain, it is an elegant hacienda-style inn with vaulted brick ceilings, Mexican-style furnishings and four guest rooms with private patios overlooking the desert. Telescopes offer lovely nighttime viewings of the sky There is a jacuzzi, a workout gym and a large common room with games, stereo and VCR. Full gourmet vegetarian breakfast included. Closed in July. ~ 11155 West Calle Pima; 520-578-3058, 866-254-0006, fax 520-578-8445; www.casatierratucson.com, e-mail info@casatierratuc son.com. DELUXE TO ULTRA-DELUXE.

For information on bed and breakfasts throughout Arizona, contact the **Arizona Association of Bed & Breakfast Inns**. ~ P.O.

Box 22086, Tucson, AZ 86002; 800-284-2589; www.bbonline.com/az/aabbi, e-mail info@arizona-bed-breakfast.com.

There is an eclectic mix of cuisine in Tucson—Southwest- and Sonoran-style Mexican fare are the specialties.

DINING

Mi Nidito is a tiny, tacky, crowded Mexican joint with great food, from enchiladas to *menudo*. Portions are generous and there are always plenty of locals lining up to fatten their waistlines. When Bill Clinton dined here, of course, he did not need to wait in line. Closed Monday and Tuesday. ~ 1813 South 4th Avenue; 520-622-5081. BUDGET TO DELUXE.

Micha's is a larger restaurant owned for many years by the Mariscal family, whose portrait is just inside the door. You won't leave here hungry—even the flour tortillas are about a foot in length. Don't miss the chimichangas, *topopo* salad or grilled shrimp fantasia. ~ 2908 South 4th Avenue; 520-623-5307, fax 520-388-9472. BUDGET TO MODERATE.

The U of A is famous worldwide for its pioneering dendrochronology program—the study of tree ring dating.

Down the street is **Delectables**, decorated with brass chandeliers and turn-of-the-20th-century oak antiques. Inside are wood tables, wood-beamed ceilings and curving tinted windows that look out onto 4th Avenue, while outside are green metal tables covered in floral tablecloths with matching chairs. This eatery offers fresh salmon and roast beef, plus salads and sandwiches. ~ 533 North 4th Avenue; 520-884-9289; www.delectables.com, e-mail delectables@delectables.com. MODERATE.

For the innovative in pizza, try **Magpies Gourmet Pizza**. Examples of their fare include The Greek with spinach, basil, garlic, piñon nuts, feta cheese, cheese and sun-dried tomatoes, or Cathy's with garlic, stewed tomatoes, mushrooms, artichokes, roasted red peppers and romano cheese. Located in a small strip center, Magpies has a contemporary look with a black-and-white tile floor, wooden chairs and modern art on the walls. Closed Sunday. ~ 605 North 4th Avenue; 520-628-1661, fax 520-798-3117; www.magpiespizza.com. BUDGET TO DELUXE.

Walk into **Café Poca Cosa** and you're bombarded with festive color. Green paint covers the ceilings, red chile peppers dot the walls, lights hang on indoor trees, and purple, green and red tiles cover the tables. The menu changes twice daily, and is written on a blackboard that's brought to the table. Dishes are home-style Mexican. Specialties include chicken breast in a tasty mango sauce, *pollo en chipotle* (chile) sauce and pork marinated in beer. Closed Sunday. ~ 88 East Broadway Boulevard; 520-622-6400. DELUXE.

At the **Arizona Inn**, you choose the ambience: formal dining room adjoining a courtyard ablaze with tiny lights in the trees, or casual dining in the lounge, on the patio or at the pool. The fare includes Continental, Southwestern, nouvelle and traditional selections. One treat is seared sea bass with rock shrimp and spinach crêpes. Weekly specials will not disappoint. ~ 2200 East Elm Street; 520-325-1541, 800-933-1093; www.arizonainn.com, e-mail reservations@arizonainn.com. ULTRA-DELUXE.

Tork's is a family-run place with only a handful of tables and delicious Middle Eastern and North African food. The *shawerma* plate with beef, chicken or lamb contains strips of meat cooked with onions and bell peppers. Other choices are the vegetarian falafel plate, hummus dip, tabbouleh and kabobs. Closed Sunday. ~ 3502 East Grant Road; 520-325-3737. BUDGET.

Buddy's Grill is a white-collar hangout. The narrow, blue-and-white room consists mainly of booths. Here, you'll find fajita salads, sandwiches, burgers cooked on a mesquite-wood grill and delicious baked French onion soup. You might also take a peek at the exhibition kitchen. ~ 4821 East Grant Road; 520-795-2226. BUDGET TO DELUXE.

It's hard to miss **Firecracker**: it's the restaurant with the huge flaming torches outside. You probably wouldn't want to miss this one anyway. The reasonably priced Pacific Rim menu might include pan-seared ahi in a spicy ginger cream sauce, or wok-charred salmon with cilantro pesto. The ingredients are always fresh and the exhibition kitchen shows off the talented kitchen staff creating unusual and tasty dishes. ~ Plaza Palomino, 2990 North Swan Road; 520-318-1118, fax 520-318-9886; www.metrorestaurants. com. MODERATE TO DELUXE.

Bentley's House of Coffee & Tea has wooden tables and chairs and the walls display rotating art shows. Food is typical café fare—soups, sandwiches, quiches—while beverages include

AUTHOR FAVORITE

It's hard to beat dining at **Anthony's in the Catalinas** with its top-notch views and ambience. The almost-floor-to-ceiling windows look over the city lights in this hacienda-style building. Dinner is served on elegant china with pale pink linens, fresh flowers and classical music playing in the background. Chandeliers hang from the vaulted, beamed ceiling and a large fireplace warms the room in winter. The Continental specialties include veal chop stuffed with prosciutto and fontina cheese, lamb Wellington and châteaubriand. Wash it down with a bottle from the extensive selection of about 1300 wines. No lunch on weekends. Reservations are recommended. ~ 6440 North Campbell Avenue; 520-299-1771. DELUXE TO ULTRA-DELUXE.

espresso, gourmet coffee and a wide range of Italian cream sodas. ~ 1730 East Speedway Boulevard; 520-795-0338, fax 520-323-6175. BUDGET.

At the **Blue Willow Restaurant,** you can either dine inside the adobe house with its cozy dining, or opt for the brick, vine-covered courtyard. Either choice is a winner. Although they serve sandwiches and salads at lunch along with full dinners, breakfast is the most popular meal here with 14 omelettes, including one with avocados, jack cheese and green chiles. ~ 2616 North Campbell Avenue; 520-327-7577, fax 520-327-9585. BUDGET TO MODERATE.

At **Coffee Etc.,** dessert and coffee reign. New York cheesecake is a favorite, served with Danish nutcream or cocoa almandine coffee. Closed Sunday. ~ 4446 South 6th Avenue; phone/fax 520-434-0900; e-mail cetc@qwest.net. BUDGET TO MODERATE.

Szechuan Omei Restaurant is a Chinese restaurant where you can choose from more than 135 entrées, including lunch specials. Decor is nothing fancy, just red tablecloths and chairs and the usual Chinese lanterns and paintings. ~ 2601 East Speedway Boulevard; 520-325-7204. BUDGET TO MODERATE.

The Sonoran-style dining room of the **Tanque Verde Guest Ranch** has picture windows facing the desert mountains, a corner fireplace and elegant mahogany tables with carved Mexican chairs. Entrées change, but may include such choices as mesquite-barbecued pork loin ribs with poblano-chile hushpuppies, duckling glazed with prickly pear cactus syrup or broiled salmon with bérnaise sauce. All meals are served. Reservations required. ~ 14301 East Speedway Boulevard; 520-296-6275, 800-234-3833; www.tanqueverderanch.com, e-mail dude@tvgr.com. ULTRA-DELUXE.

Webb's Old Spanish Trail Steak House specializes in delicious ◄ *HIDDEN* barbecue ribs and chicken, as well as steaks. At night, settle down by the picture window. There's also enclosed patio dining. Dinner only. ~ 5400 South Old Spanish Trail; 520-885-7782; e-mail webb2025@msn.com. MODERATE TO DELUXE.

For Southwestern food, try **Café Terra Cotta.** The outdoor patio is lit by miniature white lights at night, while the indoor section is decorated in terra-cotta colors and artwork by famous Southwestern names. The huge windows open onto unobstructed views of the mountains. Entrées include large prawns stuffed with herbed goat cheese and Southwestern tomato *coulis,* stuffed red and green chiles, and pizzas that are cooked in the wood-burning oven and topped with ingredients such as herbed mozzarella, lime and cilantro. ~ 3500 East Sunrise Drive; 520-577-8100; www.cafeterracotta.com, e-mail feedback@cafeterracotta.com. MODERATE TO DELUXE.

HIDDEN ►   An old-fashioned pancake house with a European feel, **Millie's Pancake Haus** is a welcoming spot for breakfast or lunch with its cozy brick and wood interior, tied-back lace curtains, displays of bric-a-brac and pleasant staff. Along with pancake choices, the menu features Russian blintzes, corn cakes, omelets and daily specials. Breakfast and lunch only. Closed Monday. Millie's has two locations. ~ 6530 Tanque Verde Road, 520-298-4250; and 7053 North Oracle Road, 520-797-8997. BUDGET.

For something special, you can't beat **Janos**, which serves French-inspired Southwestern cuisine created by award-winning chef Janos Wilder. Menus are seasonal, but typical entrées are pepito-roasted lamb loin with wild-mushroom spoon bread and ancho-chile sauce, or sesame-crusted ahi with stir-fried Napa cabbage and mango sauce. Dinner only. Closed Sunday. ~ Westin La Paloma Resort, 3770 East Sunrise Drive; 520-615-6100. ULTRA-DELUXE.

HIDDEN ►   Walk through antique, hacienda-style doors and you're inside **Tohono Chul Park Tea Room**, located in a rustic, 1940s house in the midst of Tohono Chul Park. Unless the weather is bad, opt for outdoor dining in the lush courtyard or on a patio that sits amid a wildflower landscape and offers free entertainment from the birds and other critters that come to nibble. For lunch, innovative sandwiches, soups and salads are served. Other choices are breakfast, Sunday brunch and afternoon tea. No dinner. ~ 7366 North Paseo Del Norte; 520-797-1222; www.tohonochulpark.com, e-mail grounds@tohonochulpark.com. MODERATE.

SHOPPING   If you want anything with a Southwestern flair, Tucson is where you'll find it. You'll also find shops catering to almost every need, with the majority of the artsy and antique shops downtown and various specialty shopping plazas scattered throughout the town.

Built in 1939, **Broadway Village** was one of the first shopping centers in Arizona. It houses a variety of shops in whitewashed red-brick buildings. ~ Corner of Broadway Boulevard and Country Club Road. The more unusual includes a tiny mystery book-**HIDDEN ►** shop called **Clues Unlimited**. Closed Sunday. ~ 123 South Eastbourne; 520-326-8533; www.cluesunlimited.com.

In the Broadway Village area there's **Yikes!**, a toy store with unusual gifts, small toys and books. Closed Sunday. ~ 2930 East Broadway; 520-320-5669. Next door, **Picante** sells various imported gift items, T-shirts, ethnic clothing and jewelry. Closed Sunday. ~ 2932 East Broadway; 520-320-5699.

A worthwhile stop in El Presidio District's Historic Block is the **Tucson Museum of Art gift shop**, with contemporary pottery and other artistic gifts. Closed Monday from Memorial Day through Labor Day. ~ 140 North Main Avenue; 520-624-2333; www.tucsonarts.com.

Nearby is **4th Avenue** with over 100 shops and restaurants. Shops in this older neighborhood contain vintage clothing, unique fashions, jewelry, books and art. Don't be surprised to find touches such as incense burning in the shops.

> A mature saguaro cactus can soak up enough rainwater to weigh as much as seven tons after a rainstorm, and is able to survive a two-year-long dry spell.

Antigone Books specializes in books by and about women as well as gay and lesbian literature. ~ 411 North 4th Avenue; 520-792-3715; www.antigonebooks.com.

Del Sol carries Southwestern clothes, and jewelry, and a selection of rugs made by the Zapotecs of Mexico. ~ 435 North 4th Avenue; 520-628-8765; www.delsol stores.com.

On the vintage side, stop by the **Tucson Thrift Shop**, which specializes in costumes and vintage clothing from the 1940s onward. ~ 319 North 4th Avenue; 520-623-8736.

For Mexican imports, check out what is unofficially called the Lost Barrio Warehouse District—a group of shops located in old, red-brick warehouses. **Rustica** sells Southwestern, Peruvian and Mexican furnishings and accessories. ~ 200 South Park Avenue; 520-623-4435. **Magellan Trading Company** has great buys on Mexican glassware as well as handicrafts, artifacts and furniture from Mexico, New Guinea, Indonesia and Africa. ~ 228 South Park Avenue; 520-622-4968; www.magellantraders.com.

◄ *HIDDEN*

◄ *HIDDEN*

Among the many notable downtown galleries is the **Kaibab Courtyard Shops**, which for over 50 years has been a source of collector-quality Hopi kachina dolls, Zuni fetishes, Navajo and Zapotec weavings, Mexican folk art and more. ~ 2837–41 North Campbell Avenue; 520-795-6905. Offering a wide choice of contemporary arts and crafts in a variety of media is **Obsidian Gallery**. Closed Sunday from Memorial Day to Labor Day; call ahead.~ 4320 North Campbell Avenue; 520-577-3598.

Saint Philips Plaza is a cluster of Southwest-style shops with red-tile roofs that include art galleries, clothing stores and restaurants. ~ Corner of River Street and Campbell Avenue. **Bahti Indian Arts** offers American Indian crafts such as jewelry, rugs, pottery and kachina dolls. ~ 4300 North Campbell Avenue; 520-577-0290. **El Presidio Gallery Inc.**, a large fine-arts gallery with original Southwestern art in a variety of media, has two locations. Closed Sunday. ~ 3001 East Skyline Drive, 520-299-1414; and 7000 East Tanque Verde Road, 520-733-0388.

North Campbell Avenue has a number of shopping venues. One of the most popular, judging by the ever-crowded parking lot, is **Bookman's**—*the* place for bibliophiles to browse. The owner claims the largest selection of used books and magazines in the Southwest. Bookman's also has a rare-book room and sells used magazines, records, tapes, video games, computer software and CDs. ~ 1930 East Grant Road; 520-325-5767.

A lovely place to wander and shop is **Plaza Palomino**, a shopping center without the plastic. Unusual boutiques, galleries, shops and restaurants surround the Spanish-style courtyard, which is lined with shade-giving palm trees and regularly "misted" in the summer heat. "When only the most imaginative will do," don't miss **Details & Green Shoelaces** (closed Sunday in July and August; 520-323-0222; www.detailsart.com), a gallery that defies description. Colorful, whimsical, strange and surprising, the arts and crafts here are like nothing you've ever seen. Let's just say that if you need a framed picture that doubles as a pinball machine, you've come to the right place. At **Orient East** (closed Sunday; 520-323-6250), sumptuous Asian antiques and imports are alive and well. **Maya Palace** (520-325-6411; www.mayapalacetucson.com) has it all, from comfortable, blouse outfits to swirling Mayan skirts to wedding dresses. They also have a great array of jewelry and gifts. ~ North Swan and Fort Lowell roads.

Drive farther down River Street and you'll see **River Center**, a Southwest-style shopping plaza. The stores surround a brick courtyard with a fountain and waterway. **The West** (closed Sunday; 520-299-1044) has cookbooks, cards, kids' gifts and needlework supplies, with proceeds going to local women's and children's charities. ~ Corner of River Street and Craycroft Road.

For a fun, unusual children's toy store, stop by **Mrs. Tiggy-Winkles**. ~ 4811 East Grant Road, Suite 157; 520-326-0188.

In the Plaza Palomino, **Orient East** specializes in Asian imports including lamps, furnishings, artifacts and jewelry. Closed Sunday. ~ At Swan and Fort Lowell streets; 520-323-6250.

Casas Adobes Shopping Center is yet *another* Southwest-style shopping plaza with a variety of specialty shops. ~ 7051 North Oracle Road.

A nearby favorite is **Antigua de Mexico**, a Latin American import store with Mexican Colonial and Southwestern furniture, folk art, pottery, glassware, tinware and sterling silver from Taxco. ~ 3235 West Orange Grove; 520-742-7114.

AUTHOR FAVORITE

As an art buff, I enjoy the art walks that many gallery districts regularly sponsor. Few can compare with the **Tucson Arts District** on the first and third Thursday of the month, when an "Artwalk" is held in the district, making stops at exhibit rooms, galleries and artists' studios. ~ 125 South Arizona Avenue; 520-624-9977, fax 520-624-4994; www.tucsonartsdistrict.org.

Bargain shopping in a beautiful setting describes **Foothills Mall.**
Painted clouds cover the ceiling between skylights, and a waterfall tumbles down steps from ceiling to floor. For marked-down
designer clothing, there's **Off Fifth** (520-544-0449), Sak's Fifth
Avenue's discount sister. Other outlets include **Samsonite, Nike**
and **Levis.** ~ 7401 North La Cholla Boulevard; 520-742-7191.

THE BEST BARS For alternative music—and alternative crowds   **NIGHTLIFE**
—peek into **Club Congress** inside the Hotel Congress. Tucson's
unconventional set mixes with the college crowd at this cavern-
like place with a red-and-brown-tile floor and dark walls. There's
live music Sunday, Wednesday and Friday; a deejay plays tunes
the rest of the week. Cover. ~ 311 East Congress Street; 520-622-
8848; www.hotcong.com, e-mail hotel@hotcong.com.

If you love people-watching and a good beer, head to **Gentle
Ben's Brewing Co.,** a microbrewery near campus with delicious
European-style ales. If you're there at the right time of the day,
you can see workers brewing (tours are also available). This
two-story building is furnished with recycled tables and chairs,
and there's outdoor seating where you can see and be seen.
There's deejay music on Tuesday, Thursday and Saturday, and
live music on Friday. Closed Sunday in the summer. ~ 865 East
University Boulevard; 520-624-4177; www.gentlebens.com, e-
mail realbeer@gentlebens.com.

Once a blacksmith shop and a country store, today **Cushing
Street Bar and Restaurant** is a popular spot to pass the evening.
Patrons here enjoy drinks at turn-of-the-20th-century tables and
chairs amid antiques such as a floor-to-ceiling, 1880s legal book-
case and a circa-1850 cut-glass globe above the bar. There's also
an outdoor patio. Enjoy light jazz on the weekend. Closed
Sunday and Monday. ~ 198 West Cushing Street; 520-622-7984.

Bum Steer is a casual place in a large, barnlike building containing a restaurant, several bars, a video arcade, a volleyball court
and three dancefloors (one of which is outside). Inside, everything
from cannons to airplanes hang from the vaulted roof (the staff
claims over 8000 objects are strung up). Entertainment includes
deejay-spun tunes Wednesday through Sunday and country night
on Saturday, with occasional live bands. Occasional cover. ~ 1910
North Stone Avenue; 520-884-7377, fax 520-624-0197.

Graffiti on the tables and walls is the decor at **Bob Dobbs'**   ◄ *HIDDEN*
Bar & Grill, a local hangout for the college and older crowd. A
bright, noisy place, it has indoor and outdoor seating and plenty
of televisions for catching the latest sports coverage. ~ 2501 East
6th Street; 520-325-3767.

Trophies is a popular sports bar offering pool, darts, satellite
TV and casual fare. ~ Sheraton Tucson, 5151 East Grant Road;
520-323-6262.

Laffs Comedy Club hosts everything from national to local acts. Thursday is college and military ID night. Closed Sunday and Monday. Cover. ~ 2900 East Broadway Boulevard; 520-323-8669; www.laffscomedyclub.com.

Follow the cowboy hats and neon lights and you'll end up at **Cactus Moon**, a huge place specializing in country music. Western artwork hangs on the walls and rodeos roll on movie screens. A glittering, colored light shines on the dancefloor, which is big enough for two-steppers not to be toe-steppers. Closed Sunday and Monday. Weekend cover.~ 5470 East Broadway Boulevard; 520-748-0049; www.cactusmoontucson.com, e-mail cactus moontucson@aol.com.

Berkey's Bar is a good place to hear the blues with live music all week long. A mixed crowd hangs out here, ordering drinks from the glass block bar, dancing and shooting pool. Cover Friday and Saturday. ~ 5769 East Speedway Boulevard; 520-296-1981.

The Chicago Bar offers a heady mix of live music. There's R&B on Monday and Tuesday, blues on Wednesday and Sunday, reggae on Thursday and Saturday, and rock or blues on Friday night. Chicago memorabilia covers the walls, from White Sox parking signs to hometown banners. Cover Wednesday through Saturday. ~ 5954 East Speedway Boulevard; 520-748-8169.

Tucson McGraws is a bar and dining room serving steaks and ribs. Step outside, walk down the steps and you'll land on the terrace ramada that looks toward the Santa Rita Mountains and Tucson's beautiful sunsets. ~ 4110 South Houghton Road; 520-885-3088, fax 520-886-1985.

THEATER The **Arizona Theatre Company** has been unofficially called the State Theater of Arizona and performs six or seven varied productions in Phoenix and Tucson from September through May. ~ 330 South Scott Avenue; 520-622-2823; www.arizonatheatre.org. Plays by the Arizona Theatre Company and other groups are performed in the restored Spanish Colonial revival **Temple of Music and Art** in Tucson and the **Herberger Theater Center** in Phoenix.

Gaslight Theatre offers corny musical melodramas. Patrons eat free popcorn while hissing at the villain and cheering for the

WHAT'S UP DOWNTOWN

To make up for the fact that Tucson rolls up its sidewalks relatively early, the city offers a vast amount of live music of all genres—rock, jazz, country, dance and rhythm-and-blues. These performances are generally held in venues clustered around 4th Avenue and the connecting downtown area.

hero or heroine. Many of the comedies are original, written especially for the theater. No productions on Monday ~ 7010 East Broadway Boulevard; 520-886-9428; www.gaslighttheatre.com.

Invisible Theatre has classics, musicals and Off-Broadway plays by Arizona playwrights and contemporary dramatists from September through June. ~ 1400 North 1st Avenue; 520-882-9721; www.invisibletheatre.com.

OPERA, SYMPHONY AND DANCE **Ballet Arizona** is the state's professional ballet company. They perform a repertoire of classical and contemporary works including world and national premieres from September through April. ~ 888-322-5538; www.balletaz.org.

Arizona Opera serves both Tucson and Phoenix and produces Grand Opera. The season runs from October through April, and productions have included *Don Giovanni*, *Othello* and *Madame Butterfly*. ~ 260 South Church Avenue; 520-293-4336; www.azopera.org.

For classical, pops and chamber concerts there is the **Tucson Symphony Orchestra**. Performances run from September through May. ~ 2175 North 6th Avenue; 520-792-9155, 520-882-8585 (box office); www.tucsonsymphony.org.

Centennial Hall hosts a full lineup on an international scale, from Chinese acrobatics to African dances to Broadway shows. Past performers include Itzhak Perlman, the Prague Symphony Orchestra and George Winston. ~ University of Arizona, 1020 East University Boulevard; 520-621-3341; www.uapresents.org, e-mail uapresents@arizona.edu.

GENE C. REID PARK 🚶 🚲 ⚓ This 131-acre park is a lush oasis in the desert with grassy expanses dotted with mature trees. There are a wide variety of recreational facilities here, including a recreation center, two golf courses, a swimming pool, a pond, tennis and racquetball courts and a Hi-Corbett field where major league baseball teams come for spring training. Other attractions are Reid Park Zoo and a rose garden with more than 2000 plants. The park has restrooms, picnic tables and ramadas. ~ Located between Broadway Boulevard and 22nd Street, Country Club Road and Alvernon Way; 520-791-4873, fax 520-791-4008.

PARKS

TUCSON MOUNTAIN PARK 🚶 🚲 🐎 Winding, hilly roads take you through this 20,000-acre, high-desert area brimming with ocotillo, palo verde, mesquite and saguaros and punctuated by mountains with rugged volcanic peaks. A popular spot is the Gates Pass overlook just past Speedway, where you can pull off the road and get a panoramic view of Tucson, Avra Valley and Kitt Peak, and watch Arizona's renowned sunsets. The park includes the Arizona-Sonora Desert Museum and Old Tucson Studios;

there is an admission fee to both sites. There are established picnic areas throughout the park, as well as archery and rifle ranges. (Archery hunting is allowed in season with proper permit.) ~ Off Gates Pass Road, about ten miles west of the city limits (no recreational vehicles are allowed on the road). Another entrance is on Kinney Road off Ajo Way; 520-877-6000.

▲ Gilbert Ray Campground has 146 sites, all with electric hookups; $10 per night for tents and $20 per night for RVs; information, 520-883-4200 (December through March), 520-877-6000 (year-round).

FORT LOWELL PARK 🏃 🚣 With its blend of history and recreation, Fort Lowell Park is an ideal family getaway. Fort Lowell was once a major military post and supply depot. Stroll between the trees on Cottonwood Lane and you'll see a number of ruins, including that of the adobe post hospital built in 1875. Farther down is a museum (closed Monday and Tuesday) in the reconstructed officers' quarters. The 59-acre park also has a pond with a fountain and plenty of hungry ducks around the perimeter, and a trail with marked exercise stops along the way. The park also includes tennis and racquetball courts, pool, picnic areas, lighted ball fields and shade ramadas. ~ 2900 North Craycroft Road; 520-791-4873, fax 520-791-4008.

SAGUARO NATIONAL PARK Established to protect the saguaro cactus, found mainly in Arizona, the park is divided into two segments on opposite sides of Tucson. For general information, call 520-733-5100; www.nps.gov/sagu.

Rincon Mountain District 🏃 🚴 🐎 A popular segment of Saguaro National Park is the Rincon Mountain District east of town, a 66,621-acre chunk established in 1933. Begin your tour at the visitors center, with dioramas and other exhibits of the geological and botanical history of the park. Then drive along Cactus Forest Drive, a scenic eight-mile-loop showing off tall saguaro cacti with their splayed arms. This district has more than 100 miles of hiking and equestrian trails. You'll also find picnic areas, restrooms and barbecue grills. ~ Drive east on Old Spanish Trail about three miles beyond city limits; visitors center: 520-733-5153.

Tucson Mountain District 🏃 🚴 🐎 The 24,824-acre Tucson Mountain District to the west has a visitors center with orientations to the park, exhibits, maps and books, and features the six-mile-long Bajada Loop Drive that passes dense saguaro forests and American Indian petroglyphs. There are 40 miles of hiking and equestrian trails; biking is limited to the roads. Amenities include picnic areas, restrooms and barbecue grills. ~ Off Kinney Road, two miles north of the Arizona-Sonora Desert Museum; visitors center: 520-733-5158, fax 520-733-5164.

SABINO CANYON RECREATION AREA 🚶🚲🐎 One of the most scenic spots in the region is a route that cuts through the Santa Catalina Mountains in the Coronado National Forest. You can either hike, bike or take the shuttle on a seven-and-a-half-mile roundtrip that climbs a road lined with cottonwoods, sycamores, ash and willow trees. Along the route flows Sabino Creek with its pools and waterfalls that tumble underneath arched stone bridges. The shuttle makes nine stops along the way, so you can jump on or off as you go. It will also take you on the two-and-a-half-mile trip to Bear Canyon Trail, where you then hike two more miles to Seven Falls, which cascade almost 500 feet down the side of a hill. Biking is restricted to before 9 a.m. or after 5 p.m. and is not allowed on Wednesday or Saturday. For the romantically inclined, there are moonlight rides during the full moon from April through June and September through December. Facilities in the recreation area are limited to restrooms, picnic areas, a bookstore and a visitors center. Parking fee, $5 (good at both Sabino Canyon and Mount Lemmon). ~ Located at the north end of Sabino Canyon Road after it intersects with Sunrise Drive; general information, 520-749-8700, fax 520-749-7723; www.fs.fed.us/r3/coronado, or shuttle information, 520-749-2327.

MOUNT LEMMON 🚶🚲🐎🎿⛷ In the hour's drive from Tucson to the top of Mount Lemmon, you travel from a lower Sonoran Desert zone to a Canadian zone forest, or from cacti to pine forests. For this reason, Tucsonians flock there in summer to escape the heat, and in winter to ski at Mount Lemmon Ski Valley, the southernmost ski area in the United States. If you take Catalina Highway to the top, the steep and winding mountain road will pass Rose Canyon Lake stocked with trout, and the town of Summerhaven, which is rebuilding after the 2003 Aspen fire. Once on Mount Lemmon, you can hike on 150 miles of trails. There are restrooms and picnic areas. Parking fee, $5 (good at both Sabino Canyon and Mount Lemmon). ~ Mount Lemmon is within the Coronado National Forest. Drive east on Tanque Verde Road to Catalina Highway, then head north 25 miles to Summerhaven; 520-749-8700; www.fs.fed.us/r3/coronado.

> Mount Lemmon is named after Sara Plummer Lemmon, the first woman to climb the lofty peak— in 1881 while on her honeymoon.

▲ There are tent and RV sites (no hookups) with toilets and drinking water at Rose Canyon (74 sites, $15 per night) and Spencer Canyon (62 sites, $14 per night). Molina Basin has 37 tent sites; $10 per night. Rose and Spencer canyons are closed in winter; Molina is closed in the summer.

TOHONO CHUL PARK Few tourists know about this treasure hidden in northwest Tucson. But walk down the winding paths

◄ HIDDEN

of the 49-acre park and you'll discover over 1000 species of arid climate plants, many of which are labeled, along with water fountains, grotto pond areas and a greenhouse with plants for sale. In addition, you'll find three exhibit galleries, three museums, gift shops and a tea room, as well as picnic tables, ramadas and restrooms. ~ Off Ina Road at 7366 North Paseo del Norte, about six miles north of the Tucson city limits; 520-742-6455, fax 520-579-1213; www.tohonochulpark.org, e-mail market ing@tohonochulpark.org.

CATALINA STATE PARK 🏃 🚲 🐎 This 5500-acre preserve sits in the Santa Catalina foothills. Highlights include Romero Canyon, a beautiful area with pools shaded by sycamore and oak trees, and adjacent Pusch Ridge Wilderness, home to desert bighorn sheep. The Hohokam once farmed the area, and as you walk through the park you can still see some of the pit houses and ball court ruins. Facilities include restrooms, showers, picnic tables and grills. Day-use fee, $6 per vehicle. ~ Off Route 77, about nine miles north of the city limits at 11570 North Oracle Road; 520-628-5798, fax 520-628-5797.

▲ Catalina State Park Campground has 48 tent/RV sites; $12 per night without hookups, $19 with hookups.

PICACHO PEAK STATE PARK 🏃 The most dramatic part of the park is Picacho Peak, a landmark formation that rises 1500 feet above the desert floor and can be seen for miles around. Believed to be 22 million years old—or four times as old as the Grand Canyon—Picacho Peak was used as a landmark by early explorers. It was the site of the battle of Picacho Pass during the Civil War. The 3500-acre park has seven miles of developed hiking trails that wind past saguaro cacti as well. Facilities include picnic areas, ramadas, showers and restrooms. Day-use fee, $6 per vehicle. ~ Off Route 10 (Exit 219), 40 miles north of Tucson; 520-466-3183, fax 520-466-7442.

▲ There are 85 tent/RV sites; $12 per night without hookups, $20 with electricity hookups.

▼▼▼▼▼▼▼▼▼▼▼
East of Tucson

The Wild West comes to life in this area of Arizona where murder and lynching were once considered leisure activities, poker was more popular than Sunday church services and whiskey was king. While this region is best known for infamous spots like Boot Hill and the O.K. Corral, it's also the home of historic mining towns like Bisbee, mineral spas and a cowboy hall of fame.

SIGHTS

Get on Route 10 heading east and one of the first attractions you will pass is **Colossal Cave Mountain Park**, one of the largest dry caverns in the world. Set in the Rincon Mountains, it was once home for Indians and outlaws. During 50-minute tours, hidden lights illuminate formations such as the Silent Waterfall and Kingdom of the Elves. On the premises is also a 130- year old working ranch offering trail rides, museums, and wooded picnic areas. Admission. ~ 16721 Old East Spanish Trail, Vail; 520-647-7275, fax 520-647-3299; www.colossalcave.com, e-mail info@colossalcave.com.

Farther east on Route 10 is Benson, where the **Arts & Historical Society** tells the story about how Benson grew along with the arrival of the railroad. Inside are antiques, artifacts and an old grocery store. A gift shop offers local arts and crafts. Closed Sunday and Monday and the month of August. ~ 180 South San Pedro Street, Benson; 520-586-3070.   ◄ HIDDEN

The spelunkers who discovered **Kartchner Caverns** in 1974 kept their find a secret for 14 years until they had persuaded officials to protect it as a state park. The vast cave opened to the public in 1999 after $28 million in state-of-the-art improvements, which included a wheelchair-accessible paved trail through the caverns, a computerized halogen lighting system and five sets of air-lock doors along the narrow entrance passage to prevent the desert air outside from drying up the "living" cave formations. Visitors to Arizona's largest cave find themselves in a hidden world of subterranean chambers the size of football fields dripping with calcite formations that range from delicate soda-straw stalactites up to 21 feet long and only a quarter-inch in diameter to a 58-foot-tall column that forms the centerpiece of a sound-and-light show. In dramatic contrast to the arid heat of the Chihuahuan Desert above ground, the climate inside the cave is a constant 68° and 99 percent humidity. Reservations are recommended: often tours of the cave are booked solid. Admission. ~ 2980 South Route 90, Benson; 520-586-4100, 520-586-2283 (reservations), fax 602-542-4113.

> Local legend has it that lost treasure is buried somewhere inside Colossal Cave.

On your way to the Old West towns of Bisbee and Tombstone, take a detour toward Elgin. You will enter what at first seems an oxymoron—Arizona **wine country**. But there are several wineries out here, and it's a pretty drive through the vineyards.

In the town of Elgin you'll find **The Chapel of the Blessed Mother, Consoler of the Afflicted**, a small chapel set amid grasslands, vineyards and cottonwood trees. ~ Elgin.   ◄ HIDDEN

Head south on Route 90 and you can't miss **Fort Huachuca**, a National Historic Landmark founded in 1877 to protect settlers from Apache raiders. The Fort Huachuca soldiers eventually tracked down and defeated Apache leader Geronimo. Today, this 73,000-acre installation is home to the U.S. Army Intelligence Center and School. One highlight is the Fort Huachuca Museum, located in an early 1900s building first used as a bachelor officers' quarters. Inside are military artifacts, dioramas and the history of the fort. The museum annex is across the street, and down the road is the Army Intelligence Museum. For a panoramic view of the fort and town, drive up Reservoir Hill Road. If you'd prefer picnicking, there are plenty of scenic spots amid large, old trees. ~ Sierra Vista; 520-533-3638, fax 520-533-5736.

Take Route 92 south and you'll find a place known to birding enthusiasts worldwide. **Ramsey Canyon Preserve** is home to a variety of birds, including 14 species of hummingbirds from mid-April to early September. Also commonly spotted here are white-tailed deer, gray squirrels and coatimundi. The Nature Conservancy owns this 380-acre wooded gorge set in the Huachuca Mountains. No vehicles over 18 feet are allowed. No pets, picnicking or smoking. Admission. ~ Route 92, five miles south of Sierra Vista; 520-378-2785, fax 520-620-1799; www.nature.org.

Hop on Route 90 again for the quick trip to **Bisbee** near the Mexican border. Known as the "Queen of the Copper Mines," this old mining town was the largest city between St. Louis and San Francisco during its mining heyday. Now an artists' enclave, the town is full of Victorian architecture perched on hillsides, along with funky shops and restaurants. For the full history of the town, start at the **Bisbee Mining & Historical Museum**, located in the former General Office Building of the Copper Queen Consolidated Mining Co. This is the first rural museum to become a Smithsonian affiliate. On the front lawn is old mining equipment, while inside the 1897 red-brick building are photo murals, artifacts and walk-in environments that highlight Bisbee's history. The museum also has a large display of rocks and precious minerals once housed at the Smithsonian. Admission. ~ 5 Copper Queen Plaza, Bisbee; 520-432-7071, fax 520-432-7800; www.bisbeemuseum.org, e-mail bisbeemuseum@theriver.com.

For a first-hand view of mining history, put on a slicker, hard hat and battery-pack light and hop on the underground train at the **Queen Mine Underground Tour**. An ex-miner narrates as he takes you through the Copper Queen Mine, which prospered for more than 60 years before it closed in 1944. The journey is a cool one, so bring a jacket. From here you can also take the **Lavender Open Pit Mine Tour**, a narrated, 13-mile bus tour around a 300-acre hole where more than 380 million tons of ore and tailings have been removed. In conjunction with this, the **Historic District Tour** travels through the old section of Bisbee, spotlighting such buildings as the Copper Queen Hotel and the Phythian Castle. Admission. ~ 478 North Dart Road, Bisbee; 520-432-2071, fax 520-432-6069.

Continue your time travel to the Old West at **Slaughter Ranch**, located near the Mexican border. Now a National Historic Landmark, it was once the home of John Slaughter, a former Texas Ranger, sheriff of Cochise County and one of the founders of

Douglas. He bought the fertile grassland in 1884 and developed it into a cattle ranch. Slaughter's house and half a dozen other buildings furnished to reflect the era are still on the 140-acre site. Closed Monday and Tuesday. Admission. ~ Geronimo Trail, 15 miles east of Douglas; 520-558-2474, e-mail sranch@vtc.net.

The **Gadsden Hotel** in Douglas is a National Historic Monument that opened in 1907 as a hotel for cattlemen, miners and ranchers. Step into the magnificent lobby to behold a solid white Italian-marble staircase, four marble columns with capitals decorated in 14K gold leaf, and vaulted stained-glass skylights that run its length. Several Hollywood movies have been filmed here. ~ 1046 G Avenue, Douglas; 520-364-4481, fax 520-364-4005; www.gadsdenhotel.com, e-mail rgadsden@theriver.com.

Northwest of Douglas is **Tombstone**. Prospector Ed Shieffelin staked a silver claim there in 1877 and it became a Wild, Wild West town—reputedly with saloons and gambling halls making up two of every three buildings—and in more recent years the subject of innumerable Western movies. Today the town is extremely touristy, yet almost irresistible. With its rowdy mix of history and cowboy kitsch, Tombstone is the best place in southern Arizona to watch actors stage a gun fight.

After looping off Route 10 to see Sierra Vista, Bisbee and Tombstone, get back to Route 10 and go east to Dragoon, home of the **Amerind Foundation Museum** (an archaeological research facility) and little else. This is a real treasure tucked away amidst

Old Tombstone

Born in 1877 as a silver camp, Tombstone has lived up to its nickname—the town too tough to die. Wild West legends about the Earp brothers, Doc Holliday and Bat Masterson have transformed this National Historic District into southern Arizona's busiest sightseeing destination, and each year the revenues from tourism far surpass the total amount of silver produced by the mine that lies beneath the town streets in Tombstone's heyday.

BIRD CAGE THEATRE   Most of Tombstone's early-day historic buildings are along Allen Street. At one end of the main street, the Bird Cage Theatre was built in 1881 as a gambling casino and dance hall; prostitutes plied their trade in its birdcage-like compartments. Never a dull place, the theater was the site of 16 gunfights. If you bother to count you'll find 140 bullet holes riddling the walls and ceilings. The longest poker game in the history of the West reputedly unfolded here ... it lasted eight years, five months and three days. Admission. ~ 6th and Allen streets; 520-457-3421, fax 520-457-3189; www.tombstoneaz.net, e-mail oldbirdcage@juno.com.

O.K. CORRAL   Down Allen Street from the Bird Cage is the O.K. Corral, where legend places the most famous of Tombstone's many shootouts. Life-size figures of the Earp brothers, Doc Holliday and their enemies, the Clantons, stand in the corral as a narrator describes the gunfight. (Actually, the incident did not take place here but in a nearby vacant lot, which is

the rock formations of Texas Canyon. The research facility and museum have been devoted to American Indian culture and history since they opened in 1937. Visitors walk through the Spanish Colonial revival–style buildings to see exhibits on prehistoric and historic indigenous cultures from both North and South America. The art gallery houses Western artwork, including works by Frederic Remington and William Leigh. Closed Monday and Tuesday from June through October. Admission. ~ Dragoon Road, Dragoon; 520-586-3666, fax 520-586-4679; www. amerind.org, e-mail amerind@amerind.org.

More Western history is found farther east on Route 10 in Willcox at the **Chiricahua Regional Museum and Research Center**. There's a bust of Chief Cochise, Indian and mining artifacts, and a mineral and rock collection. Closed Sunday. ~ 127 East Maley Street, Willcox; 520-384-3971.

now part of the museum.) An adjacent building showcases old Tombstone photos and memorabilia. Admission. ~ 308 Allen Street; phone/fax 520-457-3456; www.ok-corral.com, e-mail okcorral@ok-corral.com.

CRYSTAL PALACE AND SILVER NUGGET   Other notorious old houses of booze, gambling and ill repute (now restored and family-friendly) along Allen Street include the Crystal Palace and the Silver Nugget.

ROSE TREE INN MUSEUM   A huge rosebush that spreads across 8600 feet of supports is the main attraction at the Rose Tree Inn Museum, one block off the main street. Planted in 1885, the bush is an awesome sight in April, when it's covered with white blossoms. You can tour the historic adobe home containing local artifacts and period rooms. Admission. ~ 4th and Toughnut streets; 520-457-3326.

TOMBSTONE COURTHOUSE   Now an Arizona state historic park, the Tombstone Courthouse has a restored courtroom and two floors of historic exhibits that reflect the ups and downs of this once-rowdy town. The red-brick building was the town's courthouse from 1882 to 1929. Admission. ~ 3rd and Toughnut streets; 520-457-3311. Also part of the historic park is the original office of the *Tombstone Epitaph* (as locals say, every Tombstone should have an Epitaph), the second-oldest newspaper in Arizona. The monthly newspaper is still published. ~ 520-457-2211.

BOOTHILL GRAVEYARD   Finally, no visit to Tombstone would be complete without a stop at the Boothill Graveyard, where outlaws and early settlers rest side by side, their graves little more than piles of rocks marked by white metal crosses. This may be the only cemetery around with its own gift shop. ~ Route 80W; 520-457-9344.

The most famous cowboy of the area was Rex Allen, born in Willcox in 1920. The **Rex Allen Arizona Cowboy Museum** features mementos of Rex Allen's life, from his homesteading and ranch life in Willcox to his movies and television shows. Another section features the pioneer settlers and ranchers of the Willcox area. Admission. ~ 155 North Railroad Avenue, Willcox; 520-384-4583, 877-234-4111; e-mail ostark@vtc.net.

A good motel choice in Benson is the **Best Western Quail Hollow Inn,** which has 89 spacious, white-walled guest rooms with oak-finished furniture, green and mauve fabrics and artwork depicting the native quail. Amenities include refrigerators and microwaves upon request, TVs and a heated pool. Continental breakfast included. ~ 699 North Ocotillo Street, Benson; 520-586-3646, 800-322-1850, fax 520-586-7035. MODERATE.

LODGING

The majority of accommodations in Sierra Vista are along Fry Boulevard—the main commercial thoroughfare through town—and on South Route 92. **Sierra Suites** is a two-story, red-brick hotel that lures guests with complimentary breakfast. The 100 rooms face courtyards, and inside, some have mirrored sliding glass closet doors, glass tables, a chest of drawers, hairdryers, coffeemakers, refrigerators and microwaves. The price includes use of the pool and whirlpool. ~ 391 East Fry Boulevard, Sierra Vista; 520-459-4221, fax 520-459-8449; www.sierra suiteshotel.com. BUDGET TO MODERATE.

Quality Inn is a two-story, brick building with 104 rooms and a café. Lower-level guest rooms facing the pool have sliding glass doors. Most accommodations have double beds and a desk. ~ 1631 South Route 92, Sierra Vista; phone/fax 520-458-7900, 800-458-0982. BUDGET TO MODERATE.

HIDDEN ▶

For a really secluded getaway, venture out to **Ramsey Canyon Inn Bed & Breakfast**, located in the Huachuca Mountains along a winding mountain stream and adjacent to the Nature Conservancy's Ramsey Canyon Preserve and the Coronado National Forest. Accommodations consist of two fully equipped apartments and a seven-room (including one large suite) bed-and-breakfast inn, with a private bath in each room. Rates include full breakfast and homemade pies in the afternoon. ~ 29 Ramsey Canyon Road, Hereford; phone/fax 520-378-3010; www.ramseycanyoninn.com, e-mail lodging@theriver.com. DELUXE TO ULTRA-DELUXE.

Built in 1917, **Hotel La More/The Bisbee Inn** overlooks Brewery Gulch, once one of the Southwest's wildest streets. Each of the 20 rooms has handmade quilts on the beds, antique dressers with mirrors, and its own sink. Four rooms share bathrooms in the hall. Included in the rate is an all-you-can-eat breakfast. ~ 45 OK Street, Bisbee; 520-432-5131, 888-432-5131, fax 520-432-

AUTHOR FAVORITE

For beautiful scenery in a true wilderness, the **Southwest Research Station**, run by the American Museum of Natural History, provides a haven for the layperson as well as the scientist. Rooms are furnished simply and three meals a day are included in the tab. Cave Creek Canyon is known for its fabulous birdwatching. A swimming pool, volleyball court and horseshoes are available for the guests. Open to the public from mid-March through May and then again September through February. ~ Take Route 80 to Portal, then follow Cave Creek Canyon for five miles; phone/fax 520-558-2396; research.amnh.org/swrs, e-mail swrs@ amnh.org. MODERATE.

5343; www.bisbeeinn.com, e-mail bisbeeinn@aol.com. BUDGET
TO DELUXE.

If you were to make a pilgrimage to just one of the hotels in
the Southwest where John Wayne once spent the night, Bisbee's
historic **Copper Queen Hotel** would be a good choice. The Copper
Queen Mining Co. built the hotel just after the turn of the 20th
century when it was a gathering place for politicians, mining officials and travelers, including the young Teddy Roosevelt. A
plaque on one door marks the room where John Wayne stayed.
The rooms are decorated Victorian style with floral wallpaper
and tile bathrooms. The four-story building contains 48 rooms,
along with a saloon and dining room. ~ 11 Howell Avenue, Bisbee; 520-432-2216, 800-247-5829, fax 520-432-4298; www.
copperqueen.com, e-mail info@copperqueen.com. MODERATE TO
DELUXE.

School House Inn Bed and Breakfast is a large, restored, 1918
red-brick schoolhouse just above Garfield Park. The nine themed
rooms (reading, writing, arithmetic, etc.) are fairly large, and each
has a private bath with a large tub. A full breakfast is served. ~
818 Tombstone Canyon, Bisbee; phone/fax 520-432-2996, 800-
537-4333; www.virtualcities.com/ons/az/b/azb4501.htm. BUDGET
TO MODERATE.

The **Bisbee Grand Hotel** is ideally located in the main shopping area in town. The original hotel was built in 1906. There
are seven suites with private baths and six rooms. All accommodations reflect the era with period wallpaper, red carpeting, brass
beds and antiques. They also have sinks and ceiling fans. Most
of the rooms are upstairs, while downstairs is the grand Western
Saloon and Billiards Room. Rates include breakfast. ~ 61 Main
Street, Bisbee; phone/fax 520-432-5900, 800-421-1909; www.
bisbeegrandhotel.com, e-mail bisbeegrandhotel@msn.com. MOD-
ERATE TO DELUXE.

The **Jonquil Motel** is a small motor court with seven clean,
comfortable rooms. The rooms have TVs but no phones. ~ 317
Tombstone Canyon, Bisbee; 520-432-7371, fax 520-432-6915;
www.jonquilmotel.com, e-mail mail@jonquilmotel.com. BUDGET.

The six-room **Tombstone Boarding House & Lamplight
Room** is in an adobe building constructed around 1880; all
rooms have private entrances and baths. There is also a tiny tin-
clad miner's cabin that sleeps up to three people. Rooms are
tastefully decorated in pastel colors with lacy curtains and
Victorian-era furnishings. A full breakfast is served in the
Victorian dining room. In the evening, a gourmet dinner is available (at an extra charge). ~ 108 North 4th Street, Tombstone; 520-
457-3716, 877-225-1319; www.tombstoneboardinghouse.com,
e-mail info@tombstoneboardinghouse.com. BUDGET TO MODERATE.

DINING

HIDDEN ►

Horseshoe Cafe is a family-owned restaurant that has been around for more than 50 years. On the walls are Western murals by artist Vern Parker, and the posts in the café display cattle brands of Southern Arizona. A neon horseshoe on the ceiling helps light the room. Entrées include chili, sandwiches, omelettes, burgers, steaks and Mexican specialties. ~ 154 East 4th Street, Benson; phone/fax 520-586-3303. BUDGET TO DELUXE.

Speaking in relative terms, the **Thunder Mountain Inn Restaurant** is one of the more expensive places in town. Diners eat prime rib and seafood atop white tablecloths in booths divided by etched glass. ~ 1631 South Route 92, Sierra Vista; 520-458-7900. MODERATE TO DELUXE.

Stop by cozy **Grasslands Natural Foods & Café**, which looks like a miniature restaurant plopped in the middle of your kitchen. Salads, pasta salads and quiche provide a light alternative to the typical heavy burritos of the region; baked sandwiches round out the menu. Ingredients are always fresh and organic. If you're reluctant to see the end of your meal, visit their bakery, which sells olive herb sourdough, wheat germ and currant bars and homemade granola. No dinner. Closed Monday and Tuesday. ~ 3119 Route 83, Sonoita; 520-455-4770; www.grasslands bakery.com, e-mail orders@grasslandsbakery.com. BUDGET TO MODERATE.

A sleek art-deco restaurant in a historic 1907 building, **Cafe Roka** offers a wide variety of flavorful pastas and house specialties such as smoked salmon with gorgonzola. Ingredients are fresh and the service charming. Check out the original pressed-tin ceilings and the marble bar. Live music on Friday and Saturday. Call for summer hours; closed Sunday through Tuesday the rest of the year. ~ 35 Main Street, Bisbee; 520-432-5153. MODERATE.

Rosa's Little Italy is a tiny local eatery that specializes in country-style Italian fare: hearty portions of veal piccatta, fettuccini alfredo, antipasto plates and tiramisu for dessert. A good bargain, the portions are large and you get to bring your own chianti—it's BYOB. Dinner only. Closed Monday and Tuesday. ~ 7 Bisbee Road, Bisbee; 520-432-1331. MODERATE.

Enjoy Mexican or American favorites under the watchful eye of Marilyn Monroe at **Grand Cafe Restaurant**, the blonde bombshell appears in paintings, drawings and photographs exhibited throughout the eatery. Burritos, fajitas and flautas are some of the Mexican dishes while T-bone steaks and shrimp scampi are featured on the American menu. Breakfast, lunch and dinner. Closed Sunday. ~ 1119 G Avenue, Douglas; 520-364-2344. BUDGET TO MODERATE.

The **Nellie Cashman Restaurant** is housed in an 1879 building with decor to reflect the era including a stone fireplace, high wood ceilings and photos of bygone years. Although they serve sandwiches and burgers, they're best known for their homemade pies. Closed Sunday. ~ 117 South 5th Street, Tombstone; 520-457-2212. MODERATE TO DELUXE.

For the biggest hot dog in Cochise County, weighing in at half a pound and measuring a foot long, saunter over to the **Longhorn Restaurant** and order a Longhorn Dog. If that's not what you crave, they offer other big food options, including a 40-ounce steak. The decor is Western with longhorns hanging over the door and yellowing wanted posters of characters such as Billy the Kid laminated on the tables. ~ 501 East Allen Street, Tombstone; 520-457-3405. BUDGET TO MODERATE.

Singing Wind Bookshop is in the *really hidden* category. From Route 10, turn north on Ocotillo Road, then go for two and a quarter miles and turn right on West Singing Wind Road until you see the chained green gate. Don't let it stop you—just open it and drive on in (remember to close the gate behind you!) and down to the ranch house. Here, there are two huge rooms full of new books about the Southwest, Western Americana and other categories. In addition, there's a room full of children's books. ~ West Singing Wind Road and North Ocotillo Road, two and a quarter miles north of Route 10, Benson; phone/fax 520-586-2425.

SHOPPING

◄ HIDDEN

Head south to Sierra Vista and you'll discover **Misty's Gift Gallery**, one of the largest collectors' galleries in the Southwest with names that include Goebel, Hummel, Gorham, De Grazia and Perillo. There is also a gallery with original artwork, lithographs and bronzes. Closed Sunday and Monday most of the year; closed Sunday in December. ~ 228 West Fry Boulevard, Sierra Vista; 520-458-7208.

Boot Hill in Tombstone is the place where men "who died with their boots on" were frequently buried. Contrary to popular belief, Wyatt Earp's resting place is not among the cemetery's 250 historic graves.

The **Johnson Gallery** carries American Indian arts and crafts and Quezada family pottery. ~ 28 Main Street, Bisbee; 520-432-2126. Local and regional artists create the innovative and contemporary jewelry found at **The Gold Shop**. ~ 24 Main Street, Bisbee; 520-432-4557.

Poco Loco features striking hand-painted dinnerware and other pottery plus Western collectibles, furniture and jewelry. Closed Monday through Thursday in June. ~ 81 Main Street, Bisbee; 520-432-7020; www.pocoloco.com.

Allen Street is the heart of shopping in Tombstone, where you will find lots of souvenir shops mixed in with higher-quality jewelry and clothing stores. **Arlene's Southwest Silver & Gold** is a large place with American Indian jewelry and artwork including pottery, baskets, kachina dolls and rugs. ~ 404 Allen Street, Tombstone; 520-457-3344.

Gabe's Victorian Shop and Doll Museum is the oldest shop in Tombstone. The place is crammed full of dolls, dollhouse pieces, Victorian cards, collectibles and more than 250 paper dolls. In the back of the shop is a museum with dolls dating back to the 1830s. No credit cards. Admission to museum. ~ 312 Allen Street, Tombstone; 520-457-3419.

Spur Western Wear sells Western duds for the whole family. ~ 509 East Allen Street, Tombstone; 520-457-9000.

For Tombstone souvenirs, including hats, books and Western keepsakes such as cow skulls (!), check out **Tombstone Emporium.** ~ 325 Allen Street, Tombstone; 520-457-3854.

The time to travel out to the Willcox area is fall, when farms and roadside stands are selling their produce. The Willcox Chamber of Commerce (800-200-2272) has a brochure listing orchards and mills where you can stop. One is **Stout's Cider Mill**, where you can buy apples, cider, dried fruit, nuts, peaches, apple pies, chile peppers and Arizona desert preserves. ~ 1510 North Circle I Road, Willcox; 520-384-3696; www.cidermill.com.

NIGHTLIFE

HIDDEN ►

Pardners Arena Saloon & Rodeo Grounds overlooks the rodeo grounds, where events are staged five nights a week. Inside, a Western theme dominates. A lasso hangs on the door, cow skulls decorate walls, and you can warm yourself by the big rock fireplace. There are also a pool table and dancefloor, along with outdoor picnic benches. ~ 250 North Prickly Pear Street, Benson; 520-586-9983.

You want local color? You'll get it at **Jimbo's Beach Shaque**. The nightclub features two bars, pool tables and a dancefloor. And lots of locals being colorful. Cover. ~ 6755 East Route 90, Sierra Vista; 520-452-1708.

Established in 1902, **St. Elmo Bar** in historic Bisbee is a tradition around here. Memorabilia such as old maps hang on the walls, and seating is mainly stools at the counter. On weekends there's live music and dancing. Entertainment during the week is

DESERT VINTAGE

Although its first vineyards were introduced in the 17th century by Franciscan missionaries, Arizona doesn't exactly spring to mind when contemplating the great wine-growing regions of the world. It does, however, claim several varieties of grapes, including cabernet sauvignon, merlot, syrah, chardonnay, sauvignon blanc and sangiovese. Today, Arizona fosters a little over two dozen active wineries, with over 650 acres of grapes being grown to support the industry.

supplied by the CD jukebox or pool tables. ~ 36 Brewery Avenue, Bisbee; 520-432-5578.

Adjoining the Copper Queen Hotel, the **Copper Queen Saloon** is a small, dark, intimate place with some early-20th-century furnishings and live music on occasional weekends. ~ 11 Howell Avenue, Bisbee; 520-432-2216.

At the **Stock Exchange Bar**, almost one whole wall is covered with an original board from the Bisbee stock exchange. This historic building has a pressed-tin roof and worn wooden floors. There's a jukebox and occasional live music on the weekend. Downstairs is the Brewery Restaurant. ~ 15 Brewery Avenue, Bisbee; 520-432-9924.

Walk through swinging doors of **Big Nose Kate's Saloon** and you step back into the Old West. Waitresses dressed as saloon gals serve drinks. Lighted, stained-glass panels depict Tombstone's characters, and old photographs hang on the walls. On Friday you'll find live country-and-western music. Lily Langtry and Wyatt Earp once tipped their glasses here. ~ 417 East Allen Street, Tombstone; 520-457-3107; www.bignosekate.com, e-mail whisk ers@bignosekate.com.

The Crystal Palace Saloon has been restored to look like it did when it was built in the 1880s. The long, narrow room has old wood tables and red drapes underneath a copper ceiling. Live music is performed occasionally on Saturday evening and Sunday during the day. ~ 420 East Allen Street, Tombstone; 520-457-3611; www.crystalpalacesaloon.com.

CHIRICAHUA NATIONAL MONUMENT 🏃 The Chiricahua Apaches called this area the Land of the Standing-Up Rocks because throughout the park are huge rock spires, stone columns and massive rocks perched on small pedestals. Geologists believe that these formations were created as a result of explosive volcanic eruptions. For an overview of the park, drive up the winding, eight-mile-long Bonita Canyon Drive. You'll pass pine and oak-juniper forests before reaching Massai Point at the top of the Chiricahua Mountains where you can see the park, valleys and the peaks of Sugarloaf Mountain and Cochise Head. You can also explore the park on foot via about 20 miles of trails. Other attractions include historic Faraway Ranch and Stafford Cabin. There are picnic tables, restrooms and a visitors center with exhibits. Day-use fee, $5 per person (seven-day pass). ~ From Willcox, go southeast on Route 186 for 37 miles; 520-824-3560, fax 520-824-3421; www.nps.gov/chir.

▲ There are 22 sites; $12 per night. No backcountry camping is allowed within the monument.

PARKS

▼ ▼ ▼ ▼ ▼ ▼ ▼ ▼ ▼ ▼ ▼ ▼ ▼ ▼

South/West of Tucson

Far off the beaten track, southwestern Arizona is home to the world's leading astronomical center, remote ghost towns, wildlife preserves and a sanctuary dedicated to the unusual organ pipe cactus. This is also where civilization disappears and the desert blooms.

SIGHTS

Heading south on Route 19, you'll pass the retirement community of Green Valley and arrive at the **Titan Missile Museum**, the only intercontinental ballistic missile complex in the world that's open to the public. Here you'll be taken on a one-hour guided tour into the bowels of the earth, experience a countdown launch of a Titan missile and view a silo. It's an eerie excursion. Reservations are recommended. Admission. ~ 1580 West Duval Mine Road, Sahuarita; 520-625-4759.

To get away from the high-tech missiles and delve deeper into the area's history, continue farther south on Route 19 to Tubac. Here, the Spanish founded a presidio in 1752 to protect settlers from the Indians. At **Tubac Presidio State Historic Park** visitors can see the remains of the original presidio foundation, the foundation of the Spanish captain's house from the military garrison in 1750, an 1885 schoolhouse, a 1914 community hall and a museum detailing the history of Tubac. Admission. ~ Route 19, Tubac; 520-398-2252.

A few more minutes down Route 19 are the adobe ruins of a Spanish frontier mission church at the **Tumacácori National Historical Park**. Along with the museum, visitors walk through the baroque church, completed in 1822, and the nearby ruins of a circular mortuary chapel and graveyard. Since little has been built in the vicinity, walking across the grounds feels like a walk back in time. Admission. ~ Route 19, Exit 29 on Frontage Road, Tumacácori; 520-398-2341, fax 520-398-9271; www.nps.gov/tuma.

Continuing south, Route 19 hits the Mexican border. **Nogales, Mexico,** is a border town offering bargain shopping, restaurants and some sightseeing. On the other side is Nogales, Arizona. Photographs and artifacts detail the town's history at the **Pimeria Alta Historical Society Museum**, a 1914 mission-style building that once housed the city hall, police and fire departments. ~ 136 North Grand Avenue, Nogales; 520-287-4621.

HIDDEN ▶

Just off of Route 82 you'll pass by some **ghost towns**, including Harshaw and Duquesne. **Duquesne** was a mining center established around the late 1800s with a peak population of 1000 residents, including Westinghouse of Westinghouse Electric. **Harshaw** was settled around 1875 and operated about 100 mines. Today all that's left are ruins and graveyards. Some of the roads en route are extremely bumpy and rugged, so be prepared.

Tucson and the surrounding area is known as the Astronomy Capital of the World with more astronomical observatories than anywhere else. One of the most famous is the **Kitt Peak National Observatory**. Drive up a mountain road and you'll come across the observatory's gleaming white domes and its 24 telescopes. During tours you can step inside some of the telescopes, including the 18-story-high four-meter telescope. There's also a museum with exhibits on the observatory, as well as star-gazing programs. Serious astronomy buffs can spend the night on top for a steep fee. If you're planning on staying awhile, bring food—it's a long haul up the mountain and there's nothing to nibble on at the top. ~ Off Route 386, 56 miles southwest of Tucson; 520-318-8726, fax 520-318-8451; www.noao.edu, e-mail kpno@noao.edu.

> Well-known labor leader Cesar Estrada Chavez, who founded the United Farm Workers union, was born in Yuma.

Continuing to the west about 100 miles on Route 86, and then heading north on Route 85, you'll come to **Ajo**, a small scenic town whose center is a green plaza surrounded by Spanish Colonial–style buildings. It is also an old copper mining town and as such shows its scars. The **Phelps Dodge Ajo Morenci, Inc. Copper Mine** is one of the largest open-pit copper mines in the world, stretching a full mile in diameter. Although operations ceased in 1984, you can go to the pit lookout and learn about mining operations at the adjacent visitors center (call ahead). Closed May to mid-October except by appointment. ~ Route 85, Ajo; 520-387-7631; www.ajoinaz.com.

From the mine you can see the **Ajo Historical Society Museum**, located in what was once St. Catherine's Indian Mission, a stucco church built in 1942. Inside are artifacts from Ajo's history, including a blacksmith shop, dentist's office, printing shop and American Indian artifacts such as old saddles found on graves. Closed May through October, except by appointment. ~ 160 Mission Street, Ajo; 520-387-7105.

Much farther west, near the California border, is **Yuma**. Once a steamboat stop and major crossing on the Colorado River, today it's a bustling city that supports farming and basks in a subtropical climate. **Yuma Territorial Prison**, a penitentiary built between 1876 and 1909, is now a state historic park. Despite its infamous reputation, written evidence indicates that the prison was humanely administered and was a model institution for its time. Prisoners received regular medical attention and schooling was available to the convicts. Those prisoners who escaped were faced with hostile deserts and the currents of the Colorado River. The prison was closed in 1909 because of overcrowding. Today visitors walk through the gloomy cells and climb the guard tower, where one can see the Colorado River and surrounding area. Admission. ~ 1 Prison Hill Road, Yuma; 928-783-4771.

The military supply hub for the Arizona Territory is now the **Yuma Crossing State Historic Park Quartermaster Depot**, which served the Southwest until it closed in 1883. Several of the original buildings remain, including the commanding officer's quarters and Office of the Quartermaster. Admission. There's a visitors center with displays on the park's history. ~ 201 North 4th Avenue, Yuma; 928-329-0471, fax 928-782-7124.

More of Yuma's history comes to light in the **Arizona Historical Society's Sanguinetti House Museum**. Once the home of pioneer merchant E. F. Sanguinetti, it now has artifacts, photographs and furnishings of Arizona's territorial period. Just outside are colorful gardens and aviaries with exotic birds. Closed Sunday and Monday. Admission.~ 240 South Madison Avenue, Yuma; 928-782-1841, fax 928-783-0680; www.arizona historicalsociety.org.

LODGING   Located in Madera Canyon, **Santa Rita Lodge Nature Resort** is a perfect birders' getaway. Just outside the large windows in each of the 12 rooms are feeders that attract a number of bird species. Inside the rooms, charts hang with pictures of different types of hummingbirds. The lodge also offers nature programs that meet in the patio area, and staff birders will take guests on birding walks. If (gasp!) you've had enough of birding, extensive nature trails wend through the property. ~ Located 13 miles southeast of Green Valley in the Coronado National Forest; 520-625-8746, fax 520-648-1186; www.santaritalodge.com, e-mail lcollister@ theriver.com. MODERATE.

Bing Crosby was part-owner of the **Tubac Golf Resort** back in 1959. The 46 rooms and suites are decorated in a Western motif and have tiled bathrooms and patios facing the mountains; some have woodburning fireplaces. The resort has a golf course, tennis court, pool and spa, hiking trails and a full-service restaurant and bar. ~ 1 Avenida de Otero, Tubac; 520-398-2211, 800-848-7893, fax 520-398-9261; www.tubacgolfresort.com, e-mail relaxing@ tubacgolfresort.com. ULTRA-DELUXE.

Rio Rico Resort & Country Club is a beautiful resort in the San Cayatano Mountain range. All of the rooms have sliding glass doors overlooking the pool or mountains, wood-beamed ceilings, and contemporary Southwestern decor in pastel colors. Amenities include a golf course, tennis courts, horse stables, jacuzzi, exercise room, restaurant and lounge. ~ 1069 Camino Caralampi, Rio Rico; 520-281-1901, 800-288-4746, fax 520-281-7132; www. rioricoresort.com, e-mail sales@rioricoresort.com. DELUXE TO ULTRA-DELUXE.

The Stage Stop Inn is a 43-room hotel with a restaurant serving Sunday champagne brunch, a saloon and clean, comfortable rooms (some with kitchenettes) facing the pool in the middle. Movie casts and crew often stay here while filming in the area. The Western lobby showcases an antelope head above the fire-

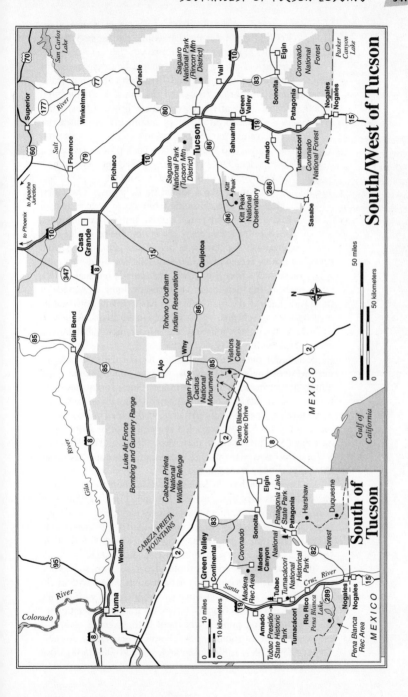

South/West of Tucson

South of Tucson

place, cattle brands on the tile floor and Western paintings on the walls. ~ 303 McKeown Avenue, Patagonia; phone/fax 520-394-2211, 800-923-2211. BUDGET TO MODERATE.

A charming old adobe that was once a boarding house for miners, **Duquesne House Bed and Breakfast** offers four comfortable suites with brick floors and mission-style architectural details. All suites have private entrances and private baths. There is also an efficiency apartment without a private entrance. A common room features a woodstove and TV. A pleasant back porch overlooks a garden. Full breakfast. ~ 357 Duquesne Avenue, Patagonia; 520-394-2732. MODERATE.

The desert town of Why, just south of Ajo, was named by irate residents tired of tourists always asking, "Why would anybody want to live here?"

Looking like a miniature dollhouse, **The Guest House Inn** is a charming white house with blue trim and a long front porch dotted with white-cushioned furniture for lazing away the hours. Phelps Dodge once entertained dignitaries at the Guest House Inn, and breakfast is now served on the 20-foot-long walnut dining table where these guests once ate. Inside, the setup is unusual, with a living room in the middle and guest rooms lining either side of the house. Each of the four bedrooms has a private bath and its own decorating scheme. ~ 700 Guest House Road, Ajo; 520-387-6133; www.guesthouseinn.biz, e-mail mcw.ghi@inetmail.att.net. MODERATE.

Built during the space races with the Russians, the theme at the **Best Western Space Age Lodge** is obvious. Hand-painted space murals accent the lobby and restaurant. Guest rooms have pictures of rockets blasting off into space and contain whitewashed wood furniture, pastel colors and large, well-lighted mirrors above the counter. There's also a pool, a spa and a coffee shop. ~ 401 East Pima Street, Gila Bend; phone/fax 928-683-2273, 800-937-8376; www.bestwesternspaceagelodge.com, e-mail spaceagelodge@aol.com BUDGET TO MODERATE.

La Fuente Inn has 96 Southwest-style rooms decorated in pastels. Rooms have VCRs, irons and ironing boards and face the grassy interior courtyard and pool. Prices include a complimentary continental breakfast, happy hour and use of the fitness room. ~ 1513 East 16th Street, Yuma; 928-329-1814, 800-841-1814, fax 928-343-2671; www.lafuenteinn.com. MODERATE.

Shilo Inn Hotel offers 134 rooms decorated in pastel colors, some with couches, patios and tile bathrooms. Suites with kitchenettes are also available. A three-story-high lobby with marble floors and mirrored columns welcomes guests. Amenities include a swimming pool, a whirlpool bath, exercise rooms, a sauna and a steam room. ~ 1550 South Castle Dome Avenue, Yuma; 928-782-9511, 800-222-2244, fax 928-783-1538. MODERATE TO DELUXE.

Even though there's not much in Amado, it's worth a stop to eat at **The Cow Palace**, a local landmark that has been around since the 1920s. While in town to shoot movies, Western stars have frequented the place, and their photos hang on the walls. Decor is rustic Western, with a wagon wheel for a chandelier and red tablecloths, carpet and curtains. Entrées carry on the theme with names such as The Trail Boss porterhouse steak and Chuck Wagon barbecue beef sandwich. ~ Off Route 19 (Exit 48), 28802 South Nogales Highway, Amado; 520-398-2201. BUDGET TO DELUXE.

DINING

◄ HIDDEN

Opened in the 1940s as a coffee shop, **Wisdom's Café** is now a restaurant crammed with old photographs, farming tools, velvet paintings, patchwork rugs and other odds and ends. You can spot it on the road by the two gigantic fiberglass chickens in front. If you can get by the chickens, try some of their Mexican food. Closed Sunday. ~ Route 19 frontage road, Tumacácori; 520-398-2397, fax 520-398-9350. BUDGET.

If you've never dined in an 1840s horse stable, stop in at **The Stables** restaurant at the Tubac Golf Resort. Actually, the place is quite nice. Inside are arched windows, cobblestone floors and pottery made by Mexicans and American Indians. Look closely and you might find Apache Indian arrowheads embedded in the restaurant's adobe walls. Dinner focuses on steak, seafood and a lavish Sunday brunch. ~ 1 Otero Road, Tubac; 520-398-2678, 800-848-7893; www.tubacgolfresort.com, e-mail relaxing@ tubacgolfresort.com. DELUXE TO ULTRA-DELUXE.

San Cayetano Restaurant in the Rio Rico Resort and Country Club offers Southwestern cuisine as well as a Sunday champagne brunch. Two walls have floor-to-ceiling windows with panoramic views of the mountains. The interior has tables and booths decorated in earth tones to fit a casual Southwestern look. Reservations are recommended. ~ 1069 Camino Caralampi, Rio Rico; 520-281-1901, 800-288-4746; www.rioricoresort.com, e-mail sales@rioricoresort.com. DELUXE.

Home Plate is a greasy spoon where the locals meet to chow down on burgers and hot and cold sandwiches. Civic-club banners circle the room and partially cover the brick walls. No dinner. ~ 277 McKeown Avenue, Patagonia; 520-394-2344. BUDGET.

◄ HIDDEN

The dining room at the **Stage Stop Inn** has the hotel's Western theme with cattle brands on the floors and a chuckwagon containing a wine display. Offerings include sandwiches, burgers, steaks, Mexican food and homemade desserts. ~ 303 McKeown Avenue, Patagonia; phone/fax 520-394-2211, 800-923-2211. MODERATE TO DELUXE.

For satisfying burgers and a variety of sandwiches on the cheap try **Lutes Casino**. The history adds ambience, as this large, dark pool hall, domino parlor and restaurant was a casino back in 1920s. ~ 221 Main Street, Yuma; 520-782-2192. BUDGET.

A ladies luncheon kind of place, **Garden Café** is next door to the Century House Museum and offers home-made sandwiches, salads and quiche. The setting is charming amidst gardens and aviaries full of birds. The Garden Café serves breakfast, lunch and Sunday brunch. Closed Monday. ~ 250 South Madison Avenue, Yuma; 928-783-1491, fax 928-343-4838. BUDGET TO MODERATE.

On June 6, 1936, the first barrel of tequila produced in the United States rolled off a Nogales production line.

In 1911, the first plane to land in Arizona did so in Yuma. Almost a century later, you can celebrate this flight of fancy at the **Yuma Landing**, a restaurant rich in aviation history. Menu offerings range from pasta to prime rib to the "Crash Landing" (two beef patties with sautéed mushrooms, bacon and Swiss cheese). Fried everything tops the appetizer list. Try not to board a plane after eating here—it might never get off the ground. Breakfast, lunch and dinner are served. ~ 195 South 4th Avenue, Yuma; 928-782-7427; www.yumalanding.com, e-mail management@yumalanding.com. MODERATE TO DELUXE.

SHOPPING About 80 shops and restaurants make up the town of **Tubac**. Although it's geared to tourists, they've managed to avoid the rubber-tomahawk syndrome and you'll find high-quality artwork. All of the shops are within walking distance and are evenly distributed along Tubac Road, Plaza Road and Calle Otero.

Tortuga Books, known throughout the Southwest, specializes in philosophy, psychology, children's books, Southwestern literature, greeting cards and CDs. ~ 19 Tubac Road, Tubac; 520-398-2807. **The Pot Shop Gallery and Rodeo June** features signed lithographs by R. C. Gorman, as well as prints, pottery and clay artwork created by Arizona artisans. ~ 16 Tubac Road, Tubac; 520-398-2898. **The Chile Pepper** offers Southwestern gourmet foods, chile food products, chile wreaths, coffees, teas and cookbooks. ~ 22 Tubac Road, Tubac; 520-398-2921. For handcrafted American Indian jewelry, kachinas, sand paintings, baskets and pottery, stop in **Old Presidio Traders**. ~ 27 Tubac Road, Tubac; 520-398-9333.

American Indian–owned and –operated, **Cloud Dancer Jewelry Studio** is a fine-art gallery with one of the largest Hopi kachina collection in Southern Arizona. The gallery also offers custom-designed jewelry with turquoise and precious gems in gold, silver and platinum settings, as well as paintings, pottery and sculpture. ~ 24-1 Tubac Road, Tubac; 520-398-2546.

To shop in the older, more historic section of town, go to Calle Iglesia. In this area you'll find **Hugh Cabot Studios & Gallery** housed in a 250-year-old adobe building that used to be a hostelry for Spanish soldiers. This internationally known artist creates Southwestern and general-interest works in several mediums and makes his home in Tubac. Closed Sunday and the month of July. ~ 10 Calle Iglesia, Tubac; 520-398-2721.

The **Tubac Country Shop** sells Mexican pottery, glassware, dishes and decorative accessories. Closed Monday. ~ Rogers Lane, Tubac; 520-398-2121.

The **Ajo Art Gallery** has a mixture of contemporary paintings by artists from across the U.S. Closed Sunday and Monday and from May through September. ~ 661 North 2nd Avenue, Ajo; 928-387-7525.

Colorado River Pottery has quite a selection of ceramics made on-site. Closed Sunday. ~ 67 West 2nd Street, Yuma; 928-343-0413, 888-410-2689; www. coloradoriverpottery.com. At the **One Percent Gallery**, George Tomkins creates decorative clay pieces. Closed Sunday and Monday. ~78 West 2nd Street, Yuma; 928-782-1934; www.claystuff.com.

NIGHTLIFE

Scenic mountain views from picture windows draw people to **Calabasas Lounge** at the Rio Rico Resort and Country Club. The contemporary, Southwest-style bar has live Top-40, jazz and dance music on Friday. ~ 1069 Camino Caralampi, Rio Rico; 520-281-1901, 800-288-4746.

Lutes Casino is one of the oldest continually owned and operated pool and domino parlors in the state. Open since 1920, the place is crammed full of farm implements, paintings and historic memorabilia. ~ 221 Main Street, Yuma; 928-782-2192; www.lutescasino.com, e-mail feedback@lutescasino.com.

For live alternative and rock bands, head on over to **Jimmie Dee's**. Antique signs and assorted knickknacks give this bar an old-timey feel. Closed Sunday. ~ 38 West 2nd Street, Yuma; 928-783-5647.

PARKS

PATAGONIA LAKE STATE PARK
The largest recreational lake in Southern Arizona (265 acres) is located in this 645-acre park. Patagonia Lake, nestled amid rolling hills, was created by the damming of Sonoita Creek in 1968. It's stocked with bass, crappie, catfish, bluegill and, in the winter, trout. A small, sandy beach lures swimmers. You can windsurf and waterski here, although waterskiing is not allowed on weekends or holidays from May through October. Because of its elevation of 3750 feet, Patagonia Lake sometimes has temperatures cooler than Tucson. The park provides picnic areas, restrooms, showers and a marina with boat rentals. Pontoon birding tours (520-287-2791) are offered on Saturday or by request (more often in spring). Day-use fee, $7. ~ Off Route 82, about 12 miles north of Nogales. Follow the signs to the park; 520-287-6965, fax 520-287-5618.

▲ There are 119 sites, including 34 RV hookups and 13 accessible by boat only; hookups are $22 per vehicle, all other sites $15 per vehicle.

PATAGONIA–SONOITA CREEK PRESERVE Nine miles north of Patagonia Lake State Park is a 312-acre sanctuary in a narrow flood plain between the Santa Rita and the Patagonia mountains. The preserve encompasses a one-and-a-half mile stretch of Sonoita Creek lined with large stands of cottonwoods—some a hundred feet tall—as well as Arizona walnut, velvet ash, willows and Texas mulberry. Birdwatchers from all over the world come here because more than 300 species of birds have been seen. It is also home to white-tailed deer, bobcat, javelina, coyote and the most endangered fish in the Southwest, the Gila Topminnow. There are restrooms and water in the preserve. Closed Monday and Tuesday. ~ From Patagonia, turn northwest off Route 82 onto 4th Avenue, then go left on Pennsylvania Avenue. When the pavement ends, cross the creek and follow the dirt road for one mile. There will be an entrance with the visitors center on your left; 520-394-2400; www.nature.org/arizona.

The staff at the Patagonia-Sonoita Creek Preserve offers guided tours of the cottonwood-willow riparian forest every Saturday morning at 9 a.m.

CORONADO NATIONAL FOREST The Coronado National Forest (www.fs.fed.us/r3/coronado) in Arizona has 1.7 million acres of public land in 12 sky islands, or mountain ranges that jut above the surrounding desert. Following are three of the highlights:

Madera Canyon 🚶 🚴 🐎 This spot is a great place for birdwatching, with more than 200 species including several varieties of woodpeckers, hawks, wrens and vultures. Driving up through the canyon the desert changes from grassland to forest. Trees on the lower slopes of the Santa Rita Mountains are mesquite, and farther up are live oaks, alligator junipers, cottonwoods and sycamores along Madera Creek. There are more than 70 miles of trails. You'll find restrooms, picnic areas and grills. ~ Located 49 miles south of Tucson. Take Route 19 south from Tucson to Green Valley's Continental Road, then go southeast for 13 miles; 520-281-2296, fax 520-670-4598.

▲ There are 13 sites at Bog Springs Campground; $10 per night per vehicle.

Pena Blanca Lake 🚶 🛥 🛥 Surrounded by oak, cottonwood and mesquite trees and light-colored bluffs, this 39-acre lake is situated at 4000 feet—making it higher and somewhat cooler than Tucson. Fishing is good for bass, bluegill, crappie, catfish and rainbow trout but because of high mercury levels, the Fish and Wildlife Department recommends that you catch and release all but trout. A trail leads around the lake. Also located here are picnic areas, pit toilets and picnic tables. ~ Located five miles north of the Mexican border. Take Route 19 south from Tucson to Ruby Road, then go west for about nine miles; 520-281-2296, fax 520-670-4598; www.fs.fed.us/r3/coronado.

▲ There are 15 sites at White Rock Campground (a quarter-mile from the lake), although there are no lake views; $5 per night per vehicle.

Parker Canyon Lake 🚣 🛥 🎣 Parker Canyon Lake is an 130-acre fishing lake west of the Huachuca Mountains and surrounded by grassy, rolling hills. Bluegill, bass, perch, trout and catfish are the common catches. To assist with the fishing there are boat rentals, bait and a fishing dock. There are also restrooms, picnic areas and a marina store. The marina is closed on Wednesday. ~ From Sonoita, take Route 83 south for 30 miles until it runs into the park; 520-378-0311, fax 520-378-0519.

▲ There are 65 sites in Lakeview Campground; $10 per night. Please note that the campground may be closed depending on funding; call for reservations and closures.

ORGAN PIPE CACTUS NATIONAL MONUMENT 🚶 🚴 This 330,000-acre refuge became a national monument in 1937 to protect the Sonoran desert plants and animals and the unique organ pipe cactus. Start at the visitors center 17 miles south of the northern entrance. Here you can see exhibits and pick up a self-guided tour pamphlet. The only paved road through the park is Route 85. If you want to get off the pavement, a good tour is the Puerto Blanco Scenic Drive, a 53-mile graded dirt loop with numbered stops described in the pamphlet. While exploring the monument, you'll pass mountains, plains, canyons, dry washes and a pond surrounded by cottonwood trees. Picnic areas and restrooms are the only facilities in the park. Day-use fee, $5. ~ The monument is located 35 miles south of Ajo, and the visitors center is at the 75-mile marker on Route 85; 520-387-6849, fax 520-387-7475; www.nps.gov/orpi.

▲ There are 208 sites in the main campground; $10 per night. Fresh water is available at the dump station, the visitors center and the campground. Primitive camping ($6 per night) is allowed at four sites in the Alamo campground and anywhere in the backcountry as long as you're a half mile from the road; you can pick up the $5 permits for backcountry camping at the visitors center. No campfires.

CABEZA PRIETA NATIONAL WILDLIFE REFUGE Established in 1939, the 860,000-acre refuge is an arid wilderness rife with cactus and mountains. Passing through the refuge is the 250-mile El Camino del Diablo (Highway of the Devil) that was pioneered by Spanish Conquistador Captain de Anza in 1774—and stretches from Mexico to California. Along the way you pass Cabeza

Prieta Mountain with its lava-topped granite peak, and Mohawk Valley with sand dunes and lava flows. Since roads here are rugged and unimproved, four-wheel-drive vehicles are required. Also, beware of the six species of rattlesnakes. Limited hunting for desert bighorn sheep is allowed in the winter. An Arizona Game and Fish permit is required. There are no facilities in the refuge; the closest groceries are in Ajo, seven miles east. The refuge is sometimes closed for inclement weather; call ahead to see if it's open. Also, three-quarters of the refuge is closed March 15th through July 15th. ~ You'll need explicit directions, which you can get when you pick up the Refuge Entry Permit at the refuge office in Ajo (1611 North 2nd Avenue). It's advisable to call ahead; 520-387-6483, fax 520-387-5359.

Cacti aren't the only things that sting in Organ Pipe Cactus National Monument—beware of rattlesnakes, gila monsters and scorpions.

▲ There are three primitive campgrounds with no facilities; no wood fires allowed; no water. Permit required.

Outdoor Adventures

Although water isn't plentiful in Southern Arizona, there are a few lakes where boats are available to rent.

BOATING

EAST OF TUCSON   Boat rentals are available at **Parker Canyon Lake**, nestled among the foothills of the Huachuca Mountains. ~ Off Route 83, 30 miles southwest of Sierra Vista; 520-455-5847.

SOUTH/WEST OF TUCSON   **Patagonia Lake State Park** offers rowboat, canoe and paddle-boat rentals. ~ Patagonia; 520-287-5545. For an excursion on the Colorado River, try a jetboat tour. **Yuma River Tours** offers boat rides past petroglyphs, homesteads, steamboat landings and mining camps. ~ 1920 Arizona Avenue; 928-783-4400.

SWIMMING

For a retreat from the heat take a plunge at one of Southern Arizona's public pools.

TUCSON   **Fort Lowell Park** has an Olympic-size pool. ~ 2900 North Craycroft Road; 520-791-2585. Dive in at **Himmel Park**. Summer only. ~ 1000 North Tucson Boulevard; 520-791-4157. Get wet at **Morris K. Udall Park**. ~ 7200 East Tanque Verde Road; 520-791-4004. **Joaquin Murieta Park** has a public pool. Summer only. ~ 1400 North Silverbell Road; 520-791-4752. Cool yourself down in **Jacobs Park**'s pool. Summer only. ~ 3300 North Fairview Avenue; 520-791-4358. Call **Tucson Parks & Recreation** for more information. ~ 520-791-4873.

BALLOON RIDES

For those without a fear of heights, there's nothing like floating above it all. Ballooning is a great way to escape the heat and get a magnificent view at the same time.

TUCSON   A Southern Arizona Balloon Excursion ascends from the Tucson area. Sunrise trips fly high enough for great views of Tucson and the Catalina Mountains and low enough to see wildlife along the Santa Cruz River. ~ 537 West Grant Road, Tucson; 520-624-3599. Another company hovering above is **Balloon America**, which offers sunrise flights over the Sonoran Desert, the Catalina mountains and the Grand Canyon. Flights operate from October through May. ~ Located near Speedway Boulevard and Houghton Road; 520-299-7744; www.balloonrideusa.com.

There's only one place to ski and snowboard in these parts—the **Mount Lemmon Ski Valley**. The southernmost ski-area in North America, Mount Lemmon offers 21 runs, equipment rental, a ski school and a restaurant. ~ 10300 East Ski Run Road, Mount Lemmon; 520-576-1321.

SKIING

If you prefer to let someone else do the walking, there are several horseback riding outfitters in the area.

RIDING STABLES

TUCSON   A Western town like Tucson wouldn't be the same without opportunities to go riding. Dudes and dudettes can saddle up at **Walking Winds and El Conquistador Riding Stables**. They offer one- to one-and-a-half-hour rides in the Catalina Mountains. Closed Monday. ~ 10000 North Oracle Road; 520-742-4200. Mount a steed at **Pusch Ridge Stables** for one-hour to overnight excursions. All meals and equipment provided. ~ 13700 North Oracle Road; 520-825-1664. Saddle up at **Pantano Riding Stables** for a guided trip into Saguaro National Park; rides last one to two hours. ~ 4450 South Houghton Road; 520-298-8980.

Mild winters make this region ideal for golfers, and aficionados can choose between a wide range of private and public courses. All courses listed for the Tucson area have club and cart rentals and golf pros available for lessons.

GOLF

TUCSON   The semiprivate **Omni Tucson National Golf Resort & Spa** has 27 holes—three 9-hole courses that can be played in different combinations. There is a pro shop and a restaurant and bar. ~ 2727 West Club Drive; 520-575-7540; www.tucsonnational.com. Swing your clubs under the sunny skies at **Starr Pass Golf Resort**, an 18-hole mountain course with long fairways, rolling greens and many elevation changes. Carts are mandatory. ~ 3645 West Starr Pass Boulevard; 520-670-0400; www.starrpasstucson.com. Work on your game at **Randolph North Municipal Golf Course**, an 18-hole course with long fairways and water hazards on six holes. The adjacent 36-hole **Del Urich Municipal Golf Course** (Randolph South Municipal Golf Course) has tall trees, lush fairways, straight holes and rolling terrain with elevated tees and greens. Both courses share a pro shop, practice area, driving range and putting green. ~ 600 South Alvernon Way; 520-791-4161.

The 18-hole executive **Dorado Golf Course** has a pro shop. ~ 6601 East Speedway Boulevard; 520-885-6751. Go for a hole in one at the public 18-hole **Arthur Pack Desert Golf Course**. ~ 9101 North Thornydale Road; 520-744-3322. The semiprivate **Lodge at Ventana** is a PGA resort course that runs through rocky canyons, arroyos and foothills; a cart is included in the green fee. ~ 6200 North Club House Lane; 520-577-1400. Beware the hazards at the 18-hole **Quail Canyon Golf Course**. ~ 5910 North Oracle Road; 520-887-6161. Tee off at the 18-hole public **El Rio Golf Course**. ~ 1400 West Speedway Boulevard; 520-791-4229. Take aim at the greens on **Fred Enke Golf Course**, an 18-hole desert course with a pro shop. ~ 8251 East Irvington Road; 520-791-2539. Situated on the bank of the Santa Cruz River, the 18-hole **Silverbell Golf Course** sports flat fairways, large greens and nine lakes. There is a pro shop. ~ 3600 North Silverbell Road; 520-791-5235.

Believe it or not, Tucson's prime golfing time is about 6 a.m., especially in the summer before the midday heat hits. For a scenic game, plan on hitting the green late in the day when shadows enhance the desert's beauty.

EAST OF TUCSON   A golfing spot east of Tucson is the 18-hole **Turquoise Valley Golf Course**. ~ 1791 West Newell Street, Bisbee; 520-432-3091. In Douglas, the 18-hole **Douglas Municipal Golf Course** has a complete pro shop, a lounge and an adjacent RV park under the same ownership, all in a desert setting surrounded by mountains. Cart rentals only. ~ 1372 East Fairway Drive; 520-364-3722.

SOUTH/WEST OF TUCSON   **Canoa Hills Golf Course** is an 18-hole semiprivate facility. ~ 1401 West Calle Urbano, Green Valley; 520-648-1880. **Pueblo Del Sol Golf Course** is another 18-hole green. ~ 2770 St. Andrews Drive, Sierra Vista; 520-378-6444. At the Resort Rio Rico, the private 18-hole PGA **Rio Rico Golf Course** was designed by Robert Trent Jones, Sr. ~ 1069 Camino Caralampi, Nogales; 520-281-8567. **Tubac Golf Resort**, an 18-hole course with lots of trees, as well as a restaurant and bar, is the premier spot in Tubac. ~ 1 Otero Road; 520-398-2211. If passing through Safford, check out the 18-hole **Mount Graham Golf Course**. ~ Golf Course Road, Safford; 928-348-3140. In Yuma you can tee off at the 18-hole **Mesa Del Sol Golf Club**. ~ 12213 Calle del Cid; 928-342-1817.

TENNIS

The dry, hot climate provides excellent court conditions all year.

TUCSON   When it's not too hot to serve, try the public tennis courts in Tucson. **Fort Lowell Park** has eight lighted public courts, as well as racquetball courts and a tennis pro; fee. ~ 2900 North Craycroft Road; 520-791-2584. You can swing a racquet at **Himmel Park**, which also has eight lighted courts; fee. ~ 1000 North Tucson Boulevard; 520-791-3276. Or try the **Randolph Tennis Center**, with 25 public courts, all lighted for night play; fee. ~ 50 South Alvernon Way; 520-791-4896. **Pima Community College** has eight lighted courts for public use on a first-come, first-served basis; classes have priority. No fee, no pro. ~ 2202 West Anklam Road; 520-206-6619.

In the mountains or along a river, on asphalt or dirt, through residential areas or among the mighty saguaro, Tucson is bicycle-friendly. If you haven't brought a bike with you, rent one in town and take to the road or trail.

BIKING

TUCSON Tucson is a very popular area for bicycling. Some favorite routes include riding on **Oracle Road** north of Ina Road, where cyclists find wide shoulders and beautiful mountain views. On the way back turn into Sun City Vistoso, a large retirement community where the roads are wide and the scenery pretty.

Another popular ride is parallel to the Santa Catalina Mountain foothills along **Sunrise Road** to Sabino Canyon, where you can climb up a challenging, four-mile road through the mountains; just beware of mountain lions in the area. Because of the tour shuttles, Sabino Canyon is only open to bicyclists before 9 a.m. and after 5 p.m., except Wednesday and Saturday when it is closed to bicyclists entirely. For more information, call 520-749-8700.

Starting on North Campbell Avenue and running along the banks of the dry Rillito River is a multi-use **asphalt trail**. Currently it's about four miles long, and more trails are added annually. The **Santa Cruz River Park** has another trail that runs about four miles on both sides of the river.

The **Saguaro National Monument**, both east and west, also offers a number of good trails, both for mountain and road bikes, as does the hilly **Tucson Mountain Park**. Both are in scenic areas studded with cactus and mountains. Another enjoyable route is along the **Old Spanish Trail** from Broadway Boulevard to Colossal Cave.

For more information and maps on bicycling in the area, contact the **City of Tucson bicycling coordinator** at 520-791-4372.

EAST OF TUCSON Good areas for bicycling can also be found outside of Tucson. Bikeable roads east of the city are **Route 90**, which you can take to Sierra Vista and then on to Bisbee, and **Route 80** through Tombstone.

SOUTH/WEST OF TUCSON A good ride is to take **Route 83** from Colossal Cave, past Sonoita and Patagonia to Nogales. This road has little traffic and wide shoulders.

Bike Rentals   You can also rent a mountain bike and buy a trail map at **Broadway Bicycles**. ~ 140 South Sarnoff Drive, Tucson; 520-296-7819. Equipment and mountain-bike rentals are available at **Tucson Bicycles**, where they also organize group rides. ~ 4743 East Sunrise Drive, Tucson; 520-577-7374. **Sabino Cycles** also will help you get set up with mountain-bike rentals. Repairs are available. ~ 7131 East Tanque Verde Road, Tucson; 520-885-3666.

HIKING   With trails lacing its many national monuments, recreation areas and state parks, Southern Arizona is built for hiking. You can view old adobe ruins, lime kilns, ancient petroglyphs and geological marvels, or scale one of the many peaks, for a stellar view of your surroundings. All distances listed for hiking trails are one way unless otherwise noted.

TUCSON   In the Rincon Mountain District in Saguaro National Park is the **Freeman Homestead Nature Trail** (1 mile), a loop that starts off the spur road to the Javelina picnic area and descends from a saguaro forest to a small wash filled with mesquite trees. Along the way you pass the ruins of an adobe house built in the 1920s.

The **Cactus Forest Trail** (7 miles) takes you though a saguaro forest between Broadway Boulevard and Old Spanish Trail. You also pass the remains of the first ranger station built in the park, and two kilns used to process lime around the turn of the 20th century.

For a trek on **Mount Lemmon**, follow the **Wilderness of Rocks Trail** (4 miles). The trailhead is a mile and a half past Ski Valley. On the way are pools along Lemmon Creek and thousands of eroded and balanced rocks.

Pima Canyon Trail (7.6 miles) in the Santa Catalina Mountains is a difficult trail that climbs from 2900 to 7255 feet through a bighorn-sheep management area. Along the way you'll pass Pima Canyon Spring and good views of Tucson and A Mountain. Beyond the spring, the trail becomes steeper and harder to follow. At the top you'll find good views of Cathedral and Window rocks. To get there, follow Christie Drive north until it dead-ends at Magee Road. Go right and park. Carry lots of water.

In the **Tucson Mountain District** the **King Canyon Trail** (3.5 miles) begins off of Kinney Road across from the Arizona-Sonora Desert Museum, then climbs up to a picnic area and beyond to the top of Wasson Peak (elevation 4687), the highest point in the area.

The short **Signal Hill Petroglyphs Trail** (.13 mile) goes up a winding path along a small hill off Golden Gate Road. At the top are rocks with ancient Indian petroglyphs on them.

The **Valley View Overlook Trail** (.75 mile) on the Bajada Loop Drive descends into two washes and ends on a scenic ridge overlooking most of Avra Valley.

Hunter Trail (2 miles) in Picacho Peak State Park offers scenic views as it climbs from 2000 to 3374 feet in elevation. The trail was named for Captain Sherod Hunter, a Confederate officer who placed lookouts at Picacho pass and was involved in the battle that occurred here in 1862.

EAST OF TUCSON   To find **Lutz Canyon Trail** (2.9 miles), drive 12 miles south of Sierra Vista on Route 92 to Ash Canyon Road. Hikers walk past old mine workings in a narrow, deep canyon with oak, juniper and Douglas fir. The trail is extremely steep. ~ Sierra Vista Ranger District: 520-378-0311.

The moderately strenuous **Crest Trail** (5.5 miles) in the **Coronado National Memorial** runs along the crest of the Huachuca Mountains, which afford a great view of northern Mexico on clear days. ~ 520-366-5515.

Within the **Chiricahua National Monument** you'll find **Massai Point Nature Trail** (.5 mile), which starts at the geology exhibit at Massai Point and takes you past a large balanced rock, a board with a description of the park's geologic story and views across Rhyolite Canyon.

Southern Arizona enjoys a reputation as one of the best birding regions in North America. Thanks in part to its scarcity of water, all birding aficionados need to do to view their prize is park themselves next to a body of water and wait.

The **Sugarloaf Trail** (.9 mile) takes you to a fire lookout at the top of Sugarloaf Mountain, the highest point within the monument.

Natural Bridge Trail (2.5 miles) begins at the Bonita Canyon scenic drive, then passes a natural rock bridge and climbs through oak and juniper woodlands to a pine forest.

Heart of Rocks Loop Trail (8-mile loop) winds through pine and fir forests and some of the park's most impressive rock formations, including Big Balanced Rock, Punch and Judy and Totem Pole.

Built as a supply artery for fire fighters stationed in the high Chiricahuas, **Greenhouse Trail** (3.5 miles) ascends 1500 feet. You'll pass Cima Cabin, the fire fighters' headquarters, and Winn Falls, which flows during the summer. To get there, go north off Cave Creek Spur Road onto Greenhouse Road and drive half a mile.

The **Coronado National Forest** offers the **South Fork Trail** (6.8 miles). Beginning off Cave Creek Road at the road end in South Fork Forest Camp three and a half miles above Portal, Arizona, it passes South Fork Cave Creek, one of the most famous bird-watching canyons in the Chiricahua Mountains and a 70-foot-tall finger of red rhyolite called Pinnacle Rock. It starts in a forest of sycamores, cypress and black walnut trees and leads to huge Douglas fir trees and the small bluffs above the South Fork Cave Creek. ~ Douglas Ranger District: 520-364-3468.

SOUTH/WEST OF TUCSON Kent Springs–Bog Springs Trail Loop (4.3 miles) within the Santa Rita Mountains climbs from 4820 feet to 6620 feet. Along the way are three seasonal springs, which create an unusually lush area with large sycamore, silver leaf oak, Arizona bamboo and walnut trees alive with birds. Exit off of Route 19 at Madera Canyon and park near the Bog Springs campground.

▼▼▼▼▼▼▼▼▼▼▼▼

Transportation

CAR

From Tucson, **Route 10** runs north toward Phoenix, then crosses **Route 8**, which heads west toward Gila Bend and Yuma. **Route 85** from Gila Bend goes south, turns into **Route 86**, cuts through the Papago Indian Reservation and goes to Tucson. South of Tucson is **Route 19** to Nogales, while the main thoroughfare east from Tucson is Route 10 toward New Mexico. Jutting south off Route 10 are **Route 83** to Sonoita, **Route 90** to Sierra Vista, **Route 191** to Douglas, and **Route 186** to Chiricahua National Monument.

AIR

Aero California, Aerolitoral, America West Airlines, American Airlines, Continental, Delta Air Lines, Northwest Airlines, Southwest and United Airlines fly into **Tucson International Airport**. ~ 520-573-8000; www.tucsonairport.org.

Yuma International Airport (928-726-5882; www.yumainin ternationalairport.com) is served by America West Express and United Express while **Sierra Vista Municipal Airport** (520-459-8575) is served by America West Express.

TRAIN

Amtrak (800-872-7245; www.amtrak.com) services the area with the "Texas Eagle" and the "Sunset Limited," stopping in Tucson at 400 East Toole Avenue (520-623-4442), in Benson at 4th and Patagonia streets, and in Yuma at 281 Gila Street.

BUS

Greyhound Bus Lines (800-231-2222; www.greyhound.com) services Tucson from around the country. ~ 2 South 4th Avenue; 520-792-3475. Other stations in Southern Arizona include Nogales at 35 North Terrace Avenue, 520-287-5628, and Yuma at 170 East 17th Place, 928-783-4403; in Benson at 680 West 4th Street, 520-586-3141; and in Willcox at 622 North Haskell Avenue; 520-384-2183.

CAR RENTALS

At Tucson International Airport are **Avis Rent A Car** (800-331-1212), **Dollar Rent A Car** (800-800-4000), **Hertz Rent A Car** (800-654-3131) and **National Car Rental** (800-227-7368).

Car-rental agencies at the Yuma International Airport are **Avis Rent A Car** (800-331-1212), **Budget Rent A Car** (800-404-8033), and **Hertz Rent A Car** (800-654-3131).

Enterprise Rent A Car serves the Sierra Vista Municipal Airport. ~ 800-325-8007.

PUBLIC TRANSIT

For extensive bus service throughout Tucson, call **Sun Tran.** ~ 520-792-9222; www.suntran.com. Local bus service in Nogales is **Dabdoub Bus Service.** ~ 520-287-7810.

TAXIS

Leading cab companies in Tucson include **Allstate Cab Co.** (520-888-2999), **Checker Cab Co.** (520-623-1133) and **Yellow Cab Co.** (520-624-6611).

In Sierra Vista try **Angel Transport.** ~ 520-452-9976.

Index

Lodging Index

Dining Index

HIDDEN GUIDES

Adventure travel or a relaxing vacation?—"Hidden" guidebooks are the only travel books in the business to provide detailed information on both. Aimed at environmentally aware travelers, our motto is "Where Vacations Meet Adventures." These books combine details on unique hotels, restaurants and sightseeing with information on camping, sports and hiking for the outdoor enthusiast.

PARADISE FAMILY GUIDES

Ideal for families traveling with kids of any age—toddlers to teenagers—Paradise Family Guides offer a blend of travel information unlike any other guides to the Hawaiian islands. With vacation ideas and tropical adventures that are sure to satisfy both action-hungry youngsters and relaxation-seeking parents, these guides meet the specific needs of each and every family member.

HIDDEN GUIDEBOOKS

____ Hidden Arizona, $16.95
____ Hidden Bahamas, $14.95
____ Hidden Baja, $14.95
____ Hidden Belize, $15.95
____ Hidden Big Island of Hawaii, $13.95
____ Hidden Boston & Cape Cod, $14.95
____ Hidden British Columbia, $18.95
____ Hidden Cancún & the Yucatán, $16.95
____ Hidden Carolinas, $17.95
____ Hidden Coast of California, $18.95
____ Hidden Colorado, $15.95
____ Hidden Disneyland, $13.95
____ Hidden Florida, $18.95
____ Hidden Florida Keys & Everglades, $13.95
____ Hidden Georgia, $16.95
____ Hidden Guatemala, $16.95
____ Hidden Hawaii, $18.95
____ Hidden Idaho, $14.95
____ Hidden Kauai, $13.95
____ Hidden Los Angeles, $14.95
____ Hidden Maine, $15.95

____ Hidden Maui, $13.95
____ Hidden Miami, $14.95
____ Hidden Montana, $15.95
____ Hidden New England, $18.95
____ Hidden New Mexico, $15.95
____ Hidden New Orleans, $14.95
____ Hidden Oahu, $13.95
____ Hidden Oregon, $15.95
____ Hidden Pacific Northwest, $18.95
____ Hidden San Diego, $14.95
____ Hidden Salt Lake City, $14.95
____ Hidden San Francisco & Northern California, $18.95
____ Hidden Seattle, $13.95
____ Hidden Southern California, $18.95
____ Hidden Southwest, $19.95
____ Hidden Tahiti, $17.95
____ Hidden Tennessee, $16.95
____ Hidden Utah, $16.95
____ Hidden Walt Disney World, $13.95
____ Hidden Washington, $15.95
____ Hidden Wine Country, $13.95
____ Hidden Wyoming, $15.95

PARADISE FAMILY GUIDES

____ Paradise Family Guides: Kaua'i, $16.95
____ Paradise Family Guides: Maui, $16.95

____ Paradise Family Guides: Big Island of Hawai'i, $16.95

Mark the book(s) you're ordering and enter the total cost here ➡ [   ]

California residents add 8.75% sales tax here ➡ [   ]

Shipping, check box for your preferred method and enter cost here ➡ [   ]

□ BOOK RATE   FREE! FREE! FREE!

□ PRIORITY MAIL/UPS GROUND   cost of postage

□ UPS OVERNIGHT OR 2-DAY AIR   cost of postage   [   ]

Billing, enter total amount due here and check method of payment ➡

□ CHECK   □ MONEY ORDER

□ VISA/MASTERCARD _____ EXP. DATE_____

NAME _____ PHONE_____

ADDRESS _____

CITY_____ STATE _____ ZIP_____

MONEY-BACK GUARANTEE ON DIRECT ORDERS PLACED THROUGH ULYSSES PRESS.

ABOUT THE AUTHOR

RICHARD HARRIS has written or co-written more than 20 other guidebooks including *Hidden Cancún and the Yucatán*, *Hidden Colorado* and *Hidden Southwest*. He has also served as contributing editor on guides for John Muir Publications, Fodor's, Birnbaum and Access guides and has written for numerous magazines including *Four Corners*, *Ritz-Carlton*, *Southwest Photographic* and *Southwest Profile*. He is past president of PEN New Mexico and an officer and director of the New Mexico Book Association.

ABOUT THE ILLUSTRATOR

GLENN KIM is a freelance illustrator residing in San Francisco. His work appears in numerous Ulysses Press titles including *Hidden Southwest*, *Hidden New Mexico* and *Hidden Belize*. He has also illustrated for the National Forest Service, several Bay Area magazines, book covers and greeting cards, as well as for advertising agencies that include Foote Cone and Belding, Hal Riney and Jacobs Fulton Design Group.